WRITING AFTER CHAUCER

BASIC READINGS IN CHAUCER AND HIS TIME
VOLUME I
GARLAND REFERENCE LIBRARY OF THE HUMANITIES
VOLUME 2040

BASIC READINGS IN CHAUCER AND HIS TIME

CHRISTIAN K. ZACHER AND PAUL E. SZARMACH, *Series Editors*

WRITING AFTER CHAUCER
*Essential Readings in Chaucer
and the Fifteenth Century*
edited by Daniel J. Pinti

Writing After Chaucer
Essential Readings in Chaucer and the Fifteenth Century

Edited by
Daniel J. Pinti

Garland Publishing, Inc.
A member of the Taylor & Francis Group
New York and London
1998

Library of Congress Cataloging-in-Publication Data

Writing after Chaucer : essential readings in Chaucer and the fifteenth century /
    edited by Daniel Pinti.
              p.   cm. — (Garland reference library of the humanities ; v. 2040.
    Basic readings in Chaucer and his time ; v. 1)
        Includes bibliographical references.
        ISBN 0-8153-2651-3 (alk. paper)
        1. English literature—Middle English, 1100–1500—History and criti-
    cism. 2. Chaucer, Geoffrey, d. 1400—Criticism and interpretation—His-
    tory. 3. Chaucer, Geoffrey, d. 1400—Appreciation—Great Britain.
    4. Chaucer, Geoffrey, d. 1400—Influence. 5. Civilization, Medieval, in litera-
    ture. 6. Manuscripts, Medieval—Great Britain. 7. Influence (Literary, artis-
    tic, etc.) 8. Fifteenth century.   I. Pinti, Daniel. II. Series: Garland reference
    library of the humanities ; vol. 2040. III. Garland reference library of the
    humanities. Basic readings in Chaucer and his time ; v. 1.
    PR293.W74   1998
    820.9'001—dc21   97-38558
                                                                        CIP

Printed on acid-free, 250-year-life paper
Manufactured in the United States of America

SERIES EDITORS' PREFACE

Basic Readings in Chaucer and His Time is a series of volumes that offers reprints of significant essays in the field, written mainly after 1950, along with some new essays as commissioned by editors of the individual volumes. The series is designed so that each volume may serve as a "first book" on the subject within the area of Chaucer studies treated, thus offering students easy access to major landmarks in the subject. There are three main branches within the series: collected essays organized according to Chaucer's work or works, essays collected from other fields that support an understanding of Chaucer in his time (e.g., art history, philosophy, or comparative literature) and special volumes addressing specific problem areas in the study of Chaucer. Each volume editor has the autonomy to select essays that reflect the current state of knowledge and that point toward future directions. Chaucer remains the major pre-modern author in English and has become a center-point where the history of literature intersects with contemporary methodologies. Basic Readings in Chaucer and His Time aims to offer an authoritative entry through its several volumes to this lively, engaging, and perduring area of study. The series is part of the remarkable flowering of Chaucer studies that has marked the last few decades, reflected in the growth of the New Chaucer Society, including its conference and publications programs; the Chaucer sessions at Kalamazoo; and the sustained activity of the Chaucer group at the Modern Language Association. At the same time, Basic Readings in Chaucer and His Time seeks to compensate for new publications patterns and changed library acquisitions policies in serials and retrospective titles by providing affordable access to significant scholarship in the field.

In this first volume to appear in the series, Daniel Pinti gathers together significant recent essays that examine the fundamental ways in which scribes, commentators, poets, and editors shaped and defined both the Chaucer canon and Chaucer's reputation in the first century after his death. Like other volumes in the series, this one is meant for those studying how Chaucer was initially received, defined, and transmitted to later eras. The volume begins with the 1979 article by Barry Windeatt that initiated scholarly realization of just how significant fifteenth-century reactions to Chaucer were for the history of Chaucer's reception. It continues with an array of important investigations of the fifteenth-century Chaucer, including contributions by John Fisher on Chaucer's role in the development of the English language, Paul Strohm on the nature of Chaucer's audiences, Louise Fradenburg on how Scots poets used the English Chaucer, and Seth Lerer on how Caxton, the first printer of Chaucer, transformed Chaucer out of a manuscript environment into the new print culture. Stephen Partridge's opening essay, the only commissioned one in the collection, is meant to introduce readers to the distinctive nature of fifteenth-century manuscript culture.

The series editors thank Daniel Pinti for composing this collection, whose subject appropriately inaugurates this series of Basic Readings in Chaucer and His Time. The series editors invite those interested to offer proposals for subsequent volumes.

Christian K. Zacher
Ohio State University

Paul E. Szarmach
Western Michigan University

Contents

Acknowledgments

Thanks are due first to the publishers and institutions which have granted permission to reprint these articles here: The Modern Language Association; The New Chaucer Society and *Studies in the Age of Chaucer* (in particular that journal's former editor, Lisa Kiser); The Pennsylvania State University Press; The University of California Press; Cambridge University Press; Duke University Press; and Princeton University Press. I wish also to thank A. C. Spearing and Louise Fradenburg for permitting their respective articles to be reprinted. The general editors of Garland's "Basic Readings in Chaucer and His Times" series, Paul Szarmach and Chris Zacher, have guided sagely and patiently a first-time editor, and I thank them both. And I would like to thank especially Stephen Partridge, who kindly agreed to write his article specifically for this anthology. His hard work is much appreciated.

It is a pleasure to acknowledge the English Department of New Mexico State University for generous financial support of this project, and to thank my departmental colleagues Stuart Brown, Reed Dasenbrock, and Diane Price Herndl for encouragement and helpful advice. I also owe a particular debt of gratitude to Dani Smith, as careful and diligent a research assistant as one could hope to find, whose work on the production of this volume has been invaluable.

My greatest debts, of course, are to my wife Maria and my son Zachary, who have given me much more than they've asked for and all that I need.

Introduction

Daniel Pinti

Sic plures penitere se postea dicunt quando mala sua et
mala per eos inducta destruere non possunt; sicut
Chawserus ante mortem suam sepe clamavit ve michi ve
michi quia revocare nec destruere jam potero illa que
male scripsi de malo et turpissimo amore hominum ad
mulieres et jam de homine in hominem continuabuntur.
Velim. Nolim. Et sic plangens mortuus.

Likewise they say that more people themselves do
penance afterwards, when they are not able to destroy
their own evil things and the evil introduced by them; just
as Chaucer often cried out before his death, "Woe to me!
Woe to me! I can neither call back nor destroy those
things I wickedly wrote concerning the evil and most foul
love of men for women, and now those things will be
perpetuated, from one person to the next. I wish. I don't
wish." And weeping thus, he died.

Dr. Thomas Gascoigne, ca. 1434-57[1]

THOMAS Gascoigne's fifteenth-century narrative of Chaucer's death,
its almost certain fictionality notwithstanding, is in its own
moralistic way a dramatic portrait of Chaucer *agonistes*. It also
represents in a condensed form some of the fifteenth-century "Chaucers" that
the scholars whose articles make up this book discuss: Chaucer the poet of
love; Chaucer the model to be followed—or, in this case, avoided; Chaucer
the writer all-too-aware of the afterlife of texts, knowingly writing for a
contemporary audience as well as for posterity.[2] In at least two important
respects, however, the picture presented in this fifteenth-century response to
Chaucer is significantly different from the others discussed in this anthology.
First, none of the other fifteenth-century writers considered here seems
especially interested in either the state of Chaucer's soul or the idea that his
works could be considered "*mala*." More intriguingly, though, Gascoigne

imagines Chaucer imagining an "infectious" literary history, one in which the production and reproduction of (his) manuscripts contaminates not poems (as traditional editorial theory might have it) but people. Yet as the essays in this collection amply bear witness, the fifteenth century's engagement with Chaucer was a much more active and creative process than Gascoigne's Chaucer might have envisioned. In other words, Gascoigne's Chaucer conceives of himself as creating and perpetuating evils, but of course it is more accurate to say that Gascoigne and his contemporaries created and perpetuated "Chaucers."

Or, as Seth Lerer puts it, "Chaucer's poetry, in a quite literal sense, *is* the product of his fifteenth-century readers and writers," and in widely varying ways all of these essays attest to this fact.[3] Readers of this collection will find that it focuses on relatively recent work on this subject of Chaucer in the fifteenth century. It does so, I think, with good reason. The earliest piece, Barry Windeatt's, dates from 1979, and "The Scribes as Chaucer's Early Critics" marks a convenient and defensible starting point for the new directions and the revaluations that have characterized current approaches to fifteenth-century Chaucer traditions. As I suggested above, the reception of Chaucer was a noticeably active process, and nowhere is this activity more visible and intriguing than in the interpretive moves performed by scribes and glossators on Chaucer's poetry. Although medieval scribes did count some bunglers among their ranks, and even the best of them surely made the occasional mistake, the recognition that many scribal "variants" represent revealing responses rather than obscuring errors is one of the most far-reaching changes in recent medieval literary studies. What Windeatt does, something that all too rarely had been done before him, is take the scribal responses to Chaucer's poetry seriously—that is, as serious sources of information about the medieval understanding as well as the misunderstanding of Chaucer. Likewise, Susan Schibanoff's "The New Reader and Female Textuality in Two Early Commentaries on Chaucer" illustrates just how powerfully productive this revaluation of scribal and glossatorial responses can be. Schibanoff's effort to "gloss the glosses" demonstrates in fascinating ways how differently medieval glossators could respond to the same poem (in this case *The Wife of Bath's Prologue and Tale*): indeed, how for one glossator that very variety of potential responses was something to be facilitated, and for another, something to be discouraged.

Together these two essays remind us that there's no way to begin to probe the complex questions surrounding Chaucer's reception in the fifteenth century without some knowledge of the manuscripts that preserve Chaucer's writing, and the one new article in this volume, Stephen Partridge's "Questions of Evidence: Manuscripts and the Early History of Chaucer's Works," is an admirably detailed overview of these all-important artifacts. In addition to providing a summary of the state of the scholarship on Chaucer's manuscripts and a helpful reading list on the subject, Partridge articulates how crucially important it is to take into account the material contexts in which Chaucer's writings are actually preserved. Partridge's article, in short, offers an up-to-date introduction to a somewhat technical but utterly essential body of knowledge, and readers of this volume—particularly those new to its subject--will find it indispensible.

That Chaucer's works contributed in important ways to the history of the English *language* as well as its literature should perhaps not be surprising, but the nature and extent of the contribution are still very much the subjects of debate. John H. Fisher's article, "A Language Policy for Lancastrian England," represents a notable contribution to this ongoing dialogue, narrating the historical connections to be found in the rise of the Lancastrian line, the "burgeoning of composition in English," and the increasing production of manuscripts of Chaucer's works. Fisher's essay also shows us (as does Partridge's) how we must not pretend that the year 1400 marks some impermeable boundary beyond which we are not to venture when considering the fifteenth-century's Chaucer. Something else that Partridge's and Fisher's articles share is an interest in questions regarding Chaucer's audiences—and what they illustrate so profoundly is the necessity of that plural. Paul Strohm's contribution to this volume, "Chaucer's Fifteenth-Century Audience and the Narrowing of the 'Chaucer Tradition'," deepens our understanding of these audiences even further. Strohm carefully describes the "dispersion" of Chaucer's original audience of knights and esquires moving in fourteenth-century court circles and the consequent broadening of Chaucer's audience and narrowing of readerly tastes as Chaucer's work moved into the fifteenth century.

It is perhaps inevitable, certainly not surprising, that the vast majority of Chaucer scholarship focuses on either *Troilus and Criseyde* or *The Canterbury Tales*,[4] and it is precisely for this reason that Julia Boffey's article on "The Reputation and Circulation of Chaucer's Lyrics in the Fifteenth Century" is so necessary to this volume. Boffey shows us, through an intensive examination of the forms in which the lyrics circulated, that in the century following Chaucer's death his lyrics were both "well-known and influential," and thus that, while certainly admired in the fifteenth century for his narrative poetry, Chaucer could be turned to as a model for lyric verse as well.[5] John Bowers' article, "*The Tale of Beryn* and *The Siege of Thebes*: Alternative Ideas of *The Canterbury Tales*" also points to the fact that what we think to be obvious or most important about Chaucer's writings is not necessarily what medieval audiences responded to or concluded. In this case it is not Chaucer's "finished" lyric poetry but his unfinished tale collection that prompts two different reader-poets, the *Beryn*-Poet and John Lydgate, to compose texts that provocatively challenge the order and implicit goals of yet another fifteenth-century "writing" of Chaucer, the justly famous Ellesmere manuscript.[6]

Bowers' article points us to the poets whose reading of Chaucer was so much a part of their own "making" of late-medieval English literature and to the concurrent, vexed questions surrounding fifteenth-century "Chaucerian" poetry. A. C. Spearing's account of the reception by fifteenth-century poets of their "Father Chaucer" charts the problem from an angle somewhat different from Bowers', first analyzing Chaucer's rather problematic representations of fathers and sons and Chaucer's own deeply ambivalent dealings with his literary forebears and then suggesting how difficult it seems to have been for poets like Lydgate to construct an individual voice alongside yet against such an indeterminate poetic "Father." The complex negotiations of poetic *auctoritas* provoked by later poets' readings of Chaucer are also addressed in different ways by Louise Fradenburg, C. David Benson, and Tim William Machan. While Spearing ends by intimating the importance of the Scots poet Robert Henryson's empowering question—"Quha wait gif all that Chauceir wrait was trew?"—the earliest of these three articles, Fradenburg's "The Scottish Chaucer," outlines in some detail a critical landscape that still provides the context in which questions of the reading of Chaucer by Middle Scots poets need to be asked. Remarking on James I's *The Kingis Quair*, Henryson's *Testament of Cresseid*, and other works of medieval Scottish literature, Fradenburg indicates the intricate process by which the English poet is appropriated for a Scottish literary past. In "Critic and Poet: What Lydgate and Henryson Did to Chaucer's *Troilus and Criseyde*," Benson distinguishes between Lydgate's adopted role as "scholarly commentator ready to annotate" and Henryson's creative "exploit[ation of] ... Chaucer's innovative literary devices." Like Bowers, although now with regard to the *Troilus* rather than the *Tales*, Benson bolsters the idea that *disparate* understandings of Chaucer in the fifteenth century need not be categorized by us as either "right" or "wrong." In a similar vein, Machan's "Textual Authority and the Works of Hoccleve, Lydgate, and Henryson " examines the various ways in which an "idea of English poetry" was conceived and accomplished in the fifteenth century by analyzing these three poets' assorted metatextual references to books and authorship in their construction of vernacular literary authority and comparing them to Chaucer's own poetic enactment of similar issues.

The last article addresses the "translation" of Chaucer into print. Today almost everyone's first encounter—indeed, almost everyone's *only* encounter—with Chaucer's writing is in a printed, usually "critical" edition of his work. Seth Lerer's essay, "At Chaucer's Tomb: Laureation and Paternity in Caxton's Criticism," demonstrates how crucial was the transformation—for us and for the late fifteenth century—of Chaucer in manuscript to Chaucer in print, and how revealing are the publisher Caxton's interpretations of Chaucer as he mediates Chaucer into an incipient print culture. Somewhat ironically, and unlike the poets discussed in some of the other essays here, Caxton is less interested in rewriting Chaucer's poetry *per se* in an effort to construct poetic *auctoritas* than in creating a "laureate" Chaucer of the purposes of literary history. For Caxton, as for Gascoigne, a patently dead Chaucer can have a distinctive utility.

In sum, the purpose of this volume is to make conveniently available to teachers, scholars, and students a range of the most provocative and influential articles on Chaucer's "afterlife" in the fifteenth century, on the scribes, glossators, poets, and editors whose reception and transmission of Chaucer's writing influence so much our own reception of it. Two final points are now in order about the scope and nature of this volume as a whole. First, the one conclusion not to be drawn from this anthology is that the essays collectively constitute *all* of the "essential readings" on the subject of Chaucer's fifteenth-century "afterlife." No editor can come away from a project like this one anything but painfully aware of what has been left out, of the fact that the final volume amounts to a useful snapshot but not an exhaustive documentary of the field. Here I take some solace in the fact that one of the things that makes each of the present essays so valuable is the thorough nature of their respective notes and bibliographies, and I am sure that anyone sincerely interested in delving further into the subject will search out the no-less-essential scholarship referred to therein.[7] And finally, the essays that are presented here testify, I believe, to the vitality of this subject and to the vigor of the debates surrounding it. It's obvious, but nonetheless "worthy for to drawen to memorie" (*CT* I.3112), that the essays embody neither critical consensus nor cacophony but rather the divergent views inherent in a rapidly developing field of Chaucer studies. If collecting these previously published articles along with Stephen Partridge's new introduction to the manuscripts encourages the continuing development of this field, then this anthology will have done its job.

NOTES

1. Martin M. Crow and Clair C. Olson, eds., *Chaucer Life-Records* (Oxford: Oxford University Press, 1966), p. 547. The translation is my own. Crow and Olson note that "This passage follows an allusion to Judas Iscariot among examples of people who had repented too late to make restitution for their sins" (p. 547).

2. On Chaucer's audiences in his own time, see Paul Strohm, *Social Chaucer* (Cambridge: Harvard University Press, 1989). Chaucer's short poem "To Adam Scryven" might be cited as evidence of Chaucer's self-conscious awareness of contemporary and future audiences, as might be the ending of *Troilus and Criseyde* (e.g., "O moral Gower, this bok I directe / To the, and to the, philosophical Strode" [V.1856-57]; "And red wherso thow [i.e., the poem] be, or elles songe, / That thow be understonde, God I beseche" [V.1797-98]). If we add Gascoigne's comment following the lines quoted above, that "idem Chawserus" was the father of Thomas Chaucer (cited in Crow and Olson, p. 543), we have a version of what Spearing characterizes as "Father Chaucer" here as well.

3. Seth Lerer, *Chaucer and His Readers: Imagining the Author in Late-Medieval England* (Princeton: Princeton University Press, 1993), p. 8.

4. For example, the annotated Chaucer bibliography for 1995 in *Studies in the Age of Chaucer* 18 (1996) lists thirty-six items related to the *Troilus*, five total for all of Chaucer's "Lyrics and Short Poems."

5. Chaucer's translations, too, did not go unnoticed or unpraised in the century after his death, and they clearly were incorporated into the narrative of his contribution to the development of the language. See, for example, Caxton's epilogue to his edition of Chaucer's *Boece*, where he describes Chaucer as the "first translatour of this sayde boke into englissh and enbelissher in making the sayd langage ornate and fayr." Lerer cites and discusses this epilogue in his article in this volume.

6. Recent research on the Ellesmere manuscript can be found in Martin Stevens and Daniel Woodward, eds., *The Ellesmere Chaucer: Essays in Interpretation* (San Marino, CA and Tokyo: Huntington Library and Yushodo Co., Ltd., 1997).

7. Here it might be useful to remind the reader of a few of the previous books that also deal with Chaucer and the fifteenth century: Ruth Morse and Barry Windeatt, eds., *Chaucer Traditions: Studies in Honour of Derek Brewer* (Cambridge and New York: Cambridge University Press, 1990); Derek Pearsall, ed., *Manuscripts and Readers in Fifteenth-Century England* (London: D. S. Brewer, 1983); D. S. Brewer, ed., *Chaucer and Chaucerians: Critical Studies in Middle English Literature* (London: Nelson, 1966); R. F. Yeager, ed., *Fifteenth-Century Studies* (Hamden: Archon Books, 1984); H. S. Bennett, *Chaucer and the Fifteenth Century* (Oxford: Oxford University Press, 1947); and Ian Robinson, *Chaucer and the English Tradition* (Cambridge: Cambridge University Press, 1972).

Questions of Evidence: Manuscripts and the Early History of Chaucer's Works

Stephen Partridge

LTHOUGH Chaucer died in the last year of the fourteenth century, virtually all the surviving manuscripts of his works date from the fifteenth.[1] The manuscripts therefore provide evidence not only for what he wrote during his lifetime, but also for how his work was read in the century after his death; thus they are among our chief means of understanding Chaucer's relationship to the fifteenth century. It is in this light that I will consider the manuscripts here. Space does not permit me to offer an introduction to the bibliography of the manuscript book, or a systematic survey of the manuscripts' dates, materials, and textual affiliations, or a comprehensive review of recent scholarship.[2] Instead, by referring to selected examples, I will highlight several aspects of pre-print culture that a student of literature might keep in mind when beginning to work with manuscript evidence. Treated with sensitivity, this evidence has the potential, often still untapped, to give us access to the history in which Chaucer's works are situated. Whatever their other reasons may be, most scholars who work with manuscripts do so in part because handling a physical artifact from the Middle Ages gives them a sense of contact with the people who lived, read, and wrote in that period that can be achieved in no other way. I hope that my readers will go on to examine Chaucerian and other medieval manuscripts for themselves in order to discover the many aspects of the medieval experience of literature which are difficult to recover from modern printed editions.

Comparing my purposes with those of an earlier introduction to the same material highlights recent developments in the study of medieval manuscripts. Even the title of E. T. Donaldson's essay, "The Manuscripts of Chaucer's Works and Their Use," is revealing; according to the essay, a scholar uses manuscripts to produce a printed edition.[3] Donaldson devotes his entire piece to explaining how an editor interprets the evidence of manuscripts, primarily the words they contain, in order to recover, so far as is possible, what Chaucer actually wrote; and how that editor then presents his conclusions, in the shape of a text, in order to make Chaucer's artistic intentions accessible to "the modern reader."[4]

Ironically, Donaldson's essay happened to appear at a time when Chaucerians, like other medievalists and literary scholars in general, were beginning to interrogate the assumptions and methods of standard editions. In addition, they were seeking new ways to incorporate the evidence contained in manuscripts and printed books into a historical understanding of literature. For Chaucerians this return to the manuscripts has led to an atmosphere of lively debate. Informed cases have been made for sharply diverging opinions on such fundamental questions as whether Chaucer actually wrote all the works attributed to him, whether he revised those works, whether he is likely to have circulated them in his own lifetime, whether he "finished" them or whether the forms familiar from modern editions were largely created by fifteenth-century "editors" supervising the scribes who copied those works. Moreover, as they have reconsidered Chaucer's own intentions, scholars have also paid extended and sympathetic attention to the many other parties who helped shape the manuscripts, such as scribes (and their supervisors), the artists who illustrated and decorated the manuscripts, patrons, and other readers.[5]

But this transformation of manuscript study has not made obsolete the editorial work Donaldson's essay describes. Barry A. Windeatt's essay on "The Scribes as Chaucer's Early Critics," which draws on material collected while preparing his edition of *Troilus and Criseyde*, shows that studying a text's transmission and reception and preparing a modern edition are complementary rather than antithetical tasks. Moreover, one should not suppose that all the traditional work with the manuscripts has been done and only waits to be reviewed or redone. For example, the Textual Notes to *The Riverside Chaucer* record the considerable number of manuscripts of the *Boece*, the *Treatise on the Astrolabe*, and the lyrics that were newly discovered between the 1950s and the 1980s.[6] The edition of the *Treatise on the Astrolabe* produced for the *Riverside* was in fact the first attempt to take account of all known manuscripts in the way Donaldson advocated. What follows, therefore, aims not to supersede Donaldson's essay but to supplement it, by focusing on those approaches to manuscript evidence which have come to the fore since it was published.

VARIATION

One of the most fundamental characteristics of Chaucer's works—and all other texts—in manuscript culture is that no two copies of the same text are identical.[7] There are many kinds of variation between manuscript copies. A scribe was liable to substitute a familiar word for one in his exemplar (the manuscript he was copying) which was unfamiliar, for example, or restore "normal" order where his exemplar's was unusual. The manuscripts were copied at a period when written English was still subject to many regional variations, and a scribe might "translate" unfamiliar forms into those of his own dialect. He might also add prepositions or pronouns to clarify the text's meaning. It is difficult or impossible to determine whether such changes were made consciously or unconsciously. Even if scribes were aware of them, they may not have considered them mistakes or faults in their work, particularly if they made the text easier to read.

Other kinds of variants were introduced as a scribe moved his eyes between his exemplar and the new manuscript. Copying a line at a time, a scribe might easily return to the wrong place in his copy, particularly if two lines began with similar or identical phrases. The result would be the omission of the intervening lines. Another common kind of mistake occurred when a scribe confused a word from a nearby line with one in the line he was copying; this might be especially likely to happen if the words sounded alike and both made good sense in context. Other variations could result when a scribe simply had trouble deciphering the handwriting in his exemplar. Difficulty reading minims, the letters used to form m, n, u, and i, was particularly common and could produce radically different but still plausible readings in a new copy. A given act of copying probably was not likely to introduce many variants of these kinds, but most surviving Chaucer manuscripts are several generations removed from the author's own copy, and so their texts contain several layers of scribal variants.

One example may give some idea of how even a seemingly minor variant can make the "Chaucer" of fifteenth-century readers significantly different from our own. In *The Clerk's Tale*, at the point when Griselda has exchanged her peasant's smock for the robes befitting a marquis's wife, *The Riverside Chaucer*, supported by the best manuscripts, reads:

> Unnethe the peple hir knew for hire fairnesse
> Whan she translated was in swich richesse.
> (IV.384-85)

Two recent and influential readings of the tale have taken their titles and significant parts of their arguments from these lines; the word "translated" has been interpreted as a crucial pun, echoing the allusions to *translatio studii* in *The Clerk's Prologue* and suggesting a metaphorical equivalence between Griselda and the tale itself.[8] But roughly a third of the manuscripts contain different words in this line, usually "transformed," a more common word which an early scribe substituted for "translated," and which was passed on to many other manuscripts thereafter. Thus a piece of wordplay integral to our contemporary understanding of the tale was invisible to a substantial number of Chaucer's early readers.

Other kinds of variants affect not single words but entire lines or passages. Some manuscripts of *The Merchant's Tale*, for example, preserve lines added to make the account of May and Damian's union in the pear tree even more obscene; these were apparently among the spurious lines to which a gentleman reader of Caxton's first edition objected. On the other hand, this entire final episode is absent from the tale in a few manuscripts, probably because an outraged scribe or reader suppressed it.[9] Similarly, the final section of *The Summoner's Tale* was omitted from quite a few copies, apparently because it also offended readers. *The Cook's Tale* was also subject to moralizing intervention; two different endings written for the tale bring Perkyn Revelour and his companions to swift justice. Another solution for the unfinished state of *The Cook's Tale*, devised very early and copied in many manuscripts, was to insert the romance of *Gamelyn* after I.4422.

Variation is especially noticeable at the ends of Chaucer's works. In addition to the examples already discussed, there are significant variations-- whether by addition, suppression, or substantial revision of text--at or near the endings of *The Parliament of Fowls*, *The House of Fame* (in Caxton's print), and the *Treatise on the Astrolabe*, among others. It is quite possible that scribes or their supervisors intervened in their texts partly for commercial reasons, to provide a superficial completeness which would make their products more marketable. There are, in turn, at least two possible reasons why they would have inherited unsatisfactory texts. First, Chaucer himself apparently left several of his works unfinished. Second, if his works circulated in separate booklets (or quires), particularly at an early phase in their transmission, endings written on the final leaves of quires may have been especially vulnerable to physical damage. The need for a superficial completeness that would satisfy a customer's inspection of a book seems also to have motivated the writing of prologues to tales for which Chaucer did not provide them; scribes apparently expected customers to assume that if some of *The Canterbury Tales* had prologues, then the work was not complete unless all had them.[10]

COLLATION AND CORRECTION

Abundant evidence in the manuscripts shows that fifteenth-century readers were often aware of the differences between copies of the same work and made judgments about which readings were preferable. Collation (the comparison of two or more copies) and correction took place in a variety of circumstances.[11] In Oxford, Bodleian Library MS Bodley 686, the scribe undertook extensive correction from his main exemplar after he had completed an initial stage of copying. He ruled additional lines for the corrections below the text area and used symbols to show where these added lines belonged in the text above.[12] We must recognize that "correction" was not merely a way to make the copy more faithful to the exemplar, for the changes in the scribe's hand suggest that he added a new, inauthentic ending to *The Cook's Tale* in the same stage of work as he supplied several omitted but authentic lines. It is also striking that the scribe made no attempt to disguise the corrections while executing what was surely a very expensive commission. Apparently their visibility was not felt to mar the appearance of pages over which the scribe had clearly taken great care; perhaps they were taken as additional evidence of his thoroughness. In another de luxe copy of the *Tales*, London, B. L. MS Harley 1758, the scribe "Cornhyll" made corrections by consulting not only his main exemplar but additional ones as well. By this process he acquired, for example, those obscene lines added to *The Merchant's Tale*, which he carefully wrote in the outer margins.[13] The scribe of Oxford, Christ Church MS 152 likewise relied on a supplementary exemplar for *Gamelyn*, which he copied in space he had originally left blank after *The Cook's Tale* and in an added quire.

Scribes could also gather exemplars and compare and choose readings before they began to write a manuscript. Ralph Hanna III has argued that such a process best explains the distinctive text of the Ellesmere manuscript; the scribes were not sophisticating their copy but rather consulting several manuscripts in order to improve their indifferent main exemplars.[14] Because collation was part of the careful preparations the scribe made before copying, Ellesmere does not have the obvious signs of collation which appear in the manuscripts discussed above; instead, Hanna was able to detect it only by comparing Ellesmere's readings with those in other early manuscripts. Occasionally one finds more obvious signs of collation even in a manuscript the scribe has prepared with great care. Blank spaces in a later manuscript of the *Tales*, Bodleian Library MS Selden B.14, suggest the scribe was hesitating over conflicting readings in multiple exemplars of *The Wife of Bath's Prologue* and never completed the final stage of work in which he would have chosen between them. Analyses of textual traditions so often reveal such conflation of readings from different exemplars, particularly in widely circulated works such as the *Tales*, that in analyzing a particular manuscript, one must always allow for this possibility.

Collation and correction might also take place after a manuscript had passed from the control of the scribe(s) who first produced it. The patron and first owner of the Paris manuscript of the *Tales*, Jean d'Angoulême, made corrections after his scribe John Duxworth was finished with his work.[15] The St. John's manuscript of *Troilus* contains many corrections over erasures in a hand both later and less polished than that of the scribe but still belonging to the fifteenth century; this hand could have been either an owner's or that of someone hired by an owner, but in any case the correction appears to have taken place at some remove from the original production of the manuscript. Additional material and annotations in several hands show that Lincoln Cathedral MS 110 was repeatedly collated with other copies of the *Tales* throughout the second half of the fifteenth century. Collation and correction in fact continued well beyond 1500, though the sources for later collation and correction were often printed books rather than other manuscripts.[16]

ATTRIBUTION

Modern readers may well be surprised to learn that those copying Chaucer's works sometimes consciously changed them, even to the point of interpolating and suppressing large portions of text. Perhaps equally foreign to a modern sensibility is the frequent failure to attribute Chaucer's works to him. Thus, for example, Chaucer's name never appears before or after his lyrics and dream poems in Bodleian Library MSS Tanner 346 and Bodley 638, and he is named only a few times in MS Fairfax 16. Likewise, the copy of *Troilus* owned by Henry V when he was Prince of Wales, Morgan MS 817, does not identify Chaucer as the author of the poem. And although more than half of the manuscripts that preserve the *Retraction* include an Explicit stating Chaucer "compiled" the *Tales*, a number of scribes omitted Chaucer's name in the course of amending or omitting the Explicit. This is especially surprising given that the *Retraction* lists many of Chaucer's works and thus, when joined with an Explicit naming him, has the effect of fixing the author's canon.

Most excerpts from *The Canterbury Tales* which appear in anthologies lack any ascription to Chaucer or any sign they have been drawn from the larger work. The usual practice in manuscripts of the entire *Tales* was to title the tales by their pilgrim tellers; these titles generally appear at the beginnings and endings of tales and prologues and sometimes in running page headings. By contrast, in the miscellanies, the tales, if they were given any titles at all, were named by their subject matter. Thus, for example, in Longleat MS 257, *The Knight's Tale* is given the title "Arcite and Palomon," and *The Clerk's Tale* is headed "Grisild." The scribe of Manchester, Chetham's Library MS 6709, while copying *The Prioress's Tale* and *The Second Nun's Tale* from Caxton's second edition, removed Caxton's titles and instead called the tales "Miraculum Beate Marie Virginis" and "Vita Sancte Cecilie." Moreover, most such manuscripts also omit any material from the pilgrimage frame which would connect the tales to particular tellers (no material from *The General Prologue* is ever excerpted in these manuscripts).[17] That such omission was intended as a way to remove the tales from the potentially ironizing "dramatic" framework is confirmed by the fact that the anthologies retain the prologues of the Prioress and the Second Nun; these, exceptionally, consist of prayers rather than dialogue between pilgrims. As a result of this treatment, the tales are removed from the context which modern readers find a crucial part of their meaning.

Yet surely it would be mistaken to take such instances as evidence of an anonymous literary culture in which an author's identity was unimportant. It is clear that the organizing idea of several of the anthologies containing the lyrics and dream-visions is Chaucer as author. The majority of the poems are by Chaucer, and what many or all of the remaining texts have in common is an indebtedness to Chaucerian genres and forms. Although the anthologies may consist largely of poems reflecting aristocratic attitudes to romantic love, they also include texts emphasizing moral or devotional themes, such as Chaucer's "Boethian" lyrics or, in the second part of Pepys 2006, *Melibee* and *The Parson's Tale*. Similarly, Chaucer-as-author motivated more ephemeral productions, such as when someone copied *Truth* into the Ellesmere flyleaves, or when *Truth* and lines from the *General Prologue* describing the Parson were written in an early manuscript of the *Boece* (B. L.

MS Additional 10340). Sometimes too the gravitational pull of Chaucer's reputation led to others' works being attributed to him; this could be either explicit or implicit, as when Lydgate's *Temple of Glass* was included, without attribution, in Gg.4.27, a manuscript clearly intended as a "collected works" of Chaucer. Occasionally those false ascriptions were sustained even after the misattributed work passed from the context of the Chaucerian anthology to a manuscript dominated by very different kinds of texts.[18]

Issues of attribution and reputation become more uncertain when we consider evidence from the earliest part of the fifteenth century. How are we to interpret, for example, the omission of Chaucer's name from the Morgan *Troilus*? If, as John Fisher proposes in "A Language Policy for Lancastrian England," the Lancastrians did seek to capitalize on Chaucer's reputation in order to help promote both English writing and their own claim to their throne, surely commissioning this manuscript was important to that strategy. Was Chaucer's reputation already so well established, and so clearly associated with the titles of his major works, that it was unnecessary to identify him as the author of *Troilus* in the manuscript itself? If so, how had that reputation been created?

BEYOND THE TEXT

So far discussion has focused on what modern readers regard as the texts of Chaucer's works—on those words in the manuscripts to which modern editors assign line numbers and which we cite in literary analysis of Chaucer's writing. But as a glance at almost any folio will show, the manuscripts contain many other elements as well; these are also important evidence for medieval readers' experience of Chaucer.[19] Titles have already been mentioned; these sometimes take the form of Incipits (as in Hengwrt's "Here bygynneth the Book of the tales of Caunterbury") or Explicits. Such Incipits and Explicits also occur at the beginnings and endings of major divisions of text, such as the books of *Troilus* and the prologues and tales in *The Canterbury Tales*. Typically the use of red ink and/or a larger, more elaborate script distinguishes these Incipits and Explicits from the text. Other features often give additional emphasis to major textual divisions. These range from full borders and demivinets (borders on 3 sides of the page) to champes (large, illuminated initials with sprays) to various kinds of smaller initials.[20] The pilgrim portraits in a few copies of the *Tales* likewise serve to mark the divisions between tales. Such means of clarifying the organization of the text often work in concert with other features. These include, for example, running titles at the tops of folios, and annotations which mark inset genres (such as lyrics in *Troilus* and the dream-visions) or provide brief summaries of a longer work.[21] Even the use of brackets or blank space to indicate stanza-divisions was part of the scribal presentation of Chaucer's texts.

Among the manuscripts of a given work, one often finds a general similarity in such features, but a greater degree of variation than in the text.

For example, in many *Tales* manuscripts the beginnings of tales are decorated more elaborately than prologues. This hierarchy remains in place even when manuscripts vary sharply in their general level of decoration. In de luxe manuscripts, a champe typically marks the beginning of a prologue, but a demivinet appears at the first line of a tale. More modest copies retain the distinction between prologue and tale by employing two different kinds of initials—though it may be that neither kind is as elaborate as a champe. There are variations from this hierarchy, however; one reason for Ellesmere's extraordinary luxury is that it includes demivinets at both prologues and tales, as well as at major divisions within the tales of the Clerk and Parson.

Many other aspects of *mise-en-page* exhibit a similar mixture of continuity and variation. As the discussion of the anthologized *Canterbury Tales* has shown, scribes sometimes changed the titles of the works they copied. But they did not do so routinely; as a result, one may well find, for a frequently copied work, more than one title in the manuscripts—but not a different one in each manuscript. A few copies of the *Treatise on the Astrolabe*, for instance, give it the charming title of "Bread and Milk for Children." By sometime in the first quarter of the fifteenth century, there had emerged at least four different traditions for the Incipits and Explicits of *The Canterbury Tales*. Though later scribes sometimes translated these from English into Latin or French, or introduced small variations in wording, they generally based their Incipits and Explicits on these traditions. The mixture of continuity and variation appears in other aspects of *mise-en-page* as well. A series of marginal annotations, often Latin citations from Chaucer's sources, entered the textual tradition of *The Canterbury Tales* at a quite early stage and continued to be copied in many manuscripts throughout the fifteenth century. But scribes sometimes failed to copy them at all, or copied only some of them, through either systematic selection or simple carelessness. Yet they also added to what they found in their exemplars.[22] The manuscripts preserve several different series of scribal summaries to *The Knight's Tale*, for example. Features of *mise-en-page*, like passages of the text, could be acquired through collation; the scribe of Bodleian Library MS Rawlinson poet 141 drew on University of Chicago MS 564 of the *Tales* for text and some glosses, but gathered many additional glosses from a manuscript resembling Ellesmere and B. L. Additional MS 35286. Moreover, such aspects of *mise-en-page* could be added long after the original scribe had finished work; for example, two or more readers added running page heads to folios which lacked them in B. L. MS Harley 7334, a very early copy of the *Tales*. The manuscripts also include many signs of attention to particular passages—underlining, pointing hands, brackets, as well as "nota bene" and other remarks—written by readers during the fifteenth and sixteenth centuries.

Although some extratextual features enter the tradition so late they cannot possibly be connected to Chaucer himself, others are present in the earliest surviving manuscripts and in many others as well. Scholarly discussion about whether any of these can be attributed to Chaucer has still not proceeded very far. It is hard to imagine Chaucer would not have provided some elements of layout for his longer works, in particular, but because we cannot apply some of the tests, such as metrical ones, which are often used to distinguish authorial from scribal readings in the text, and because scribes and readers added or modified features of *mise-en-page* so readily, it is also hard to be confident that these features derived from Chaucer's own copy without scribal interference.

There is another side to the question of attribution for extratextual features; that is, how were they perceived by early readers? When we make judgments about attribution, we do so partly by comparing readings in many manuscripts. But no fifteenth-century reader had access to so much information. If his or her manuscript contained marginal summaries or citations from Chaucer's sources, what status were they judged to have? In an age preoccupied, as Tim Machan has pointed out, with textual authority, were both text and gloss believed to carry Chaucer's authority?[23] Did it matter to early readers whether or not such features were to be ascribed to Chaucer? The varying amounts of care taken in copying them may reflect early readers' different levels of interest in extratextual features.

THE MAKERS OF BOOKS

At this point we should consider the status and relationships of those involved in producing books. Recent investigations have undermined the model of shops or scriptoria which shaped earlier scholarship on the manuscripts.[24] Craftsmen in the book trade had begun to congregate in the area near St. Paul's in London by about the middle of the fourteenth century, and many of the de luxe Chaucer manuscripts were probably produced here, but "a book made for the commercial trade in London, such as the Hengwrt and Ellesmere manuscripts, was more probably the joint product of work done in many different places, with each stage in a book's creation occurring in a different artisan's shop."[25] Copies of even the most popular vernacular texts were made on a commission or bespoke basis. The materials of books were too expensive, and the demand too unpredictable, for stationers to have produced copies "on spec," and so we cannot imagine readers browsing among readymade copies in the window of a shop. Expense and uncertain demand also make it unlikely that scribes kept exemplars on hand. Rather, the customer may often have been responsible for supplying an exemplar of the text he or she wished to have copied. As a result, a customer could play a greater role in determining the shape of a book than he or she does in print culture. This seems especially true with respect to the anthologies of dream poems and short poems, where the choice of texts was probably largely up to the customer.

Similarly, alliances among the various craftsmen needed to produce de luxe or intermediate-level copies seem to have been developed in response to specific commissions. In de luxe copies decoration (and illustration, if any) constituted a significant part of the customer's expense, and the artists may well have supervised the scribes in the execution of high-end commissions. For even the most accomplished scribes, the copying of vernacular works may well have been a sideline, as their main source of work was probably the copying of Latin works such as books of hours or even of legal or government documents. In manuscripts written by more than one scribe we can often infer—from correction, from other finishing work such as rubrication, or from the apportioning of text for copying—that one scribe acted as supervisor of the others. But this relationship may well have existed only for this particular piece of work, probably because the "supervisor" was the one who received the original commission and then parceled out some of the work to others. It is best not to suppose any individual consistently acted as the "corrector," for instance, of other scribes' work.

Production of English manuscripts was by no means limited to this London book trade. Those involved in producing university texts at Oxford would have been available for the copying of vernacular literature and so would scribes in other cities and towns, who were probably also employed primarily in copying Latin texts. Such producers would have been especially dependent on their customers for texts, some of which they probably obtained in London.[26] Significant numbers of manuscripts were also produced in noncommercial environments. In the large households of the provincial gentry, clerks engaged in a variety of administrative tasks might have been asked to copy literary texts—probably a very small part of their duties. Some copies were made in religious establishments. In all of these circumstances the writers might have decorated the manuscripts themselves or may have called on the services of local or itinerant artisans. Finally, some readers copied texts for themselves. The Findern manuscript preserves the work of not one but many such readers.

Copies of Chaucer's works clearly passed readily between these various environments. Dialectal variation shows that they were disseminated throughout much of the British Isles during the fifteenth century. Bodleian Library MS Selden B.24, for example, an anthology including *Troilus*, the *Parliament of Fowls*, and several lyrics along with works by others, was produced in Scotland late in the century (or possibly early in the sixteenth). A now-battered copy of the *Tales*, B. L. Additional MS 25718, apparently was written in Ireland in the second quarter of the fifteenth century. Other kinds of evidence show that those in religious houses or making copies for themselves drew on the same exemplars as scribes in commercial environments. For instance, annotations and Incipits to several of Chaucer's works in B. L. MS Harley 7333, a large anthology apparently prepared in or for a house of Austin canons at Leicester, show that these texts ultimately derive from John Shirley, who had close connections to the London book trade.[27] The three anthologies which form the "Oxford group" are usually highly similar in their texts but clearly differed sharply in their expense and circumstances of production. Fairfax 16 has de luxe decoration, including gold leaf and a full-page illustration; Tanner 346 was written by accomplished scribes but has more modest decoration; while the entirely unadorned Bodley 638 must have been written by "Lyty" for his own use and his family's.

AUTHORS AND MANUSCRIPT PRODUCTION

We know much less than we would like to about what role an author would have played in the production of books. In general, we might imagine a number of possible interactions involving an author, those producing copies, and the person for whom a manuscript was intended—whether a patron of a work, a customer for a particular copy, or someone to whom the author wished to present a copy. For example, an author seeking copies for friends or others who had expressed interest, or for more public presentation to a prestigious recipient (perhaps in hopes of financial reward) might have commissioned a number of manuscripts. But if a person of means had commissioned a literary work, such as a translation, he or she might instead have been responsible for initial circulation. Having devoted some resources to supporting the author's or translator's work, a patron might well attempt to win some recognition for his patronage by commissioning copies for presentation to others. Then, once a work had begun to circulate and acquire a reputation, the primary demand for manuscripts might have come from readers seeking their own copies. But this would not necessarily have ended the involvement of the patron (if there was one) and author, since if they were still accessible, either the scribes or their customers might have turned to them for exemplars.

Relative to the number of surviving Middle English manuscripts, we have little evidence which would help us make more definite statements about these transactions; most obviously helpful would be more documentary records of payment for the making of books, or more manuscripts which we could be confident were overseen by authors. We have hundreds of documents which name Chaucer, but none acknowledges that he wrote poetry; and we have few if any manuscripts produced in his lifetime. As a result, we are forced to make inferences from his works about his relationships with scribes and with the possible recipients of copies. For instance, we know from allusions in the poem itself and in later passages listing his works that in *The Book of the Duchess*, Chaucer commemorated Blanche of Lancaster and her husband's love for her. And we have a record of John of Gaunt's grant of an annuity to Chaucer in 1374, within a few years of Blanche's death. But the record does not mention the poem, so we can only infer that the payment was an award for it. If we do so, it would also seem logical to suppose Chaucer oversaw preparation of a copy and presented it to John of Gaunt. The earliest surviving copy of *The Book of the Duchess*, however, dates from the second quarter of the fifteenth century, perhaps 70 years after the poem was written, and we have no good basis for imagining what relationship if any that copy might bear to the hypothesized presentation manuscript.

Our literary evidence for Chaucer's possible role in book production and presentation is often vague and contradictory and, as in the case of *The Book of the Duchess*, often difficult to reconcile with the history of his works visible in the manuscripts. In the case of the *Treatise on the Astrolabe*, the number of manuscripts, rather than their paucity, surprises us; in the first line Chaucer states that he wrote at the request of his son Lewis, about as informal a "commission" as one can imagine, yet the work clearly achieved early and wide circulation. In famous lines at the end of *Troilus*, Chaucer directs "this book" to "moral Gower" and "philosophical Strode" (V.1856-57). But the compliment to Queen Anne at I.171, the poem's frequent addresses to an implied audience of "lovers," and the account, however fictionalized, of the poem's reception in the Prologue to the *Legend of Good Women* all suggest the poem was "presented" to an audience of rather different status and attitudes than Gower's and Strode's. The two earliest surviving copies, Corpus and Morgan, likewise argue an audience of the highest class. Lines 496-97 in the F prologue of the *Legend* seem to provide the clearest evidence that one of Chaucer's poems was intended for a royal patron, but the lines' omission from the revised G Prologue and the incompleteness of the surviving text raise doubts that the commission was fulfilled. Several short poems—*Scogan, Bukton, Purse, Stedfastnesse*, and *Truth*—give us some of our most specific information about occasions and recipients. But if we suppose copies of such poems were presented to their recipients on single leaves or in small booklets, we still confront difficult questions about how they might have been used to produce later anthologies like those in which the poems survive. How well would such small booklets have survived, even for the few decades that passed between their composition and the dates when we know they were being collected in anthologies? How would those making the manuscripts have known about and obtained exemplars after such a passage of time?

Questions also arise when we turn to Chaucer's remarks about scribes in *Troilus* (V.1793-98) and in the poem to *Adam Scriveyn*. The lines in *Troilus* imply that Chaucer foresaw, with some apprehension, his texts passing out of his control as scribes produced copies. In the poem to *Adam Scriveyn*, Chaucer portrays himself as involved in the making of copies of *Troilus* and the *Boece*, acting as a corrector of scribal errors. But the brief poem does not make clear for whom the copies are being made; it does not allude to any of the presentation scenarios of *Troilus* or the *Legend*, and so those copies may have been intended for Chaucer's own use rather than for others'. Given this lack of conclusive evidence, it is hardly surprising that Chaucerians sharply disagree about the nature, the number, and the dates of the lost manuscripts behind those which survive.

There are other kinds of evidence which also deserve to be considered in any hypothesis about the canon's "prehistory." Other writers alluded to or quoted Chaucer's works in the fourteenth century; we can be most confident about Usk's *Testament of Love*, of about 1387, and Clanvowe in *The Book of Cupid*, written in the late 1380s or the 1390s. Beyond mention of specific titles or reference to specific lines, we must acknowledge that these writers have absorbed an entire idiom which Chaucer had introduced into English; Clanvowe, for example, while writing in a five-line stanza never employed by Chaucer, did write in the pentameter line which Chaucer had shown could succeed as a basic medium for English poetry. English poetry written very soon after Chaucer's death (at the latest), such as the early works of Hoccleve and Lydgate, likewise reflects that thorough absorption of Chaucerian forms and themes. Finally, Chaucer's allusions to his own works, in the lists of the *Legend*, the "Wordes of the Host" before the *Man of Law's Tale*, and the *Retractions*, as well as his allusion to the Wife of Bath in *Bukton*, should not be left out of account; they constitute some evidence that copies of those works were already in circulation.

In order to reconcile this literary evidence with the lack of surviving fourteenth-century manuscripts, some have proposed that Chaucer's works circulated in his lifetime only within a well-defined, limited community in London, consisting of men much like himself as well as people of higher status who were associated with the royal court.[28] The lack of evidence for Chaucer's public presentation of his works—the kind of event typically portrayed in medieval presentation miniatures—has, along with the lack of pre-1400 manuscripts, made scholars reluctant to characterize Chaucer's possible circulation of his works as publication. Certainly, the poet's offering of copies to a small circle of friends of his own social status would not have had the same cultural value as presentation to a royal or other highly prestigious patron. But for the production of manuscript copies, the two kinds of presentation have essentially the same significance; in each case the text would have been released from the strict control of the author and become available for further copying. As soon as the text circulated beyond that "first degree of separation" from Chaucer—perhaps when friends wished to make copies for their friends—then his work may well have passed into the commercial environment of the London artisans, for this would have been one obvious place to turn for anyone possessing an exemplar and wishing to make a copy. There is no *a priori* reason to suppose this would have happened only after Chaucer's death. In print culture, the distinction between coterie circulation and publication is connected to a change in medium, from manuscript or typescript to print. In manuscript culture, where there was no such change in medium, the distinction between the two kinds of circulation was much less clear.

REVISION AND TEXTUAL TRADITIONS

Manuscript culture also requires us to reconsider our notion of revision.[29] The technology and economy of print culture discourage frequent authorial revision. So long as copies of a book remain on hand, a modern publisher will be reluctant to print a revised edition that would make them obsolete. In addition, much of the cost of a printed work derives from the labor required to set type; having made this investment, a printer or publisher finds it advantageous to make as many copies as possible from one set of type, because he or she incurs considerable costs for even the smallest revisions if they require resetting type. Thus a publisher will often wait several years, in order to collect enough corrections and revisions to justify the investment, before resetting a work and publishing a corrected or revised edition.

But in the production of manuscript copies, this set of financial constraints did not obtain. Nothing in the economy of publication discouraged authors from constantly making changes to their works and having these incorporated into subsequent copies—as indeed, after a work had passed from an author's control, there was no financial consideration to prevent the scribes themselves or their patrons from making changes to the text being reproduced. Authors may in fact have regarded the preparation of every new copy under their supervision as an opportunity to introduce changes, of whatever nature and extent, into their works. For this reason we cannot reserve the term "revision" only for the kind of systematic authorial reconsideration which is usually required for the production of a distinct edition in print culture.

Thus if we are to suppose Chaucer had any involvement in the production of copies for circulation, we must allow for the possibility that those copies varied partly as a result of his revisions. Let us return, for example, to those manuscripts which do not include the final "pear-tree" episode of *The Merchant's Tale*. When we look at that tale in isolation, the obvious explanation for the absence of these lines appears to be scribal suppression due to their scandalous content . But these three manuscripts also lack several other passages in Fragments IV and V we consider authentic and which are found in most reliable manuscripts as well as in modern editions. It is much harder to attribute the lack of these other pieces of text to scribal discomfort with their content; moreover, these manuscripts are marked by extensive variation within the confines of Fragments IV and V, rather than, say, widespread suppression of bawdy passages throughout the work. It is possible that those who produced the exemplar behind these three manuscripts simply never had access to those passages, including the conclusion of *The Merchant's Tale*, because they were working with a copy or copies which represented an early stage of Chaucer's intentions.

While there is no evidence in the *Tales* or any other work of a comprehensive line-by-line revision, there are occasionally intriguing small variants which might be explained as Chaucerian rather than scribal. For example, in the line in *The Clerk's Tale* discussed above, we can confidently attribute the reading "transformed" to scribal substitution for the less familar "translated." But a few manuscripts—including those three which lack the conclusion of *The Merchant's Tale*—include a third reading for this line, "transmuwed." This word does not appear to have been any more common than "translated" in the sense in which it is used here, and so the editorial principle of the "harder reading" cannot be invoked to attribute either word to scribal substitution. Moreover, the word "transmuwed" is an anglicization of the word which appears at this point in one of Chaucer's sources for *The*

Clerk's Tale, a French version of the Griselda story. It therefore seems possible that "transmuwed" represents Chaucer's earliest intentions and that he changed this word to "translated" at a later stage—perhaps a stage at which he also embarked on larger-scale rearrangements and additions in Fragments IV and V. Not only textual editors but also those studying variation as evidence for reception must consider authorial revision as a possible source of variation.[30]

MATTERS OF SURVIVAL

The relative abundance of manuscript evidence for Chaucer's works can make it easy to forget a fact already touched on in the preceding discussion of their "prehistory": that evidence is irreparably incomplete. In some cases, a small remnant survives of what must have been a substantial codex. For instance, the hand of the scribe who wrote the Hengwrt and Ellesmere manuscripts of the *Tales* appears also on a single, battered leaf containing a few lines of *Troilus and Criseyde*; thus we have only the slimmest fragment of a codex which was probably accurate in its readings and may have contributed significantly to the early dissemination of the poem. Similarly, two fragmentary manuscripts of the *Tales*, the Merthyr fragment and the single leaf of Cambridge U. L. MS Kk.1.3, date from the first 10 to 15 years of the fifteenth century and contain highly accurate texts.[31] To judge by size, layout, and contents, both *represent* complete codices of the *Tales* which contained a wealth of information, like that in extant codices, but to which we no longer have access.

But these tangible artifacts do not by themselves give us an adequate idea of how much has been lost. We can also infer the existence of lost copies from the textual relationships among those we have. When two (or more) copies are very similar but one is not copied from another, it is most plausible to suppose they were copied from a common original which has been lost. Typically the copies preserve certain kinds of evidence more or less faithfully--textual variants, distinctive linguistic forms, Incipits and Explicits, glosses--but not other kinds, such as indications of ownership (coats of arms, for example, or names scribbled in the margins or endleaves) and programs of illustration.[32]

Even when conditions would seem most favorable for their preservation, manuscripts have been lost. Consider, for example, Hoccleve's *Regiment of Princes*. Passages in the poem and a miniature in an early copy make it clear that Hoccleve prepared a manuscript for presentation to Henry, Prince of Wales, for whom he had written the work. Hoccleve also saw that other manuscripts were produced for presentation. An additional envoi preserved in later manuscripts shows that one of these was intended for John, Duke of Bedford, an important bibliophile. Many copies of the poem are extant, some written in Hoccleve's lifetime and at least two probably under his direction. The manuscripts presented to the Prince of Wales and the Duke of Bedford, however, do not seem to have survived.[33]

Because we do not know when and how Chaucer's texts passed from his control into the hands of those making copies for sale, it is difficult even to guess at the nature and quantity of the manuscripts which have been lost. It would be conservative to suppose that for any Chaucerian text we have lost at least half the copies which once existed. An editor of *The House of Fame* proposes a hypothesis of five or more lost copies to explain the relations of the three surviving manuscripts and one early print.[34] Fifteenth-century wills—themselves a very partial record of book ownership—record Chaucer manuscripts which cannot be identified with any of those which survive.[35] A survival rate of one in three to five seems a reasonable conjecture, and one in ten not impossible for some texts.

We can imagine any number of reasons for the destruction of copies. If Chaucer did present a manuscript of *The Book of the Duchess* to John of Gaunt, it may well have perished in the burning of the Duke's palace in London, the Savoy, during the English Rising of 1381. Michael J. Bennett adduces a number of possible reasons for the early loss of many cultural artifacts created under the patronage of the court of Richard II.[36] In addition, Chaucer manuscripts, like many others, were vulnerable as a result of the civil wars which ravaged England in the fifteenth century, the advent of printing, and Henry VIII's dissolution of the monasteries. The rat-gnawed leaves of the Hengwrt manuscript remind us of more mundane threats. But we should not assume that even those manuscripts which survived these trials were necessarily safe once antiquarian collecting had begun in the late sixteenth and seventeenth centuries. John Stow's brief note on fol. 82^v of Fairfax 16, at the end of Lydgate's *Temple of Glass*, "Here lacketh .6. leves that are in Joseph Holland's Boke," shows Stow gathered information about the whereabouts of various copies and compared their texts—still essential scholarly activities. It must be weighed in the balance, however, with the notes which appear on fol. 1 of this treasury of Chaucer's dream poems and lyrics: "I bought this att Gloucester | 8 Sept 1650 C. Fairfax | intendinge to exchange itt for a better booke."

PATTERNS

Having sounded this note of warning, I will conclude by offering a few generalizations. Parts of the preceding discussion have touched on the diversity of the Chaucer manuscripts—in materials and expense, in where they were produced, in their contents and the ways they present them, in their fidelity to what we judge Chaucer actually wrote. The point is less bland than it might seem, and worth emphasizing. Consider, for example, their level of decoration. The Ellesmere is one of the most lavish English literary manuscripts, and roughly half of the *Tales* manuscripts include demivinets and gold leaf, while the others include many standard commercial copies and a few modest books apparently made up by readers for their own use.[37] The Corpus *Troilus*, if completed, would have exceeded even Ellesmere, but some copies of the poem were written largely or entirely on paper and without any decoration at all. Chaucer's works are thus well represented throughout the entire range of books used for English literary texts. The picture is different for the poems of his contemporaries: Gower's *Confessio Amantis* is much more often accompanied by miniatures, and only a third of the copies have little or no decoration, while almost all copies of the various recensions of *Piers Plowman* have minor decoration or none at all.[38]

Although there is one attempt at a "collected works" (Cambridge U. L. Gg.4.27), and a few other anthologies are also exceptions, the manuscripts generally observe a tripartite division of Chaucer's literary works. The *Tales* are the main or sole contents of the manuscripts in which they appear, as is *Troilus* in the codices which contain it; the dream-visions and shorter poems appear together in still other manuscripts. The *Astrolabe* appears separately from all of these, often in collections of astronomical and astrological material. The *Boece* is usually isolated from Chaucer's works, though it appears together with one or more shorter poems in three copies. Outside anthologies such as those of the "Oxford group," one is struck by the apparently ephemeral existence of the lyrics, as they are sometimes copied at the ends of much longer works or in the blank spaces at the ends of quires.

The *Tales*, *Troilus*, and the dream-visions and shorter poems tend to appear only with other works of particular, well-defined types, which might be characterized as those suited to "metropolitan" taste, such as the works of Hoccleve, Lydgate, and Clanvowe. This pattern obtains even when the material circumstances of production vary widely—whether in London, a religious house, or a household of the country gentry. Chaucer's poetry almost never appears with that of the Alliterative Revival, the tail-rhyme romances, or *Piers Plowman*.

Unlike the poems of the Alliterative Revival, which almost always survive only in single copies, almost all of Chaucer's works survive in more than one manuscript, and some are among the most widely attested texts in Middle English. There are well over 50 largely intact manuscripts of the *Tales*; about twice as many as for any other of his works; of these, the ones that survive most often are the *Astrolabe*, *Truth*, *Troilus*, and the *Parliament of Fowls*. These numbers do not necessarily reflect the numbers of copies that existed in the fifteenth century. The *Tales* and *Troilus* might survive in larger quantities, relative to the number that once existed, because they occupied an entire book. The prose works might have been perceived as less relevant to Chaucer's reputation as "court poet" and so of less interest to the sixteenth and seventeenth-century antiquarians who sought out and preserved copies of the poems.

Only for the *Tales*, *Boece*, and the *Astrolabe* are there significant numbers of copies from the first quarter of the fifteenth century. For several of the longer works—the *Tales*, *Troilus*, and the *Astrolabe*—more copies appear to date to the second quarter of the century than to any other. This chronological concentration is even more clear if we define an "extended second quarter" of c. 1420-60. That *Boece* is an exception, with most copies dating to the first quarter or early in the second, may be significant; the prose translation may have been superseded by John Walton's versification of Chaucer's work. By contrast to the longer works, the manuscripts containing the dream-visions and short poems tend to be later, almost all dating from the second half of the century.

This pattern of dates suggests the *Tales*, among the last works to be written, may have been among the first to achieve wide circulation, and may have helped to create a demand for Chaucer's other poetry. (Quite possibly interest in *Boece* and the *Astrolabe* was not so dependent on the development of an audience for vernacular literary texts.) But here we confront once again a conflict between manuscript evidence and the early allusions to Chaucer, which often invoke the dream poems, lyrics, or *Troilus*. This may suggest a disparity between the aspects of Chaucer's art that appealed most to other writers, centered in the capital, and those most popular with a broader audience, especially that beyond London. The *Tales* contain some elements, such as the religious and moral tales and the romances, of the kinds people may have been used to reading in English by the end of the fourteenth century and which continued to become more popular in course of the fifteenth. Once the *Tales* had helped to make Chaucer familiar to a heterogeneous readership, its members may have been prepared to seek out and read his other works, even if these poems invoked a more specifically metropolitan audience.

This is offered merely to illustrate the kind of argument that might be developed from certain general patterns in the manuscript evidence. But every manuscript is in some way exceptional and therefore worth knowing.

SUGGESTIONS FOR FURTHER READING

Those new to the study of medieval manuscripts might begin with D. C. Greetham, *Textual Scholarship* (New York: Garland, 1992); chapters 2 and 4 provide basic introductions to the bibliography (i. e., the materials and structure) of the manuscript book, and to the history of Western scripts. (The book also contains an extensive bibliography.) More detailed discussions can be found in Sandra Hindman and James Douglas Farquhar, *Pen to Press* ([College Park:] Art Department, University of Maryland; [Baltimore:] Department of the History of Art, Johns Hopkins University, 1977), especially chapter 1, "The Manuscript as a Book"; and in Bernhard Bischoff, *Latin Paleography*, trans. Dáibhí ó Cróinín and David Ganz (Cambridge: Cambridge University Press, 1990). A general introduction to illumination, such as J. J. G. Alexander, *Medieval Illuminators and Their Methods of Work* (New Haven and London: Yale University Press, 1992), will also be useful. The essential discussion of English writing in the later Middle Ages is M. B. Parkes, *English Cursive Book Hands* (revised rpt. London: Scolar Press, 1979). Beverly Boyd, *Chaucer and the Medieval Book* (San Marino: Huntington Library, 1973), offers an introduction oriented specifically to the reader of Chaucer; it is now somewhat dated in light of the large volume of new research on the topic. *Sixty Bokes Olde and Newe*, ed. David Anderson (Knoxville, Tenn.: The New Chaucer Society, University of Tennessee, Knoxville, 1986), includes information about manuscript and printed copies of works by Chaucer and other medieval writers in collections in the eastern U. S, with many illustrations. *Book Production and Publishing in Britain 1375-1475*, edited by Jeremy Griffiths and Derek Pearsall (Cambridge: Cambridge University Press, 1989), summarizes much recent work on the "conditions of literature" during the years when Chaucer was writing and his works were circulating in manuscript. I have drawn on several of its chapters in preparing this essay.

After becoming familiar with the basic terms and history, one should work at the earliest opportunity with the published facsimiles of the major Chaucer manuscripts. There is an additional reason for this: firsthand experience of manuscripts is an essential prerequisite for intelligent use and evaluation of the other kinds of materials discussed below, such as descriptions and transcriptions of manuscripts, and arguments which interpret their evidence. (Ultimately, work with manuscripts themselves is in turn necessary for effective use of facsimiles.) In addition to those listed in the Textual Notes to *The Riverside Chaucer* (Boston: Houghton Mifflin, 1987), p. 1117, the following facsimiles have appeared: *The Pierpont Morgan Library Manuscript M.817: A Facsimile*, intro. Jeanne Krochalis, The facsimile series of the works of Geoffrey Chaucer, vol. 4 (Norman, Okla.: Pilgrim Books, 1986); *Manuscript Trinity R.3.19: A Facsimile*, intro. Brådford Y. Fletcher, The facsimile series, vol. 5 (Norman, Okla.: Pilgrim Books, 1987); *The New Ellesmere Chaucer Facsimile*, eds. Martin Stevens and Daniel Woodward (San Marino: Huntington Library, and Tokyo: Yushodo, 1995). More widely available than the last is *The Ellesmere Chaucer: A Working Facsimile*, intro. Ralph Hanna III (Cambridge: D. S. Brewer, 1989), which actually reproduces an earlier, non-photographic facsimile of Ellesmere. *The Wife of Bath's Prologue on CD-ROM*, ed. Peter Robinson (Cambridge: Cambridge University Press, 1996) includes images of the *WBP* in all manuscripts. Boydell and Brewer will publish a facsimile of Oxford, Bodleian Library MS Selden B.24, with an introduction by Julia Boffey and A. S. G. Edwards, in 1997. The introductions to these facsimiles offer a wealth of information about the manuscripts and amount to a short course in how to interpret and evaluate their evidence.

It would, of course, be a mistake to limit oneself to Chaucer manuscripts; there have also been published facsimiles of other important Middle English manuscripts such as Bodleian Library MSS Douce 104 and Bodley 851 of *Piers Plowman*, the Lincoln Thornton manuscript, the Auchinleck manuscript, and B. L. MS Harley 2253, which contains the "Harley lyrics." Many medieval manuscripts are available in microfilm; copies of films made for the British Manuscripts Project during World War II can be ordered from the Library of Congress, and newer microfilms of certain collections have been published in recent years. It can be somewhat harder to use microfilms than published facsimiles, but they are less expensive and give one access to a far wider range of texts.

The bibliography of printed material relating to the manuscripts, like that of virtually all aspects of Chaucer studies, is vast. The Annotated Bibliography of Chaucer published each year in *Studies in the Age of Chaucer* includes a section on Manuscript and Textual Studies. These may be used to supplement the bibliographies in N. F. Blake, *The Textual Tradition of The Canterbury Tales* (London: Arnold, 1985); *Troilus and Criseyde*, ed. B. A. Windeatt (London and New York: Longman, 1984); *The Legend of Good Women*, eds. George Kane and J. M. Cowen (East Lansing, Mich.: Colleagues Press, 1995); Julia Boffey, "The Reputation and Circulation of Chaucer's Lyrics in the Fifteenth Century," *Chaucer Review* 28 (1993), 23-40, reprinted in this volume; and the facsimiles cited above. M. C. Seymour, *A Catalogue of Chaucer Manuscripts, Vol. I: Works Before the Canterbury Tales* (Aldershot: Scolar Press, 1995) has been sharply criticized; see the review by A. S. G. Edwards in *Review of English Studies* n. s. xlviii (1997), 82-84. The essays in *The Ellesmere Chaucer: Essays in Interpretation*, eds. Martin Stevens and Daniel Woodward (San Marino: Huntington Library, and Tokyo: Yushodo, 1995) contain many references to relevant publications, but the book does not include a bibliography.

The Textual Notes to *The Riverside Chaucer* contain information about the locations of manuscripts, brief analyses of the textual traditions for the various works, citations of the most important scholarship, and selective lists of variant readings. More detailed discussions can often be found in editions of individual works, such as the volumes of the Variorum Chaucer. Windeatt's edition of *Troilus*, and the Kane/Cowen edition of the *LGW*, provide complete lists of variants. Daniel Mosser's "Bibliographical Notes" in *The Wife of Bath's Prologue on CD-ROM* update and supplement but do not yet supersede the descriptions in Volume I of *The Text of The Canterbury Tales*, eds. J. M. Manly and Edith Rickert (Chicago: University of Chicago Press, 1940). The CD-ROM gives one access to a comprehensive corpus of variants for that particular part of the *Tales*; Manly and Rickert give variants from all manuscripts for all of the *Tales*, but their listing is selective, and many readers have found their presentation of the variants forbidding. A more summary outline of the information appears in Sir William McCormick, *The Manuscripts of The Canterbury Tales: A Critical Description of Their Contents* (Oxford: Clarendon Press, 1933), a helpful but underused resource.

From the 1860s to the early part of this century, the Chaucer Society published transcriptions of many of the most important manuscripts; *The Riverside Chaucer* lists the numbers in which transcriptions appeared, at the Textual Notes to each work. While the Chaucer Society transcriptions are not completely reliable in matters of detail, they do present the textual variation among different copies of the same work in a way which some readers find more accessible than an edition's corpus of variants. The Chaucer Society also issued many other publications related to the manuscripts, such as facsimiles of selected folios, and monographs on textual issues—for example, the extent and nature of Chaucer's possible revisions in the *Tales, Troilus,* and the *LGW*—which set the terms for debates that continue to this day. Another early study posing questions that still engage scholars is Aage Brusendorff's *The Chaucer Tradition* (London: Humphrey Milford, 1925).

Disagreement about the *Tales* has been particularly vocal. N. F. Blake, in *The Textual Tradition of The Canterbury Tales,* and Charles A. Owen Jr., in *The Manuscripts of The Canterbury Tales* (Cambridge: D. S. Brewer, 1991), discuss the evidence at length in order to pursue specific hypotheses which have proved controversial. Derek Pearsall's account of the manuscripts in *The Canterbury Tales* (London: Allen and Unwin, 1985) is similar but not identical to Blake's. A critique of Blake's arguments, in particular, is offered by Ralph Hanna III in "The Hengwrt Manuscript and the Canon of *The Canterbury Tales," English Manuscript Studies* 1 (1989), 64-84; this and other important essays on, for example, the textual traditions of *Troilus* and *Truth,* are reprinted in Hanna's *Pursuing History* (Stanford: Stanford University Press, 1996). Larry D. Benson's "The Order of *The Canterbury Tales," Studies in the Age of Chaucer* 3 (1981), 77-120, proposes a hypothesis based on rather different assumptions than those of Blake or Owen. Daniel S. Silvia, "Some Fifteenth-Century Manuscripts of the *Canterbury Tales,"* in *Chaucer and Middle English Studies in Honour of Rossell Hope Robbins,* ed. Beryl Rowland (London: Allen and Unwin, 1974), pp. 153-163, focuses on the miscellanies which contain one or a few tales.

In his edition of *Troilus,* Windeatt presents his arguments about the text of the poem, which overturned R. K. Root's long-accepted idea that the poem exists in three Chaucerian recensions. Stephen A. Barney, in chapter 6 of *Studies in Troilus: Chaucer's Text, Meter, and Diction* (East Lansing, Mi.: Colleagues Press, 1993) reviews the subsequent controversy while siding with Windeatt on this particular question. Chaucerians have long supposed the G Prologue to the *Legend of Good Women* represents Chaucer's revision of the F Prologue, undertaken several years later partly in response to Queen Anne's death. But that view has been challenged from two different perspectives by William A. Quinn in *Chaucer's Rehersynges* (Washington, D. C.: Catholic University of America Press, 1994) and by Joseph A. Dane in "The Notions of Text and Variant in the Prologue to Chaucer's *Legend of Good Women:* MS Gg, Lines 127-38," *PBSA* 87 (1993), 65-80.

As several of the essays in the present volume testify, the manuscripts have been drawn on increasingly as evidence for the reception of Chaucer. As part of this trend, there have appeared new editions and transcriptions of manuscript material often omitted from modern printed editions of Chaucer's texts. John M. Bowers has edited *The Canterbury Tales: Fifteenth-Century Continuations and Additions* (Kalamazoo: Western Michigan University, 1992) for the TEAMS Middle English Texts series. *The Wife of Bath's Prologue on CD-ROM* includes transcriptions of the glosses and an introductory essay reviewing the scholarly debate about them. "The Manuscript Glosses to Chaucer's *Troilus and Criseyde"* have been edited by

C. David Benson and B. A. Windeatt in *Chaucer Review* 25 (1990), 33-53 . Seth Lerer's *Chaucer and His Readers* (Princeton: Princeton University Press, 1993) is distinctive for the scope of its arguments and for its combination of manuscript evidence with other kinds, such as the ways Chaucer's admirers and imitators responded to his reputation in their poetry. Most of the essays in *The Ellesmere Chaucer: Essays in Interpretation* are concerned with reception and transmission of Chaucer's text, rather than with traditional editorial questions about such matters as the relative authority of various witnesses or the readings of particular lines.

Of many publications on the recent revisionary thinking about editorial assumptions and procedures, only a very few can be cited here. The essays in *Editing Chaucer: The Great Tradition*, ed. Paul Ruggiers (Norman, Okla.: Pilgrim Books, 1984) consider the ways editors from Caxton to the twentieth century have presented Chaucer's texts, including how they made use of particular manuscripts. Barney's *Studies in Troilus* uses examples of specific textual problems to give a lucid picture of how a modern editor works. For overviews of the state of play in various fields, see *Scholarly Editing*, ed. D. C. Greetham (New York: Modern Language Association of America, 1995), including the chapter by A. S. G. Edwards on "Middle English Literature," pp. 184-203. Tim William Machan offers a more extended and theoretical reconsideration in *Textual Criticism and Middle English Texts* (Charlottesville and London: University Press of Virginia, 1994). John M. Bowers cogently poses fundamental questions about the transmission and editing of Middle English texts in "Hoccleve's Two Copies of *Lerne to Dye*: Implications for Textual Critics," *PBSA* 83 (1989), 437-72. Two collections offer a range of perspectives on editorial problems relating to many Middle English texts: *Medieval Literature: Texts and Interpretation*, ed. Tim William Machan (Binghamton, New York: Medieval and Renaissance Texts and Studies, 1991), and *Crux and Controversy in Middle English Textual Criticism*, eds. A. J. Minnis and Charlotte Brewer (Cambridge: D. S. Brewer, 1992). Jerome McGann's *A Critique of Modern Textual Criticism* (Chicago: University of Chicago Press, 1983) has influenced thinking about many areas of English and American literature.

NOTES

1. *The Equatorie of the Planetis*, which may or may not be Chaucer's, dates from the 1390s. Only a very few manuscripts of works that are certainly Chaucer's have ever been ascribed to the 1390s, and no such ascription is now widely accepted. A small number of the manuscripts were written in the sixteenth century.

2. I direct this essay primarily to those who have read Chaucer in modern printed editions but have no experience of medieval manuscripts beyond reproductions of single leaves or museum and library exhibitions of early books. The Suggestions for Further Reading at the end of this essay includes introductions to textual and manuscript studies as well as publications more

specifically relevant to the manuscripts of Chaucer's works. To avoid duplication, I have not cited the standard resources in my footnotes; instead I have used these only to cite publications on specific problems discussed in this essay.

3. The essay can be found in *Geoffrey Chaucer*, ed. Derek Brewer (Athens, Ohio: Ohio University Press, 1975), pp. 85-108.

4. As Donaldson put it in the subtitle of his innovative edition, *Chaucer's Poetry: An Anthology for the Modern Reader*, 2nd ed. (New York: Ronald Press, 1975).

5. Among the strongest stimuli for such revisionary work were the two major, collaborative editorial projects of The Variorum Chaucer and *The Riverside Chaucer*, and publication of manuscript facsimiles.

6. *The Riverside Chaucer*, ed. Larry D. Benson (Boston: Houghton Mifflin, 1987). All references to Chaucer's works are to this edition.

7. Paul Zumthor uses the term *mouvance* for this aspect of texts in manuscript culture: "By *mouvance* I mean to indicate that any work, in its manuscript tradition, appears as a constellation of elements, each of which may be the object of variations in the course of time or across space. The notion of *mouvance* implies that the work has no authentic text properly speaking, but that it is constituted by an abstract scheme, materialized in an unstable way from manuscript to manuscript, from performance to performance"; *Speaking of the Middle Ages*, trans. Sarah White (Lincoln and London: University of Nebraska Press, 1986), n. 49, p. 96.

8. Carolyn Dinshaw, "Griselda Translated," in *Chaucer's Sexual Poetics* (Madison: University of Wisconsin Press, 1989), pp. 132-55, and David Wallace, "'Whan she translated was': A Chaucerian Critique of the Petrarchan Academy," in *Literary Practice and Social Change in Britain 1380-1530*, ed. Lee Patterson (Berkeley, Los Angeles, and London: University of California Press, 1990), pp. 156-215. My information about the variant forms of this line comes from J. Burke Severs, "Did Chaucer Revise the Clerk's Tale?," *Speculum* 21 (1946), 295-302.

9. See A. S. G. Edwards, "*The Merchant's Tale* and Moral Chaucer," *Modern Language Quarterly* 51 (1990), 409-26.

10. The addition of the romance of *Beryn* and its prologue, discussed by John Bowers in this volume, cannot be attributed simply to commercial motives. A dislike for unfinished narratives may also have been a matter of personal taste; Jean d'Angoulème's manuscript of the *Tales*, Paris, B. N. MS fonds anglais 39, omits or abbreviates all of the unfinished tales.

11. I am not using "collation" here to refer to the assembly of copies, the sense which may be more familiar to readers from printing and photocopying.

12. For a well-illustrated study of correction in another manuscript of the *Tales*, see Daniel W. Mosser, "The Two Scribes of the Cardigan Manuscript and the 'Evidence' of Scribal Supervision and Shop Production," *Studies in Bibliography* 39 (1986), 112-125.

13. For discussion and a photograph of the relevant folio, see Rosalind

Field, "'Superfluous Ribaldry': Spurious Lines in the *Merchant's Tale*," *Chaucer Review* 28 (1994), 353-67, esp. pp. 357-58.

14. "(The) Editing (of) the Ellesmere Text," in *The Ellesmere Chaucer: Essays in Interpretation*, eds. Martin Stevens and Daniel Woodward (San Marino: Huntington Library; Tokyo: Yushodo), pp. 225-43.

15. See Paul Strohm, "Jean of Angoulême: A Fifteenth-Century Reader of Chaucer," *Neuphilologische Mitteilungen* 72 (1971), 69-76.

16. Correction is a scribal practice which deserves more detailed study than it has so far received. Sixteenth- and seventeenth-century collation and annotation of Chaucer manuscripts has received almost no systematic attention in print, though the material is abundant.

17. The most notable exceptions to my generalizations in this paragraph are Pepys 2006 (part 2) and B. L. MS Harley 1239, which acknowledge the dramatic framework and/or Chaucer's authorship more openly than most of the others. Significantly, these are the only two of the anthologies which are devoted to works by Chaucer; the others are typically moral and devotional collections containing such tales as those of the Prioress, Clerk, Second Nun, Man of Law, Monk, and Parson, as well as the *Melibee*.

18. For a study of one such brief piece mistakenly attributed to Chaucer in some manuscripts, see Julia Boffey, "Proverbial Chaucer and the Chaucer Canon," in *Reading from the Margins*, ed. Seth Lerer (San Marino: Huntington Library, 1996), pp. 37-47.

19. The classic treatment is M. B. Parkes, "The Influence of the Concepts of *Ordinatio* and *Compilatio* on the Development of the Book," in *Medieval Learning and Literature*, eds. J. J. G. Alexander and M. T. Gibson (Oxford: Clarendon Press, 1976), pp. 115-41.

20. For these terms see Kathleen L. Scott, "Limning and Book-producing Terms and Signs *in situ* in Late-Medieval English Manuscripts: A First Listing," in *New Science out of Old Books*, eds. Richard Beadle and A. J. Piper (Aldershot: Scolar Press, 1995), pp. 142-88.

21. Ardis Butterfield presents a valuable study of the annotations to *Troilus* in "*Mise-en-page* in the *Troilus* Manuscripts: Chaucer and French Manuscript Culture," in *Reading from the Margins*, ed. Lerer, pp. 49-80.

22. This was the case in the manuscript "behind" Egerton 2864, one of the manuscripts discussed by Susan Schibanoff in "The New Reader and Female Textuality in Two Early Commentaries on Chaucer"; the scribe of that exemplar inherited Latin glosses in several parts of the *Tales* and added his own to *The Wife of Bath's Prologue*. Butterfield, *op. cit.*, describes the "layers" of annotation added to the *Troilus* manuscripts during the fifteenth century.

23. See Tim William Machan, "Textual Authority and the Works of Hoccleve, Lydgate, and Henryson," reprinted in this volume.

24. An influential refutation of that model was presented by A. I. Doyle and M. B. Parkes, in "The Production of Copies of the *Canterbury Tales* and the *Confessio Amantis* in the Early Fifteenth Century," in *Medieval Scribes, Manuscripts, and Libraries: Essays Presented to N. R. Ker*, ed. M. B. Parkes

and A. G. Watson (London: Scolar Press, 1978), pp. 163-215. The "new science" of vernacular paleography, in which Doyle and Parkes have been the chief pioneers, has transformed our ability to determine the number of hands in a given manuscript and to identify the same scribal hand in more than one manuscript. Thus it has been possible to reconsider thoroughly the social circumstances of manuscript production.

25. C. Paul Christianson, "A Community of Book Artisans in Chaucer's London," *Viator* 20 (1989), 207-18, p. 210.

26. Ralph Hanna III, in "Sir Thomas Berkeley and His Patronage," *Speculum* 64 (1989), 878-916, discusses the passage of literary texts between London and other parts of England at pp. 906-13.

27. For John Shirley, see most recently Seth Lerer, *Chaucer and His Readers* (Princeton: Princeton University Press, 1993), pp. 117-46; for MS Harley 7333, see pp. 122-29. Lerer's account draws partly on older descriptions of Harley 7333, which are now in need of revision.

28. As Julia Boffey points out in "The Reputation and Circulation of Chaucer's Lyrics in the Fifteenth Century," the discrepancy between manuscript and literary evidence for circulation of some of Chaucer's poems continues well into the fifteenth century.

29. Robert K. Root's "Publication Before Printing," *PMLA* 28 (1913), 417-31, remains a useful outline of the issues discussed in the following paragraphs.

30. As it happens, I think scribal excision is the better explanation for the absence of the final episode from *The Merchant's Tale*, though the absence of the other passages from Fragments IV-V does argue for a distinct authorial state of the text. Thus this example shows that even when there is good evidence for authorial variants, one cannot rule out the possibility of scribal variants.

31. For plates and analysis of the Hatfield fragment of *Troilus* and CUL MS Kk.1.3, see A. I. Doyle, "The Copyist of the Ellesmere *Canterbury Tales*," in Stevens and Woodward, eds., *The Ellesmere Chaucer*, pp. 49-67.

32. So the glosses Schibanoff analyzes in two late fifteenth-century manuscripts of the *Tales* (B. L. MSS Additional 5140 and Egerton 2864) probably were first devised around mid-century, in a lost manuscript from which these two later ones were derived.

33. For the date and circumstances of Hoccleve's writing of *The Regiment of Princes*, see J. A. Burrow, *Thomas Hoccleve* (Aldershot: Variorum, 1994) and Derek Pearsall, "Hoccleve's *Regement of Princes*: The Poetics of Royal Self-Representation," *Speculum* 69 (1994), 386-410. For the evidence of a Bedford presentation manuscript, see Marcia Smith Marzec, "The Latin Marginalia of *The Regiment of Princes* as an Aid to Stemmatic Analysis," *Text* 3 (1987), 269-84, p. 271.

34. A. S. G. Edwards, "The Text of Chaucer's *House of Fame*: Editing and Authority," *Poetica* 29-30 (1989), 80-92. Tim William Machan argues it is unlikely many copies of the *Boece* have been lost, in "The *Consolation* Tradition and the Text of Chaucer's *Boece*," *PBSA* 91 (1997), 31-50.

35. For one such will see Malcolm Richardson, "The Earliest Known Owners of *Canterbury Tales* MSS and Chaucer's Secondary Audience," *Chaucer Review* 25 (1990), 17-32.

36. Michael J. Bennett, "The Court of Richard II and the Promotion of Literature," in *Chaucer's England*, ed. Barbara Hanawalt (Minneapolis: University of Minnesota Press, 1992), pp. 3-20. Bennett mentions the destruction of the palace at Sheen after the death of Queen Anne; the loss of ships returning from the elaborate celebrations near Calais of Richard's marriage to Isabel of France; and "the circumstances of his return to England" immediately before he was deposed, which "left royal treasure dispersed in Dublin and a whole series of western seaports" (p. 15). Bennett's essay dissents from the recent trend of scholarly skepticism about Richard's cultural patronage, and we have no evidence, of course, that Chaucer manuscripts were among the objects destroyed on these occasions.

37. See A. S. G. Edwards and Derek Pearsall, "The Manuscripts of the Major English Poetic Texts," in *Book Production and Publishing in Britain 1375-1475*, eds. Jeremy Griffiths and Derek Pearsall (Cambridge: Cambridge University Press, 1989), pp. 257-78. In a chart on p. 270, they count seven copies of the *Tales* with miniatures, 23 with "elaborate" decoration, and 27 with "minor or none."

38. Edwards and Pearsall, *ibid.*, p. 270.

The Scribes as Chaucer's Early Critics

B. A. Windeatt

This essay first appeared in Studies in the Age of Chaucer *1 (1979): 119-41.*

'I nel noȝt scorne,' quod Scripture; 'but scryueynes lye . . .'[1]

'**B**UT scryueynes lye....' We hesitate, and the hesitation lies behind all attempts at editing medieval mss. An author's text is conceived of as something pure which, once entrusted to the medium of the scribes, becomes inaccurate because it passes through secondary minds who distort everything they transmit.[2] The author's original is "corrupted" and "contaminated," as the technical vocabulary of editing expresses itself through metaphors of moral degeneration from purity of text. The scribes can comfortably be characterized for editing purposes: they are either harmless in proportion to their doltishness, or dangerous in proportion to such intelligence as they may show. Indeed, medieval poets are themselves critical of their scribes, and with some justice from their point of view.[3] But like the modern editor, the medieval poet is concerned to use the scribes as means to an end. For both poet and editor any scribal influence on the text is by definition unwanted, and in the medieval circumstances of copying mss there are many such unwanted influences. But most modern admirers of Chaucer do not come to his work as editors, and it is possible that they can use the means offered by the scribes to rather different ends. The scribal responses to Chaucer's poetry, which are implicit in the variants offered by the mss for any work, are not to be despised as the equivalent of mere printing errors. The result of a completely different process, they are different in kind and in their literary implications. In ignoring the context of scribal responses in which medieval texts are preserved to us in the mss, the modern reader may waste a valuable resource. With varying levels of attainment, the scribes—as the near-contemporaries of Chaucer—can offer us the earliest line-by-line literary criticism of Chaucer's poetry, a reaction to what in the poet's text makes it distinctive and remarkable in its own time.[4]

The common, lowly view of scribes stems from considering them en masse as the intervening medium which stands between us and a completely accurate reflection of the original poet's intentions. But when the work of individual scribes is examined, their achievements in response to the difficulties of a text are sometimes (but not, of course, always!) impressive and arresting. Yet it is not surprising that men who could read and write to gain their living and who, in the very exercise of their craft, were often exposed to a range of literary material should show some literary intelligence and feel for what they are copying. Within their times the scribes are reading men. They may not be thinking men, but their minds are the courses through which runs the literary language of their day in order to achieve its literary form. Much evidence for contemporary literary response can be ignored in misvaluing those opinions of the scribes which are embodied in their texts of the Chaucer works they have copied.[5]

While there is no doubt of the appreciation of Chaucer as poet among his contemporaries and immediate successors, the precise nature of that appreciation is more elusive, because of the terms used by the poet's admirers. Remarks like Henry Scogan's about Chaucer's poetry ("That in his langage was so curious") have been eagerly seized upon.[6] But such comments give an overall impression of Chaucer's poetic rather than analyzing what was so special in it for his contemporaries. Their comments summarize, but do not aim to recreate a detailed response to the texture of the poetry which would approximate more to modern critical analysis. Yet the behaviour of the scribes in mss of Chaucer's works offers line-by-line a contemporary response to his poetry. The scribes are men of some literacy and some sense of what is current in the forms of contemporary language, and they work through texts necessarily in a line-by-line way, forced into close confrontation with the form of the poems. Their reactions to the poetry they are transcribing are their equivalent of literary analysis, in that they can reveal to us exactly what the scribes found difficult and unusual in Chaucer's work. It is not likely that all scribes are worth attending to in all lines: their intelligence and sensitivity will vary enormously.[7] Scribal critical response as reflected through misunderstanding or interference will be at very various levels of consideredness as literary response, but this does not affect its interest. The instinctive reaction and judgment which cuts across accuracy to the exemplar has an intrinsic value. The scribal rewriting reflects a sense of what is out of the ordinary and needs to be "made normal." It is often an unconscious criticism, an inverse criticism, but a criticism nevertheless, of how the poetry functions and how it stands in relation to the customary and ordinary in contemporary language.

Scribal transcribing is a form of writing which constitutes an "active reading," an active reading which involves judgment-through-variation on the difficulties and peculiarities of what it encounters. In the age of print an author speaks directly to each reader through his multiply- reproduced text, whereas each manuscript offers a text already "read," and as such a document of some critical interest. The literary response of the scribes gains rather than is limited by the way that it springs from this process of copying the original. The scribes' response is inevitably conditioned by their circumstances as transcribers, and this distinguishes them from the individual reader, whose response is not given recorded form through the need to write out his own copy of the text. Yet as the successive redactions of the great medieval romances can show, in the Middle Ages the most vigorous form of literary criticism expresses itself through the re-writing of a received text, and in little the individual scribe's transcription of a poetic work by Chaucer can reproduce some of this creative, critical activity. Indeed, their line-by-line response is of special value for estimating contemporary appreciation of Chaucer's poetic, precisely because his verse lines are composed with especially close and carefully contrived texture (as his own worries about textual distortion show at the end of the *Troilus*, V, 1793-98). Because the scribes remain copyists as well as readers, the literary interest of their own work needs to be distinguished from their more mechanical errors and difficulties of transcription. But the nature of the variants themselves can suggest how much the scribes were engaged by both the content and the form of what they were transmitting.

Unlike *Piers Plowman*, there is relatively little controversial material in Chaucer's works to invite participation by scribes stimulated by their own prejudices and convictions.[8] Sometimes a scribe gives some hint of topical prejudice, as when Criseyde criticizes those who tolerate jealousy "And wolde a busshel venym al excusen" (III, 1025),[9] which one scribe rewrites "... a *beschop* venym" (Gg).[10] But there is a kind of "narrative" participation, in which the scribe becomes involved with the spirit of a scene and its presentation of character or event. Such involvement with the text by the scribes shows in itself the power of the poem they were transcribing to suggest its own standards and values. It is relatively unusual for scribes to go completely counter to the implications of a passage, as when one scribe rewrites a line of the *Troilus* consummation scene ("This Troilus in armes gan hire streyne," III, 1205) into "This Troylus hir swetty in armis tweyne ..." (H5). When Pandarus visits Criseyde next morning, Chaucer's line "And Pandarus gan under for to prie" (III, 1571) is rewritten by one scribe so that the uncle begins "in for to pryke" (Gg) .

But participation by the scribes which is of wider literary interest does show an active extension in their own minds of the scenes of the narrative and of the moral view implied by the poem's tone. Thus, when Criseyde rebukes Troilus gently for his "jealousy" Chaucer's text has her say "Now were it worthi that ye were ybete" (III, 1169), and the scribe of R has added the comment in his margin "Ye *with* a Fether". This participation by the scribe is an endearingly sentimental response to Criseyde's sympathetic authoritativeness here. The scribe has reacted in keeping with the delicate tones of his original text. In the next line, where all other mss record that "Troilus gan sorwfully to sike" (1170) at this speech of Criseyde's, R alone visualizes instead the embarrassment of his hero at the heroine's rebuke ("the Troylys gan changen al his hewe . . .). Similarly, when Chaucer describes the fainted Criseyde with "Hire eyen throwen upward to hire hed" (IV, 1159), one scribe visualizes the scene himself and writes instead that her eyes were "blensched vpward to hir heede" (Ad).

Such variation is of value in illustrating how some sensitive scribes were involved with their texts to the extent of occasionally improving and elaborating them in ways which show the larger influence of the text upon them. A scribe may magnify the emotional force of the original scene by his participation. When Troilus imagines that the wind from the Greek camp consists of Criseyde's sighs, Chaucer has him say "And hardily this wynd that more and moore / Thus stoundemele encresseth in my face . . ." (V, 673-74), but one scribe rewrites "þus stormyal encresith . . ." (Gg). Some scribes also enter into the characters' direct speech to re-express it more forcibly. Chaucer's prayer for Troilus in the stew ("Now blisful Venus thow me grace sende . . ." III, 705) becomes "Now Venus prey I thow me grace sende" (R). The scribe has identified with the speaker and emphasizes the hero's role in the prayer. This same identification and association with the characters will lead a scribe to adapt Chaucer's lines "Who shal now yeven comfort to my peyne? / Allas, no wight . . ." (IV, 318-19) by writing instead "Alas I not. . ." (H5). Or again, when Troilus urges Pandarus to tell him which of his sisters he desires "To han for thyn and lat me thanne allone" (III, 413) one scribe instead has Troilus say more directly "I speke for the and lat me . . ." (H4). The scribe steps into his text here to express more immediately the intentions of the character speaking. This association with the poem's *dramatis personae* leads the same scribe to change Chaucer's "And Lord so thanne gan gronen Troilus" (III, 206) into ". . . tho gan grone seli Troilus" (H4). It is as if the scribe's interest in the poem's narrative situations overcomes his attention to the more balanced and indirect manner of expression in his exemplar. To us, such variation conveys the activeness of the scribes' response in reading, and it also shows by contrast the care Chaucer takes to express the force of his characters' feelings through the often intricately organized pattern of his poetic form.

In most mss of Chaucer's works intrusion of a whole invented line to replace the probably authentic version is relatively rare. Scribal interference with the form of Chaucer's text is focussed more closely, and this helps locate where the scribes' main critical response to Chaucer's poetry occurs. Although scribes certainly show themselves capable of replacing existing lines with their own metrical fabrications, this is not—relative to the number of lines being copied—a very frequent feature of the scribal response to the text. But this feature has nevertheless the value of revealing the scribes' reaction to their task at greater length than usual. Thus, in the third proem to *Troilus* one scribe is concerned to restate his text more emphatically, regardless of sense, so that Chaucer's "Ye folk a lawe han set in universe" (III, 36) becomes "I wot youre lawis ben on and not dyvers" (H5), which is a more directly emphatic version of the poet's line. Later in Book III Chaucer follows his definition of Fortune ("That under God ye ben oure hierdes," III, 619) with "Though to us bestes ben the causes wrie," but the same scribe expands more explicitly on the "hierdes" idea: "And ledyn vs alle bothe low and hye" (H5). The scribe prefers to explain the difficult idea and supplement it with a formulaic paired phrase. Similarly, the unusual line "That privete go with us in this cas" is difficult enough to be glossed by Chaucer himself in the next line ("That is to seyn that thow us nevere wreye," III, 283-84). But this difficult context provokes one scribe to rewrite the second line more emphatically to paraphrase the first ("For no myschef thou neu*er* vs thre bewreye," H4). Such instances of the scribes' involvement with the poems being copied indicate the type of nonsubstantive variation which can concern us here as signs of scribal consideration and criticism of Chaucer's poetry. Evidence for what struck contemporaries as distinctive in Chaucer's poetry emerges firstly in the particularly sustained reactions in the mss to some aspects of Chaucer's diction and secondly, in the scribes' recurrent difficulties in responding to the individual qualities of the syntax of his poetry.

II

Most scribal response to Chaucer's text usually focusses on a limited number of words within the body of the line. It is at such points that the scribes are often registering their reactions to the very concise containment of sense within a highly compact verse-form. The mss provide very widespread evidence for verbal substitution by the scribes, substitutions which reflect their sense of the difficulty and unusualness of the diction in their exemplar.

When the poet's own line "But whan the cok, comune astrologer . . ." (TC III, 1415) is bungled by one scribe into ". . . the cok come aftyr longere" (Gg), the origin of this type of substitution may have been a more mechanical slip, a confusion over a few letters of a difficult phrase. But it is a confusion which brings home how frequently unusual and difficult Chaucer's diction was for his contemporary readers. Indeed, the English expression "comune astrologer" is explained by a Latin gloss ("vulgarus astrologus") in the margins of some mss (H1 Ph S2). This tendency for scribes to gloss their text in cases of what strikes them as strange or awkward diction offers a valuable guide to their response to the diction of Chaucer's poetry. For the couplet

> Were I a god ye shulden sterve as yerne
> That heren wel this man wol no thing yerne
> (TC III, 151-52)

H5 reads "sterve as *faste*" and S1 glosses "yerne" in 152 as *desire* in the margin, while H1 goes one further and includes the gloss in the text ("no thyng desire ȝerne"). A number of variants indicate how the scribes' sense of the difficulty of their exemplar has led to helpful glosses and notes, some of which have then been absorbed into the text. For the phrase "al is untrewe / That men of yelpe" (TC III, 306-07), J reads "That men of boste yelpe".

Here, as so often, the striking figurative sense of Chaucer's diction has brought the scribes' expository tendencies into play.

Many mss show a developed sense of providing glosses for difficult, unusual terms, and suggest that Chaucer's poetry was being read by readers with a considerable concern for the meaning of texts of which the diction was often "curious" to them. The unusual terms in a line like "The gold-ytressed Phebus heighe on-lofte" (TC V, 8) or "The laurer-crowned Phebus with his heete" (V, 1107) provoke glosses from the scribes. H4 has "auricomus" and "sol" above the line over 'gold-ytressed" and "Phebus", while H2 reads "The auricomus tressed Phebus . . ." and "The laurer laurgerus crouned Phebus . . .". The poetic circumlocutions in lines like "Syn that the sone of Ecuba the queene" (TC V, 12) or "Of which the sone of Tideus took hede" (V, 88) move the scribe of Cp to write ". . . the sone I Troilus of Ecuba . . ." and "the sone Diomede of Tideus".[11] For the line "Soth is that under God ye ben oure hierdes" (TC III, 619), H4 glosses "hierdes" with ".i. gouernours", and this nicely expresses the position of many scribes. The scribe senses the difficulty of an unusual expression and supplies an alternative which evinces significant powers of vocabulary, but yet offers a rather imprecise appreciation of the term actually being glossed in the text. There is straightforward, informative glossing: "wyerdes" (TC III, 617) is glossed as "destine" by several scribes in the margin or between the lines, and with "That jalousye, allas! that wikked wyvere" (III, 1010) several mss have absorbed the gloss within their text ("þe wikkid serpent wythir," H2 Ph). Unusual and figurative uses of English words will draw explanations from the scribes, so that for "Allas, that he al hool or of hym slyvere" (TC III, 1013) H4 has the interlined gloss ".i. pars" over "slyvere". Yet the difficulties of Chaucer's compressed and unusual expressions were still not prevented even by the presence of the glosses: for *Troilus* III, 1194 ("To whom this tale sucre be or soot") H4 reads "sugre be or swote .i. bitter".

But throughout the mss the scribes demonstrate considerable powers of diction in paraphrasing the sense of their exemplars. Some of the *Troilus* variants reveal the preference of individual scribes for a more Latinate diction than the poem itself demands. For "This knowen folk that han *ysuffred* peyne" (V, 415), H3 reads *endurede*. For "And ek the bet from sorwe hym *to releve*"(V, 1042), Ph reads *to refreyne*. The text of one *Troilus* ms (H2) shows a sustained tendency to latinize the diction of its exemplar. For "Al this have I myself *yet thought* ful ofte" (IV, 542), H2 reads *ymagened yet*. For "And if she *wilneth* fro the for to passe" (IV, 615), H2 reads *desir*. For "On Troilus iset so *wonder* faste" (IV, 674), H2 reads *merueilously*. In "Hym to *withholde* of wepyng atte leeste" (V, 76), H2 has *restreine from*. In "*My red* is this, syn thow kanst wel endite" (V, 1292), H2 reads *My counseill*, while in V, 1468 ("*Wrak* hire in a wonder cruel wise"), H2 has instead *Venged*. These few instances must stand to represent a much wider tendency in this and other mss.

The scribes' considerable sense of the verbal originality of their texts is revealed by their tendency to substitute synonyms, and rather easier words of similar shape.[12] For the *Troilus* line "And al the *richesse* of his sikes sore" (III, 349), H4 reads *tresour*, and for "*Revesten* hem in grene when that May is" (353), the same scribe reads *Reioisyn*. When Troilus is brought back from his faint the unusual verb in "Hym to *revoken* she did al hire peyne" (III, 1118) is rewritten as *revyuen* by some scribes (H4 H5). The scribes' responses pick out for the modern reader the points of difficulty for the contemporary reader of Chaucer's diction in lines like ". . . and though no manere routhe / *Commeve* yow . . ." (V, 1385-86), which is rewritten as *Remorde* (H2 H4). Or again, scribal response registers the unusualness of less conspicuously difficult lines like "*So confus* that he nyste what to seye" (IV, 356) which one scribe will change into *So pensyf* (H5). In many such cases, the scribe is guessing at the meaning from the context, as when Troilus cries "Thow moost me first *transmewen* in a stoon" (IV, 467) and some scribes have *graue* (H2) or *close* (H4); or when Troilus's tears run "As licour out of a *lambic* ful faste" (IV, 520) and one scribe reads *lampe* (Ad) and another *well* (H4). Here scribes are concerned to make plainer the difficult meaning, as they are when "the grete tour / *Resouneth* of his yowlyng and clamour" (*CT* I, 1277-78)[13] becomes *Dynned* (Ii), or when "In *redoutynge* of Mars and of his glorie" (2050) becomes *recordyng* (d*) or *remembraunce* (Ii). Yet the scribes' own sense of the relative force of the diction they use is not to be disparaged: when Griselda is described "*conformynge* hire to that the markys liked" (*CT* IV, 546) the variant reading *consentynge* (E1) seems just an easier paraphrase, but another reading *constreynyng* (Fi-N1-Ra^2-Ra^4-Tc^2) suggests the capacity of scribes to paraphrase their exemplars with diction which is often neither harder nor easier in itself. An important aspect of Chaucer's poetic achievement for his contemporaries is revealed by the difficulties of the scribes in always appreciating the particularly appropriate twist that its poetic context in a line gives to much of Chaucer's diction.

There is no lack of evidence for the scribes' literacy and their resources of diction, yet often these resources are being employed because they do not understand the peculiar nature of their text's originality. Thus, Troilus quickly deals with the letter he has used to get rid of Deiphebus and Helen ("That gan ful lightly of the lettre pace," III, 220). The version of this line in H4 ("That tenquire aftir the lett*er* was desirous") uses quite a high style and shows the literacy of the scribe, yet says the opposite of what the exemplar means, presumably due to misunderstanding of *pace*. It is not simply the obviously difficult, Romance parts of Chaucer's vocabulary which cause his scribes difficulty: for the scene with Pandarus and Criseyde in the bedroom ("And *poked* evere his nece new and newe," III, 116) H2 and Ph read "And *procurid* euer . . .". Tersely unexpected expressions in Chaucer's poetic cause the scribes difficulties in their own way, so that when Criseyde is described as loving Troilus "al nere he malapert or made it tough" (III, 87) one scribal reader replaces this last problematical expression by "or made a vowe" (H2).

In this way the scribes' substitutions give recorded form to the way that Chaucer's poetry was distinguished for his contemporary and early readers by its many poetic uses of figurative expressions. Thus, for the revelation in

Troilus III, 1216 ("*Men drynken* ofte peyne and gret distresse") one scribe has instead *Men suffre* (H4). If Chaucer's text has the compactly figurative advice "Be naught to rakel theigh thow sitte warme" (III, 1630), one scribe will modify the image into the simple ". . . fele it warme" (Du). When Troilus is compared to a wounded bull ("Now her, now ther, *idarted* to the herte," IV, 240), one scribe replaces the unusual idea with *perishid* (H5) and so loses the peculiar figurative intensity of the poet's original. Again, when the wasting Troilus is described ("He so *defet* was that no manere man / Unneth hym myghte knowen . . ." V, 1219-20) some scribes prefer a more descriptive term like *disfigured* (Gg) or *dissassid* (H4). For Chaucer's "the bente moone with hire hornes pale" (III, 624) the scribe of H4 feels the need for a gloss above the line over "bente" (".i. curua"), and H5 avoids the difficulty by replacing "hente" with the conventionally descriptive, non figurative "beautefull". Again, in the line "But feste hym with a fewe wordes white" (III, 901) the figurative sense of the verb is ducked by several scribes who prefer "But feffe hym . . ." (H2 Gg S1). When Chaucer's "O cruel day, accusour of the joie" (III, 1450) becomes for one scribe "a cursour . . ." (Gg) the unusual sense has given way to the more literally obvious in a context of recriminations. If Criseyde complains that a bushel of venom is excused in jealous behaviour "For that o greyn of love is on it shove" (III, 1026) the force and roughness of the image embodied in the verb is replaced by one scribe (". . . is in it sowe," H2), for whom the imagery of the bushel and the grain is less convincing than the more familiar associations of grain with the sowing of seed. This scribal trend to substitute a more literal expression registers that frequent sense of the compact and usually expressed imagery embedded in Chaucer's poetry. When Troilus declares "O soule lurkynge in this wo unneste" (IV, 305) some mss have a marginal gloss "go out of þi neste" (Du H1 S1). But evidently without such help from their own exemplars, other mss turn the unusual verb into a noun ("wrecchydness," H3; "woful nest," H4R) or alter to an adjective ("wo vnhonest," Ph Ad). Another ms misreads the earlier image too ("O soule berkyng in this wo," H2), and it is clear that Chaucer's distinctive imagery enacted in his verbs struck his scribal readers as a very novel feature of his poetic style. The comparably distinctive verb in Criseyde's oath not to eat "Til I my soule out of my breste unshethe" (IV, 776) was probably one of the stimuli behind the variant line "Troil*us* my sorwre out of myn brest conueye" (Gg).[14]

The scribes can be observed pervasively engaged in so registering their sense of the figurative force of Chaucer's poetic language. They respond to Chaucer's distinctive use of verbs, so that when Troilus "neigh ded for smert gan bresten out to rore" (IV, 373) one scribe will write "to groon" (Du). But a line like "Ayeins that vice for to ben a labbe / Al seyde men soth . . ." (III, 300) will also be stripped of its artistry to become "Declaryn that men auhte not to labbyn" (H4). Indeed, at a more limited level of variation, the scribes often pass over minor instances of Chaucer's distinctively figurative or abstract diction, so that "Wheras at leiser al this *heighe* matere" (III, 516) will become ". . . al his hol mateere" (H4), and "May in no perfit *selynesse* be" (III, 831) becomes "sekirnesse" (H4), which is the more obvious reading in the context.

Much scribal response can generally be termed clichéd, in that it moves Chaucer's diction and syntax back from his poeticization of language towards more established patterns and associations. In the scribal reaction to Chaucer's texts there is a marked trend towards sentimentalizing clichés among the variations. Such variation has often been stimulated by the mood and tone of the particular poem being copied, yet each instance of scribal cliché in itself has the power to illustrate by contrast the balance which Chaucer's own poetry preserves in its use of conventional language. Thus, it is Chaucer who writes "This Diomede as fressh as *braunche* in May" (V, 844) and a scribe reads instead *rose* (Gg). When Chaucer has "And to youre trouthe ay I me recomande" (V, 1414) this same scribe will write ". . . to ʒoure hertis pete" (Gg). In *The Knight's Tale* line ". . . lyk the loueris maladye / of *Hereos*" (*CT*, I 1373-74) one scribe reads *hertes boote* (Ha³). Where Chaucer describes Troilus returning home ("He softe into his bed gan for to slynke," III, 1535) one scribe rewrites this as the hero's emotional response ("He soft gan in his herte to shrinke," Du). When Pandarus declares "Swich fir by proces shal of kynde colde" (IV, 418), a scribe prefers a familiar set phrase (". . . shal of caris colde," Ph). The scribes' tendency to the more obvious and familiar associations of words can suggest the newness of Chaucer's own uses of words: "The morwen com and gostly for to speke" (V, 1030) becomes the more obvious "shortly" (R), or "Withinne a paved *parlour*" (II, 82) becomes ". . . *floor*" (Du). When Troilus and Criseyde saw that day "Gan for taproche as they by sygnes knewe" (III, 1696) one scribe rewrites this line so that day "His briht hornys in euery wiket gan shewe" (H4). Here the scribe participates eagerly in the narrative of sun-rise, yet expresses it in a cliché associated with the moon. This instance well represents the recurrent response of the scribes, who bring out the force of a passage through familiar set-phrases even at variance with the precise meaning of the context they are elaborating.

The mss reveal a marked tendency in the scribes to think in pairs of related ideas, so that a word in Chaucer's poem may bring in a set-phrase of which that word is a part. Thus, Troilus's request to Criseyde ("Ye wolde somtyme frendly on me see," III, 130) becomes "Ye wold some tyme on me rewe and se" (H2). Such clichés are part of the trend to bring out more explicitly the understated emphases of the poet's original, so that "This passeth al that herte may bythynke" (III, 1694) becomes ". . . hert may speke or thynk" (H5), or "Knew at the fulle and waited on it ay" (III, 534) becomes ". . . wayted eu*ere* & ay" (R). When in *The Knight's Tale* "He gan to loken vp with eyen lighte" (1783) some scribes write "blake and lighte" (Ha⁴ Ii) and some "blake and blith" (Ne N1). The scribal introduction of such repetitive clichéd emphases illuminates the way that, by contrast, Chaucer both uses but controls conventional emotional language in a way that gives it an economic effectiveness. Chaucer's "I have hem don dishonour weylaway" (V, 1066) becomes "dishonour & velony" (Gg), or the poet's "For how sholde I my lif an houre save?" (III, 1476) becomes "my lif and honour save" (Du). In both cases, the scribes are more used to thinking in set-phrases than in attending to the economy of Chaucer's lines. The distinction between the scribes' sense of conventional language and the poet's deployment of it is best revealed by the scribal misunderstandings of contexts where Chaucer himself uses paired ideas in his lines. Thus, where Chaucer writes "For al the gold atwixen sonne and se" (V, 886) one scribe writes ". . . londe and see" (H3), and where Chaucer has "His herte ay with the first and with the beste" (V, 839), some scribes have instead "& with þe laste" (H2 H4). These scribal reactions show how even where Chaucer himself uses conventional language he is still avoiding the associations which seem the more obvious ones to his contemporary readers.[15]

A recurrent feature of the scribes' response to the texts of Chaucer's poetry is their tendency—by small additions to the lines—to bring out more explicitly the sense of the passages that they are transcribing. Scribal reactions stress the quantity and extent, the duration and direction of many events and actions in their exemplars. As a pervasive contemporary response in reading Chaucer's poetry they suggest the distinctiveness of a style in which the poet intended to leave some of his meaning understated. When Troilus prays to the gods ("For nevere man was to yow goddes holde," III, 1259), a scribe re-expresses this "to you goddes more holde" (H3), bringing out explicitly the understood emphasis of the original. When Criseyde wishes Troilus "To telle me the fyn of his entente" (III, 125), one scribe stresses "his hol entent" (H4), or when Pandarus regrets "And I hire em and traitour eke yfeere" (III, 273), H4 emphasizes "em & traitour bothe in fere."

The scribes' more explicit stress on the speed and direction of events offers their own critique of what often struck them as unusual in the syntax of Chaucer's poetry. When Pandarus swears to Criseyde that "He nolde nevere comen ther she were" (III, 567) if she insists on leaving despite the storm, some scribes have written instead ". . . nevere come more ayen þere" (H2 Ph), and one has "nolde neuere aftir cum . . ." (H5). In Chaucer's line "For fere of which men wenen lese here lyves" (V, 381), the scribe of Du writes "oft lees." When Pandarus declares there is nobody "That evere wiste that she dide amys" (III, 270), one scribe pushes the emphasis even further by saying ". . . ded ȝet amys" (Ph). Or when we hear "That after sharpe shoures ben victories" (III, 1064), several scribes make this more sweeping by saying "bene oft victorie" (Ph H2). When Criseyde promises "She wolde come, ye, but she nyste whenne" (V, 1428), one scribe emphasizes "nyst neuere whan" (Ph).

The scribal variations reveal a comparable concern to make directions and movements in the narratives more explicit than Chaucer leaves them in his own style. Thus in Chaucer's line "His hed to the wal, his body to the grounde" (IV, 244), a scribe writes "dovn to the grovnde" (H3), or in the oath "And I with body and soule synke in helle" (IV, 1554), one ms has "doun to hell" (H4). The poet's own "But in a rees to Troilus he wente" (IV, 350) becomes "faste went" (H2 H5), while to the line "And fer his hed over the wal he leyde" (V, 1145), one scribe adds helpfully "out ouer" (Ph).

This type of scribal involvement with the poem's text reflects a significant critical response by the scribes because it illuminates the unusual conciseness with which Chaucer suggests by understatement the force and quantity of developments in his poetry. If Chaucer's Pandarus describes himself as "swich a meene / As maken wommen unto men to comen" (III, 255), which is then transcribed by one scribe "As makyn men and wymmen togidir comyn" (Ph), this brings out how the poet's meaning is sensitively ordered and understated within his metrical form. A Chaucer text can make restraint in expression into a poetic resource which distinguishes Chaucer's poetry from normal contemporary usage. From the scribes' responses, it was a resource which Chaucer's contemporaries noticed strongly.

III

In the wider range of scribal responses to aspects of compression and brevity in the poetry, the variableness of the mss presents a further kind of literary reading of the contemporary distinctiveness of Chaucer's style. The attentive reading necessitated by the syntax of Chaucer's poetry has always been demanding, as is shown by those scribal glosses which convey to the reader what the poet has assumed is understood in the larger flow of his sense, where the compressed form of one line may depend on the sense of another. Thus, where Chaucer's text reads "And dredeles, his ire, day and nyght / Ful cruwely the Grekis ay aboughte" (V, 1755-56), the scribe of H4 writes "his troily ire" to make the subject plain. When Criseyde concludes a long outburst on jealousy ("And that excuse I for the gentilesse," III, 1036) and then starts a new stanza ("And som so ful of furie is and despit," 1037) the scribe of H4 writes "ielosi" above the line over *that* and *som*, in case the reader has not followed what Chaucer's long flow of sense is about. Again, when Troilus exclaims on his lady's eyes ("Though ther be mercy writen in youre cheere, / God woot, the text ful hard is soth to fyndel!" III, 1356-57), the H4 scribe has written the note "mis*er*cor" above *text*. The figurative connection between the two lines is of a difficulty which the scribe evidently feels he must make clearer to the reader of his ms than the poet himself is concerned to do within his own style in the poem.

These scribal aids to the contemporary reader of Chaucer's poetry reveal that one part of the distinctive specialness of Chaucer's poetic style lay in the peculiar form of some lines, which were units in a larger syntactical whole spanning a number of lines. The individual line may often seem incomplete as a consequence, even though it may be very concisely expressed in order to fit the verse form. The scribal readers' reaction to this aspect of Chaucer's conciseness is expressed through their tendency to introduce into their own versions of individual lines the implied verb, or the implied subject or object of the sentence, which the compactness of Chaucer's style has avoided. The scribes are persistently dissatisfied with lines such as III, 1421 ("With herte soor to Troilus thus seyde"), which are consequently found adapted by some mss into ". . . to Troilus þus she saide" (Du Ph). This provides the pronoun that Chaucer's line has not included. The numerous variations of this type in the mss are little problem editorially, and intrinsically of little interest, except in that they collectively illustrate an aspect of Chaucer's style which scribes evidently and recurrently find unusual. When Troilus "To Pandarus on knowes fil adown" (III, 1592), it is a predictable scribal response that some mss will read "fell he doune" (Du H4). An authentic line like "But certeyn is som manere jalousie / Is excusable . . ." (III, 1030) will be rewritten "But sertayn ther is sum maner of ielosye" (H5). The scribe prefers the individual line to be more self-contained than it often is in Chaucer's poetic syntax and reacts against the poet's own omissions.

The introduction of verbs into lines where they have been omitted by the poet also gives recorded form to the scribes' strong sensation of the exceptional brevity and conciseness of Chaucer's constructions in the syntax of his poetry. It is a scribe who can give us some contemporary perspective on how Chaucer's lines may have given the impression of an especially poetic degree of contrivance in his own times. To a characteristic line like ". . . oon the gentileste / That evere was and oon the worthieste" (V, 1056-57) one scribe will write "euer *there was*" (H4) and another will expand on the verb with "þat euere *was born* . . ." (Gg). For where the verb is held over until a later line or is understood from above, many scribes will introduce a verb into the "incomplete" line. Chaucer's "And it pronounced by the president" (IV, 213) becomes "pronounsid was" (H4), or the authentic "To get ayeyn Criseyde brighte of hewe" (V, 1573) is rewritten as "Criseyde þat was bright of hewe" (Ph). The terseness of Chaucer's own constructions proves a temptation for scribes to expand to that greater syntactical fullness which they prefer so persistently that it must have been more natural and normal to them. Chaucer's line "So cruel wende I nought youre herte ywis" (V, 1685) becomes "ȝoure hert had be Iwis" (Gg). The brevity of Criseyde's promise ("Now certes, em, tomorwe and I hym se," III, 809) is expanded into ". . . and y may hym se" (Ph H2), and Chaucer's description "that twenty thousand tymes er she lette" (III, 473) becomes ". . . or she wolde lette" (Du). Most recurrently the scribes move to supplement the poet's holding over of the verb. In the couplet:

> If this were wist, my lif lay in balaunce,
> And youre honour, God shilde us fro meschaunce . . .
>
> (IV, 1560-61)

one scribe reads "And your honour loste" (H2). And when Criseyde declares "It sate me wel bet ay in a cave / To bidde" (II, 117-18), this becomes "ay ben in a caue" in one ms (H3) and "to ben in a cave" in two others (H4 H5).

One major further area of the scribes' implicitly critical response to the nature of Chaucer's poetry involves the marked variableness over word-order which is found in the mss.[16] Variation over word-order within Chaucer's verse lines is one of the most frequent differences between mss. If a scribe copied by memorizing one line at a time, his allegiance to his copy would be strongest at the beginning of the line and at the rhyme, with its own mnemonic effect. The scribe's accuracy to his copy would be least strong precisely in that central area of the line which is just where the significant, yet often delicately slight, distinctions in Chaucer's word-order often occur. Variations in the middle of lines often suggest that while the line was being held in the scribe's mind, it tended to revert to more familiar word-order than Chaucer had originally given it.   The demands of rhyme and metre frequently require Chaucer to adapt a certain stylization of the order of his sense, in order to reconcile it to its context. The responses of the scribes can enable modern readers to gain some sense of how the order of Chaucer's lines distinguished itself to contemporary readers as "poetic" and "difficult" when set against the expectations of more ordinary written English.

The mss of Chaucer's works present numerous cases where the scribes react to the poet's departures from a more predictable English word-order, always with the proviso that the word-order of Middle English is not so pre-defined as it has later tended to become. But a Chaucer line like "He seith hym told is of a frend of his" (III, 796) becomes in one ms: "He seith it is told hym of . . ." (Gg). There are very many instances where, even within the limited compass of several words, Chaucer prefers to shift the order away from its most obvious sequences. There are almost as many instances where the scribes notice such features by altering them. Thus, "Than every tyme he that hath in memorie" (III, 829) becomes for some scribes the more obvious "every tyme he hath þat . . ." (H2 R S2). Many such variations over word-order depend on a difference of only one or two words. Chaucer's line "Quod Pandarus, 'It tyme is that we wende'" (III, 208) is rewritten by some scribes "'It is tyme tham.. .'" (Ad C1 Du H3 R), or again the authentic "Syn that yow list it skile is to be so" (III, 646) is turned into "it is skil" (Ad). It needs only a brief lapse of concentration by scribes when memorizing the whole line for a movement towards a more usual English word-order to occur: Chaucer's "For wel I woot thow menest wel parde" (III, 337) will become "For I wot wel . . ." (Gg 115). The difficulty for the scribes lies in the nature of Chaucer's style, which depends on small distinctions in the order of often undistinctive words. Chaucer writes "Thow woost how longe ich it forbar to seye" (III, 365), but a scribe will prefer to write "y forbare hit" (Ph). Chaucer will write "So koude he hym governe in swich servyse" (III, 475), but a scribe writes instead "So koude he gouerne hym" (R).

In brief, as the scribe held in his head and copied a line like "That wel unneth it don shal us duresse" (V, 399), there would be a tendency for his copy to come out as "it schal don" (Gg H3 H4 R). Yet the extent of scribal support for the authentic patterns of word-order suggests the scribes recognized these as a distinctive part of Chaucer's style which many tried to maintain. But Chaucer's word-order was repeatedly departing in small ways from more normal usage both for metrical and stylistic reasons. Within the verse lines with their rhyme patterns, scribal changes in word-order represent a very limited move to ordinary word-order, so that "She myght on hym han loked at the leste" (III, 1160) becomes "She myght han loked on hym . . ." (R). But in much of Chaucer's poetry the author's slight modification of word-order in this way is part of the dignity of verse through which form matches theme. It is this distinctive quality in Chaucer's poetic language which the scribal divergences can bring out for the later reader. It is part of the *Troilus* style that Pandarus should declare "Dulcarnoun called is 'flemyng of wrecches'" (III, 933) and not "Dulcarnon is called . . ." (H3 H5 S2), for here the inversion matches the extraordinary nature of everything else in the line he is expressing. By inversion, Chaucer lends a specialness and consequent dignity to the simplest descriptions of very strong emotional reactions and commitments. The scribes' reversion to a more prosaic order brings out by contrast the effectiveness of such inversion in Chaucer's hands. Chaucer's "Which that I nevere do shal eft for other" (III, 251) is changed into "y shal neu*er*e do" by H2 H5 Ph. "If sorwe it putte out of hire remembraunce" (III, 968) becomes "Yif sorwe putte it . . ." (H4), and "That bitternesse assaied was byforn" (III, 1220) becomes for one scribe "was assaied byforn" (Cp). By inversion the simple actions of the lovers are given a solemnity ("In which a ruby set was lik an herte," III, 1371) which is lost on those scribes who write instead "was sette like" (H2 H3). For the inversion of syntax draws a special attention to the actions described, so that Criseyde's solemn charge to Troilus "And that ye me wolde han as faste in mynde" (III, 1506) becomes more ordinary when some scribes rewrite it as "ye wold me haue" (Du H2 Ph), or "ye wolde haue me" (H5 R). Similarly, Griselda's response ("And she agayn answerde in pacience," *CT* IV, 813) is copied by one scribe as "answerde agayn" (E1). The accuracy of the scribes to these authentic word orders is often impressive: only one ms (Cp) changes Criseyde's wish "That I honour may have and he plesaunce" (III, 944) into "That I may haue honour . . ." Yet the distinctiveness and consequent difficulty of this aspect of Chaucer's poetic style for his contemporaries is revealed in the recurrent divergences by the scribes as they read and copy.

It is the essential flexibility of the way Chaucer uses the resources of English within his poetry that repeatedly disconcerts the scribes, who tend to read a small space of the text at a time. The relation between lines often escaped the copyists, and their adaptations reflect Chaucer's distinctive achievement in creating an especially sinewy poetic syntax which stretches across a series of lines to form verse-paragraphs. The poet's characteristic couplet for Troilus:

> In vayn fro this forth have ich eyen tweye
> Ifourmed, syn youre vertu is aweye . . .
> (IV, 314-15)

confuses scribes who do not see the connection between "Ifourmed syn . . ." and the preceding line. One scribe writes desperately "Ne for medecyne ʒour vertu is away" (Ad) and another has "I for medycyn . . ." (Gg). Both are making the best of a construction which they do not understand as it unfolds itself over more than one line. Both replace the distinctive verbal texture of the original by stressing what they take to be the incurable despair conveyed by the context.

The evidence in the mss of scribal response to Chaucer's poetry reveals how difficult they found it to cope with this flexibly various approach to syntax by the poet. Chaucer's verse lines show very varying degrees of density and tautness of construction, depending on the particular balance between the material and the verse form in any one line. Pervasively the scribes fill out the syntax of Chaucer's compressed lines, to the destruction of the syllabic content of those lines. This is especially true of the scribes' response to Chaucer's deployment in his poetry of relative constructions. The mss show innumerable instances where the scribe is moved to insert that relative pronoun which Chaucer's poetic style depends on omitting. To the modern reader of a ms, this can bring home how forcibly Chaucer's contemporaries were evidently struck by the unusual spareness and tautness of the way Chaucer often reconciled his material with his form. For a line like Chaucer's "For ther is nothyng myghte hym bettre plese" (III, 886) some scribes will write "þat might" (Du H4), and for Chaucer's "For wel woot I in wise folk that vice" (III, 327) some mss have instead "þat in wyse" (H2 Ph). To a compact authentic line like "Allas, I ne hadde ibrought hire in hire sherte" (IV, 96), one scribe will add "Alas þat . . ." (H5). Yet because Chaucer is flexible in response to his verse form, there are by contrast many occasions where the form of his own lines depends on relative constructions, and in many lines scribes will clip the exceptionally fuller syntax that Chaucer requires. In a line like "Yet wist I nevere wel what that he mente" (III, 126) four mss will omit "that" (Du H3 H4 S2). Chaucer's style in a feature like use of relative pronouns is governed by the needs of the poetic context. As a poet in his own times, Chaucer's distinctive use of language is often represented by such unusually flexible adaptation of language to a poetic context, and this is evidently so distinctive that its detail is not consistently grasped by his contemporaries.

To read all the extant mss for a Chaucer poem is like taking up—to look at the same object—a number of sets of binoculars each adjusted to somebody else's eyesight. Each set is focused differently in the fine detail of its account of the text. For the editor the medieval poem is accordingly something of an aspiration, a hardest idea, somewhere between, behind, or above the network of available scribal variations in any given line. Chaucer's poems survive for each line somewhere mid-way in a band of possible scribal variation on either side. The scribes differ frequently amongst themselves over the grammatical forms of the poetry they are copying and over its minutiae of expression, so that the precise form of the poem seems unfocused. Few scribes are as incompetently casual as Gg in V, 994:

> This word to yow ynough suffisen oughte . . . (V, 994)
> Þis is word Inow for ʒow suffiseþ it nouʒt   (Gg).

But the mss frequently differ over the exact forms of verbs, especially the modal auxiliaries;[17] over tenses; over dative verb constructions;[18] over use of the infinitive with or without *to*; over use of the negative;[19] over the singular or plural nature of nouns. In their many differences over details of expression the scribes diverge from their exemplar in ways which collectively give recorded form to their response to a very distinctive feature of Chaucer's "curious" style: its dependence on a fine precision with which grammatical form is dovetailed into accommodation with verse form. It is to the challenge for Chaucer's early readers of this precise poetic form that the blurring found to some varying extent in every ms bears contemporary witness.

There is no need to credit the scribes' reading of Chaucer with an authority which intrinsically it does not merit, in order nevertheless to learn from it something of the response to Chaucer's poetic achievement in or near his own times. Most assessments of scribes have been formed by editors, and by definition a scribe only acquires any existence where he differs from his author. It is the author who is the ultimate goal of our attention. Yet with authors now very distant in the past, who were recognized as major original artists within their own times, it is helpful to regain some sense of how their contemporaries would themselves define the nature of that originality. It is in this that the responses of the scribes, however unconscious, can have a significant role for the modern reader of Chaucer. It is intrinsically unlikely that so much evidence from so many diverse and necessarily literate near-contemporaries of the poet should have no potential value as contemporary commentary, line-by-line, upon the quality of the poetry that it transmits. To ignore the evidence of the scribes except in so far as it can be categorized for the editorial purpose of determining originality is to pursue a modern ambition to create a text free from its scribal medium. This is in itself essentially a falsification of how the poem was almost universally first read, through the medium of scribal copies with all their built-in adaptations and interpretations of the poet's intentions. Scribal variation has its own value, as witness to what the intelligent reader made of Chaucer's poetry at a time when, in one sense, that poetry can scarcely have been more thoroughly read and appreciated, in that it was subjected to the process of repeated re-making and reinterpretation through being copied. By definition the literary criticism of the scribes is, editorially speaking, "easy" and "bad," and in proportion as it is so it has the power to heighten our own critical awareness, by showing how distinctively hard and difficultly good Chaucer's "curious" poetry could seem to his contemporaries and to his age.

NOTES

1. *Piers Plowman: The B Version*, X 337, ed. C. Kane and E. T. Donaldson (London, 1977).

2. See B. Blakey, "The Scribal Process," in *Medieval Miscellany Presented to Eugène Vinaver*, ed. F. Whitehead etc. (Manchester, 1965), pp.

19-27, and E. Vinaver, "Principles of Textual Emendation," in *Studies in French Language and Medieval Literature presented to Prof. Mildred K. Pope* (Manchester, 1939), pp. 351-69. For an account of recent thinking on editing, see Anne Hudson's chapter "Middle English," in *Editing Medieval Texts*, ed. A. G. Rigg (New York, 1977), pp. 34-57.

3. With Chaucer's remarks to "Adam Scriveyn," cf. Petrarch in *De Librorum Copia*, in *Petrarch: Four Dialogues for Scholars*, ed. and trans. C. H. Rawski (Western Reserve Univ. Press, 1967), esp. pp. 34-37. On the author's role, see S. J. Williams, "An Author's Role in Fourteenth Century Book Production," *Romania*, 90 (1969), 433-54; H. C. Schulz, "Thomas Hoccleve Scribe," *Speculum*, 12 (1937), 71-81; P. J. Lucas, "John Capgrave, OSA (1393-1464), Scribe and 'Publisher'," *Transactions of the Cambridge Bibliographical Society*, 5 (1969), 1-35.

4. Because of the numbers of Chaucer mss the present study focusses mainly on the results of collations of all the mss of *Troilus*.

5. For characterization of how scribes respond to the nature of their poetic exemplar, see *Piers Plowman: The A Version*, ed. G. Kane (London, 1960), "Editorial Resources and Methods," pp. 115-72.

6. *Chaucerian and Other Pieces*, ed. W. W. Skeat (Oxford, 1897), p. 239. Cf. also P. Strohm, "Jean of Angoulême: A Fifteenth Century Reader of Chaucer," *Neuphilologische Mitteilungen*, 72 (1971), 69-76.

7. On aspects of scribal behaviour, see N. Davis, "Scribal Variation in Late Fifteenth Century English," *Mélanges de Linguistique et de Philologie: Fernand Mossé in Memoriam* (Paris, 1959), pp. 95-103; G. L. Brook, "A Piece of Evidence for the Study of Middle English Spelling," *NM*, 73 (1972), 25-28. See also M. C. Seymour, "A Fifteenth Century East Anglian Scribe," *Medium Aevum*, 37 (1968), 166-73; and J. C. Hirsh, "Author and Scribe in *The Book of Margery Kempe*," *Medium Aevum*, 44 (1975), 145-50. For another scribe at work, see G. H. Russell and V. Nathan, "A *Piers Plowman* Manuscript now in the Huntington Library," *Huntington Library Quarterly*, 26 (1963), 119-30.

8. See Kane, *The A Version*, p. 136 ff.

9. The text of *TC* is cited from F. N. Robinson, *The Complete Works of Geoffrey Chaucer*, 2nd edn. (London, 1957), with some punctuation omitted, and variants are cited from the mss, with sigils as in *The Book of Troilus and Criseyde*, ed. R K. Root (Princeton, 1926), except that A becomes Ad and D becomes Du.

10. All italics are, of course, my own.

11. On Cp, see M. B. Parkes, "Palaeographical Description and Commentary," in *Troilus and Criseyde: A Facsimile of Corpus Christi College Cambridge MS. 61* (Cambridge: D. S. Brewer, 1977).

12. With the scribes' feeling for synonym, cf. the recent suggestions about medieval attitudes to English diction in N. F. Blake, *The English Language in Medieval Literature* (London, 1977), chs. 4-7. Cf. also J. J. Murphy, "Literary Implications of Instruction in the Verbal Arts in Fourteenth Century England," *Leeds Studies in English* NS 1 (1967), 119-35.

13. All quotation is from *The Text of the Canterbury Tales*, ed. J. M. Manly and E. Rickert (Chicago, 1940). See also A. I. Doyle and M. B. Parkes, "The Production of Copies of the *Canterbury Tales* and *Confessio Amantis* in the early fifteenth century," in *Medieval Scribes, Manuscripts and Libraries: Essays Presented to N. R. Ker*, ed. M. B. Parkes and Andrew G. Watson (London, 1978), pp. 163-210.

14. For Chaucer's verbs in *un-*, see N. Davis, "Chaucer and Fourteenth Century English," in *Geoffrey Chaucer: Writers and Their Background*, ed. D. S. Brewer (London, 1974); see also R. W. V. Elliot, *Chaucer's English* (London, 1974).

15. Formulaic cliché marks scribal variation over prayers and oaths in the text: "I thank it God was torned to gladnesse" (III, 1400) becomes "Blyssyd be god was . . ." (H5); and one oath is replaced by another: "Ris up for by *myn hed* she shal not goon"(IV, 593) becomes *my treuthe* (Ad) or *my feith* (H4). On formulaic diction, see W. E. Holland, "Formulaic Diction and the Descent of a Middle English Romance," *Speculum*, 48 (1973), 89-109; and M. Tyssens, "Le style oral et les ateliers de copistes," in *Melangés M. Delbouille*, Vol. II (Gembloux, 1964). Cf. further S. T. Knight, "Oral Transmission of *Sir Launfal*," *Medium Aevum*, 38 (1969), 164-70; and A. McIntosh, "The Textual Transmission of the Alliterative *Morte Arthure*," in *English and Medieval Studies presented to J. R. R. Tolkien* (London, 1902), pp. 231-40.

16. See George Thomson, "Simplex Ordo," *Classical Quarterly*, 15 (1965), 161-75.

17. See S. Ono, "Chaucer's Variants and What They Tell Us: Fluctuation in the Use of Modal Auxiliaries," *Studies in English Literature* (Tokyo), English Number 1969, 51-74.

18. For "And wold of that hym missed han ben sesed" (III, 445), 10 mss read the easier *he missed*.

19. For uncertainty over use of *ne*, see T. F. Mustanoja, *A Middle English Syntax* (Helsinki, 1960), pp. 339-41.

The New Reader and Female Textuality in Two Early Commentaries on Chaucer

Susan Schibanoff

This essay first appeared in Studies in the Age of Chaucer *10 (1988): 71-108.*

THE anonymous glosses or marginal annotations that appear in almost half of the fifty-eight complete manuscripts of *The Canterbury Tales* provide a rich—but neglected—source of reader response to Chaucer's poetry. Although Chaucerians have begun to explore how Chaucer's contemporaries reacted to his works, we have been slow to examine these glosses.[1] Several obvious reasons for our relative disregard of them come to mind. Perhaps the most important is that access to these marginalia remains difficult.[2] But even were this material ready to hand in facsimile or edited form, we would still have to struggle to interpret the kind of response to Chaucer's text that we find in most glosses. Only in rare cases do these marginalia make direct comment on Chaucer's text: "verum est" is one glossator's unequivocal assent to the Wife of Bath's claim that no man can swear as boldly as a woman can, and "nota bene" signals another glossator's obvious interest in, if not precise attitude toward, a proverb in *The Knight's Tale*.[3] In equally unambiguous fashion, another glossator registers moral disapproval of the misplaced kiss in *The Miller's Tale* by means of the marginal warning "nota malum quid."[4] And, citing Proverbs 21:19 ("Better to live alone in the desert than with a nagging and ill-tempered wife"), yet another glossator makes it quite clear that he prefers silent and agreeable women.[5]

More often, however, the glosses on *The Canterbury Tales* do not offer us such straightforward commentary, and as modern readers we find ourselves in the ironic position of having to gloss the glosses, that is, of having to explicate their meaning or significance. In particular, we must interpret the source gloss, by far the most common type of marginal annotation on *The Canterbury Tales*.[6] This gloss commonly occurs in one of three forms: it names (correctly or incorrectly) the source or analogue of a passage in Chaucer's *Tales*, as in the Ellesmere gloss, "Valerius libro 6° folio 14°," on *The Wife of Bath's Prologue* 643; it gives the Latin text of the source or analogue but no title nor author, as in the Ellesmere gloss, "Quis pinxit leonem," on lines 692, "Who peyntede the leon, tel me who"; or it quotes both the Latin text and the title of the source or analogue, as in the Ellesmere gloss, "Ne des mulieri nequam veniam prodeundi ecclesiastici 25°," on lines 657-58, "[Whoso] suffereth his wyf to go seken halwes, / Is worthy to be hanged on the galwes."[7]

Earlier Chaucer scholars (as well as some recent ones) concluded that such glosses had merely a decorative function. Aage Brusendorff and J. S. P. Tatlock, for instance, viewed the source gloss as an indication of the medieval "love of learning" and fondness for citing authorities rather than as a specific comment on or response to the text.[8] The latest writer on this subject, Graham D. Caie, however, has taken the opposite view, arguing that the source gloss not only contains the glossator's remark on the text but aims to shape the response of subsequent readers of the text as well:

> Were [source glosses] included merely for decoration, to give the *Tales* an aura of authority, or because the medieval scribe enjoyed quoting the Latin source? [No.] . . . They were in fact comments on the tale to guide the reader's interpretation. Even to note a source reference has the effect of arresting the reader and drawing his attention to the original when he might otherwise pass on with no more than a hazy flicker of recognition. By boldly placing the glosses (side by side with the text) in as large a hand as the text, the glossator prompts the reader to compare the interpretive context of the quotation, thus remembering its usual application.[9]

We who now take for granted such critical activities as interpreting variorum editions[10] have little difficulty agreeing with Caie that all texts— even fourteenth- and fifteenth-century bibliographical marginalia—have a subtext, or, in this case, may constitute a paratext. We may also be quite comfortable viewing the source gloss as an example of what we would now call "intertextuality" and what Chaucer called "new corn" from "old fields," that is, the critical concept recently explored by Barthes, Bloom, and others that texts are largely made out of prior texts.[11] And, with Walter J. Ong, we may even accept the idea that the language itself of most glosses—Latin— has a significance that we may interpret or explain.[12] In this current critical climate the older view of these glosses as "meaningless" embellishment is not likely to engage our attention or to deter our exegesis of them.

Even if we agree with Caie, however, that the mere act of noting a source constitutes a response to the text, we have yet to determine the specific nature of that response. To do so, we must consider audience, for Caie partly bases his interpretation of the glosses as moral guides for readers on an unstated assumption about the characteristics of this audience. When he maintains that the source gloss reminds the reader of the "usual"—the complete or orthodox—version or application of a traditional text and thus exposes the way Chaucer's fictional characters partly quote, misquote, or otherwise abuse these texts, he has in mind not a learned but a "lewed" audience. For instance, when the Wife of Bath selectively paraphrases Paul's marital teaching in 1 Corinthians 7:4—"I have the power durynge al my lyf / Upon his propre body, and noght he / Right thus the Apostel tolde it unto me" (*WBP* 158-60)—Caie detects an "indignant" flood of corrective source glosses that unmask and "damn" this "perverse" use of Scripture before the reader's eyes:

> The Egerton 2864 glossator quotes 1 Cor. 7:3 "Let the husband render unto the wife due benevolence: and likewise also the wife unto the husband," thus stressing the fact that love in marriage is reciprocal. Many other manuscript glosses add to her statement "I have the power . . . upon his propre body" the all-important conclusion, "the wife hath not power of her own body, but the husband" (1 Cor. 7:4). A number of the glosses comment on this gross perversion of Scripture by quoting Paul's admonition in Ephesians 5:22-24: "Wives submit yourselves unto your husbands, as unto the Lord. For the husband is head of the wife, even as Christ is head of the Church: and he is the Saviour of the body."[13]

Clearly Caie's interpretation of the source glosses assumes a reader in need of the most elementary instruction, as I think it is safe to assume anyone in the Middle Ages with but a dim recollection of the Pauline marital policies of Corinthians would be, for this was one of the most popular and commonplace of late-medieval scriptural texts. Such "readers" were no doubt uneducated, what we would call illiterate or nonliterate. Like the readers of a much earlier age, this audience would continue to listen to the recitation of texts, although what they heard now was read aloud from a written script rather than orally composed. Thus Caie's putative audience would most likely consist of what I call "old" readers, not of the "new" educated and private readers of manuscripts whose emergence was well under way during Chaucer's era.

How likely is it that these old readers, who would not have held manuscripts in their hands, knew of the Chaucer glossa? And even if they did, how plausible is it that they would read Latin, the traditional language of marginal annotation?[14] It seems improbable that a reciter of the *Tales* also voiced its marginalia to "ear-readers," or a listening audience. The gloss, as well as its descendant the footnote,[15] seems to be designed for the new reader, the visual reader, and most likely the actual audience of the Chaucer glosses were "eye-readers," the educated and elite: wealthy patrons who ordered manuscripts of the *Tales* and the family, friends, and others who had access to their libraries; scribes, editors, and others in the "book" trade; poets and scholars; and, of course, other glossators.

If the source gloss was written for an educated, literate audience—for new readers—then it would not likely serve the primary purpose Caie maintains it does, as a reminder of the orthodox version or usage of a well-known passage from the Bible, for this audience would not require such prompting. This audience would know its Paul well enough that the sort of elementary scriptural guidance Caie hypothesizes would be superfluous, as it evidently is for Chaucer's Pardoner.[16] To avoid this apparent contradiction between the form of the gloss and its function, I think we must examine the source gloss more fully and assume for it an audience of new readers rather than one of old readers.

The assumption of such an audience encourages us to open our eyes to two particular glosses that are also about the new reader. Such self-consciousness and self-reflexiveness should not surprise us, for the glosses in question annotate a section of *The Canterbury Tales* that understandably attracts marginal comment on the new reader: *The Wife of Bath's Prologue* and *Tale*. Alison's "bookishness"—a woman's literal and metaphorical taking of texts into her own hands—dramatizes an extreme act of new reading to which the two glossators we shall examine below have different reactions. One sees in the Wife's "textuality" the promise and the other the threat of this emerging late-medieval audience. As well as revealing to us a fifteenth-century conflict over new reading, juxtaposing these commentaries offers us a means of interpreting the otherwise inscrutable source annotation, which must be our first task in glossing these glosses.

The two commentaries in question occur in manuscripts Ellesmere (ca. 1400-10) and Egerton 2864 (ca. 1460-80). Although the glosses in Egerton 2864 are not original but derive from an earlier, nonextant manuscript,[17] both they and the Ellesmere glosses were copied wholesale at one time. Thus, even if multiple authors lie behind these marginalia, each appears in its respective manuscript as a single, unified gloss. We may therefore conceive of two individual and specific authors of these commentaries, as evidently the scribes or supervisors of these manuscripts wished readers to regard them.

When considered in isolation, the Ellesmere marginalia on the Wife's *Prologue* do not appear to make any particular response to the text. Most— 34 of 43—are source glosses and take one of the three forms I outlined earlier. Approximately half of these source glosses concentrate on the first 162 lines of the *Prologue*, the Wife's so-called sermon on marriage, and the rest spread out over the remaining 600-odd lines of the *Prologue*, the Wife's narration of her marital experiences. None of the marginal notes offers direct comment on the text, no "verum est," "nota bene," "nota malum quid," or any other passage such as the one I quote above from Proverbs 21:19 that clearly indicates the glossator's attitude or response to the text. Nor do any of Ellesmere's source glosses underline, as Caie implies they do,[18] the Wife's misuse or abuse of an "auctoritee." When, for instance, the Wife quotes Paul in part so that he appears to command only husbands to obey wives (*WBP* 153ff.), the Ellesmere glossator does not supply the remaining part of the Apostle's command that wives also obey husbands. Instead, he echoes the Wife's partial quotation of Paul with a similar partial quotation of his own: "He who has a wife is regarded as a debtor, and is said to be uncircumcised, to be the servant of his wife, and like bad servants, to be bound."[19] Considered in isolation, then, the Ellesmere glosses yield no obvious response to the text, and, since it is unlikely that they are meant to inform an audience already cognizant of common source materials, we might be tempted to conclude with Tatlock and Brusendorff that these marginalia are "meaningless" embellishment.

When, however, we view the Ellesmere gloss on the Wife's *Prologue* in the context of the Egerton 2864 gloss, some obvious contours of meaning or response begin to emerge from its apparently featureless ground. Unlike that in the Ellesmere glosses we have just considered, unquestionably clear is the nature of the Egerton glossator's response to the Wife's text. We cannot mistake this annotator's outrage and indignation over the Wife's *Prologue*, an attitude negative enough to prompt him to compose (or borrow from a now nonextant source) a unique set of marginalia with which to excoriate Alison's immorality and vice. Because, to date, we have not considered the Egerton glosses on the *Prologue* as an individual and independent set of annotations but have treated them as adjunct to or part of the Ellesmere glosses, I shall outline them in detail to establish their separate identity. And although some of the Egerton glosses constitute a complex response to the Wife's text, I shall focus first on those that make overt moral condemnation of the Wife's behavior and actions. This series of comments occurs in the latter or narrative section of the *Prologue* and is unique to the Egerton manuscript.[20] Having examined the Egerton gloss in its own right, I then return to the Ellesmere gloss and read it "interglosally," that is, interpret it in light of its generic counterpart, Egerton 2864.

As the Wife begins the story of her life with five husbands, the Egerton glossator remains unobtrusive for some time, largely restricting his comments to bibliographical annotations that cite the Latin version and sources of antifeminist gibes the Wife's husbands threw at her (e.g., at *WBP* 278, 363, 371, 401).[21] But patience, scholarly pose, and self-restraint soon wear thin. When the Wife launches into a celebration of her ability to outtalk her men and requite her husbands word for word (*WBP* 419-25), the Egerton glossator drops the calm, detached mien of scholar-bibliographer and attempts to shout the Wife down in a series of marginal remarks taken from Scripture and intended to silence noisy women: "It is the stupid who are fluent with calumny" (Prov. 10:18, second half); "Better to live in a corner of the house top than have a nagging wife and brawling household" (Prov.

21:9); "Better to live alone in the desert than with a nagging and ill-tempered wife" (Prov. 21:19); "As the climbing of a sandy way is to the feet of the aged, so is a wife full of tongue [to a quiet man]" (Ecclus. 25:27).[22] And, having finally joined verbal battle with the Wife, the Egerton glossator continues to shout her down and to cite chapter and verse against her throughout the remainder of her narrative.

When the Wife wistfully recalls her youth—her singing, her drinking, and her "ragerye"—with the remark that it tickles her about the "herte roote" to remember how she has had her world in her time (*WBP* 455-73), the Egerton glossator thunders against her with a series of somber and sobering admonitions: "Woe to you who are mighty to drink wine" (Isa. 5:22, first half); "Woe to you that rise up early in the morning to follow drunkenness, and to drink until the evening, to be inflamed with wine" (Isa. 5:11); "A drunken woman is a great wrath and her reproach and shame shall not be hid" (Ecclus. 26:11); "Turn from the wayward impulses of youth" (2 Tim. 2:22, first half).[23] When Alison candidly admits that she told her "gossib" even more secrets than she did her parish priest (*WBP* 533), her commentator warns husbands never to rely on their wives' ability to be discreet: "Seal your lips even from the wife of your bosom" (Mic. 7:5, second half).[24] And when the Wife complains that she hated both listening to Jankyn's endless proverbs and having her vices pointed out to her (*WBP* 660ff.), the Egerton annotator takes a page from Jankyn's book: he too cites a long series of proverbs on the virtues of accepting correction and the vices of neglecting reproof (Prov. 3:11, 9:7, 10:17, 12:1, 13:18, 15:10, and 15:32).

As the Wife nears the conclusion of her marital narrative, relating how she ripped pages out of Jankyn's book and they traded blows (*WBP* 790ff.), the somewhat weary-sounding Egerton glossator remarks that evil women do try men's souls: "A wicked woman abateth the courage and maketh a heavy countenance and a wounded heart" (Ecclus. 25:31).[25] Nevertheless, this glossator is determined to have the last word in his verbal duel with Alison—and does. As the Wife ends her story by telling us that Jankyn gave her control over their marriage and that they never debated again (*WBP* 813ff.), the Egerton glossator pulls her own text out from under her feet with a contradictory bit of conventional wisdom: "A woman, if she have superiority, is contrary to her husband" (Ecclus. 25:30).[26]

As this series of marginalia on the latter half of the Wife's *Prologue* makes evident, the Egerton glossator sees Alison as the stereotypical alewife and rails against her traditional shrewish vices. Yet within this conventional response to the "wicked wife," a more subtle and perhaps significant conflict occurs between Alison and her commentator: a battle over who shall control the text and "auctoritee," who shall have the right to interpret or gloss. Obvious indications of this struggle lie in the marginalia—again unique to the Egerton manuscript—at lines 688-710 and 346-47. In the former passage the Wife declares that it is "an impossible" for clerics to write well of women and that books of "wikked wyves" such as the one her fifth husband reads to her result from clerical prejudice against women. Or, as the Wife succinctly puts it, "Who peyntede the leon, tel me who?" (*WBP* 692). But no sooner has the Wife characterized, interpreted, analyzed, and hence controlled written authority on the nature of women than the Egerton glossator steps in to wrest control away from her. In response to her complaint about clerical bias against women, he tries to undercut the Wife's credibility by citing the first half of Proverbs 31:10 ("Who shall find a valiant woman?"),[27] the verse that begins the longer biblical text known as the "praise of a wise wife." This is, we should note, the sole instance in the Egerton glosses in which the glossator writes well of women (or quotes a scriptural passage that does so). He does so, of course, not to praise women but to deny the Wife's knowledge of, and hence her right to interpret, written authority.

Another conflict over glossing occurs in the Egerton marginalia at lines 346-47. But here the struggle is more complex, for it involves three parties—the Wife, her initial three old husbands, and the Egerton glossator. First, the Wife narrates how her old husbands warned her that fancy attire endangers women's chastity and how, to "enforce" their caveat, they glossed it with the Apostle Paul's command to women in 1 Timothy 2:9: "'In habit maad with chastitee and shame / Ye wommen shul apparaille yow,' quod he, / 'And noght in tressed heer and gay perree, / As perles, ne with gold, ne clothes riche'" (*WBP* 342-45). The Wife, however, asserts that she will heed neither the "text" of her husbands' warning nor their "rubriche" (*WBP* 346), the Pauline gloss with which they justify their own words to her. Neither, she concludes, deserves a gnat's worth of her attention. But the Egerton glossator does not allow the Wife to win this battle with her husbands so easily. Not only does he restore their Pauline gloss that the Wife summarily dismissed ("Similiter et mulieres in habitu ornato verecundia et sobrietate ornante se non in totis crinibus aut argento aut margaritis vel veste preciosa etc apostolus ad thymotheum," fol. 85v), but he goes on to give another gloss, this time from the Apostle Peter:

> [Similarly, let wives be subject to their husbands; so that even if any do not believe the word, they may without word be won through the behavior of their wives,] / observing reverently your chaste behavior. / Let not theirs be the outward adornment of braiding the hair, or wearing gold, or of putting on robes.[28]

In league with the Wife's former husbands, then, the Egerton glossator reinstates the Pauline gloss, but, by means of the second gloss that he adds, he announces that he alone has final word on—and control of—the text.[29]

These two examples of the Egerton commentator's struggle with the Wife for control of the text suggest a way of interpreting the remainder of the gloss and of gaining an overall sense of its significance. The rest of the Egerton gloss annotates the first section of the *Prologue* (lines 1-162), the Wife's so-called sermon on marriage. Unlike the latter part of the gloss I outlined above, which makes unequivocal moral comment on the Wife's actions and behavior, this section contains only source glosses and on its own appears to offer no particular response to the text. It is, however, an unusually full and, we might say, energetic gloss: nineteen individual marginalia on the Wife's 162 lines, some of which cite multiple biblical verses. If we bear in mind the evident enthusiasm the Egerton glossator holds for textual citation as well as the context we have already observed of opposition to the Wife for her behavior and her desire to interpret texts herself, this opening section of the gloss begins to lose its "flatness" and take on more obvious contours of response.

For example, the initial Egerton gloss (*WBP* 11) at first appears to be little more than a "decorative" bibliographical reference. On closer and contextual examination, however, we may see that it represents a choice, hence an attitude or response, by the glossator. That is, the Wife opens her *Prologue* with a discussion of the way a particular biblical passage (John 2:1-2) is interpreted or glossed: she has been told, she says, that Christ's appearance at only one wedding (at Cana in Galilee) means that one marriage alone is sanctioned for the Christian. The Wife, of course, rejects this reading of the wedding at Cana as a "sharp word for the nones" (line 14). She argues that, although men "glosen up and doun" about the number of marriages permissible to the Christian, nowhere has she ever heard an express "diffinicioun" of this number or limitation on it. Alison, in other words, demands the right to interpret Scripture herself, in this case not to gloss but to read "expressly" or literally. And it comes as no surprise that the way she reads justifies multiple marriage: the Apostle has told her that as a widow she is free to remarry, so "welcome the sixte, whan that evere he shal" (line 45).

Presumably at this point the glossator of the Wife's *Prologue* has at least one of two choices to make to supply a bibliographical reference. He might cite the biblical text in question (John 2:1-2), or he might cite the interpretation of this passage that the Wife says she has heard and rejected— in other words, the gloss that interprets the wedding at Cana as a mandate against multiple marriage (as, for instance, does Jerome in the *Adversus Jovinianum* (1.40): ". . . by going once to a marriage [Christ] taught that men should only marry once"). Which choice the glossator makes, I suggest, results from an attitude toward the Wife's text and also constitutes a response to it. If the glossator cites the biblical text, emphasis falls on Scripture, and our attention focuses on the contrast between Holy Word and human words, or, in this case, between sacred text and Alison's profane reading of it. But if, on the other hand, he cites another reader's reading of the biblical passage, then our attention focuses on how this reader and the Wife interpret the same text, and we compare mortal reader with mortal reader. No matter how authoritative or "correct" one reading may be judged to be, both readers are equal in the sense that the annotator accords each the right or privilege to attempt to gloss the text.

As we might expect by now, the Egerton glossator does not cite another reader's interpretation and thus grants no such equality to the Wife. Instead, he chooses to cite the biblical text—"a marriage took place at Cana of

Galilee, and the mother of Jesus was there. Now Jesus too was invited to the marriage and also his disciples"[30]—and thus focuses our attention on the tonal differences between the sonorous rhythms of the Gospel and the cacophonous splutterings of Alison's human—and indignant—response ("Herkne eek, lo, which a sharp word for the nones" [*WBP* 14]). By citing Scripture only, the Egerton glossator takes a kind of possession or custodianship of Holy Word, edging the Wife into the subordinate position of one whose rights to "own" the text by glossing it are at best questionable. Such a gloss, then, is not, as it might first appear, mere adornment but a subtle anticipation of the overt attempt to gain textual control that later emerges in the Egerton marginalia at lines 346-47 and 688-710.

As Manly and Rickert observe, throughout the Wife's *Prologue* the Egerton glossator often gives the fullest bibliographical references of any annotator.[31] The more significant difference for us to observe, though, is that with but a few exceptions he quotes Scripture only, whereas other glosses, such as those in the Ellesmere, often cite profane or secular literature— Jerome's *Adversus Jovinianum*, classical authors, astrological treatises, proverbial wisdom, Aesopic fables, and the like. In many instances, like the one discussed above (*WBP* 11), the effect of Egerton's scriptural source gloss is to claim for the glossator a primary relationship with Holy Word that undermines the Wife's attempt to make the text fit her experience by glossing it "up and down." As such, then, the source glosses that open the Egerton commentary on the *Prologue* take on a definite contour of response to the Wife, a contour that elevates into open hostility soon enough.

Significantly, it is not the Wife's sexuality per se that draws the Egerton glossator's heaviest fire but her "textuality," her insistence on the right to interpret Scripture. This should not surprise us, for as *The Canterbury Tales* itself depicts again and again, professional rivalry is a constant of human interaction, be it among fictional millers and reeves, friars and summoners, or between an actual fifteenth-century glossator and a "textual" Wife. And, as I suggest below, this last conflict dramatizes a much larger social and religious controversy over another kind of "new" reading that had already begun in Chaucer's time and would continue far beyond it: lay reading of the vernacular Bible.

Examined as a distinct and discrete example of its genre and assuming an educated audience, the Egerton gloss not only yields its own particular meaning or significance but can help define the major contours of such glosses as the Ellesmere, which, as we briefly explored above, appear featureless upon first reading. We may now observe, for instance, that the Ellesmere glossator never makes direct comment on the Wife, unlike the Egerton glossator who, by the middle of the *Prologue*, excoriates Alison's errant ways. Presumably the Ellesmere annotator finds Alison's behavior unremarkable. Nor does he struggle for textual control in the overt fashion of the Egerton glossator at *WBP* 346-47 and 688-710. Instead, the Ellesmere glossator is largely content to echo or augment the Wife's text, offering Latin versions of her words, explaining further her discussion of astrological phenomena, and the like. And, consistent with these differences from the Egerton gloss, the Ellesmere marginalia display a yet much more fundamental dissimilarity: whenever the Ellesmere glossator must make the choice we discussed above between citing Holy Writ or a secular text, he chooses secular text, human interpretation. And thus, unlike his counterpart, the Ellesmere commentator allows Alison the right to gloss Scripture and draws our attention to the subject of how different readers read the same text.

The work the Ellesmere glossator quotes most often is the *Epistola adversus Jovinianum*, which contains Jerome's interpretation of the Apostle's pronouncements on marriage. Of Ellesmere's thirty-four source glosses, twenty-four cite Jerome, and many of them invite us to compare the different ways in which the Wife and, as she calls him, the "clerk at Rome" (*WBP* 672), gloss the same text. For instance, in the Wife's way of reading, the Bible neither commands nor instructs Christians to limit the number of their marriages, whereas the Ellesmere gloss gives us Jerome's very different interpretation of this matter: "[Jesus] by going only once to a marriage . . . taught that men should marry only once" (*Adv. Jov.* 1.40).[32] Or, in the Wife's interpretation, "conseillyng is no commandment" (*WBP* 67, 73, 82); therefore, Paul's counsel on the preferability of virginity to marriage (1 Cor. 7:25) has no force for her. For Jerome, however, the Apostle's counsel does have force, or so the Ellesmere glossator implies in his citation from the *Adversus Jovinianum* (1.12) at *WBP* 73: "Paul, 'concerning virgins I have no commandment, but I give my judgment,' et cetera."[33] Or, when the Wife reads 1 Corinthians 7:27 ("Art thou bound to a wife? Do not seek to be freed. Art thou freed from a wife? Do not seek a wife"), she hears the first part of the verse more loudly than the second, and it justifies her own belief that women should rule marriages and that men should be their "dettours" and "thrals." Jerome, however, the Ellesmere glossator would have us understand in the gloss at *WBP* 155, is more attuned to the second part of the Corinthians verse, echoing its disparagement and discouragement of marriage: "He who has a wife is regarded as a debtor, and is said to be uncircumcised, to be the servant of his wife, and like bad servants to be bound" (*Adv. Jov.* 1.12).[34]

In emphasizing the very different ways these two readers read, the Ellesmere glossator invites us to consider the issues of relativity and contextuality in interpretation and the inclination of readers to read as their situations dictate. He also encourages us to take a sympathetic view of the Wife, to understand, perhaps, how her traditionally subservient role might incline her to interpret the Bible as validating female sovereignty in marriage, just as we may appreciate how the clerk at Rome, the future saint, seeks scriptural precedents for the superiority of celibacy over marriage. But on several occasions the Ellesmere glossator goes beyond implicit sympathy for the Wife to explicit, even if ironic, support for her way of reading. And, with a touch of humor uncharacteristic of his genre, he even goes so far as to enlist a most improbable ally in support of the Wife's way of reading— Saint Jerome himself.

An example of the Ellesmere glossator's support of the Wife occurs as she argues that her choice of marriage over virginity or celibacy has scriptural justification. Ignoring the first part of 1 Corinthians 7:7 ("For I would that you were all as I am myself") and quoting the second part ("each one has his own gift from God, one in this way, and another in that"), the Wife fashions a text (*WBP* 103-104) to imply that all "gifts"—marriage, virginity, celibacy—are equal in the eyes of God . And the Ellesmere glossator evidently affirms the Wife's attempt to reread Scripture in this way, for he supplies a Latin version of her partial quotation of Paul's words ("Unusquisque proprium habet donum ex deo alius quidem sic alius autem sic") and nothing else. In contrast, the Egerton glossator thwarts Alison's attempt to mold the text in her own image and to her own advantage. Citing the first part of 1 Corinthians 12:4 ("There are varieties of gifts") and then Alison's partial text on gifts,[35] the Egerton commentator asserts that there is a hierarchy of "gifts" the Wife ignores as she takes Scripture into her own hands.

Not only does the Ellesmere glossator echo the Wife's rewritten text, but in one ironic instance he makes an original contribution to her radical new book on marriage. The passage in question is both the finale and climax of the Wife's "sermon" on matrimony: Alison boldly announces that her husbands shall be subservient to her and suffer tribulation on her account because the Apostle (Paul) has decreed both that wives should have power over their husbands' bodies and that husbands should love their wives well (*WBP* 155-62). Alison creates this text, of course, by carefully selecting only those biblical verses that, taken out of context, appear to support her goal of dominance in marriage and by ignoring the many that would oppose it. This is the text that evidently strikes one member of her audience—the Pardoner, an expert manipulator of scriptural verse himself—as so outrageous that he is compelled to break in and halt her construction of it.

Another member of the Wife's audience, however, neither interrupts nor protests her text but echoes and, in fact, augments it: the Ellesmere glossator. At *WBP* 158 he imitates the highly selective text that the Wife has cobbled together in justification of female-dominated marriage: "and if you take a wife you do not sin yet such will have tribulation of the flesh etc.[1 Cor. 7:28, in part]; And the husband does not have the power of his body but the wife [1 Cor. 7:4, second part]; And, husbands, love your wives [Eph. 5:25, first part, or Col. 3:19, first part]."[36] And, in the same gloss the Ellesmere annotator also amplifies the Wife's text with a passage that apparently she does not know and that occurs in the most ironic source possible, the *Adversus Jovinianum*, Jerome's own "book" on marriage with which the Wife has so often been at odds throughout her *Prologue*: "And also if you are your wife's servant, be not sad upon that account."[37] Thus, with Jerome's own words (taken out of context, of course) advocating cheerful submission to women, the Ellesmere commentator ironically cheers the Wife on as she reaches the triumphant conclusion of her case for female sovereignty in marriage.

This same pattern of the Egerton glossator battling with the Wife for control of the text and the Ellesmere glossator supporting her creation of the text continues in Alison's tale of the old hag and the rapist knight. Here again the Egerton glossator reacts more negatively to female textuality than to sexuality. He has nothing to say on the central folklore motif of the tale, the choice between wives who are fair but unfaithful as opposed to wives who are foul but faithful. Nor does he engage in the snubs of women for their vanity and indiscretion that other commentators on the *Tale* occasionally do.[38] Instead the Egerton glossator continues to concern himself with the use of written authority, in this case the hag's employment (or nonemployment) of biblical quotations to gloss her self-justifying sermon on the virtues of age, poverty, lowly status or natural "gentillesse," and physical ugliness.

When the hag first meets the rapist knight as he searches for the answer to the question of what women want most, she attempts to establish her credentials for aiding him (and to defend her old age) by means of the proverbial remark that "'olde folk kan muchel thynge'" (*WBT* 1004). Although this bit of conventional lore suffices to convince the knight of the hag's qualifications, such an unauthoritative comment evidently strikes the Egerton glossator as less than persuasive, and he immediately "textualizes" the hag's traditional wisdom by citing a scriptural authority on the subject of age. Not only does he display his own erudition, but he undercuts the hag's self-defense by quoting a passage that conflicts with her implication that knowledge is a natural or automatic function of "elde": "O how comely is wisdom for the aged, and understanding and counsel to men of honor. Much experience is the crown of old men, etc. Ecclesiasticus" (Ecclus. 25:7-8).[39]

After the hag has married the knight, however, and found him to be a reluctant lover, hiding himself "as an owle" all day, she does begin to "textualize" her approach to him. First she defends her lowly social status by calling her husband's attention to what Dante, Cicero, Valerius, Boethius, and Seneca had to write in favor of natural gentility. Throughout this longish lecture (*WBT* 1109-77), with its frequent allusions to and quotations of secular authorities, the Egerton glossator remains silent. It is not until the hag begins her defense of poverty and refers to Scripture that we hear from him again. Characteristically, here he struggles with the hag for control of the text, rivaling her biblical allusion with a quite different citation of his own. Paraphrasing a passage such as 2 Corinthians 8:9 ("For you know the graciousness of our Lord Jesus Christ—how, being rich, he became poor for our sakes, that by his poverty you might become rich"), the hag reminds her husband that "the hye God, on whom that we bileve, / In wilful poverte chees to lyve his lyf" (*WBT* 1178-79). The Egerton glossator finds the hag's gloss inappropriate, incorrect, or insufficient, and so next to it he adds his own scriptural quotation that stresses not how the "hye God" himself chose poverty but how God favors the poor: "Has not God chosen the poor of this world [?] James the Apostle" (middle part, James 2:5).[40]

Finally, as the hag finishes her so-called curtain lecture, which is actually a dissuasion of her husband's celibacy, she returns to the praise of "elde." Once again, however, her ability to recall relevant textual authorities fails her. She concludes that, even though "noon auctoritee / were in noon book," noble people would still honor the old, and someday, she guesses, she will find an author whom she can quote to this effect (*WBT* 1207-12). The Egerton glossator, of course, cannot resist the temptation to stud the hag's deficient text with biblical citations. He quotes not one but two scriptural passages on "elde," once more underscoring the hag's ignorance. More important, he again undercuts her argument, choosing passages that employ a more complex—and conditional—view of the virtues of age than does the hag, as if to suggest that her praise of "elde" is either simplistic or self-serving: "Old age is a crown of dignity when it is found in the ways of justice. Proverbs of Solomon [Prov. 16:31]. For venerable old age is not that of long time, nor counted by the number of years. Wisdom" [first half, Wisd. of Sol. 4:8].[41]

As he did earlier in the Wife's *Prologue*, in the *Tale* the Egerton glossator battles with a female sermonizer, the hag, for control of the text. And once again he has the last word, in this case the last textual citation (at *WBT* 1207). Almost immediately afterward, the hag leaves her books, her "auctours," and her lecture behind and fades into a folktale milieu in which she is magically transformed into a beautiful young woman. No doubt the Egerton glossator is relieved to see her exit from his erudite world of texts and sermons, but it is clear that his counterpart, the Ellesmere glossator, does not share this sentiment. As in the Wife's *Prologue*, his gloss on the *Tale* not only supports the hag's textuality but augments it.

The Ellesmere commentator concentrates his textual citations on a twenty-line section (*WBT* 1182-1202) of the hag's *dissuasio* promoting the virtues of poverty. This is the most "bookish" section of her lecture; it abounds in quotations of secular authorities, about which the Egerton glossator has nothing to say. The Ellesmere annotator's remarks here, however, literally support the hag's textuality. His first gloss (at *WBT* 1182) gives the Latin version of the hag's quotation from Seneca; his second gloss (at line 1186) cites a biblical passage that corresponds to the hag's argument that "he that coveiteth is a povre wight"; his third gloss (at line 1193) provides the Latin form of the hag's citation from Juvenal; and similarly, his fourth gloss (at line 1195) supplies the Latin version of the hag's statement that "poverte is hateful good."[42]

The Ellesmere glossator also offers (perhaps ironically again) one "auctor" who augments the hag's lecture on the virtues of poverty and the evils of wealth: Jerome. As the hag concludes her remarks on poverty, she argues that it increases "sapience" and provides a utilitarian lens (a "spectacle," line 1202) through which one may discover both God and true friends. In support of this metaphor, the Ellesmere glossator adds a passage from the *Adversus Jovinianum* (2.9) that illustrates how, in Jerome's words, some have abandoned riches to pursue virtue and philosophy: "Hence Crates the Theban, after throwing into the sea a considerable weight of gold, exclaimed, 'Go to the bottom, ye evil lusts: I will drown you that you may not drown me.'"[43]

In one other respect as well the Ellesmere glossator emphasizes—and increases—the "textuality" of the hag's *dissuasio*: throughout her lecture he adds marginal headings that articulate its constituent parts. These rubrics ("De generositate" at line 1109, "De paupertate" at line 1177, "De Senectute" at line 1207, "De turpitudine" at line 1213), in addition to earlier brief annotations ("Titus liueus," line 930, and "exemplum," line 1146), accord a "bookish" status to the hag's performance, indexing it as if it were a school text to which a (new) reader might wish to return to reconsider or borrow its comments on "gentillesse," poverty, age, and foulness. In contrast, the Egerton glossator rubricizes only two sections of the hag's *dissuasio* and does so in a grammatically inconsistent fashion: "Descripcio generositatis" (line 1109, fol. 95v); and "Nota de paupertate" (line 1175, fol. 96v).

Thus the pattern of glossing the Wife's *Prologue* extends into the *Tale*: the Egerton glossator continues to struggle for control over the text, while his Ellesmere counterpart supports and augments the construction of the text, in this instance one that argues a woman's case for being worthy of her husband's attention. And when the Ellesmere glossator enlists the *Adversus Jovinianum* in the service of the hag's *dissuasio* of male celibacy in the *Tale*, he reminds us of the earlier outrageous situation in the *Prologue* in which he made Jerome not only defend marriage but advocate female sovereignty in marriage. Because these two particular Ellesmere marginalia are so ironic in similar ways, and because as a whole the Ellesmere gloss on the Wife's *Prologue* and *Tale* supports "free" reading and plurality of interpretation to the extent that it appears to encourage Alison literally to take the text into her own hands, we cannot help but wonder who the Ellesmere glossator is and why he takes such a seemingly modern attitude toward readers and reading.

We know that, compared to the Egerton glossator, this annotator finds exuberant sexuality, verbosity, even arrogance unremarkable in a woman, or at least in the Wife of Bath, and thus has no marginal comments to make about them. Also unlike the Egerton glossator, this reader allows the Wife to control her own text and never challenges her power. Instead, he shows more interest in the way different readers read and focuses our attention on the many questions such relativity and contextuality raise. As some of the unique marginalia in the Ellesmere gloss indicate, this reader also possesses a decided interest in astrology and the effect of the stars on human character and destiny as well as a more limited acquaintance with the classics,[44] both secular subjects on which the Egerton glossator never draws. And finally, still unlike the Egerton glossator, this commentator displays a certain flair for wit and irony and composed this gloss early, probably sometime before 1410.[45]

In short, the Ellesmere glossator sounds much like Chaucer himself, and some scholars maintain that the Ellesmere glossator *is* Chaucer. In 1925, Chaucerians began to propose the poet's authorship of various of the Ellesmere glosses.[46] Several proponents have done so on the grounds that certain of these marginalia represent authorial "working" memoranda, Chaucer's notes to himself concerning passages that he wished later to add, expand, or double-check. Subsequently, this argument continues, scribes copied Chaucer's marginal jottings from the now lost autograph manuscript into our extant copies of the *Tales*. As persistent as the attempt to prove Chaucerian authorship of the glosses has been, it nevertheless has its critics, including Manly and Rickert and more recently Charles A. Owen, Jr.,[47] whose general argument against the likelihood of Chaucerian authorship of Ellesmere glosses emanates from the relationship he establishes between the glossing patterns in the earlier Hengwrt and later Ellesmere manuscripts. He sees the glossator of these two manuscripts as "surely the same person" (p. 243), one who first annotated the Hengwrt manuscript and then the Ellesmere manuscript and who thus could not be Chaucer. This glossator, Owen continues, did not find marginalia in his exemplar but invented them to "create the aura of authority" (p. 241) for the Hengwrt. He then reproduced, as well as expanded, his self-devised Hengwrt glosses in the later Ellesmere manuscript as he became more intent on "giv[ing] us assurance that we are in touch with authority" (p. 243), which is also part of what Owen sees as the Ellesmere editor's design to create an "appearance of completeness" (p. 243) for his book.

Owen's point that the Ellesmere manuscript aims to present itself as a "complete" and "finished" product—as a "book that would satisfy contemporary expectations" (p. 247)—is, I think, a convincing one. And someone who annotated both the Hengwrt and Ellesmere manuscripts could not, of course, also be Chaucer. But that does not rule out the possibility that this glossator attempts to sound like Chaucer in the Ellesmere manuscript. That is, along with the reordering of fragments to smooth over uncertainties and gaps, I suggest that another part of the "hoax" of the Ellesmere manuscript may be the invention of pseudo-Chaucerian glosses, glosses meant to appear as authentic. Such authorial—as opposed to editorial or scribal—marginalia would be important in creating the aura of authority for the Ellesmere manuscript, because by Chaucer's time new readers may have expected secular authors to annotate their own works.

Boccaccio, for instance, composed his own glosses and rubrics and informed his readers that he did so. In the *Decameron* he claims authorship of the plot-summary rubrics that preface the 100 individual *novella*: ". . . whoso goes a-reading among these stories, let him pass over those that vex him, and read those that please him. That none may be misled, each [story] bears on its brow the epitome of that which it hides in its bosom."[48] And in the *Teseide*, Boccaccio again claims authorship of the extensive glosses when, for example, he equates himself, as the unrequited lover of Fiammetta, with the lovesick Palamon: "I am that man," Boccaccio tells his readers in a gloss.[49] Dante, of course, had popularized the idea of self-exegesis in both the *Convivio* and the *Vita nuova*, and it is now assumed that the fashion spread to Chaucer's English contemporaries. The glosses to Gower's *Confessio Amantis*, for instance, are thought to be authorial rather than scribal or editorial.[50]

We may never know for sure which medieval secular authors composed their own glosses. But I think we can speculate that by Chaucer's time a tradition—and presumably some expectation—of authorial marginalia in secular literature existed. If this is the case, then the obvious resemblances between the Ellesmere glosses and Chaucer's interests and tone may be not coincidental but deliberate. The Ellesmere gloss may represent, in other words, a contemporary reader's idea of what Chaucer might have said about his own text, how he might have read it himself. Hoax though he may be, this "Chaucer" can nevertheless tell us something important about Chaucer and readers during a crucial period of transition in the history of reading.[51]

This period is what Walter J. Ong calls "manuscript culture," as distinct from the earlier oral and later print eras,[52] and it includes the gradual shift from public to private audiences that was well underway in Chaucer's time. During much of the transitional or manuscript phase, the older form of reading—listening to works narrated aloud, even if these works were now written rather than orally composed—and the newer form of silent reading, overlapped one another (some readers, of course, literate ones, utilized both fashions, on certain occasions reading privately and on others listening to written works recited). While we have no statistics on the proportions of these modes of reading during Chaucer's era,[53] Ruth Crosby deduces that fourteenth-century authors continued to write with both audiences in mind.[54] Not until the fifteenth century do we find authors addressing only a silent audience, a readership, although Ong notes that some of the conventions of writing to the dual audience persist long beyond the demise of the old reader.[55] In Chaucer we may find evidence of mixed modes of reading in the existence of the glosses, designed for private readers, and, assuming they are accurate rather than conventional, in the manuscript illuminations we have of Chaucer evidently reciting his works, in one instance (Corpus Christi College, Cambridge, MS 61) to a court audience.[56] This visual depiction of Chaucerian old readers is, of course, designed for the eyes of Chaucerian new readers, the same audience who would see the glosses.

Unquestionably, Chaucer was aware of public and private audiences, but we also need to consider here what attitudes he held toward them as a poet. He seems positively inclined to the imaginative possibilities of private reading when, for instance, he begins his early dream visions with episodes of new reading—narrators who fall asleep poring over their manuscripts and dream wondrous dreams about their reading.[57] But we may also detect a Chaucerian parody of the private reader when May of *The Merchant's Tale* literally encloses herself in a privy to read her love letter from Damian. Individual Chaucerian episodes of old reading come in for similarly diverse treatment. Chaucer displays the persuasive power of public reading on the audience when, for instance, Criseyde hears Antigone's song, which sways her to grant Troilus's suit. But Chaucer also exposes the ironic deficiencies of old reading when Criseyde sits listening to the recitation of a romance from a book in which, had she held it in her own hands and read it all the way through, she might have found written the ending of the story of Troy, that is, her own story.[58]

Chaucer's attitude to new and old reading was bound to be complex, even contradictory, as these examples suggest, for such a response befits a transitional era. Yet if we enlarge our angle of vision to consider not only the occasional fictional readers within Chaucer's works but Chaucer's conception of *us* as audience, a different and more consistent pattern of response forms up. As Ong phrases it, "The writer's audience is always a fiction,"[59] an audience constructed in the writer's imagination. This fictional audience cannot serve as reliable historical evidence anymore than can the depictions of an internal audience I cited above, for either one may or may not reflect the actual audience. But it can enlighten us about what and how a writer thinks about the audience.

If we examine the writer's audience in Chaucer—or what role we are asked to play—we find that it reveals Chaucer's gradual artistic usage of new reading, an acceptance and approval of it that I have suggested "Chaucer's" treatment of this subject in the Wife of Bath commentary echoes. The first signs of this endorsement occur when Chaucer's narrators become aware of the possibilities of misinterpretation by readers—new readers—and full acceptance of new reading occurs in *The Canterbury Tales*, whose narrator fictionalizes both an internal and an external audience in complete control of the text, that is, an audience of new readers par excellence. Since it is largely Chaucer's narrators who construct the concept of audience—old or new—in a given work, we might first consider how medieval narrators themselves are in fact a product of the shift from old to new reading.

As Franz Bäuml has observed, written narrative creates distance between author and the actual audience.[60] One of the initial consequences of this separation, I suggest, was authorial fear of misinterpretation by readers and the creation of an internal device, the fictional narrator-poet, to reprovide the writer with at least an imagined direct access to the audience.[61] While the medieval maxim, "Vox audita perit, littera scripta manet" ("The heard voice perishes, the written word endures") indicates the ephemeral nature of old reading, it is also true that old readers came under more authorial regulation than did new readers.[62] Poets who recited their own works (as evidently many did even as late as Chaucer's time)[63] might utilize such extratextual means as gesture, tone, pace, even impromptu commentary and improvisation to communicate nuances of meaning and intention to a listening audience.[64] Ong remarks that "most persons could get into written form few if any of the complicated and nuanced meanings they regularly convey orally."[65] New readers, of course, could not be influenced by such methods of communication, nor could the writer even know (and correct, if necessary) their readings of a work.

As private reading became more and more common, medieval authors developed an artistic device within the text itself to reproduce their former role as reciter of the work and determiner of its meaning: the fictional narrator-poet who first appears in secular literature of the twelfth century. Many times, as when, for instance, the narrator-poet "allegorizes" the work, these figures now seem crude or didactic to us because they do, in fact, bear the heavy burden of "explaining" the actual poet to us. In a sense, the device of narrator-poet functions as a gloss on the text to communicate the writer's meaning to distant new readers. Initially at least, this narrator-poet creates and participates in the fiction of the work—whatever the reality of the actual situation—that the audience consists of old readers, that is, readers to whom the poet, through the narrator, can still explain and appeal directly and who therefore never threaten to misread the work. Eventually, however, narrators may come to conceive of their audience as new readers. When they do so, their own roles begin to change in complex but interrelated ways: on the one hand, narrators may lose their "anxiety of influence" and, like the new readers to whom they now write, become much more innovative with their own sources; on the other hand, they may lose their power and authority and become unreliable, ironic, and uncertain of their abilities to make themselves understood, just as they fear new readers will misinterpret them.[66]

This shift in audience conception helps explain the development of the Chaucerian narrator that Donald R. Howard outlines in "Chaucer the Man."[67] Howard delineates both the increasing "strangeness" of Chaucer's narrator— his distance from his audience—and his growing originality and artistic independence (or at least the pose of such freedom) as we progress from early to late works. The pivotal point in this transformation of the narrator from the nearby and "wide-eyed" figure who merely transmits his "auctour" into the distant one who fashions his own work Howard locates in *Troilus and Criseyde*. There, he argues, the narrator "is no longer the conventional dreamer of the earlier poems—he is a *reader*" (p. 340), and one of the common experiences of those who read is "aesthetic distance" from the illusion of what they read. While I agree with Howard's overall paradigm concerning the development of the narrator in Chaucer's works, I would note that Chaucer's narrators, dreamers or not, *always* pose as readers, whether (as new readers) they read to themselves or (as performers of their works) read aloud to us. And I would also suggest that the turning point in the narrator's development, although it occurs in the *Troilus*, involves not so much this figure's self-conception or pose as his conception of the fictional audience. That is, as we, the fictional audience, are transformed from old to new readers over the course of Chaucer's works and thus distanced from the narrator, there is a corresponding increase in both the narrator's originality and his anxiety over our misinterpretation of his text.[68]

Chaucer's earliest narrators, those of the dream visions, fictionalize an audience of old readers, one that does not threaten the poet with private reading and the potential misunderstanding of his works. Each dream vision narrator-poet signals this conception of audience by beginning his work with an episode of reading aloud to us: the narrator of *The Book of the Duchess* recites Ovid's tale of Seys and Alcyone; the narrator of *The House of Fame*, Virgil's Dido and Aeneas story; and the narrator of *The Parliament of Fowls*, Macrobius's *Somnium Scipionis*. As part of his function with old readers, each narrator-poet also takes it upon himself to instruct, guide, and explain to the listening audience: "And hyt was soth, for everydel / I wol anon ryght telle thee why," the *Duchess* narrator informs us (lines 846-47); "Now herkeneth, every maner man / That Englissh understonde kan, / And listeneth of my drem to lere," the *Fame* narrator instructs us (lines 509-11); and "The lyf so short, the craft so long to lerne, / Th'assay so hard, so sharp the conquerynge, / The dredful joye, alwey that slit so yerne: / Al this mene I by Love," the *Parliament* narrator explains to us (lines 1-4).[69]

The *Fame* narrator in particular can afford to poke fun at himself for being a new, silent reader—one who sits and reads his texts "also domb as any stoon" (line 656)—because he remains in control of us old readers; he expertly guides us, for instance, through the library in the *House of Fame*, transforming his book learning into an oral mnemonic form appropriate for nonreaders, that is, his fictionalized listening audience. While as actual modern readers we may experience difficulties interpreting Chaucer's early poems, the narrators themselves express little fear of misinterpretation, for they conceive of us as old readers and find themselves to be effective devices for maintaining contact with us and thus control over us. In fact, the narrator of *The House of Fame* warns us that it would require nothing less than outright malice, presumption, hate, scorn, envy, or other such villainy for us to "mysdeme" him (lines 92-97), and he plunges into the story of his dream with all the confidence that having "Jesus God" on his side affords him. His caveat may be ironic, for the narrator possibly precludes our misinterpreting him by refusing to finish his tale, yet the more significant point here is that he feels close enough to his audience to shape its response.

In *Troilus and Criseyde*, however, Chaucer's narrator-poet begins to lose this sense of connection to the audience; now he sometimes conceives of us as private and distant rather than as public and accessible. For the most part, this new conception of audience liberates the narrator-poet. Instead of having to recite the entire Troy legend, he can, for instance, send us off to read Homer or Dares or Dictys on our own; he can also refer his new readers to "other bokes" (5.1776) to learn of Criseyde's flaws, which frees him to concentrate on her virtues. Fictionalizing his audience as new readers accentuates the narrator-poet's own freedom to act as a new reader. That is, he licenses himself to give us a new reading of Criseyde, to select and shape his own written sources as he will. Conveniently, he cannot find in his books the answers to such controversial questions about Criseyde as whether or not she believed Pandarus's lies about Troilus (3.575) or how long it was before she took up with Diomede (5.1086). He perhaps even thinks of himself as far distant enough from any authorial control over how he himself reads to invent an author (Lollius) as well as his own individual interpretation of a controversial character. Even though Chaucer's narrators have been new readers from the start, it is when they begin to think of us similarly that they take fullest advantage of the liberties of "textuality."

But new reading also has its liabilities, and we find several warning notes about them in the *Troilus*. For one, as the narrator-poet begins to conceive of us as reading rather than listening to his words, his authority diminishes, and his uncertainty about his poetic abilities grows. Still thinking of us as listeners, the narrator-poet first admits that he knows little of love and that perhaps some of us who "felyng han in loves art" (3.1333) may wish to correct his words on the subject. But by the end of the work, as he begins to fictionalize us as "rederes" (5.270), the narrator-poet loses almost all confidence in his ability to communicate; his "wit" is now completely insufficient to describe for us Troilus's woe. Echoing this discordant note about new reading is Chaucer the poet as he bids farewell to his "litel bok" at the end of the *Troilus*. He first prays that scribes copy his works accurately, and then, as he remembers the two audiences, old and new, that will read his work, the possibility of its misinterpretation briefly flits across Chaucer's mind: "And red wherso thow be, or elles songe, / That thow be understonde, God I biseche!" (5.1797-98).

These nagging worries about miscommunication and misreading in the *Troilus* develop into a major problem in its sequel and companion piece, *The Legend of Good Women*. For the most part, our new reading liberated the *Troilus* narrator, but it oppresses the *Legend* narrator, for it causes the misreading Chaucer earlier feared. When he wrote the *Troilus* and translated the *Romance of the Rose*, the *Legend* narrator tells us, he intended to praise women and to further the cause of love, yet now he finds that at least one private reader, the God of Love, has interpreted the matter differently. And, furthermore, this reader, who makes his complaint directly to the narrator, will not allow his private reading to be glossed over, to be canceled by the author's statement of intentions: "Thow maist yt nat denye, / For in pleyn text, withouten nede of glose, / Thou hast translated the Romaunce of the Rose, / That is an heresye ayeins my lawe, / And makest wise folk from me withdrawe" (*LGW* G 326-31).[70] As his penance, the *Legend* narrator must become a reader again himself, returning to comb through his "sixty bokes olde and newe" until he finds some tales of worthy women to tell.

While the vagaries of individual reader's responses cause the *Legend* narrator considerable consternation and the obligatory composition of a work in praise of women, the last of Chaucer's narrators (the pilgrim Chaucer) not only accommodates himself to new reading but makes art of it. He no longer fears misinterpretation; in fact, "misreading"—or idiosyncratic and individual response—becomes the very substance of his poetry. Chaucer signals this attitude toward new reading in several ways. For one, his narrator-poet does not, as we might expect, address—much less lead, guide, or control—the internal audience of the work, the assemblage of pilgrims, but joins that audience as an equal. He maintains that his role is simply to record what he hears. He has no power over who says what, and he enlists both Plato and Christ to justify his function as mere reporter in this work (*GP* 739-41). At the same time as the narrator fictionally surrenders any control he might have over tale-telling on the pilgrimage, he gives the external audience of the *Tales*—we who hold his work in our hands—complete authority to read and interpret as we will. If we do not like churl's tales, he warns us before the Miller's fabliau, "turne over the [manuscript] leef and chese another tale" (*GP* 3177).

The narrator's occasional uncertainty, his ineptness, and, in particular, his anonymity and invisibility during the course of the *Tales* also reflect his fictionalization of us as a distant and disparate group of readers whom he can no longer see or "read," much less influence. To his credit, he makes a virtue of necessity, or rather makes art of our "unreadability." That is, *The Canterbury Tales* proceeds as a series of texts that the internal audience of pilgrims interprets. Sometimes these readings take the form of pilgrims' comments in response to a tale in the links and sometimes the form of entire tales. One of the most common observations about *The Canterbury Tales* is how dramatically appropriate these latter responses are. Two churls, the Miller and the Reeve, for instance, tell churls' tales in response to the Knight's story of noble love; three men, the Clerk, the Merchant, and the Franklin, respond as a cleric, an unhappy husband, and an idealistic gentleman might be expected to the Wife's tale of female sovereignty in marriage. From another angle, however, such dramatically suitable tales also represent idiosyncratic and contextual interpretations, "misreadings" akin to those that new readers were likely to make. But in *The Canterbury Tales* such new reading does not threaten art, as it did in the *Legend*; it *is* art.

An equally common observation about the other form of response in the *Tales,* the occasional brief comments found in the links, is how it appears to misinterpret Chaucer's art. Harry Bailly, for instance, seems to "underread" the narrator's tale of Thopas when he condemns it as a dismal performance and to "overread" the Man of Law's story of Constance when he praises it as a "thrifty" tale. We often try to explain away the Host's apparent misinterpretations by arguing that artistic standards and tastes in the Middle Ages differ from ours, that, unlike us, medieval readers may have preferred didactic pieces to humorous parodies. Yet I think we might do better simply to let the misinterpretations stand as such, for I believe that Chaucer accepted the fact that readers read differently from one another and from the author. Although a comic one, Harry Bailly is the artistic correlative of the new reader; he interprets as he will, even when (perhaps especially when) such reading evidently misunderstands Chaucer the pilgrim's own art altogether.

That in *The Canterbury Tales* Chaucer came to accept and utilize the artistic possibilities of "misreading" inherent in new reading receives support in the *Retraction,* Chaucer's final self-exegesis. There, in the style of the reciting author who lectures the old reader, he informs us how to interpret such early works as *The Parliament of Fowls* and *The House of Fame*: we are to read them as promoting "worldly vanitees." But he does not give us instruction on how to read *The Canterbury Tales*. Instead, he envisions us as new readers who must—and will—determine for ourselves which of the tales of Canterbury "sownen into synne." New reading, then, not only creates art but can require its practitioners to exercise moral judgment about art.

Ironically, Chaucer's endorsement of new reading occurs in a work whose internal audience, the Canterbury pilgrims, functions as old readers who listen to one another's works and even compose these works orally (although, in some cases, such as the Clerk's, this composition requires the conscious recollection of written texts the narrator has read).[71] In part, convention (e.g., Boccaccio's *Decameron*) and practical concerns call for pilgrims who listen to one another rather than read one another. *The Canterbury Tales* could not easily fit itself to the fiction of written *querelle* or epistolary battle in which Christine de Pisan participated. Yet Chaucer uses his old readers to define and highlight the characteristics, from an author's point of view, of new reading. What is always so surprising to me about *The Canterbury Tales* is how little direct response the pilgrims actually receive from one another. To be sure, the Reeve takes immediate offense at the Miller's tale, the Host explodes at the Pardoner, the Knight breaks off the Monk's tale, etc. But many tales are greeted with silence, an eerie quiet where we might expect someone to voice a reaction, to say or do something, as the inner audience unfailingly does, for instance, at the conclusion of each tale in Marguerite de Navarre's *Heptameron*. In making these old readers unexpectedly silent and "unreadable," I think Chaucer depicts for us what it was like for an author to write to a new reader, and that may help us understand why the need to fictionalize—to see and hear—the audience became so important for the medieval writer. At the same time, Chaucer's paradoxical hybrid of the unreadable old reader may represent his granting to all audiences the freedom to determine meaning, to be beyond the author's grasp—or gesture, tone, and like influences.

More to the point here, though, is Chaucer's attribution of the characteristics of new reading to one old reader in particular, the Wife of Bath, who listens to Jankyn's book of wicked wives and registers an altogether different reaction to it from his. Because her reading differs so much from the conventional reception of this antifeminist material, she emblemizes the new reader par excellence even though, ironically, Alison appears to be an ear-reader, not an eye-reader. Her literal act of taking the book into her own hands demonstrates the power of new reading and dramatizes her female textuality, her rewriting of both Paul's teaching on marriage and the conventional antifeminist *dissuasio* of marriage that Alison refashions into a *dissuasio* of male celibacy. Because the Wife of Bath is perhaps the preeminent example of the new reader in *The Canterbury Tales*, "Chaucer's" Ellesmere gloss on the Wife also concerns itself with new reading. And approves it. I believe that Chaucer himself also supported new reading for the additional reason [than] that he allows us to see how Alison's various "misreadings," "misinterpretations," and "misunderstandings" all lead her to re-create herself fictionally at the end of the tale as a woman who might live in "parfit joye" with the men around her rather than in the constant conflict and strife that have been her lot. The need to fictionalize, to make stories about ourselves and others, was important not only to the medieval author but to everyday people as well and perhaps, for Chaucer, to medieval women in particular.

For Chaucer and "Chaucer," new reading and female textuality appear to be nearly synonymous, and they hold great promise, both human and artistic. But to "Chaucer's" colleague, the Egerton glossator, to whom we may now turn our attention briefly, they present a very different side, as we have seen above. Why does this commentator react so differently—so negatively—to new readers and to female textuality? If, as Manly and Rickert hypothesize,[72] the Egerton gloss was composed by a "learned cleric," then we have an immediate context in which to understand his opposition to new reading, for it is closely allied to another kind of "new reading" that threatened the Church during the latter Middle Ages: the reading of the translated or vernacularized Scripture by the laity. It was not, of course, reading itself that presented problems to the Church but the fear that new lay readers would go beyond mere reading and interpret Holy Writ for themselves. As the clergy well recognized, the technology of new reading—the privately owned manuscript—aided and abetted lay reading of the Bible, for it provided the necessary means to engage secretly in this proscribed activity. The typical image of the Lollard heretic is not the old reader who might hear a priest read the Bible in English and form some unacceptable interpretation of it but the new reader who has access to books and reads privately, even clandestinely.[73]

In the Egerton glossator's struggle with the Wife to control scriptural text, there is evidence of the late-medieval conflict over whether interpretation of "auctoritee" would remain in the hands of the clergy or pass, as it later did, into the hands of the laity. It is also important to realize, however, that the Egerton glossator's opposition to new reading of Scripture would include vigorous resistance to female textuality. We have only recently begun to understand that one of the particular threats of translation and hence "laicization" of Scripture was that it would make the text accessible to female readers.[74] And these new readers, in the eyes of the clergy, presented a greater threat to Church authority than did male lay readers, for women alone were barred from teaching or preaching Holy Word. The Egerton glossator's antifeminist response to the Wife, then, in part results from his era and his profession, which incline him to see a female glossator as a special abomination that required the sort of energetic opposition we find in his gloss.

One final marginalium in the Egerton gloss deserves our attention here because it shows us a somewhat different association between women and new reading that this commentator draws. This gloss occurs in *The Manciple's Tale*, the fable of Phoebus, his adulterous wife, and the telltale crow that opens with the narrator's illustrations of the vanity of attempting to bridle female sensuality. No matter how much you tame a bird, the Manciple argues, it still flies his cage at the first chance; no matter how much milk you feed a cat, it still prefers to hunt mice; and the she-wolf, when in heat, mates with the "lewedeste" male that she can find. Having cited these examples, the Manciple next tells us that they refer to "thise men / that been untrewe" and not to women (*ManT* 187-88). Presumably this remark is ironic, for the Manciple's examples emanate from his earlier musing on the "verray nycetee" of trying to tame a "shrewe," as "writen olde clerkes in hir lyves" (lines 150-54). It is possible, however, to read the Manciple's disclaimer at lines 187-88 in a different light, for instance, to interpret it as the deliberate, even if contradictory, cover-up of a narrator who suddenly realizes that his antifeminism is showing too much .[75] Whatever the case, Chaucer lets the reader decide how to interpret this remark, as his well-known ambiguity and irony often invite us to do in the later poetry.

The Egerton glossator, however, cancels the choice Chaucer affords us. He selects the "correct" interpretation of the Manciple's words: "per antifrasim quedam figura que est per contrarium" (line 187, fol. 256r). Understand, the Egerton annotator instructs us, that the Manciple employs the rhetorical figure of antiphrasis. Therefore, the right way to read his comment is "by opposites." In other words, the Manciple does implicate women in his examples, not men. Not only does the Ellesmere glossator refrain from such instruction and allow readers to decide what the Manciple says about women, but this is the sole instance I have found in any gloss on *The Canterbury Tales* that literally tells us how to read a passage.[76] It is also one of the few instances in the Egerton gloss that displays any concern with secular as opposed to scriptural matters. It is significant, I think, that the Egerton glossator worries not only that new female readers are more dangerous than new male readers but that new reading—uncontrolled, unglossed interpretation—may create new attitudes toward women.

Although probably composed within fifty years of each other, the Ellesmere and Egerton commentaries on the Wife of Bath function in opposite ways—in one, to support the plurality of interpretation that female textuality contributes to and represents and, in the other, to condemn it. Unlike its later counterpart, the Ellesmere gloss on the Wife's *Prologue* and *Tale* is, finally, an antigloss, for it empowers readers, not authors and "auctoritees," to determine, even create, meaning. And it is the antigloss that would eventually win the day.[77] In Chaucer it triumphed soon enough: the earliest extant printed editions of the *Tales* (Caxton's in 1478 and Thynne's in 1532) reproduce none of the marginalia that annotate more than half of the manuscripts.[78] Despite the tendency of early publishers to reproduce many features of manuscripts in printed books,[79] Caxton and Thynne appear to realize that the gloss has no place in the new book, a work designed for private reading.[80] More prophetic than these early printers, however, are Chaucer and "Chaucer," for they both accepted and endorsed new reading as well as female textuality, an achievement all the more impressive because it occurred in an era that could also express the most vigorous opposition to— indeed, burn as relapsed heretics—bookish women who took the text into their own hands.[81]

NOTES

1. See, for instance, the following articles in *Studies in the Age of Chaucer* alone: B. A. Windeatt, "The Scribes as Early Chaucer Critics," 1 (1979): 119-41; Anne Middleton, "The Clerk and His Tale: Some Literary Contexts," 2 (1980): 121-50; Beryl Rowland, "*Pronuntiatio* and Its Effect on Chaucer's Audience," 4 (1982): 33-51; Paul Strohm, "Chaucer's Fifteenth-

Century Audience and the Narrowing of the 'Chaucer Tradition,'" 4 (1982): 3-32; John M. Bowers, *"The Tale of Beryn* and *The Siege of Thebes*: Alternative Ideas of *The Canterbury Tales*," 7 (1985): 23-50; and Charlotte C. Morse, "The Exemplary Griselda," 7 (1985): 51-86. But, as Derek Pearsall remarks, "more needs to be done" to assess readers' reactions to Chaucer, and he urges the "meticulous study of particular manuscripts and their marginalia, since "such comments are important, especially in the absence of other kinds of information, for the evidence they provide of a reader's critical response to Chaucer in the fifteenth century" ("Texts, Textual Criticism, and Fifteenth Century Manuscript Production," in Robert F. Yeager, ed., *Fifteenth-Century Studies: Recent Essays* [Hamden, Conn.: Archon, 1984], pp. 130-31). My article takes up Pearsall's call to see in the glosses readers' interpretations of Chaucer rather than, as has often been the case so far, evidence with which to settle such paleographical questions as the chronology of manuscripts of the *Tales* or such literary issues as Chaucer's sources, methods of revision, and so forth.

2. In their descriptions of "special features" of manuscripts of the *Tales* (vol. 1, passim) and their chapter on glosses (3.483-527), John M. Manly and Edith Rickert, eds., *The Text of the "Canterbury Tales"* (Chicago: University of Chicago Press, 1940), indicate which Chaucer manuscripts are glossed. The glosses themselves, however, have not been edited, nor is there a complete transcription or facsimile of all of them. Eight of the glosses on Chaucer manuscripts have been fully transcribed by F. J. Furnivall: Ellesmere, Hengwrt 154, Cambridge University Gg.4.27, Corpus Christi 198, Petworth, and Lansdowne 851 in *The Six-Text Edition of Chaucer's Canterbury Tales*, Chaucer Society Publications, 1st ser. (London: N. Trübner, 1868-77); Harley 7334 in *The Harleian MS 7334 of the Canterbury Tales*, Chaucer Society Publications, 1st ser., vol. 73 (London: Kegan Paul, Trench, Trübner, 1885); and Cambridge University Dd.4.24 in *The Cambridge MS Dd iv, 24 of the Canterbury Tales*, Chaucer Society Publications, 1st ser., vol. 95 (London: Kegan Paul, Trench, Trübner, 1901). Paul G. Ruggiers, ed., *The Canterbury Tales: A Facsimile and Transcription of the Hengwrt Manuscripts, with Variants from the Ellesmere Manuscripts*, vol. 1 in Paul G. Ruggiers and Donald C. Baker, gen. eds., *A Variorum Edition of the Works of Geoffrey Chaucer* (Norman: University of Oklahoma Press, 1979), gives the most recent transcriptions of the Hengwrt and Ellesmere glosses. Editors of the individual volumes in the *Variorum Chaucer* now being published print selected glosses, usually with an eye toward establishing the textual affiliations of Chaucer's works. And Manly and Rickert, *Text*, 3.483-527, includes all of the Ellesmere glosses as well as a generous selection of other glosses. But they make no claim to completeness, and in many instances, rather than transcribe a non-Ellesmere gloss, they simply indicate its source. When they indicate a biblical source (e.g., 1 Cor. 7:4 at *WBP* 158), Manly and Rickert often do not note that the actual gloss in a given manuscript contains only half the verse, as does, for instance, Egerton 2864 . Such a practice has evidently misled scholars who

rely upon their work for the specific wording of unpublished glosses (see n. 13 below).

3. These glosses occur, respectively, at *WBP* 228 and *KnT* 1255 in Cambridge University Dd.4.24, transcribed by Furnivall, ed., *The Cambridge MS*, pp. 173, 38.

4. Hengwrt 154 gloss on *MilT* 37 34, transcribed by Ruggiers, ed., *Facsimile*, p. 190.

5. Egerton 2864 gloss on *WBP* 419: " . . . Et postea melius est habitare in terra deserta quam cum muliere rixosa et iracunda. . . ," fol. 87r. (In this and all subsequent glosses I transcribe from Egerton 2864, I silently expand abbreviations. Below I continue to give a modern translation of the gloss in my text and the original gloss in my notes. Although there are three Egerton manuscripts of the *Tales*, my use of the designation "Egerton" refers always to 2864. Below I explain my assumptions of male authorship of this gloss.)

6. Manly and Rickert, eds., *Text*, 2.483, refer to this kind of gloss as one of "reference" or as a gloss "citing sources." Charles A. Owen, Jr., "The Alternative Reading of *The Canterbury Tales*: Chaucer's Text and the Early Manuscripts," *PMLA* 97 (1982): 239, refers to it as the gloss that "provides us with sources. . ., performing functions that in a modern book would be relegated to footnotes." For brevity's sake, I use the term "source gloss" to refer to this type of annotation.

7. These and all subsequent quotations of the Ellesmere glosses are from Ruggiers, ed., *Facsimile*; below I give a modern translation of the Ellesmere gloss in my text, and the original from Ruggiers in my notes. All quotations of Chaucer's text are from F. N. Robinson, ed., *The Works of Geoffrey Chaucer*, 2d ed. (Boston: Houghton Mifflin, 1957).

8. See Aage Brusendorff, *The Chaucer Tradition* (London: Milford, 1925), p. 127; and J. S. P. Tatlock, "The *Canterbury Tales* in 1400," *PMLA* 50 (1935): 103.

9. "The Significance of Marginal Glosses in the Earliest Manuscripts of *The Canterbury Tales*" in David Lyle Jeffrey, ed., *Chaucer and Scriptural Tradition* (Ottawa: University of Ottawa Press, 1984), p. 77. For earlier versions of this argument see Graham D. Caie, "The Significance of the Early Chaucer Manuscript Glosses (with Special Reference to the *Wife of Bath's Prologue*)." *ChauR* 10 (1976): 350-60: and Graham D. Caie, "The Significance of the Glosses in the Earliest Manuscripts of *The Canterbury Tales*," in Stig Johannson and Bjorn Tysdahl, eds., *Papers from the First Nordic Conference for English Studies, Oslo, 17-19 September 1980* (Oslo: University of Oslo, Institute of English Studies, 1981), pp. 25-34.

10. See Stanley E. Fish, "Interpreting the *Variorum*," *CritI* 2 (1975): 465-85 (reprinted in Stanley Fish, ed., *Is There a Text in This Class? The Authority of Interpretive Communities* [Cambridge, Mass.: Harvard University Press, 1980], pp. 147-73); and Stanley E. Fish, "Interpreting 'Interpreting the *Variorum*,'" *CritI* 3 (1976): 191-96.

11. See, for instance, Harold Bloom, "The Breaking of Form," in Geoffrey Hartman, ed., *Deconstruction and Criticism* (New York: Seabury

Press, 1979), pp. 1-38; and Roland Barthes, "From Work to Text," in Stephen Heath, ed. and trans., *Image-Music-Text* (New York: Hill and Wang, 1977), pp. 155-64.

12. In Walter J. Ong, "Latin Language Study as a Renaissance Puberty Rite," *SP* 56 (1959): 103-24, Ong interprets the use of Latin as "a kind of badge of masculine identity."

13. Caie, "Significance of the Early Chaucer Manuscript Glosses," p. 355 and nn. 23-24, to which Caie refers readers in his most recent work ("The Significance of Marginal Glosses," p. 76 n. 3) for examples of glosses that refresh audience's "hazy" recollections of the "usual application" or full version of a text. Other than Egerton 2864, however, Caie does not actually document which manuscripts contain glosses at *WBP* 158ff. that quote all of 1 Cor. 7:3 (or 7:4) or that quote Eph. 5:22 (or its echo in Col. 3:18), and I cannot find any transcribed manuscript listed above in n. 2 that does so. In fact, there are at least five manuscripts with glosses that quote 1 Cor. 7:4 in part in the same fashion that the Wife selectively paraphrases it: Ellesmere, "Item vir corporis sui non habet potestatem set vxor," "And the husband does not have power of his own body but the wife" (Ruggiers, ed., *Facsimile*, p. 234); Selden Arch. B. 14, "Ad Corinthios vij° vir sui corporis non habet potestatem set mulier &c," repeated without "&c" in Petworth and Lansdowne 851 (Furnivall, ed., *Six-Text Edition*, pr . 4, Chaucer Society Publications, 1st ser., vol. 25 [1872], p. 338): and Egerton 2864, "Item vir corporis sui non habet potestatem set vxor," fol. 83v. Furthermore, the Egerton glossator does not quote 1 Cor. 7:3 in the complete—hence "corrective"—manner that Caie alleges but rather quotes in the same partial fashion the Wife herself might ("Uxori vir debitum reddat apostolus ad corinthios," fol. 83v, "Let the husband render to the wife her due, the Apostle to the Corinthians"); and the Egerton 2864 glossator quotes neither Eph. 5:22-24 nor Col. 3:18, as Caie states in n. 24 (Caie's misquotation of the Egerton glosses is due, no doubt, to Manly and Rickert's occasional errors and abbreviated method of listing non-Ellesmere glosses; see above, n. 2). Thus, although the validity of Caie's specific conclusion that a number of glossators found the Wife guilty of "gross perversion of Scripture" awaits the documentation of his evidence, I still wish to consider here his general theory about the function of glosses because I believe that it contains assumptions about audience that are important for us to examine.

14. "Indexing" marginalia, or rubrics that summarize the plot, however, often occur in the vernacular, see, e.g., the Ellesmere glosses on *KnT* 2221, 2297, 2349, 2374.

15. The complete history of the development of gloss into footnote has not been written, but aspects of it are discussed by Charles Plummer, "On the Colophons and Marginalia of Irish Scribes," *PBA* 12 (1926): 11-42; Hugh Kenner, *Flaubert, Joyce and Beckett: The Stoic Comedians* (London: W. H. Allen, 1964), pp. 39-40; Lawrence Lipking, "The Marginal Gloss" *CritI* 4 (1977): 699-55; and Shari Benstock, "At the Margin of Discourse: Footnotes in the Fictional Text," *PMLA* 98 (1983): 204-25.

16. The Pardoner ironically labels the Wife a "noble prechour" (*WBP* 165) without the benefit of a marginal gloss to remind him that she uses the Pauline text in an unorthodox fashion.

17. Manly and Rickert note that the glosses in both Additional 5140 and Egerton 2864 had an "immediate common ancestor" (*Text*, 1.146).

18. Caie, "The Significance of Marginal Glosses," p. 76.

19. "Qui vxorem habet et debitor dicitur et esse in prepucio et seruus vxoris et quod malorum seruorum est alligatus," identified by Manly and Rickert, eds., *Text*, 3.497, as Jerome's quotation of Paul in the former's *Adversus Jovinianum* 1.12 (the translation in my text is from W. H. Fremantle, ed., *St. Jerome: Letters and Select Works*, in Philip Schaff and Henry Wace, eds., A Select Library of Nicene and Post-Nicene Fathers of the Christian Church, 2d ser., vol. 6 [Grand Rapids, Mich. William B. Erdmanns, n.d.], p. 356; all subsequent translations of Jerome are also from Fremantle).

20. Manly and Rickert, eds., *Text* 1.31, note, however, that there is "close agreement" between Egerton 2864 and Additional 5140 glosses, with the implication that the latter borrowed from the former or from their nonextant common ancestor.

21. At *WBP* 278, "Tecta jugiter perstillantia mulier litigiosa parabolae Salamonis et postea tecta perstillantia in die frigoris et litigiosa mulier comparuntur qui retinet eam quasi qui ventum teneat et oleum dextere sue vocabit," fol. 85r; at *WBP* 363, "per tria movetur terra per quartum quod non potest sustinere per [servum] cum regnaverit per stultum cum saturatus fuerit cibo per odiosam mulierem cum in matrimonio fuerit assumpta et per ancillam cum fuerit heres domine sue parabolae Salamonis," fol. 86r; at *WBP* 371, "Tria sunt insaturabilia et quartum quod numquam dicit sufficit parabolae Salamonis," fol. 86r; and, at *WBP* 401, "versus ffallere nere flere cepit deus in muliere," fol. 86v.

22. "Qui profert contumeliam insipiens est parabolae Salamonis et postea melius est sedere in angulo domatis quam cum muliere litigiosa et in domo communi Et postea melius est habitare in terra deserta quam cum muliere rixosa et iracunda et alibi ascensus arenosus in pedibus veterani sic mulier linguata. . .," fol. 87r. Although the manuscript is cut off and the marginalium is not entirely legible, this gloss goes on to quote a version of the first half of James 3:8 (not, as Manly and Rickert mistakenly list it, Gen.3:8): "but no man can subdue the tongue."

23. "Ve qui potentes estes ad bibendum vinum etc. . . . Ve qui consurgitis mane ad ebrietatem sectandem et potandum usque ad vesperam etc. . . . Mulier ebriosa ira magna et contumelia et turpitudo illius non tegetur. . . . Juvenilia autem desideria fuge apostolus ad titum," fol. 87v.

24. "Ab ea que dormit in sino tuo custodi claustra oris tui Michee prophete," fol. 88r.

25. "Cor humile et facies tristis et plaga mortis [*sic*] mulier nequam Ecclesiasticus," fol. 91r.

26. "mulier si primatum habeat contraria est viro suo Ecclesiasticus," fol. 91v.

27. "Mulierem fortem quis inveniet parabolae Salamonis," fol. 90r. Since the rarity—perhaps uniqueness—of this gloss is important to my argument below, I must point out that Caie's statement that "the *glosses* quote Proverbs 31, 10" ("The Significance of the Early Chaucer Manuscript Glosses," p. 353, italics mine) is unsubstantiated. None of the transcribed manuscripts listed above in n. 2, or any other mentioned by Manly and Rickert (*Text*, 3.500), contains this gloss.

28. 1 Peter 3:1-3. The Egerton gloss quotes only verses 2-3 in full: "per alibi considerantes in timore castam conversationem vestram quarum sit non extrinsecus capillatura aut circumdacio auri aut indumenti vestimentorum cultus etc jacobi [*sic*] apostolus," fols. 85v-86r.

29. The Ellesmere and other manuscripts also contain the Pauline gloss (see Manly and Rickert, eds., *Text*, 3.496, 498), but they do not have the additional Petrine gloss.

30. "Nuptiae factae sunt in Chana galilee et erat mater Jhesu ibi Vocatus autem Jhesu et discipuli eius ad nuptias etc," fol. 81v.

31. Manly and Rickert, eds., *Text*, 3.496, 525.

32. "Qui enim semel iuit ad nupcias docuit semel esse nubendum," at *WBP* 13.

33. "Paulus de virginibus preceptum non habeo consilium autem do et cetera."

34. "Qui vxorem habet et debitor dicitur et esse in prepicio et seruus vxoris et quod malorum seruorum est alligatus."

35. "Divisiones gratiarum sunt apostolus ad corinthios Vnus quisque proprium donum habet ex deo alius quidem sic alius vero sic apostolus ad corinthios," fol. 82v.

36. ". . .Item si acceperis vxorem non peccasti tribulacionem tamen carnis habebunt huiusmodi et cetera Item vir corporis sui non habet potestatem set vxor Item viri diligite vxores vestras."

37. "Et iterum seruus vxoris es noli propter hoc habere tristiciam . . . ," from *Adv. Jov.* 1.11 (not, as Manly and Rickert list it, 1.13,16).

38. E.g., "Nota de muliere" at *WBP* 966 in Trinity Cambridge R.3.15 (Manly and Rickert, eds., *Text*, 2.503); and "verum est" at *WBP* 930 in Cambridge Dd.4.24 (Furnivall, ed., *Cambridge MS*, p. 199).

39. "Quam speciosa veteranis sapiencia et gloriosis intellectus et consilium corona senum multa perita etc. Ecclesiasticus," fol. 94r.

40. "nonne deus elegit pauperes in hoc mundo jacobi apostoli," fol. 96v.

41. "Corona dignitatis senectus que in viis iustiniae reperietur parabolae Salomonis Et alibi senectus enim venerabilis est non diuturna neque numero Annorum computata Sapienciae," fol. 96v.

42. "Seneca in epistola / Honesta res est leta paupertas" (at *WBT* 1182); "Pauper est qui eget eo quod non habet sed qui non habet nec appetit habere ille diues est de quo intelligitur id Apocalypsis 3° dicis quia diues sum" (at *WBT* 1186); "Cantabit vacuus coram latrone viator et nocte ad lumen trepidabit Arundinis vmbram" (at *WBT* 1193); and "Secundus Philosophus Paupertas est odibile bonum sanitatis mater curarum remocio sapientie

reparatrix possessio sine calumpnia" (at *WBT* 1195).

43. "Vnde et Crates ille Thebanus Proiecto in mari non perno auri pondere Abite inquit pessime male cupiditates ego vos mergam ne ipse mergar a vobis" (at *WBT* 1202).

44. See, e.g., the glosses at *WBP* 460, 498, 609, 643, 702, 705.

45. As Manly and Rickert, eds., *Text*, 1.152, note, the Ellesmere manuscript was evidently planned in advance to accommodate its annotations, for it leaves considerable space for the marginalia, which never overlap the text or squeeze onto the page in the cramped and distorted fashion that they sometimes do in Hengwrt or Egerton (see A. I. Doyle and M. B. Parkes, "Paleographical Introduction," in Ruggiers, ed., *Facsimile*, pp. xxxiii-xxxiv). This suggests, although it does not prove, that the Ellesmere commentary predates the actual execution of the manuscript, ca. 1410.

46. See Brusendorff, *Chaucer Tradition*, pp. 82, 127-29. Others who attribute certain glosses to Chaucer include J. S. P. Tatlock, "The *Canterbury Tales* in 1400," p. 103; Germaine Dempster, "Chaucer at Work on the Complaint in the *Franklin's Tale*," *MLN* 52 (1937): 16-23; Germaine Dempster, "A Further Note on Dorigen's Exempla," *MLN* 54 (1939): 137-38; Germaine Dempster, "Chaucer's Manuscript of Petrarch's Version of the Griselda Story," *MP* 41 (1943): 6-16; Daniel S. Silvia, Jr., "Glosses to the *Canterbury Tales* from St. Jerome's *Epistola Adversus Jovinianum*," *SP* 62 (1965): 28-39; Robert Enzer Lewis, "Glosses to the *Man of Law's Tale* from Pope Innocent III's *De Miseria Humane Conditionis*," *SP* 64 (1967): 1-16, John P. Brennan, "Reflections on a Gloss to the *Prioress's Tale* from Jerome's *Adversus Jovinianum*," *SP* 70 (1973): 243-51. In "The Significance of the Glosses in the Earliest Manuscripts of *The Canterbury Tales*," p. 27, Caie suggests that "many [glosses] were written by Chaucer or a contemporary"; later, in "The Significance of Marginal Glosses," p. 76, he maintains the same position.

47. Manly and Rickert do identify a few glosses that Chaucer perhaps wrote himself, but they attribute "certainly" to his hand only the gloss from the *Thebaid* at *GP* 858 (see *Text*, 3.525-27). Owen argues his case against Chaucerian authorship in "Alternative Reading" (subsequent references to Owen's Article are cited parenthetically by page number in my text).

48. Trans. J. M. Rigg (1930; rpt. NewYork: Dutton, 1973), 2.348.

49. Trans. Bernadette Marie McCoy (New York: Medieval Text Association, 1974), p. 95 (gloss on 3.35). For a discussion of this passage as ironic hoax, see Robert Hollander, "The Validity of Boccaccio's Self-Exegesis in His *Teseide*," *M&H* 8 (1977): 174-75. In general, Hollander argues that Boccaccio designed the gloss to offer readers "an interpretive clue as to his purpose in his poem" (p. 164). Silvia, "Glosses to the *Canterbury Tales*," p. 38, briefly notes the relevance of Boccaccio's glosses to Chaucer's. R. A. Pratt, "Conjectures Regarding Chaucer's Manuscript of the 'Teseida,'" *SP* 42 (1945): 759, concludes that Chaucer's copy "did not contain Boccaccio's commentary," although Piero Boitani has reexamined the evidence and maintains that the chances are that Chaucer knew the

commentary, or at least part of it" (*Chaucer and Boccaccio*, Medium Aevum Monographs, n.s., 8 [1977]: 115).

50. See Alastair Minnis, "'Moral Gower' and Medieval Literary Theory," p. 53, and Derek Pearsall, "The Gower Tradition," p. 182, both in A. J. Minnis, ed., *Gower's* Confessio Amantis: *Responses and Reassessments* (Cambridge: D. S. Brewer, 1983), and Russell A. Peck's review of the last (*Speculum* 61 [1986]: 182).

51. In this respect, then, I disagree with Owen, "Alternative Reading," p. 241, that the "adornment" of the Ellesmere manuscript "contributes little of substance to the reader's experience, however much it may help to create the aura of authority." A. I. Doyle and M. B. Parkes, "The Production of Copies of the *Canterbury Tales* and the *Confessio Amantis* in the Early Fifteenth Century," in M. B. Parkes and Andrew G. Watson, eds., *Medieval Scribes Manuscripts and Libraries: Essays Presented to N. R. Ker* (London: Scolar Press, 1978), p.191, find editorial apparatus substantive in the sense that it can offer an early reading of a work, a view I share: "by careful planning of the layout of the [Ellesmere] manuscript—much more than in Hengwrt or its exemplar—thus making exceptionally generous provision for the apparatus, and by furnishing headings, running titles and illustrations, by what a twentieth-century reader would regard as an 'editorial process,' someone has emphasized his own interpretation of the work."

52. Walter J. Ong, *Orality and Literacy: The Technologizing of the Word* (New York: Methuen, 1982), p. 119. As Katherine O'Brien O'Keefe, "Orality and the Developing Text of Caedmon's *Hymn*," *Speculum* 62 (1987): 1-20, most recently reminds us, manuscript culture presents interesting hybrids of the 'pure' states of orality and literacy.

53. There is, however, a variety of evidence to suggest that new reading was well established in the fourteenth century. For instance, M. B. Parkes, "The Literacy of the Laity," in David Daiches and Anthony Thorlby, eds., *The Medieval World* (London: Aldus Books, 1973), p. 557, notes that a fourteenth-century discussion of the value of teaching new reading "would be pointless if by that time [new] reading had not already become something of habit." M. T. Clanchy, *From Memory to Written Record: England, 1066-1307* (Cambridge, Mass.: [Harvard University Press], 1979), p. 105, observes that "the emphasis in [book] production had moved by 1300 from large liturgical folios to small intelligible manuals." The former, Clanchy continues, "were intended to be placed on lecterns and displayed or read aloud in monastic communities," whereas the latter "were designed for individual private study, if they were academic books, or meditation, if they were religious." And John Ahern, "Binding the Book: Hermeneutics and Manuscript Production in *Paradiso* 33," *PMLA* 97 (1982): 800, explains how Dante's serial publication procedures encouraged private ownership—and, presumably, private reading—of the text of the *Commedia*. Numerous exempla of pre-1400 new (or silent, ocular) reading are given by Paul Saenger, "Silent Reading: Its Impact on Late Medieval Script and Society," *Viator* 13 (1982): 367-414. On medieval literacy in general, see James

Westfall Thompson, *The Literacy of the Laity in the Middle Ages*, University of California Publications in Education, vol. 9 (Berkeley, 1939; rpt., New York, 1963); and V. H. Galbraith, "The Literacy of Medieval English Kings," *PBA* 21(1935): 201-38. And on literacy rates in the late fifteenth century, see H. S. Bennett, *English Books and Readers, 1475 to 1557* (Cambridge: Cambridge University Press, 1952), pp. 19-29, 54-64.

54. Ruth Crosby, "Oral Delivery in the Middle Ages," *Speculum* 11 (1936): 100 and n. 3. See also H. J. Chaytor, *From Script to Print: An Introduction to Medieval Vernacular Literature* (New York: October House, 1967), chaps. 2, 6; and William Nelson, "From 'Listen, Lordings' to 'Dear Reader,'" *UTQ* 46 (1976-77): 111-24.

55. Ong, *Orality and Literacy*, pp. 103, 115-16.

56. For a facsimile of this illumination, see M. B. Parkes and Elizabeth Salter, intro., Troilus and Criseyde *by Geoffrey Chaucer: A Facsimile of Corpus Christi College Cambridge MS 61* (Cambridge: D. S. Brewer, 1978), fol. lv. Salter remarks that it has become "traditional to believe that . . . [this] miniature . . . describes, with retrospective authority, . . . the historical role of Chaucer as court-entertainer, delivering his poetry to a sophisticated and appreciative audience" (p. 15), and she attributes the speaker's lack of a text to the frontispiece's reliance upon the conventions of "preaching miniatures" (p. 17). See also Margaret Galway, "The *Troilus* Frontispiece," *MLR* 44 (1949): 161-77; and D. A. Pearsall, "The *Troilus* Frontispiece and Chaucer's Audience," *YES* 7 (1977): 68-74.

57. Marshall W. Stearns, "Chaucer Mentions a Book," *MLN* 57 (1942): 28-31, notes that the mention of book reading was an unconventional device in dream visions before Chaucer. See also Paula Neuss, "Images of Writing and the Book in Chaucer's Poetry," *RES*, n.s., 32 (1981): 385-97.

58. If, of course, as Alain Renoir, "Thebes, Troy, Criseyde and Pandarus: An Instance of Chaucerian Irony," *SN* 32 (1960): 14-17, argues, Criseyde's version of the story of Thebes was also bound with the *Roman de Troie*, as sometimes was the case.

59. Walter J. Ong, "The Writer's Audience Is Always a Fiction," *PMLA* 90 (1975): 9-21.

60. Franz Bäuml, "Varieties and Consequences of Medieval Literacy and Illiteracy," *Speculum* 55 (1980): 250: ". . .not only in a physical sense is the distance greater between fixed text and writing author or reading reciter than between oral poem and oral poet, but also in a perceptual sense—form and content of a written narrative can be manipulated by the writing author or scribe and the reciting reader to a much greater extent than a traditional oral poem by a performing oral poet."

61. Bäuml, ibid., 252 n. 43, sees the development of the "poetic I" as an "automatic and inevitable consequence of the independent existence of the written text," but not specifically as a result of the authorial fear of misinterpretation that I maintain accompanies the fixed text. See also Franz Bäuml, "Transformations of the Heroine: From Epic Heard to Epic Read," in Rosmarie Thee Morewedge, ed., *The Role of Woman in the Middle Ages*

(Albany: State University of New York, 1975), p. 34.

62. As I argue, however, in "Taking the Gold out of Egypt: The Art of Reading as a Woman," in Elizabeth A. Flynn and Patrocinio P. Schweickart, eds., *Gender and Reading: Essays on Readers, Texts, and Contexts* (Baltimore, Md.: Johns Hopkins University Press, 1986), pp. 88-91, probably the least regulated "reader" is the auditor in *fully* oral culture, for the absence of the fixed text provides the greatest freedom of interpretation to the audience. The readers under most control would seem to be old readers of manuscript culture, for they are subject both to the fixed or written text and to the reciting author.

63. Crosby, "Oral Delivery," pp. 94-96.

64. Salter, in Parkes and Salter, intro., Troilus and Criseyde: *A Facsimile*, pp. 17-18, provides evidence that the speaker's use of hand gestures was a familiar feature of court-entertainer miniatures, a device also borrowed from preaching miniatures. (See n . 56 above.)

65. Ong, "The Writer's Audience," p. 10.

66. Ironic and unreliable narrators do, of course, appear as early as Chrétien de Troyes, and early Chaucerian narrators still fictionalize the audience as old readers; thus the development I describe takes an uneven course within individual writers as well as over the several centuries between Chrétien and Chaucer.

67. Donald R. Howard, "Chaucer the Man," *PMLA* 80 (1965): 337-43. Subsequent quotation of this article is cited parenthetically by page number in the text. I have not yet been able to see Howard's 1987 biography of Chaucer.

68. Cf. Derek Brewer, "Chaucer's Poetic Style," in Piero Boitani and Jill Mann, eds., *The Cambridge Chaucer Companion* (Cambridge: Cambridge University Press, 1986), p. 228: "Literacy supplies much of [Chaucer's] subject-matter, and some of his form (for example, Chaucer's development of a narrator-figure . . . can be seen as the result of the detachment of the poet from his audience which is effected by literacy)."

69. Although these examples use language —"telle," "herkeneth," "listeneth"—that suggests a reciting poet and a listening audience, I would not regard such phrases alone as proof that the narrator conceives of the fictional audience as old readers. As Ruth Crosby, "Chaucer and the Custom of Oral Delivery," *Speculum* 13 (1938): 416-17, cautions us, Chaucer sometimes uses "read" to mean 'declare" or "tell," just as "speak" or "tell" may mean "write." And there are, of course, instances in which the narrator advises the fictional audience to read—"rede Virgile in Eneydos, / Or the Epistle of Ovyde" (*HF* 378-79)—and it is unclear exactly which kind of reading Chaucer had in mind in such instances, reading as we understand it now or having the work recited aloud to one. Because of these difficulties, my ideas about whether the fictional audience is cast into the role of new or old readers are based only partly upon general and ambiguous terms such as "read" and "tell." The rest of the decision rests on the narrator's concern with misinterpretation and other aspects of his relationship to the audience. When,

however, the narrator tells us to take a certain book in our hands or to turn over the leaf and choose another tale, I regard this as more conclusive evidence about his conception of audience.

70. Jesse M. Gellrich, *The Idea of the Book in the Middle Ages: Language Theory, Mythology, and Fiction* (Ithaca, N.Y: Cornell University Press, 1985), p. 219, concludes that the God of Love "hears only what he wants to hear." I would agree, except that I would stress that the God of Love reads only what he wants to read and that new reading makes this freedom to "misread"—to interpret individualistically—possible.

71. Cf. Donald R. Howard, *The Idea of the "Canterbury Tales"* (Berkeley: University of California Press, 1976). p. 66: the *Tales* "has voiceness because the author addresses us directly and himself rehearses tales told aloud by others: we seem to hear his and the pilgrims' voices, we presume oral delivery."

72. Manly and Rickert, eds., *Text*, 3.525.

73. Janet Coleman, *Medieval Readers and Writers, 1350-1400* (New York: Columbia University Press, 1981), pp. 209-11, remarks that in the fifteenth century "heresy was understood as being caused by the possession of vernacular books and the ability to read them" and that *De heretico comburendo*, which sent some Lollard heretics to the stake, "drew attention to lay literacy as a fundamental aspect of their sedition." For an excellent recent discussion of the relationships between literacy and heresy in an earlier era, see Brian Stock, "Textual Communities," in his *The Implications of Literacy: Written Language and Models of Interpretation in the Eleventh and Twelfth Centuries* (Princeton, NJ.: Princeton University Press, 1983), pp. 88-240.

74. Claire Cross, "'Great Reasoners in Scripture': The Activities of Women Lollards, 1380-1530," in Derek Baker, ed., *Medieval Women*, Studies in Church History, Subsidia, vol. I Oxford: Blackwell, 1978), pp. 359-80 (in the same volume see also Anthony Goodman, "The Piety of John Brunham's Daughter, of Lynn," pp. 354-55, for a discussion of Margery Kempe's "usurpation" of the priestly prerogatives of quoting and glossing Holy Writ).

75. And some readers simply label the Manciple's statement ridiculous, e.g., R. M. Luminansky, *Of Sondry Folk: The Dramatic Principle in the Canterbury Tales* (Austin: University of Texas Press, 1955), p. 239.

76. For a related incident of "disambiguation" regarding another of Chaucer's poems, see Lee W. Patterson, "Ambiguity and Interpretation: A Fifteenth-Century Reading of *Troilus and Criseyde*," *Speculum* 54 (1979): 297-330.

77. On Chaucer's satirical attitude toward "glosynge," see Mary Carruthers, "Letter and Gloss in the Friar's and Summoner's Tales," *JNT* 2 (1972): 208-14. Lawrence Besserman, "'Glosynge is a Glorious Thyng': Chaucer's Biblical Exegesis," in Jeffrey, *Chaucer and Scriptural Tradition*, p. 68, comments that "Chaucer lived at a time when glossing the Bible was acquiring a very bad name." He also reminds us that "Chaucer himself was a gifted translator of the Bible, not relying on the Wycliffite versions but

working independently from the Vulgate, which he must have owned," although such activity was not yet labelled heretical (see Anne Hudson, "The Debate on Bible Translation, Oxford 1401," *EHR* 90 [1975]: 17).

78. Instead, each editor added his own preface to the *Tales*, which includes commentary on Chaucer. See Beverly Boyd, "William Caxton (1422?-1491)," p. 13, and James E. Blodgett, "William Thynne (d. 1546)," pp. 35-36, in Paul G. Ruggiers, ed., *Editing Chaucer: The Great Tradition* (Norman, Okla.: Pilgrim Books, 1984).

79. Elizabeth Eisenstein, *The Printing Press as an Agent of Cultural Change: Communications and Cultural Transformations in Early-Modern Europe* (New York: Cambridge University Press, 1980), p. 51.

80. By 1598, in Thomas Speght's edition of the *Tales* however, we do find a transformed version of the gloss cropping up again in the form of the editor's "arguments" or introductions to individual tales. J. A. Burrow, "*Sir Thopas* in the Sixteenth Century," in Douglas Gray and E. G. Stanley, eds., *Middle English Studies Presented to Norman Davis in Honour of His Seventieth Birthday* (Oxford: Clarendon Press, 1983), p. 91, observes that Speght's argument to *Thopas* constitutes literary criticism, or a form of instruction about how to read the work that follows. The history of the development of the marginal gloss into the independent piece of literary criticism has not yet been written, but we may observe briefly that, after Speght, reading instructions soon disappear again from the margins of printed secular works, which, as I have argued above, are hostile to such overt and direct regulation of reading. By 1617, Richard Braithwaite had separated commentary from text in his *Comment Upon the Two Tales of . . . Chaucer*. Like the old gloss, this commentary explicates *The Miller's Tale* and the Wife's *Prologue* in line-by-line fashion, but, significantly, the commentary no longer exists in the margins of the actual text of Chaucer to demand the reader's consideration. Instead, the reader of Chaucer must voluntarily seek out Braithwaite's commentary. Such reading instructions as footnotes and introductions remain in texts today, but none of them has the prominence— and influence during the *actual* reading experience—that the medieval marginal gloss did. Ironically, marginalia, which in some cases attempted to stabilize—or even petrify—our interpretations of written texts, were themselves ephemeral, for they tended to be lost in the copying and cut off during rebinding (see n. 22 above, and Richard H. Rouse and Mary A. Rouse, "*Statim invenire*: Schools, Preachers, and New Attitudes to the Page," in Robert L. Benson and Giles Constable with Carol D. Lanham, eds., *Renaissance and Renewal in the Twelfth Century* [Cambridge, Mass.: Harvard University Press, 1982], p. 209).

81. Gellrich,*The Idea of the Book*, p. 247, concludes that the allegory of reading in Chaucer "open[s] the way for rereading," a view with which I agree, except that here, as in n. 70 above, I would specify that "rereading" is, in fact, "new reading."

I wish to thank Stuart Palmer, Dean of the College of Liberal Arts, University of New Hampshire, for providing the travel funds necessary for first-hand study of fifteenth-century manuscript glosses.

A Language Policy for Lancastrian England

John H. Fisher

This essay first appeared in PMLA *107 (1992): 1168-80.*

HOW did English become the national language of England? From the Norman Conquest until after 1400, French was the official language of England—not because any law had been passed to make it so but because it was the native language of all those who held office. As Sir John Fortescue explained in 1460, in *De Laudibus Legum Anglie* (I give the English translation by Stanley Chrimes of Fortescue's Latin):

> [A]fter the French had, by duke William the Conqueror, obtained the land, they would not permit advocates to plead their causes unless in the language they themselves knew, which all advocates do in France, even in the court and parliament there. Similarly, after their arrival in England, the French did not accept accounts of their revenues, unless in their own idiom, lest they should be deceived thereby. They took no pleasure in hunting, nor in other recreations, such as games of dice or ball, unless carried on in their own language. So the English contracted the same habit from frequenting such company, so that they to this day speak the French language in such games and accounting. (115)

From 1066 until 1217, England was the property of the dukes of Normandy, who were in turn subjects of the kings of France. The French connection was so strong that when Pope Innocent III divested Duke Jean, whom we call King John, of his lordship, he ordered the French king to carry out the sentence; and when the barons fell out with John over the implementation of the Magna Charta, they offered the English crown to King Louis of France, who came over to England to take possession. England ceased to be a province of France when William Marshall defeated King Louis in the Battle of Lincoln in 1217.

We think of the period from 1066 to 1350 as culturally barren in England, but some of the most important literature of that period was produced for the Anglo-Norman aristocracy that flourished on both sides of the Channel. *Chanson de Roland*, Arthurian romances, troubadour lyrics, the first French play, French sermons, saints' lives, and chronicles are found in insular manuscripts and were probably written in England, and some of the finest French writers—Chrétien de Troyes, Marie de France, Robert Grosseteste, and in Chaucer's time Jean Froissart, John Mandeville, and John Gower—wrote French in England for Anglo-Norman audiences (Merilees; Legge).

The fourteenth century saw the beginning of the rebirth of English cultural independence, but the reigns of Edward III and Richard II, 1327-99, were the high point of the influence of French culture in England (Johnson; Vale; Matthew). As Ruskin observes in *The Stones of Venice*, it is when a culture is decaying that it articulates itself most clearly. After King John lost Normandy, he and his successors still claimed lordship over France south of the Loire, for which they were obliged to do homage to the French king. And beginning with Edward III, for a hundred years the English kings asserted, and tried to implement, their sovereignty over France.

This was the great era of French influence throughout Europe. The geographical centrality of France, the wealth and population its fertile lands generated in an agricultural economy, its supremacy in chivalry, when a knight in armor was equivalent to a modern tank, made France the superpower of the Continent. But a superpower in the medieval tribal sense. Until long after Chaucer's death there was no unified "France," only a kaleidoscope of competing dukedoms, of which the English were merely the most disruptive. French nationalism is not considered to have begun to emerge until Joan of Arc (c. 1430), whereas English nationalism began to emerge in the 1340s, with Edward III. Even though most of the energy of France during this period of cultural ascendancy was spent on internal conflict, enough was left to spill over onto its neighbors. When the pope and his curia moved to Avignon in 1309, France became the seat of religious as well as secular supremacy. Its modes of combat, architecture, religion, literature, dress, food, and manners set the standard everywhere, and especially in England, which had for so long been an integral part of France.

Men of the English aristocracy regularly married Continental wives and married their own daughters off to Continental husbands. King Edward's wife, Philippa, came from Hainault in modern Belgium. Froissart served as her secretary from 1361 until her death in 1369 and while in England began collecting material for his chronicle of the Hundred Years' War. Chaucer's wife, Philippa, and her sister Katherine were the daughters of a French knight, Sir Paon de Roet, who came to England in the retinue of Queen Philippa. One wonders what the domestic language was in Sir Paon's household, in which Philippa grew up, and what Chaucer's own domestic language may have been when he married the daughter of a French knight.

Katherine married Sir Thomas Swynford and became the mistress, and eventually the wife, of John of Gaunt and mother of Henry Beaufort and his brothers, who, I argue, played an important part in the reestablishment of English.

Below this international aristocratic stratum, the English commonality were beginning to assert their own culture. It was English-speaking longbowmen who had cut down the French chivalry at Crécy and Poitiers. An argument used in the English parliaments of 1295, 1344, 1346, and 1376 for support in the wars against France was that French victory would annihilate the English language (Fisher, "Chancery and the Emergence" 879). The Rolls of Parliament were regularly in Latin and French, but occasional entries indicate that the discussion was in English. In an entry of 1426, the exposition is in Latin, but the lines spoken by the witnesses are in English. In another of 1432, the clerks of the Royal Chapel present a petition in Latin, but the introduction is in English. In 1362 the clerks admitted for the first time that Parliament was addressed in English, and in the same year Parliament decreed that all legal proceedings had to be carried on in English because the litigants could not understand French. As a matter of fact, this statute was not enforced, and the common-law courts continued to plead in French until 1731, but that is another story.[1]

Evidently by the 1360s most oral exchange in commerce and government must have been carried on in English, but the records were still kept in Latin and French. Formal education was in Latin, and the writing masters who taught English clerks the secretarial skills of *ars dictaminis* taught them in Latin and French. Virtually all religious and cultural writings intended for any kind of circulation were in Latin or French. Such records as we have of the libraries of Edward III and Richard II and other books mentioned in wills and inventories before 1400 are exclusively Latin and French. A. S. G. Edwards and Derek Pearsall estimate that there are extant only some thirty manuscripts of secular poetry in English written before 1400 and that nearly all are personal productions, like Cotton Nero A.X of the *Gawain* poems, King's College 13 of *William of Palerne*, and Bodley 264 of the *Alexander*. A. I. Doyle has pointed out that the few extant manuscripts of secular poetry in English before 1400 are by household scribes writing in provincial dialects, not by professional scribes in London. The courtesy literature that distinguished the gentle from the churl was virtually all in French (Nicholls).

It is the politics of the movement of the written language from Latin and French to English that concerns me here. We are not now talking about when secular poetry began to be composed in English. From 1300 on, and particularly after 1350, more and more literature was composed in English, but clearly there was no audience that caused these English writings to be copied and disseminated. All the manuscripts of Geoffrey Chaucer, John Mandeville, John Trevisa, John Barbour, Laurence Minot, and other fourteenth-century secular English authors date from after 1400. Gower might be regarded as an exception because one of the two earliest manuscripts of *Confessio Amantis* (the Stafford manuscript, now Huntington

El 26.A.17) seems to be dedicated to Henry Bolingbroke before he became king in 1399, but that is grist to my mill.

A great deal has been written about the emergence of writing in English after 1350, perhaps best in *A History of the English Language* by Albert Baugh, now revised and updated by Thomas Cable, but like all others, Baugh and Cable write as if English just happened. They trace a gradual accretion of statements about English and documents in English that reveal an undirected, populist movement. The model of Chaucer used to be given a large role in this transition, and Derek Pearsall gives Lydgate almost as much importance in conferring prestige on literary English. But neither Baugh and Cable nor Pearsall, nor any others who have discussed the matter, point to the significance of the relation between the specific date at which manuscripts of English writings began to multiply and the date of the Lancastrian usurpation of the throne, in September 1399. Until 1400 we have virtually no manuscripts of poetry in English that were commercially prepared and intended for circulation. Immediately after 1400 we have the manuscripts of Gower, Chaucer, and other fourteenth-century writers and the compositions and manuscripts of Lydgate; Hoccleve; Clanvowe; Scogan; John Walton; Edward, Duke of York; and other fifteenth-century writers. After 1420 the libraries of Sir Richard Beauchamp, Sir Thomas Chaworth, Sir Edmund Rede, and Sir John Paston contained manuscripts by Chaucer and Lydgate as well as other courtly and didactic writings in English (Doyle).

I do not believe that this sudden burst of production in English after 1400 was simply a natural evolution. I think that it was encouraged by Henry IV, and even more by Henry V, as a deliberate policy intended to engage the support of Parliament and the English citizenry for a questionable usurpation of the throne. The publication of Chaucer's poems and his enshrinement as the perfecter of rhetoric in English were central to this effort. The evidence is circumstantial. King Henry, Prince Henry, Henry Beaufort, John Lydgate, Thomas Chaucer, and Thomas Hoccleve did not keep diaries about their plans and motives, but the associations and dates warrant examination.

The fragility of the reign of Henry IV is well known (Wylie, vol. 1; Harriss, *Cardinal*, ch. 2). During the first four years he had to contend with three rebellions of barons who rejected his title to the throne. He countered these by appealing to the commons for support, thus ultimately strengthening parliamentary government. One aspect of this appeal was increased use of the English vernacular. The earliest English entry in the Rolls of Parliament is the 1388 petition of the Mercers Guild printed by Chambers and Daunt, but the next English entries are the 1397 address of Judge Rickhill concerning the impeachment of the duke of Gloucester, which precipitated the downfall of Richard II; two 1399 addresses by Chief Justice Thirnyng regarding the deposition of Richard; and—most important of all—Henry's own challenge to the throne on 30 September 1399 (Fisher, "Chancery and the Emergence" 880). The only conceivable reason for these entries to be recorded in English at a time when the official entries in the Rolls were still uniformly in Latin and French was to appeal to the commons.

John Gower says that Richard II encouraged him to write the *Confessio Amantis* in English (Fisher, *Gower* 9-11), but the earliest manuscript (Huntington El.26, mentioned above) appears to have been presented to Henry Bolingbroke upon his return from France in 1399. It is illuminated with the lion recognizance of John of Gaunt and the swan of Thomas of Gloucester, which Bolingbroke assumed immediately after the murder of Gloucester. The absence of royal emblems indicates that the manuscript was completed before Henry's coronation. Immediately after the coronation, Gower composed *In Praise of Peace*, a poem in English warning Henry not to presume on the right of conquest but to seek peace and to rule with pity (Fisher, *Gower* 132-33). Between the time of Henry's accession and Gower's death in 1408, Gower commissioned perhaps ten manuscripts of his *Confessio* and other English poems. Richard Firth Green in *Poets and Princepleasers* has a good deal to say about Gower's support of Henry's usurpation.

In 1393 Henry had given Gower a collar with a swan pendant, apparently as a reward for Gower's support of Thomas of Gloucester, and soon after his coronation he granted Gower two pipes of wine yearly (21 Nov. 1399). At nearly the same time (13 Oct. 1399[2]), the King doubled Chaucer's annuity from Richard to £20 and granted to Hoccleve, then a young clerk in privy seal, an annuity of £10 (12 Nov. 1399). Henry IV may have made these grants for the writers' civil service rather than for their poetry, but his benefactions to Gower, Chaucer, and Hoccleve all three certainly qualify him as a supporter of English poets.

Our attention now shifts to Henry V who came to the throne in 1413. The entries in the Rolls of Parliament under Henry IV continued to be mostly in French, and Henry V continued to use French for his correspondence as Prince of Wales and during the first three years of his reign. His effort to secure the support of the commons in Parliament was even more strenuous than that of his father: in 1414 he granted that their statutes should be made without altering the language of the petitions on which the statutes were based. There is no recorded evidence that this elevated the use of English, but petitions and the actions upon them are the primary constituents of the Rolls of Parliament, whose earliest entry in English is the mercers' petition of 1388, as mentioned above. Henry V's success at Agincourt in 1415, after so many years of failure in the wars with France, reinforced English nationalism, and in 1416, as the king began to assemble his forces to make good his claim to the French throne, he addressed five proclamations in English to the citizens of London, requesting supplies and commanding soldiers and sailors to assemble for the invasion.[3] These are the first royal proclamations in English since the proclamation of Henry III in 1258 and that had been the only one since the last English proclamation of William the Conqueror in 1087. Most significant, upon reaching France on 12 August 1417, Henry addressed his first missive in English to his chancellor, and from that time until his death in 1422 he used English in nearly all his correspondence with the government and the citizens of London and other

English cities. The use of English by Henry V marks the turning point in establishing English as the national language of England. Its effect is reflected in the familiar entry of 1422 in the abstract book of the Brewers Guild explaining their change of record keeping from Latin to English:

> Whereas our mother-tongue, to wit the English tongue, hath in modern days begun to be honorably enlarged and adorned, for that our most excellent lord, King Henry V, hath in his letters missive and divers affairs touching his own person, more willingly chosen to declare the secrets of his will, for the better understanding of his people, hath with a diligent mind procured the common idiom (setting aside others) to be commended by the exercise of writing; and there are many of our craft of Brewers who have the knowledge of writing and reading in the said English idiom, but in others, to wit, the Latin and French, before these times used, they do not in any wise understand. For which causes with many others, it being considered how that the greater part of the Lords and trusty Commons have begun to make their matters to be noted down in our mother tongue, so we also in our craft, following in some manner their steps, have decreed to commit to memory the needful things which concern us [in English].
>
> (Chambers and Daunt 139)

This momentous decision is recorded in Latin, but in the 1420s the Brewers and other guilds did switch their record keeping to English; and the chancery dialect, modeled in many ways on Henry's own idiom and spelling (Richardson; Fisher, Richardson, and Fisher), became the prestige written language (Samuels). Chambers and Daunt edited many of these documents in their *Book of London English*, and John Fisher, Malcolm Richardson, and Jane Fisher edited Henry's signet letters and other English chancery documents in their *Anthology of Chancery English*.

This is the documented historical record, but I believe that the transformation of the language of government and business would not have been possible without more than a decade of preparation and propaganda. Let us go back to 1398, when Prince Henry was eleven years old. According to a tradition commencing with the Chronicle of John Rous, completed in 1477, Henry Beaufort (son of John of Gaunt and Katherine Swynford and therefore half brother to Henry IV, son of John of Gaunt and Blanche of Lancaster) was tutor to Prince Henry at Queen's College, Oxford. The relationships with Beaufort and the university are not mentioned in any other chronicle, and Rous's account—coming, as it does, some eighty years after the event—is rightly regarded as questionable evidence. It may be pointed out, however, that since Rous was born in 1411 and at Oxford by 1425, his testimony is more current than the 1477 date of his chronicle might indicate. Nineteenth-century biographers accepted both relationships (e.g., Armitage-Smith 414; Towle 170-71); recent biographers accept the tutorship but not the prince's residence at Oxford (e.g., Harriss, *Cardinal* 9; Hutchinson 18; Seward 4). The careful conclusion of the entry on Beaufort in the *Dictionary of National Biography* suggests why Harriss and others have accepted the tutorship:

> [Beaufort] is said to have been the tutor of the Prince of Wales. He certainly exercised considerable influence over him. While the king was in a great measure guided by Arundel, the prince attached himself to the younger and more popular party of which [Beaufort] was the head.

In the entry on Henry V, the *DNB* narrows the inference:

> The tradition that he was educated at Queen's College, Oxford, under the care of his uncle Henry Beaufort . . . first appears in the "Chronicle of John Rous" (ed. Hearne, p. 207). Beaufort was chancellor [of Oxford] in 1398, and, if the statement is correct, the prince's residence at Oxford must have fallen in this year. There is, however, no record relating to Henry at Queen's College.

Again the evidence is circumstantial. The political association between Henry and Beaufort from 1403 onward, abundantly detailed and documented in Harriss's *Cardinal Beaufort*, was so constant and familiar that biographers feel they must accept a personal relationship, hence the tutorship; but the lack of any record at Oxford makes them shy away from the Queen's College association. One might ask, Why accept one half of Rous's statement but not the other? And would it have been that unusual for the college records not to mention a boy of eleven—even a prince— staying with his uncle and having no official connection with Oxford? Hutchinson (17) and Seward (3) never consider where and when the tutorship that they accept might have occurred. As the *DNB* observes, the best possibility is 1398, when Beaufort was chancellor of Oxford.

In the fall of 1398, at the age of twenty-three, Henry Beaufort was made Bishop of Lincoln and began his service with the king. But Harriss surmises that Beaufort still spent a good deal of time in Oxford until 1403, when he was appointed chancellor of England for the first time (*Cardinal* 8, 12, 19). He served as chancellor four times— under Henry IV, V, and VI—becoming the richest man in England and supplying enormous sums to support the war in France. Until his death in 1447, according to the historian William Stubbs, "he held the strings of English policy" (3: 143). K. B. McFarlane's essay "At the Deathbed of Cardinal Beaufort" is a fascinating overview of Beaufort's wealth and influence (115-38).

Prince Henry was not at Oxford continuously after 1398. In October of that year King Richard, after banishing Henry Bolingbroke and confiscating the Lancastrian holdings, called the prince to court and in January 1399 took young Henry with him on his expedition to Ireland. There Henry remained until his victorious father sent a ship for him the next October. After Henry had been created Prince of Wales on 15 October 1399, he is reported at Chester and in Wales with the troops from time to time, but until 1403 his connection with the Welsh wars was nominal. The actual operations were in the imperious hands of Sir Henry Percy (Hotspur). It was the rebellion of the Percys that led to Prince Henry's appointment in March 1403 as King's Lieutenant of the Marches of Wales, making him at sixteen commander in chief in fact as well as in name (Harriss, *Cardinal* 15; Seward 18). We have no continuous account of Prince Henry's whereabouts between October 1399 and March 1403. In the same month that the prince assumed military command, Henry Beaufort was named chancellor of England for the first time. So whatever period there could have been for Henry Beaufort and Prince Henry to contemplate the place of English in Lancastrian policy would have been in whatever intervals they may have passed together at Queen's College and elsewhere between 1398 and 1403.

During this five years Thomas Chaucer was settling into his manor at Ewelme, about ten miles from Oxford.[4] Thomas was the son of Philippa Chaucer, the sister of Katherine Swynford. We will not here go into the question of whether his father was Geoffrey Chaucer or John of Gaunt, but Thomas was at least first cousin to the Beauforts and may have been an unacknowledged half brother of both the Beauforts and the king (Fisher, *Importance* 19-23). His amazing career points in this direction. In 1395 he was married to a wealthy heiress, Maud Bergersh, through whom he acquired Ewelme and many other valuable properties, and he was showered with honors from the moment Henry IV assumed the throne: in 1399 he was appointed Constable of Wallingford Castle, in 1400 Sheriff of Oxfordshire, in 1402 King's Butler, with responsibility not only for procuring and dispensing the wine for the royal household but also for collecting petty customs, the tax on wine imports throughout the kingdom. He sat as member of Parliament for Oxfordshire in 1401 and in thirteen other parliaments. He was Speaker for the Commons in the Parliament of 1407 and in three other parliaments and remained, until his death in 1434, an important intermediary between the commons and the king.

A third member of Prince Henry's putative Oxford circle between 1398 and 1403 may have been John Lydgate. We know that he was at Gloucester College, Oxford, in 1406 from a letter by the prince to the abbot and chapter of Bury Saint Edmunds asking them to allow Lydgate to continue his studies at Oxford (Pearsall 29), and John Norton-Smith supposes that Lydgate was in residence there from 1397 to 1408 (195).

Thomas Chaucer was one of Lydgate's longtime patrons, and by all accounts the two sustained a pleasant relationship at Ewelme (see Schirmer; Pearsall; and Ebin). Thomas's manor was the salon for a literate Lancastrian circle much interested in English poetry, from whose members Lydgate received several commissions. In the complimentary *Balade at the Departyng of Thomas Chaucer into France*, he extolled Thomas as his "maister dere," the same term he applied several times to Geoffrey. The "balade" to Thomas Chaucer, like the close relationship between Prince Henry and Henry Beaufort, is circumstantial evidence for an association dating back to college. An Oxford association of the prince, his tutor, his cousin, and the budding poet-apologist for the house of Lancaster could have been the time and place when the seeds for the self-conscious cultivation of English as the national language were planted. And the first sprout of that momentous plan may have been the decision to organize and publish the poetry of Geoffrey Chaucer.

There are no extant manuscripts of Chaucer's poems dating from before his death in 1400, and it is the general (though by no means universal) opinion today that he died without commissioning a presentation copy of a single one of his works (Fisher, "Animadversions"). Why we do not know, since presentation of an elaborate manuscript to a patron was the accepted method of publication in the Middle Ages (Root). Chaucer's failure to publish, or the loss of all his presentation manuscripts, is one of the great mysteries of early English literary culture. Furthermore, the textual evidence seems to indicate that Chaucer fully finished very few of his works, either poetry or prose (Fisher, "Animadversions"; Blake; Windeatt). He was living in Westminster during the first two years of the fateful 1398-1403 period, presumably surrounded by copies of works that were well known to the courtly and commercial circles of London from oral presentations dating back over thirty years but that had never been published because of his own diffidence and because of the lack of prestige of English as a cultivated language. Everyone spoke English, but writing in English was simply not couth.

This is not an unusual sociolinguistic situation. It was exhibited in Montreal and India and Norway at the beginning of this century.[5] In Montreal most of the population spoke French, but business and commercial writing was largely in English. In Norway most of the population spoke Norwegian dialects but wrote Danish. In India most of the population spoke Prakrit dialects, of which Hindi was the most widespread, but official writing was in English. In these cultures in the nineteenth century and for some time afterward, the populace generally spoke native dialects, but official and polite writing was in nonnative prestige languages. So it was with England until after 1400.

French, Norwegian, and Hindi are now official languages in these cultures and are exemplified by increasingly sophisticated literatures. But the elevation of these languages is not the result merely of demographic and economic evolution. It reflects deliberate political decisions. We have ample evidence about these decisions today, but the absence of evidence for the England of 1400 does not mean that the process was different at that time. England had persisted in its bilingual situation, with French as the official language and English as a patois, for four hundred years, two hundred after the Battle of Lincoln made the country politically independent and sixty after the beginning of the Hundred Years' War made France its enemy. It seems likely that bilingualism might have persisted for much longer if it had not been for a deliberate decision by some influential authority.

Henry V was such an authority. Much has been made of his charisma as a national hero, of his cultivation of nationalism, of his communication with Parliament and the citizenry (Harriss, *Henry V*). It took him three years after his accession to implement the use of English in his signet letters. This action can hardly have been casual and unpremeditated. There is a persistent medieval tradition that official languages were inaugurated by kings--by King Alfred in Anglo-Saxon England (Richards), by Philip the Fair in France (Brunot 1: 370), by Alphonse X in Spain (Wolff 178; Fisher, "European Chancelleries"). Modern linguists tend to discount this tradition and to attribute sociolinguistic developments to impersonal demographic and economic forces. I do not deny the importance of such forces, but I think that (whatever the process in Montreal) the development of Norwegian would not have proceeded as it did without the leadership of Knud Knudsen and Ivar Asen, nor of Hindi without the leadership of B. J. Tilak and Mahatma Gandi (see n5). Einar Haugen discusses specifically the role of the language planner and cites the names of language planners in northern European countries and in Greece and Turkey (168-70). The history of the developments of all official languages for which there is documentation show that such developments do not occur without influential leadership and deliberate political process.

The outburst of copying and composing in English that began soon after 1400 can best be explained as a deliberately instigated activity that laid the groundwork for the political actions of 1416-22. That Chaucer should be chosen as the cynosure for this movement would not be at all surprising. He was of both the royal and the commercial circles, son of a vintner and a close relative by marriage to King Henry IV, Prince Henry, and the Beauforts. His vernacular poetry had already attracted attention by Thomas Usk, Henry Scogan, John Clanvowe, and other contemporaries in England and by Eustach Deschamps in France. Norman Blake, developing the arguments of J. S. P. Tatlock, Germaine Dempster, A. I. Doyle, Malcolm Parkes, and others, has given a persuasive account of the evolution of the text of the *Canterbury Tales* from the initial effort to make sense of the foul papers in the Hengwrt manuscript to the fully edited text in the Ellesmere manuscript. He envisages this process of development through five or six versions as progressing under the direction of a group of editors working to give a veneer of completeness to papers that Chaucer had left in disarray at the time of his death.

The most sumptuous of all Chaucer manuscripts, Ellesmere, written by the same scribe as Hengwrt, is associated by its illuminations and scrimshaw with Thomas Chaucer, whom Manly and Rickert propose as "logically the person to have made what was clearly intended as an authoritative text" (1: 159). Thomas would presumably have had opportunities to visit with his father during the poet's last years in Westminster and to arrange for the Hengwrt scribe to begin making an initial compilation from the foul papers. He and his friends (Henry Beaufort, Prince Henry?) could have gone over the result with the scribe and engaged another scribe to produce the Corpus version; then gone through a similar process with that and with the Harlean, Lansdowne, and two Cambridge versions—I am using Blake's scenario. With the last two they approached completion: Cambridge Dd achieved the Ellesmere order for the tales, and Cambridge Gg introduced the first illustrations of the pilgrims. Having got to this stage, Thomas Chaucer could have arranged for the original scribe to produce the Ellesmere manuscript, incorporating all the editorial "improvements" arrived at throughout the several versions.

This process would have been expensive, but Thomas Chaucer had the money to pay for it. Doyle and Parkes give a fascinating account of a group of five scribes working in London and Westminster in the first quarter of the century who produced eight of the earliest manuscripts of the *Canterbury Tales*, including four of those that Blake treats in his scenario of the evolution of the text (Hg, El, Cp, and Ha). One or more of the same group of scribes also produced a copy of *Troylus and Criseyde*, seven copies of *Confessio Amantis*, a copy of *Piers Plowman*, a copy of John Trevisa's translation of Bartholomaeus Anglicus, and three manuscripts of the writings of Thomas Hoccleve. Indeed, as one of the group himself, Hoccleve cooperated in producing the Trinity College manuscript of *Confessio Amantis* that Doyle and Parkes use as the touchstone for their analysis.

Doyle and Parkes's evidence indicates that the London book trade at the beginning of the fifteenth century was still very informal. The shifting associations among the scribes militates against the notion of bookshops employing regular staffs of copyists. It appears, instead, that books were produced under individual contract. The contractors were called "stationers" because they were stationary; that is, they had shops where they could be reached. Paul Christianson is assembling evidence of these shops clustered around Saint Paul's Church in London. There the stationers accepted commissions from patrons for books or other documents, which they copied themselves and hired other scribes to help with. The assistants worked on a piecework basis, fascicle by fascicle, in their own rooms. When the copying was complete, the stationer would assemble the fascicles and send them out to the limners to be decorated, and eventually to the binders to be bound. Most of the piecework clerks would be, like Hoccleve, regularly employed in governmental or commercial offices. Some, like Doyle and Parkes's scribe D, might be free-lance scriveners.

This commercial method of book production had begun long before 1400, but until then its products in England had all been in Latin or French. We have no evidence that the switch to English was stimulated by any policy of Henry IV, Prince Henry, or Henry Beaufort. None of the manuscripts by the five scribes identified by Doyle and Parkes reveals any connection with royalty, but royalty and aristocracy were patrons for English manuscripts. The Morgan manuscript of *Troylus and Criseyde* has on its first page the arms of Prince Henry while he was still Prince of Wales. And the English poetry composed at the beginning of the century shows that Prince Henry was considered a patron and Geoffrey Chaucer the initiator. G. L. Harriss observes that Hoccleve's *Regement of Princes* was completed in 1411 and Lydgate's *Troy Book* was commissioned in 1412, precisely the years "in which the prince, at the head of a council of his own choosing and virtually without reference to his father, was carrying through a sustained programme of 'bone governance' to which he had pledged himself in the parliament of January 1410" (*Henry V* 9). Part of the "bone governance" may have been the enhancement of the position of English.

This takes us back to the third member of the putative Oxford circle, John Lydgate. Lydgate's dedication of the *Troy Book* comes as close as anything we have to attributing to Prince Henry a nationalistic policy for enhancing the use of English. The prince, Lydgate says,

> Whyche me comaunded the drery pitus fate
> Of hem of Troye in englysche to translate
>
> . . . .
> By-cause he wolde that to hyge and lowe
> The noble story openly wer knowe
> In oure tonge, aboute in every age,
> And y-writen as wel in oure langage
> As in latyn or in frensche it is;
> That of the story the trouthe we nat mys
> No more than doth eche other nacioun:
> This was the fyn of his entencioun.
> (*Troy Book*, Pro. 105-06, 111-18)

Schirmer identifies the Tanner D.2 manuscript of this poem as the possible presentation copy to Henry himself (50). Lydgate's *Life of Our Lady* is likewise in one manuscript ascribed to the "excitation and stirryng of our worshipful prince, kyng Harry the fifthe." Even though Pearsall doubts the validity of this ascription, because the work was never finished and contains no internal reference to the patron such as Lydgate usually makes (Pearsall 286), the ascription manifests recognition of Henry's patronage of English letters.

What is most significant to my argument, however, is Lydgate's acknowledgment that his version of the Troy story expands on Chaucer's model:

> The hoole story Chaucer kan yow telle
> Yif that ye liste, no man bet alyve,
> Nor the processe halfe so wel discryve,
> For he owre englishe gilte with his sawes,
> Rude and boistous firste be olde dawes,
> That was ful fer from al perfeccioun,
> And but of litel reputaticoun,
> Til that he cam & thorug his poetrie,

Gan oure tonge firste to magnifie,
And adourne it with his elloquence—
To whom honour, laude, & reverence,
Thorug-oute this londe yove be & songe,
So that the laurer of oure englishe tonge
Be to hym yove for his excellence,
Rigt as whilom by ful hige sentence
Perpetuelly for a memorial.
                    (*Troy Book* 3.4234-19)

Two of Lydgate's earliest poems, *The Complaint of the Black Knight* and *The Flour of Curtesye*, dated by Schirmer between 1400 and 1402— during the fateful 1398-1403 period—are acts of homage to Chaucer (Schirmer 34, 37). The acknowledgment in *The Flour of Curtesye* suggests that they may have been composed very soon after Chaucer's death:

Ever as I can supprise in myn herte
Alway with feare betwyxt drede and shame
Leste oute of lose, any worde asterte
In this metre, to make it seme lame,
Chaucer is deed that had suche a name
Of fayre makyng that [was] without wene
Fayrest in our tonge, as the Laurer grene.

We may assay forto countrefete
His gay style but it wyl not be;
The welle is drie, with the lycoure swete....
                    (Spurgeon 1.15)

In *The Churl and the Bird* (c. 1408), a beast fable somewhat like the *Nun's Priest's Tale*, Lydgate again does obeisance to Chaucer's precedence in creating an English that could stand beside French:

Go gentill quayer, and Recommaunde me
Unto my maistir with humble affectioun
Beseke hym lowly of mercy and pite
Of thy rude makyng to have compassioun
And as touching thy translacioun
Oute of frensh / hough ever the englisshe be
Al thing is saide undir correctioun
With supportacioun of your benignite.
                    (Spurgeon 1.15)

Schirmer observes that these poems, like most others by Lydgate, must have been written in response to commissions, but he does not venture who the patrons might have been (31, 37). I would like to think that the poems were commissioned by Henry Beaufort and Prince Henry at the same time that they were encouraging Thomas Chaucer to bring out his father's works.

The *Temple of Glas,* another early work acknowledging Chaucer's inspiration, could likewise have been composed in response to the Oxford inspiration. In addition, Lydgate pays tribute to his master Chaucer in the *Serpent of Division* (c. 1420) and the *Siege of Thebes* (c. 1422), whose patrons are not identified; in the *Pilgrimage of the Life of Man* (c. 1427), written for Thomas Montacute, the husband of Chaucer's granddaughter Alice; and in the *Fall of Princes* (c. 1431), for Humphry, duke of Gloucester, the youngest brother of Henry V. The list of Lydgate's patrons reads like a Who's Who of both the courtly and the commercial circles in England, suggesting influential support from the Lancastrian affinity for the cultivation of English. If this support stemmed from policy established at Oxford about 1400 by Henry Beaufort and Prince Henry—a resolve to elevate the prestige of English and to display Chaucer's poetry as the cynosure of this elevation—then John Lydgate could be considered the public relations agent for this policy.

And Lydgate was not alone in his promotional efforts. I have already mentioned Thomas Hoccleve as one of the scribes in the cohort that was turning out commercial manuscripts in English. Hoccleve's relation to the emergence of English is peculiar. As a clerk in the Westminster office of the privy seal, he should have been party to the introduction of English into chancery. But after he retired from the office, about 1425, he compiled a formulary with examples of different kinds of instruments issued by the privy seal office. These examples are all in French or Latin, but between folios 36 and 37 there is a scrap of vellum in Hoccleve's hand with one of the earliest statements about chancery procedure, showing that chancery was a cultivated style:

> In a precedende write word by word and leter by leter titel
> by titel as the copie is & than look ther be aplid ther on in
> the chauncerie & that the write be retourned unto the
> chauncerie and begin thus . . .
> (Fisher, "Chancery Standard" 141)

The instructions go on, in increasingly illegible script, to address themselves to Latin formulas. Hoccleve's professional languages were always, like Chaucer's, Latin and French, while, like Chaucer, he wrote his poetry in English. Like Lydgate, Hoccleve acknowledged Prince Henry as the patron of English and Chaucer as its initiator. *The Regement of Princes* begins with a warm dedication to "[h]ye and noble prince excellent" (2017) and speaks of the prince's grandfather, John of Gaunt, and father, Henry IV (3347-53), indicating that the poem was completed before 1413, when Prince Henry ascended to the throne. Halfway through the dedication comes the first reference to Chaucer: "Mi dere maistir—god his soule quyte!—/ And fadir, Chaucer, fayn wolde han me taght; / But I was dul and lerned lite or naght"

(2077-79). The dedication ends with more compliments to the prince and good wishes for his reign, leading into what Jerome Mitchell has called "virtually the first full-fledged English manual of instruction for a prince" (31), which was of great interest to the public (more than forty manuscripts are extant) because the behavior of the king was the only context in which people of that period could conceive of social amelioration. The discussion continues to be punctuated with direct exhortations to Prince Henry both to be virtuous and to pay Hoccleve his annuity. Near the end, under the heading "take counsel," comes the most explicit tribute to Chaucer, accompanied by the famous picture that is thought to be the exemplar for the Ellesmere and other contemporary portraits:

> The firste fyndere of our faire langage,
> Hath seyde in caas semblable, & othir moo,
> So hyly wel, that it is my dotage
> ffor to expresse or touche any of thoo.
> Alasse! my fadir fro the worlde is goo—
> Be thou my advoket for hym, hevenes quene!
> (Regement 4978-83)

Hoccleve wrote five other poems addressed to Henry V after the king ascended to the throne.

Much more could be written—indeed, has been written (e.g., Bennett)—about the efflorescence of composition and multiplication of manuscripts in English in the first quarter of the fifteenth century. I have said nothing about Henry Scogan's *Moral Balade*, addressed to Prince Henry and his brothers, which also acknowledges "my maister Chaucer." But my line of argument is by this time evident. Hoccleve, no more than Lydgate, [n]ever articulated for the Lancastrian rulers a policy of encouraging the development of English as a national language or of citing Chaucer as the exemplar for such a policy. But we have the documentary and literary evidence of what happened. The linkage of praise for Prince Henry as a model ruler concerned about the use of English and of master Chaucer as the "firste fyndere of our faire langage"; the sudden appearance of manuscripts of the *Canterbury Tales, Troylus and Criseyde*, and other English writings composed earlier but never before published; the conversion to English of the signet clerks of Henry V, the chancery clerks, and eventually the guild clerks; and the burgeoning of composition in English and the patronage of that literature by the Lancastrian court circle—these are concurrent historical events. The only question is whether the concurrence was coincidental or deliberate.

All linguistic changes of this sort for which we have documentation—in Norway, India, Canada, Finland, Israel, or elsewhere—have been the result of deliberate, official policy. There is no reason to suppose that the situation was different in England. Policy in the Middle Ages originated with the king, who worked with the advice of influential counselors (Scanlon). As we look at England between 1399 and 1422, we see Henry IV and Henry V attempting to establish their shaky administration by appealing to Parliament, the Beaufort brothers and Thomas Chaucer providing counsel and support, the poetry of Thomas's father being cited as the cynosure of cultivated English, and Henry V beginning to use English for his official missives. An association of Prince Henry, Henry Beaufort, Thomas Chaucer, and John Lydgate at Oxford and Ewelme between 1398 and 1403 would have offered an appropriate opportunity for the initiation of a plan to cultivate English as the official and prestige language of the nation. Oh to have been a cricket on the hearth at Queen's College and Ewelme Manor to have heard the talk that went round the fire in those years![6]

NOTES

1. Pollock and Maitland summarize the history of English legal language (1:80-87). Fisher gives citations for the English records in the Rolls of Parliament and statistics on the increasing number of English entries in the Rolls, from one in 1403 to fifteen in 1449 ("Chancery and the Emergence" 880).
2. The date on the vellum is 13 Oct. 1399, but Ferris shows that the grant was made in Feb. 1400 and backdated to Oct. 1399.
3. The 1416 proclamations and later English missives from Henry V in the London Corporation's Letter Books are printed by Riley.
4. 0n Thomas Chaucer, see Ruud; Baugh; Roskell; Crow and Olson 541-44. The *DNB* gives a substantial listing of Thomas's many grants and offices, as do Wylie and Waugh, app. E, and McFarlane 96-101. On the close association between Thomas Chaucer and Henry Beaufort, see Harriss, *Cardinal* 20 and index.
5. Heller discusses the development of French as the official language in Montreal; Haugen the development of Norwegian Riksmal (ch. 6); and Misra the spread of Hindi. Grillo treats peripheral and prestige languages in Great Britain and France. Wardhaugh treats not only the rise to dominance of English in Great Britain and French in France but the competition of languages for dominance in Belgium, Switzerland, Canada, and African countries. Cooper devotes a whole volume to the politics of language change.
6. This essay began as a convocation address at Indiana State University, Terre Haute, in April 1991. It develops material presented in *The Importance of Chaucer*.

WORKS CITED

Armitage-Smith, Sidney. *John of Gaunt*. 1904. New York: Barnes, 1964.
Baugh, Albert C. "Kirk's Life Records of Chaucer." *PMLA* 47 (1932): 461-515.
Baugh, Albert C., and Thomas Cable. *A History of The English Language*. 3rd ed. New York: Prentice, 1978.

Bennett, H. S. *Chaucer and the Fifteenth Century.* Oxford: Clarendon-Oxford UP, 1947.

Blake, Norman. *The Textual Tradition of the* Canterbury Tales. London: Arnold, 1985.

Brunot, Ferdinand. *Histoire de la langue francaise.* 1900-10. Paris: Colin, 1966. 5 vols.

Chambers, R. W., and Marjorie Daunt. *A Book of London English.* Oxford: Clarendon-Oxford UP, 1931.

Christianson, C. Paul. "Evidence for the Study of London's Late Medieval Manuscript Book Trade." Griffiths and Pearsall 87-108.

Cooper, Robert L. *Language Spread: Studies in Diffusion and Social Change.* Bloomington: Indiana UP, 1982.

Crow, M. M ., and Clair Olson. *Chaucer Life Records.* Oxford: Clarendon-Oxford UP, 1966.

Doyle, A. I. "English Books in and out of Court from Edward III to Henry VII." *English Court Culture in the Later Middle Ages.* Ed. V. J. Scattergood and J. W. Sherborne. New York: St. Martin's, 1983. 163-82.

Doyle, A. I., and Malcolm Parkes. "The Production of Copies of the *Canterbury Tales* and the *Confessio Amantis* in the Early Fifteenth Century." *Medieval Scribes, Manuscripts, and Libraries: Essays Presented to N. R. Ker.* Ed. M. Parkes and A. G. Watson. London: Scholar, 1978. 163-210.

Ebin, Lois. *John Lydgate.* New York: Twayne, 1985.

Edwards, A. S. G., and Derek Pearsall. "The Manuscripts of the Major English Poetic Texts." Griffiths and Pearsall 257-78.

Ferris, Sumner. "The Date of Chaucer's Final Annuity and of 'The Complaint to His Empty Purse.'" *Modern Philology* 65 (1967): 45-52.

Fisher, John H. "Animadversions on the Text of Chaucer, 1985." *Speculum* 63 (1988): 779-83.

--------." Chancery and the Emergence of Standard Written English in the Fifteenth Century." *Speculum* 52 (1977): 870-99.

--------." Chancery Standard and Modern Written English." *Journal of the Society of Archivists* 6 (1979): 136-44.

--------." European Chancelleries and the Rise of Standard Written Languages." *Proceedings of the Illinois Medieval Association 3.* Ed. Ruth E. Hamilton and David L. Wagner. DeKalb: Northern Illinois U, 1986. 1-34.

--------. *The Importance of Chaucer.* Carbondale: Southern Illinois UP, 1992.

--------. *John Gower.* New York: New York UP, 1964.

Fisher, John H., Malcolm Richardson, and Jane L. Fisher. *An Anthology of Chancery English.* Knoxville: U of Tennessee P, 1984.

Fortescue, John. *De Laudibus Legum Anglie.* Ed. and trans. S. B. Chrimes. Cambridge: Cambridge UP, 1947.

Green, Richard Firth. *Poets and Princepleasers.* Toronto: U of Toronto P, 1980.

Griffiths, J. J., and Derek Pearsall, eds. *Book Production and Publishing in Britain, 1375-1475.* Cambridge: Cambridge UP, 1989.

Grillo, R. D. *Dominant Languages: Language and Hierarchy in Britain and France.* Cambridge: Cambridge UP, 1989.

Gumperz, John J. *Language and Social Identity.* Cambridge: Cambridge UP, 1982.

Harriss, G. L. *Cardinal Beaufort.* Oxford: Clarendon-Oxford UP, 1988.

--------. *Henry V: The Practice of Kingship.* Oxford: Oxford UP, 1985.

Haugen, Einar. *The Ecology of Language: Essays by Einar Haugen.* Selected and introd. Anwar S. Dil. Stanford: Stanford UP, 1972.

Heller, Monica S. "Negotiations of Language Choice in Montreal." Gumperz 108-18.

Hoccleve, Thomas. *The Regement of Princes.* Vol. 3 of *Hoccleve's Works* Ed. F. J. Furnivall. ES 72. Oxford: EETS, 1897.

Hutchinson, Harold. *Henry V: A Biography.* New York: Day, 1967.

Johnson, Paul. *The Life and Times of Edward III.* London: Wiedenfeld, 1973.

Legge, Mary Dominica. *Anglo-Norman Literature and Its Background.* Oxford: Clarendon-Oxford UP, 1963.

Lydgate, John. *Troy Book.* Ed. Henry Bergen. ES 97. Oxford: EETS, 1906.

Manly, J. M., and Edith Rickert. *The Text of the* Canterbury Tales. 8 vols. Chicago: U of Chicago P, 1940.

Matthew, Gervase. *The Court of Richard II.* London: Murray, 1968.

McFarlane, K. B. *England in The Fifteenth Century: Collected Essays.* London: Hambledon, 1981.

Merilees, Brian. "Anglo-Norman Literature." *Dictionary of the Middle Ages.* Vol. 1. New York: Scribner's, 1982.

Misra, Bal Govind. "Language Spread in a Multilingual Setting: The Spread of Hindi as a Case Study." *Language Spread: Studies in Diffusion and Social Change.* Ed. Robert L. Cooper. Bloomington: Indiana UP, 1982. 148-57.

Mitchell, Jerome. *Thomas Hoccleve.* Urbana: U of Illinois P, 1968.

Nicholls, Jonathan. *The Matter of Courtesy.* Cambridge: Brewer, 1985.

Norton-Smith, John. *John Lydgate: Poems.* Oxford: Clarendon-Oxford UP, 1960.

Pearsall, Derek. *John Lydgate.* Charlottesville: U of Virginia P, 1970.

Pollock, Frederick, and Frederic William Maitland. *The History of English Law.* 2nd ed. 2 vols. Cambridge: Cambridge UP, 1968.

Richards, Mary P. "Elements of Written Standard in the Old English Laws." *Standardizing English: Essays in the History of Language Change in Honor of John Hurt Fisher.* Ed. Joseph B. Trahern, Jr. Knoxville: U of Tennessee P, 1989. 1-22.

Richardson, Malcolm. "Henry V, the English Chancery, and Chancery English." *Speculum* 55 (1980): 726-50.

Riley, H. T., ed. *Memorials of London and London Life*. London: Longman, 1868.

Root, R. K. "Publication before Printing." *PMLA* 28 (1913): 417-31.

Roskell, J. S. "Thomas Chaucer of Ewelme." *Parliaments and Politics in Late Medieval England*. London: Hambledon, 1983. 151-92.

Ruud, Martin B. *Thomas Chaucer*. U of Minnesota Studies in Lang. and Lit. 9. Minneapolis: U of Minnesota, 1926.

Samuels, M. L. "Some Applications of Middle English Dialectology." *Historical Linguistics*. Ed. Roger Lass. New York: Holt, 1969. 404-18.

Scanlon, Larry. "The King's Two Voices: Narrative and Power in Hoccleve's *Regement of Princes*." *Literary Practice and Social Change in Britainin, 1380-1530*. Ed. Lee Patterson. Berkeley: U of California P, 1990. 216-47.

Schirmer, Walter. *John Lydgate*. Trans. Ann E. Keep. Berkeley: U of California P, 1961.

Scogan, Henry. *Moral Balade*. *The Complete Works of Geoffrey Chaucer*. Ed. W. W. Skeat. Vol. 7. Oxford: Clarendon-Oxford UP, 1894. xli. 7 vols.

Seward, Desmond. *Henry V Warlord*. London: Sidgwick, 1987.

Spurgeon, Caroline F. *Five Hundred Years of Chaucer Criticism and Allusion*. 3 vols. 1908-17. New York: Russell, 1960.

Stubbs, William. *The Constitutional History of England*. 3 vols. Oxford: Clarendon-Oxford UP, 1874-78.

Towle, George M. *The History of Henry V*. New York: Appleton, 1866.

Vale, Juliet. *Edward III and Chivalry*. Cambridge: Brewer, 1982.

Wardhaugh, Ronald. *Languages in Competition: Dominance, Diversity, and Decline*. Oxford: Blackwell, 1987.

Windeatt, Barry, ed. *Troilus and Criseyde*. By Geoffrey Chaucer. London: Longman, 1984.

Wolff, Philippe. *Western Languages*. Trans. F. Partridge. London: Wiedenfeld, 1971.

Wylie, James Hamilton. *History of England under Henry the Fourth*. 2 vols. 1884. New York: AMS, 1969.

Wylie, James H., and W. T. Waugh. *The Reign of Henry V*. 3 vols. 1914-29. New York: Greenwood, 1968.

Chaucer's Fifteenth-Century Audience and the Narrowing of the "Chaucer Tradition"

Paul Strohm

This essay first appeared in Studies in the Age of Chaucer *4 (1982): 3-32.*

THE principal responsibility of any theory of literary history is to account for stylistic change.[1] The shortcoming of a wholly enclosed history of the interrelations of literary texts is that it has no persuasive way to account for the challenge or supplantation of tradition by countertradition, for the replacement of one form or genre by another, for the revival of a form or style whose time might seem wholly to have passed. Presumably, none of us still believes in the "evolutionary" model of the progression of texts, in which forms and styles pass from youthful vitality to full maturity to senescence, are born and die out, according to some imperative inherent in their own genetic structure. Yet, in its failure to produce a more satisfactory account of stylistic change, the self-enclosed history of texts causes us to behave as if this evolutionary model still possessed explanatory force. If we are to develop more efficacious models, we must enlarge the scope of our consideration from the interrelationships of literary texts to include the historical and social environments in which they were composed or written, heard or read.

One promising link between literary works and their environments is through the aesthetics of reception, with its interest in the relationship between artistic styles and their literary publics. Hans-Robert Jauss has demonstrated the pertinence of reception-aesthetics to the analysis of medieval literature, in his theory that a literary work is received by contemporary readers or hearers within their historically-conditioned "horizon of expectations."[2] Still more relevant to a discussion of stylistic change are the theories of Arnold Hauser, with his recognition that audiences of different social composition (and different expectations and tastes) may co-exist or overlap or succeed each other.[3] In his view, writers within a period and even individual writers within their careers engage in various stylistic experiments, but a particular style is perpetuated when it finds its "point of attachment" in the encouragement of a socially-defined class or group of readers. So long as the position of this group is secure, the style it encourages is likely to persist; displacement of the group may have consequences for artistic style. One corollary of this view is that the emergence of a new style is likely to be associated with the emergence of a new group. Another is that the eclipse of a style is likely to be associated with a major deterioration in the position of the group. Hauser's is essentially a theory of reception. To be sure, his hypothesis of a connection between stylistic tendencies and the different social levels of a society has possible implications for the genesis of works, if we were to seek them.[4] Finally, though, he has most to tell us about why some styles, once available, flourish, while others, equally available, decline.

These introductory comments are meant to frame the discussion of a particular issue in literary history: the striking narrowing in the decades immediately following Chaucer's death of what has been called the "Chaucer tradition."[5] His literary legacy upon his death in 1400 was, after all, an almost incomparably rich one, encompassing the courtly *dits* and lays and love-visions of his early period; the morality and good counsel of Boethius and *Melibee* and *The Parson's Tale*; such richly reflective narratives as *Troilus* and *The Knight's Tale*; and finally the full stylistic variety inherent in the bold formal and thematic juxtapositions of *The Canterbury Tales*. Further, he did not lack for would-be and self-proclaimed followers and disciples, some of whom were to produce substantial quantities of verse. Yet one must be struck by the apparent inability of his artistic legatees to claim more than a small portion of their inheritance. As frequently noted, Chaucer's fifteenth-century followers neglect his mature works of greatest formal and thematic complexity, in favor of a comparatively narrow range of *dits amoureux* and visions in the manner of continental France. To be sure, manuscripts of *Troilus* and *The Canterbury Tales* were in active circulation throughout the period. Yet from the point of view of literary influence, these major works were, as R. H. Robbins has pointed out, essentially *sans issue*.[6]

General explanations for the inability of the writers of the early fifteenth century to draw upon the full Chaucer legacy have, of course, been offered. A particularly frequent observation is that no writer of Chaucer's genius was available to succeed him—a point which is undoubtedly correct, but still insufficient to explain the near-absence even of feeble attempts to emulate his confident juxtaposition of a full range of styles and themes. Other explanations at a broad level of generality involve such considerations as national and local turmoil and brigandage associated with the dynastic struggles of the century—but one doubts that writers of potential talent spent all or even any of their time worrying about which side to choose in the shifting factional struggles of Lancaster and York. My own thesis is that the first place to look in order to understand the vicissitudes of the Chaucer tradition in the early years of the fifteenth century is to the individual and collective histories of those fourteenth-century readers who most immediately encouraged his literary talent. In general harmony with the theories of Hauser, I would expect the long-term fortunes of a particular kind of poetry supported by a definable social group to be affected by any marked alterations in the composition or situation of that group.

I. The Dispersion of Chaucer's Primary Audience

In the last few years, several persons have independently arrived at new and remarkably similar conclusions about the social composition of Chaucer's primary or immediate audience. In "Chaucer's Audience," I argued that his immediate public or "point of attachment" was a group of persons in social situations rather comparable to his own—knights and esquires of the household of Richard II or otherwise prominent in court circles (such as Clifford, Clanvowe, Vache, Scogan, and Bukton), together with a handful of lawyers, chancery figures, and other civil servants (including Gower, Strode, and in some qualified respects Usk and later Hoccleve).[7] My argument was not that *all* of Chaucer's immediate readers came from such a milieu; one must concede the connections between *The Book of The Duchess* and the household of the aristocratic John of Gaunt and the possible interest of Richard II and Queen Anne in *The Legend of Good Women* as well as the possibility that certain of Chaucer's acquaintances among the merchant classes of London would have admired his work. Yet the unusual *concentration* of members of Chaucer's immediate audience in this one "circle" of courtiers and civil servants seemed to me quite clearly illustrated by references within his own poetry, by literary imitations (like John Clanvowe's *Boke of Cupide*), and by other explicitly literary activities (such as Lewis Clifford's interaction with both Deschamps and Chaucer). A very similar analysis of the social composition of Chaucer's immediate public was simultaneously advanced by Derek Pearsall, in two different publications. In "The 'Troilus' Frontispiece and Chaucer's Audience" he argued that "We might do well to look beyond the entourage of king and nobility for Chaucer's audience, to the multitude of household knights and officials, career diplomats and civil servants, who constitute the "court" in its wider sense, that is, the national administration and its metropolitan milieu.[8] This argument was further developed in "The Chaucer Circle," a subchapter of *Old and Middle English Poetry*, with particular reference to the so-called "Lollard Knights," to government and city officials like Hoccleve and Usk, and to London intellectual circles.[9] Additional support for the notion of such an immediate public has been offered in studies of Chaucer's epistles to Scogan and Bukton by Alfred David and R. T. Lenaghan, with their emphasis on the implied social relationship between Chaucer and the recipients of his good-humored verses.[10] Anne Middleton has endorsed essentially the same view in her "Chaucer's 'New Men' and the Good of Literature in the

Canterbury Tales," pursuing an analysis of the views of those pilgrims who held most in common with the position of his presumed audience.[11]

Given the amount of independent agreement on this view of Chaucer's audience, both in recent studies and in such background studies as those of T. F. Tout,[12] I feel justified in treating it as an established position.[13] On the reflection of several years, I would propose just one adjustment in the frame, involving a recognition of the rather large difference in the social situations of the Chamber knights (and especially the propertied ones like Montagu) and such lesser officials and clerks as Usk and Hoccleve. I would still assert the essential homogeneity of this group, especially since most of the Chamber knights attained landed security only through marriages related to their Court service. Yet the social profile of this group might best be expressed through R. T. Lenaghan's 'two-tiered' characterization of the social context of *Lenvoy a Scogan* as "the civil service of Richard II, a bureaucracy of clerks and a fellowship of gentlemen" (p. 46). With Montagu and Clifford and Beauchamp we encounter gentlemen who were something more than clerks, and with Usk and Hoccleve we encounter clerks who were just barely gentlemen. Yet, in a broad sense, all were civil servants of the court of Richard II or its environs. All or most would have been at least glancingly acquainted. All—with the possible exception of Montagu and one or two others— were primarily committed to English in a court which was still French-speaking in its highest social reaches.[14] All finally constituted a social and literary "circle" in an unusually pronounced and verifiable sense.

If one accepts the proposition that the existence of such a sympathetic social and literary circle had something to do with the breadth and confidence of Chaucer's mature poetic achievement, then one must also suppose that its dispersion would have had something to do with the failure of the transmission of Chaucer's achievement through the first decades of the fifteenth century. Certainly, such a dispersion took place, in the years immediately preceding and following Chaucer's death in 1400—not for any single reason, but for a combination of reasons.

One is always tempted to invoke the broadest political and cultural terms to explain a general phenomenon like the dispersion of a literary public. Here, for example, my own first impulse was to suggest that the dynastic uncertainties of the century had an unsettling effect on cultural life, or that the economic depression of the century somehow eroded the capacity of the lesser gentry for the enjoyment of *belles lettres.* Such broad theories turn out, however, to be of minimal assistance in addressing the particular problem of the dispersion of Chaucer's audience. After all, dynastic uncertainties did not prevent Henry Vl and others from endowing colleges at Cambridge and Oxford, or Humphrey Duke of Gloucester and others from patronizing classic letters, nor did the economic constraints of the century limit the copying and circulation of manuscripts of *The Canterbury Tales* or of Shirley's genteel anthologies. Clearly, a phenomenon as delicate as the status of a social and cultural group is best addressed not at the "macro" level of general causes, but at the "micro" level of individual careers.

Even when considering the watershed year of 1400, in which Henry IV consolidated his rule, one finds considerable variation in the situations of the members of Chaucer's circle. Some were old men, obviously ready in any event to retire from the political and cultural scene; some were dead already; some were forced into retirement as a result of the dynastic change; others—including Chaucer himself, in the last months of his life—made the transition smoothly or even advantageously.[15] Finally, I see no alternative but to look case-by-case at their individual circumstances in and around the year 1400. The persons whom I will consider include five Chamber-knights of Richard II (Sturry, Clifford, Clanvowe, Montagu, and Vache); two knights or esquires in royal service, in positions somewhat closer to Chaucer's own (Scogan, Bukton); an Oxford philosopher or London lawyer (Strode); and three fellow poets, one with ties to the rural gentry (Gower) and two civil servants less well placed than Chaucer himself (Usk, Hoccleve).

Richard Sturry was acquainted with Chaucer,[16] and frequently in the company of Clanvowe and Clifford. His literary involvements include his close acquaintance with Froissart and his willingness to act as intermediary between Froissart and Richard II for the presentation of a volume of Froissart's love poems,[17] as well as his own possession of a copy of the *Roman de la Rose*.[18] A half-generation older than Chaucer, he was evidently dead by 1395.[19]

As a subsidiary aspect of his distinguished diplomatic career, Lewis Clifford acted as a literary intermediary between Deschamps and Chaucer, who sent "par Clifford" the balade to "grant translateur, noble Geffroy Chaucier."[20] His will, in which he left devotional books including his "Book of Tribulacion" to his daughter and to his son-in-law Vache, is printed in Dugdale.[21] Since he was born after 1330, Clifford's withdrawal from the world of affairs would be explicable by age alone—though he evidently did experience at least some difficulty in securing his earlier, highly advantageous grants in the years between the accession of Henry IV and his own death in 1414.[22]

John Clanvowe, born in or about 1341, was an author in English of a devotional treatise and also of the first poem which might be called 'Chaucerian.' (Thomas Clanvowe, possibly his nephew, has been proposed for authorship as well, but the early fifteenth-century dating by Furnivall and Skeat based on the assumption that its title was borrowed from a work by Hoccleve seems unconvincing.)[23] Accepting the arguments of V. J. Scattergood, I would place its *terminus a quo* at about 1386, based on its imitation of *The Knight's Tale*, *The Parlement of Foules*, and *The Legend of Good Women*, and the *terminus ad quem* at 1391, the year of his death near Constantinople.[24]

John Montagu was born in 1351 and became the one undeniable aristocrat of the group when he was elevated to the Earldom of Salisbury in 1397. An author himself, he was praised by Christine de Pisan as not only a lover of poetry but a "gracieux ditteur," and his relations with her included an arrangement to raise her son Jean in his own household.[25] His own poems were presumably written in French, appropriately reflecting the fact that the King and the aristocracy of the court (as opposed to most of the Chamber knights and the remaining members of Chaucer's immediate circle) were almost undoubtedly speakers of French in preference to English, rather than the reverse.[26] All his poems are now lost, or at least lost in anonymity. Montagu was the one member of Chaucer's circle who may be said not to have made the transition to Henry's reign at all; at liberty through Henry's general policy of amnesty toward Richard's former dukes, Montagu lost his head as a result of his participation in the abortive uprising of January, 1400[27]—an event bitterly reported by Christine.

Clifford's son-in-law Philip de la Vache was the dedicatee of Chaucer's short poem of consolation "Truth," in which a certain warmth and a pun on the name Vache relieve the stern Boethian message. Vache was born in 1346, was a Chamber knight by 1374, and was active in Richard's service; the poem may have been written in response to reversals he suffered during Richard's eclipse, 1386-89.[28] While the summit of his career was probably his elevation to Garter knight in 1399 (following Clifford in 1398), he appears not to have suffered unduly by Henry's seizure of the crown. Rickert notes that "During the first part of Henry's reign, he seems to have been in active service, though there is no sign of any very close connection with the Court" (p. 220). He was exempted from formal duties, entering into a life of retirement in 1403, and died in 1408.

Henry Scogan, a Norfolk squire born about 1361, was (along with Bukton and Vache) addressed in one of the short balades which are so valuable for giving us a glimpse of the intimate and playfully serious manner in which Chaucer addressed his familiars. At any rate, Scogan was certainly closer to Chaucer's station than the Chamber knights—though even he was somewhat better situated than Chaucer, as suggested by Chaucer's Envoy in which Scogan is seen as kneeling "at the stremes hed," while Chaucer waits downstream. Also a poet of sorts, Scogan wrote a gravely serious "Moral Balade," apparently addressed to the sons of Henry IV and quoting Chaucer's "Gentilesse," three times identifying him as his 'mayster' in terms presumably less conventional than such epithets usually are.[29] The tradition has grown up, apparently from Scogan's reference to "My noble sones, and eek my lordes dere," that he was the tutor of Henry's sons, though no definitive evidence in such forms as issue rolls seems to exist.[30] Whatever our final conclusion on this point, he certainly seems to have flourished in the period between the accession of Henry and his death in 1407.

The debate has continued as to whether the Bukton who received Chaucer's good-humored balade on "the sorwe and wo that is in mariage" and who evidently knew other works including *The Wife of Bath's Prologue* was Sir Peter Bukton of York (1350-1414) or Sir Robert of Suffolk (d. 1408).[31] The points at dispute are admirably summarized by Robinson in his edition of Chaucer (p. 864), but need not be settled here. For this present purpose of determining the situation of Chaucer's audience around and after 1400, we might note only that each continued to flourish into the early years of the new century—though Sir Peter was more about the Court during Henry IV's reign than Sir Robert, most of whose activities centered in Suffolk.

Uncertainty likewise prevails as to whether Chaucer's "philosophical Strode" from the Envoy to *Troilus* was the Oxford philosopher (a fellow of Merton College before 1360 who took part in controversy with Wyclif), or the successful London lawyer who was sergeant of the City of London 1375-85 and who died in 1387, and whether these were in fact the same person. Ernest Kuhl has argued that they were, pointing out that Wyclif was associated in business dealings with the London lawyer, and that "Ralph Strode of Oxford disappears when a Ralph Strode of London appears on the records."[32] I am more inclined to agree with T. F. Tout, who points out that "if the one Ralph Strode did all these things he was a very remarkable man."[33] My own suspicion is that the two were separate, and that Chaucer's relations were with the London lawyer who was his associate in the Brembre faction.[34] Why then "philosophical Strode"? The answer to this question may reside in the characteristically wry tone of Chaucer's envoys and dedications. Occurring at the point of Chaucer's tonally-mixed withdrawal from his own poem, the dedication to "moral Gower" and "philosophical Strode" might well involve affectionate play. (Certainly, as Alfred David has pointed out to me in conversation, the reference to "moral Gower" may be consistent with his light twitting of Gower in the Prologue to *The Man of Law's Tale*.) Perhaps the reference to "philosophical Strode" is therefore intended in a spirit of partial jest to associate his lawyer-acquaintance with the famous academic namesake. Whatever conclusion one draws, however, again has limited applicability to the subject at hand; the lawyer's death in 1387 puts him out of the picture before the end of the century, and the Oxford philosopher (if separate) is unlikely to have lived much longer than that.

"Moral Gower" and Chaucer may or may not have quarreled, as an earlier generation of critics supposed, but they certainly interacted. John Fisher has well shown the influence of Gower on the scope and moral themes of *The Canterbury Tales*,[35] and Alfred David has described the ultimately friendly tonalities running through Chaucer's dissection of Gower's more genteel poetical standards.[36] The slightly competitive currents running through Gower's admonition to Chaucer at the end of the 1392-93 version of the *Confessio* and Chaucer's attribution to the Man of Law of mock dismay at the "unkynde abhomynacions" inherent in subjects treated by Gower are not exactly friendly in the easy vein of Chaucer's poems to Scogan and Bukton, but they certainly argue for an important literary association in the 1380's and 1390's. Of course, Gower was some ten years older than Chaucer,[37] and—with the exception of some revisions to the *Confessio* and some overtly Lancastrian political poems at the end of the century—had finished the most active segment of his literary career by 1390, when he was about 60 years of age. Although he outlived Chaucer by some eight years, these were not eight years of literary activity, or years in which he would have been likely to attract a discipleship. Although Gower had laid a foundation for Lancastrian favor in his 1392-93 revision of the *Confessio* and in the *Cronica* and other poems at the end of the century, by 1400 his literary career was through.

While more closely aligned with the country gentry than with the court, and hence not exactly of Chaucer's immediate milieu, Gower did share Chaucer's rank of *esquire* and the two may be thought approximate social equals. If one accepts a "tiered" conception of Chaucer's public, with gentlemen at one extreme and clerks at the other, then both Gower and Chaucer might have fallen fairly near the social middle—though in the final analysis each was more gentleman than clerk. In a lower tier of those who were clerks first and hardly gentlemen at all were Chaucer's disciples and fellow writers Usk and Hoccleve. While each was employed about or by the court, neither was as securely situated as was Chaucer himself. As with Chaucer, neither was primarily a writer; Usk was deeply and rather shadily involved in London faction-politics in the 1380's, and Hoccleve was a clerk of Privy Seal from 1387-88 until 1427. Yet each, to a more considerable extent than Chaucer, sought security or advancement from his writing. Writing of Usk in the *DNB*, Henry Bradley notes that "a florid eulogy of 'Troilus and Creseide' is introduced in an awkward manner which suggests that it was written for a special purpose,"[38] and this aura of special purpose clings to the productions of both. Usk's *Testament* did him no good, and he was beheaded in 1388; Hoccleve, nearly two generations younger, may have enjoyed some modest patronage as a result of his writing, but he seems never to have known ease between his birth around 1370 and his death sometime in the 1440's.[39] Each claimed to have been a follower of Chaucer, and Hoccleve claimed to be a friend. While claims of special intimacy may have sprung only from a desire for legitimation,[40] each was nevertheless much influenced by the example of Chaucer's poetry, and Usk in the 1380's and Hoccleve thereafter may be thought to typify one element of Chaucer's literary circle.

Despite the necessary brevity of this survey, it illustrates the instability of any literary "circle" or "primary public." Few members of Chaucer's circle outlived him, and fewer still continued to be active after his death. Sturry was dead by 1395; Clifford was inactive after 1400; Clanvowe died in 1391; Montagu was beheaded in 1400; Vache was inactive after 1403; Scogan wrote his "Moral Balade" during the reign of Henry IV, but died in 1407; neither Strode is likely to have lived beyond 1387; Gower was inactive after 1400; Usk died in 1388; Hoccleve alone carried on in vigorous fashion after the first decade of the fifteenth century.

The reader might suspect that I am on the brink of the unexceptional observation that one's friends and associates die, many around the time of one's death and all sooner or later. Certainly, the impact of retirement and death on Chaucer's immediate circle is similar to that which we would expect in the case of any writer. But the crucial question is not whether Chaucer's immediate public changed composition in the way that any public must, but whether it or some similarly-composed public *survived at all* into the early years of the fifteenth century. The distinction I am drawing here is between a public which renews itself through reasonable turnover in its membership, and a public which ceases to exist. Available evidence suggests that Chaucer's public did indeed fail to renew itself, and that by the early years of the fifteenth century it had ceased to exist as a public likely or able to provide a setting encouraging to the creation of literary works. The end of the active careers of Chaucer's associates signals also the end of a particular literary milieu.

While the Lancastrian supplantation of Richard II did not eliminate Chaucer's circle overnight, it did create new circumstances which threatened the maintenance of such a circle. Even though Henry IV adopted a policy unusual in its clemency toward former followers of Richard,[41] the years between 1399 and 1408 were nevertheless marked by an unusual number of requests for exemptions from duties of state, and (as Edith Rickert has pointed out) these exemptions include many names of Richard's courtiers.[42] Presumably the high rate of such retirements was assured after the abortive rebellion of the former dukes in which Montagu perished in 1400, but other aspects of Lancastrian rule also assured the supplantation of Richard's followers. As E. F. Jacob has indicated (p. 439), the Lancastrians were always a virtual "pauper government" with respect to funds, and poverty undoubtedly contributed to Henry IV's reliance on his own duchy servants for administrative assistance (pp. 30-31). Just as his administrative support tended to come less from the court than his own duchy, so did his counselors tend to come more from the ranks of the nobility of the kingdom than from a palace entourage; Jacob comments (p. 6) that the policy of the nobility in the early years of Henry's reign was "to get the king out of the hands of a courtier or palace entourage, to emphasize his dependence on a ministerial nobility." Reinvolvement of the nobility—as well as the prolonged absences of Henry V in France and the long minority of Henry VI—led to the increasing importance of the continual council of magnates as the true governing authority of the country (pp. 426-36). While the mechanism of a council headed by the king or a lieutenant or a protector turned out to be reasonably efficient, it did not really constitute or encourage a court in any way similar to that of Richard II. A minor aspect of this shift of the institutions of governance away from the court—but a major one for understanding the disappearance of anything resembling a "Chaucer circle" in the fifteenth century—is the eclipse of the Chamber. According to Tout, even Richard had not sought to use his Chamber knights for autocratic purposes, and from the end of his reign until the establishment of the Tudor monarchy the Chamber was of limited importance in the government of the realm.[43] Thus, throughout most of the fifteenth century, the institution that had been more central than any other in drawing together a group of persons sympathetic to Chaucer's poetry virtually ceased to be.

The breakup of Chaucer's circle undermined the possibility of familiar poetry of the sort that Chaucer wrote for his circle. Whether the familiarity is explicit, as in the good-humored epistles to Scogan and Bukton,[44] or implicit, as in the created voice in which he addresses the audience of the *Tales*, Chaucer normally wrote within a secure sense of an audience of social equals and near-equals—who despite occasional unease with the bolder of his stylistic experiments—constituted a sympathetic and receptive group. Only rarely, as in "Complaint to his Purse" and some of the longer works possibly directed to royalty or aristocracy such as *The Book of the Duchess, The Legend of Good Women,* and *Melibee* can he be said to have written for a "special purpose." But, if Chaucer wrote for a generally sympathetic circle, his most immediate continuators give us the impression of writing from the outside, looking in. If Chaucer addressed his clear superiors only occasionally and obliquely, poets of the first decade of the fifteenth century like Henry Scogan and—especially—Hoccleve and Lydgate seem to address them constantly and explicitly. For, as Derek Brewer comments of Hoccleve and Lydgate, "they were merely on the fringes of that courtly centre of power and prestige of which Chaucer was a full member."[45] With Hoccleve's constant quest for security and Lydgate's attempt to become, in effect, England's first professional poet,[46] each seems constantly to write with "special purpose." Occasionally, such purposes were a spur to ingenuity, as in Hoccleve's confessional "Male Regle" (in which repentant self-disclosure is mobilized as an argument for payment of his annuity, to cure both body and purse) and his arresting "Complaint" (which candidly addresses the subject of his mental illness, in part with the motive of underscoring his return to good health and full capacity). More often, though, writing in the explicit hope of preferment or for noble patrons had the effect of flattening tone and discouraging experiment, as in Lydgate's lengthy commissioned translations and compositions for Henry V, Humphrey Duke of Gloucester, the Earl of Salisbury, and others.

No one would argue that Hoccleve or Lydgate, however "encouraged" by a sympathetic literary circle, could have equalled the range and stylistic variety of Chaucer's later poetry. Even if something very close to Chaucer's own circle had continued to exist, it would presumably not have been open to Hoccleve or Lydgate in the particular sense in which it had been to Chaucer, with all his points of professional and social entry to the court. Yet one can still imagine certain benefits to the poetry of Hoccleve or Lydgate if either had been able to find a sympathetic circle. If Hoccleve had chosen to write for his "fellows of the prive seale"[47] or if Lydgate had identified a congenial audience among monks at Bury and clerics at Oxford, their poetry might not have become more "Chaucerian," but it would have benefited from some of the confident familiarity of Chaucer's tone.

II. THE BROADENING OF CHAUCER'S FIFTEENTH-CENTURY AUDIENCE AND THE NARROWING OF HIS TRADITION

The successful author of any century must experience (and endure) the transition from a "primary" or intended public to a larger, "secondary" audience which receives and enjoys the author's works in circumstances over which he or she has little control. This transition was, of course, underscored in the case of the later medieval author, who had some first-hand contact with a primary public (whether through oral performance or through loaned or presentation manuscripts) and for whom the wider distribution of works in manuscript form must have been a disjunction indeed. It was further underscored in Chaucer's own case, because of the rapid dissolution around 1400 of his immediate circle, which effectively ceased to be available either as a "point of attachment" for new work in his manner or as a continuing locus of his own fifteenth-century readership. Chaucer's works had undoubtedly begun to find their way to an enlarged secondary audience during the last years of his life, but this natural process was abruptly and inevitably accelerated by his death, the dispersion of his primary audience, and the formation of an altered public for literature in the early years of the fifteenth century. The members of Chaucer's secondary audience were at once more widely distributed geographically and more disparate socially than Chaucer's primary audience, and more narrow in their taste for particular facets of Chaucer's poetic achievement. The narrowing of their attraction to particular facets of the Chaucer legacy is (as critics have frequently observed) evidenced both in the kinds of "Chaucerian" poetry they encouraged and in the elements of Chaucer's own corpus which they apparently enjoyed. Paradoxically, for all their increased geographical and social latitude, the members of this new audience seem to have inclined strongly toward works which they perceived in some usually nebulous sense as "courtly" or "of the court."

While the "courtly" style of life was obviously something of a fiction in the first decades of the fifteenth century, it by no means ceased altogether. Actually, it was radically decentralized, into the households of the brothers of Henry V, of Queen Margaret, and of magnates such as the Duke of Suffolk. Much of the original poetry written in the period certainly seems courtly in its points of reference, to the extent that it strikes the reader as coterie verse, written for a very small court circle or cluster of court circles—though it remains oddly lacking in evidence of any particular milieu.[48] Robbins, who has spent considerable time reviewing the original poetry of the period, characterizes the court verse of the fifteenth century as comprising two or three hundred short lyrics structured on the lover's salutation or complaint, together with a cluster of longer love poems extending these devices, all composed "for intellectual and social diversion and amorous dalliance among a miniscule elite group."[49] The presumption that such poems were directed at such a group is fortified by the character of the "Chaucerian" poetry written soon after his death: for example, Hoccleve's "Letter of Cupid" (1402) is directed at a court audience which is figured by the "gentil kinrede" of subject-lovers which he addresses, and Scogan's "Moral Balade" (1406-07) is addressed to the sons of Henry IV. The fact that such noble *ditteurs* as Charles d'Orleans and the Duke of Suffolk were active participants in the perpetuation of this tradition of love-poetry (admixed with small doses of morality and advice to princes) further supports the notion that such verse was composed for and by a very restricted social coterie.

Still, while verse embodying courtly views may have been produced within a coterie, the audience for such verse ultimately extended well beyond such boundaries. Even R. F. Green, who has recently presented an extremely vigorous argument for the courtly locus of production and enjoyment of fifteenth-century poetry, is prepared to concede a merchant-class element within the apparently courtly audience—with the proviso that the taste of the middle-class segment was indistinguishable from that of other, socially-superior members.[50] The most useful conceptualization of the situation which I have encountered is that of Derek Pearsall, who distinguishes between 'court poetry' produced in and for a court environment and 'courtly poetry' reflecting its values but disseminated among an enlarged public.[51] Even though productions of court or courtly households were undoubtedly seized upon for dissemination, the ultimate audience of "Chaucerian" poetry in the fifteenth century was undoubtedly "courtly" in Pearsall's sense rather than strictly "of the court." Such an expanded audience is apparently envisioned by John Shirley, who aimed the mid-fifteenth century manuscript compilations of his scriptorium at a general audience of "bothe the gret and the commune" (i.e., the "commonality" or middle class), and who—while mentioning the nobility in his prefaces—seems to have been well aware of the potential market opening for him in the emerging middle-class reading public.[52]

When this enlarged, socially-mixed audience encountered Chaucer, its affection or nostalgia for the courtly style apparently limited its attraction to many aspects of his work. With Muscatine, I view the essence of Chaucer's mature poetic achievement as a poetic style which "has within it an extraordinary variety, which derives from the great range of Chaucer's themes and the way in which his style supports or expresses them."[53] Certainly, early fifteenth-century writers were not unaware of the breadth of his stylistic and thematic range. While Lydgate and others most typically praise him as a "noble rethor," Lydgate was also capable of describing the range of *The Canterbury Tales* in this fashion:

> Some of desport / some of moralite
> Some of knyghthode / love and gentillesse,
> And some also of parfit holynesse,
> And some also in soth / of Ribaudye. . . .[54]

Yet in point of fact, the range of possible *endytings* described by Lydgate was narrowed in the practice of professed fifteenth-century Chaucerians to some "moralite" (in the form of advice to princes), some "holynesse" (in the form of saints' lives and related genres), and a considerable amount of "knyghthode / loue and gentillesse." "Desport"—let alone "ribaudye"—was out the window, and only a very narrow segment of Chaucer's literary heritage was claimed by those to whom he had bequeathed it.[55]

I will not repeat Robbins' and Green's previously-cited characterizations of the conservatism of mid-fifteenth century "courtly" literature, with its stress on traditional themes and its emphasis on those genres treating *fin amour,* advice to princes, and morality. I might note, however, that a further indication of the conservatism of the audience for courtly literature is the relatively small number of new pieces which actually found their way into circulation. One notices in the Shirlean compilations, for example, how little of his material was recent or written especially for his audience. His assurances to his readers run in the opposite direction, emphasizing virtuous material:

> As wryten haue thees olde clerkis
> That been appreuede in alle hir werkis
> By oure eldres here to fore. . . . [56]

All medieval writers agree that poetry is intended to foster memory of past achievements, but Shirley appears to accept this commonplace in a particularly literal and restrictive sense. The backward-looking quality of Shirley's selections is apparent in all of his manuscripts, such as MS. Addit. 16165 which includes the following works: Chaucer's translation of Boethius; a translation of Trevisa's *Nichodemus*; Edward Duke of York's hunting treatise *Master of Game*; a prose *Regula sacerdotis*; Lydgate's *Complaint of the Black Knight*; and "other balades" including Lydgate's *Dream of a Lover*, Chaucer's *Anelida and Arcite* in two parts, Lydgate's *Invocation to St. Anne* and *Departing of Thomas Chaucer* and other short poems. (Closest to contemporaneity on this list is Lydgate, who may have survived as a very old man when the manuscript was compiled. But Lydgate was recognized by his contemporaries as a writer in traditional modes, and his major achievements were by this point far behind him.)

Attention to little known works like *Anelida and Arcite* might seem strange, but it is part of a pattern which emerges as we look at the range of Chaucer's pieces in existing Shirlean compilations: *Anelida* is included three times, along with the *Complaint of Mars,* the *Complaint of Venus*, the *Complaint unto Pity, Fortune, Truth, Gentilesse,* and the *Complaint of Chaucer to His Purse.* Needless to say, Shirley shows no desire in such selections to challenge his audience of "all thoo that beon gentile of birthe or of condicions,"[57] but rather to assist their aspirations, to lead them in a reassuring way to an already-existing world of taste and gentility which they seek but have not previously known.

The narrowing of the Chaucer tradition reflected in the short poems chosen for fifteenth-century circulation seems at first to be contradicted by the relatively large number of surviving manuscripts of the complete or nearly-complete *Canterbury Tales.*[58] The existence of some sixty of these manuscripts would seem to indicate at least some continued capacity for enjoyment of the full range of his achievement throughout the century. These manuscripts seem, as well, to have reached a broader social range of readers than ever heard or read his poetry during his lifetime. Yet an examination of the fifteenth-century manuscript tradition of *The Canterbury Tales* raises as much doubt as encouragement about the nature of their reception in the fifteenth century.

The dispersion of Chaucer's late fourteenth-century literary circle is reflected in patterns of manuscript ownership. While no single group or locale can be identified through the evidence of early manuscripts, the six reasonably complete surviving manuscripts of the *Tales* probably written before 1420 all seem to have been owned by persons with social positions more or less similar to those of Chaucer's original circle. Evidence gathered by Manly and Rickert connects El with the Duke of Exeter or the Duke of Bedford (and Hg with the Ellesmere scribe), Ha[4] with a "person of importance who had it made in a shop," Cp and La with the Burley family, and Dd with the Hungerford family, whose membership included the Lord Treasurer Walter Hungerford (d. 1449).[59] Thereafter, the spread of manuscript ownership through additional strata of society was rapid. In the second half of the century, owners range from Richard III (then Duke of Gloucester) through a variety of merchants, auditors, and clerks. This broadening-out in the direction of the urban middle classes is most visible in fifteenth-century wills, of which the first two instances are a bequest of the *Tales* from Richard Sotheworth to John Stopyndon (both clerks in Chancery) and from John Frinchele to William Holgrave (both citizens and tailors of London).[60]

Lydgate imagined in his *Troy Book* that adept readers of *Troilus* (who "konnyng hath his tracis for to swe") might turn up "in borwe or toun, village or cite."[61] While his is an undoubtedly sentimentalized view, the fact that fifteenth-century manuscripts of the *Tales* received wide social and geographical circulation might be taken as evidence of heightened receptivity on the part of enlightened individuals. Other evidence suggests, though, that the *Tales* were preserved reasonably intact more out of respect for Chaucer's secure reputation as a founder and upholder of the institution of English letters, than because the full range of his literary achievement was necessarily enjoyed. Certainly, all modern readers are struck by the traditionalism inherent in fifteenth-century judgments of Chaucer as translator, compiler, rhetorician, and refiner of the language, and Shirley further develops this view in his headnote for the mid-century MS. Harley 7333 of the *Tales* in which he presents them as "stories of olde tymis passed ... wiche beon compilid ... by the laureal and moste famous poete that euer was to fore him as in themvelisshing of oure rude moders englisshe tonge."[62] Of course, the real question is how individual readers would have responded to individual tales, or to the mix of tales, and here extremely limited evidence requires the most cautious evaluation. Only one fifteenth-century reader— Jean of Angoulême—has actually left traces of his experience, in the form of comments written in the Paris MS. fonds anglais 39 of the Bibliothèque Nationale, which was written under his direction. In a separate discussion, I have suggested that his tastes were quite traditional, including a strong endorsement of *The Knight's Tale* as "valde bona" (presumably for its use of familiar materials and balancing of *solace* and *sentence*) and rejection as "valde absurda" of the more experimental *Squire's Tale* and *Canon's Yeoman's Tale*, as well as other tales more lopsided in the direction either of *solace* or *sentence*.[63] Fortunately, more particular evidence of the taste both of Chaucer's immediate fourteenth-century circle and his enlarged fifteenth-century public has been developed by Charles A. Owen, Jr. and by Daniel S. Silvia.[64]

Basing his conclusions on the number of independent textual traditions of individual tales existing at the time of Chaucer's death or soon after, Owen has gauged the relative popularity of different tales. Allowing for such factors as probable date of completion (with the earlier tales having more possibility of independent circulation), he finds that the most popular tales among Chaucer's contemporaries were *The Franklin's Tale, Prioress' Tale, Pardoner's Tale, Shipman's Tale, Canon's Yeoman's Tale,* and *Miller's Tale.* On the other hand, tales with few independent textual traditions, indicating that they circulated mainly within collections, include *The Man of Law's Tale, Friar's Tale, Summoner's Tale, Melibeus, Squire's Tale, Clerk's Tale, Second Nun's Tale, Monk's Tale, Manciple's Tale,* and *Parson's Tale.* These findings are in sharp contrast to the evidence of fifteenth-century popularity which Owen and more recently Silvia derive from fifteenth-century "anthologies" of free-standing tales. The most frequent appearances in the course of the fifteenth century belong to *The Clerk's Tale* (6), *Prioress' Tale* (5), and *Melibeus* (5), together with *The Second Nun's Tale* (2), *Monk's Tale* (2), and *Parson's Tale* (2). *The Franklin's Tale* appears only once and *The Pardoner's Tale, Shipman's Tale, Canon's Yeoman's Tale,* and *Miller's Tale* not at all. In his fuller analysis of this fifteenth-century phenomenon, Silvia points out that all the anthologized pieces belong to one of two traditions, which he labels "courtly" and "moral" (p. 155). Certainly, a massive shift in taste has occurred, from tales which tend to the generically and thematically problematic to tales which support traditional assumptions both in their firm delineation of genre and in their theme.

Opposing the tales of the Franklin, Pardoner, Shipman, Canon's Yeoman, and Miller to those of the Clerk, Monk, Second Nun, and Parson, and to *Melibee,* one immediately notices several distinctions between the two clusters.

Granting that Chaucer always adjusts his sources in one way or another and is never content merely to translate or adapt, one may still divide his tales according to the relative independence with which he structures them. By this standard, his most 'original' tales would be those of the Squire (even though written in the exotic traditions of *Floris and Blancheflour* and other popular narratives), the Franklin (for all its pretense of following the form of the Breton lay), and the Canon's Yeoman, and perhaps those of the Miller (with its elaboration of the French *fabliau* tradition and its possible new fusion of two pre-existing plots), the Merchant, and Chaucer's own *Sir Thopas* (which, as generalized parody, follows no one analogue). By the same standard, Chaucer's least independent tales would include, in addition to *Melibeus,* those of the Knight, Man of Law, Clerk, Physician, Prioress,

Monk, Second Nun, Manciple, and Parson (though, as in *The Miller's Tale*, Chaucer may have fused two free-standing sources in this latter treatise). The point of this distinction is not, of course, to praise or blame Chaucer according to some anachronistic standard of "originality," since in *The Knight's Tale* and elsewhere his perspective on very authoritative material is fully original. The point is to say something about the audience's own previous familiarity with the materials of the tales popular in the two centuries. The tales most circulated in the fourteenth century—including those of the Franklin, Canon's Yeoman, and Miller—would have been among Chaucer's most independent and would have possessed an effect of "first encounter," with all the charged excitement which accompanies such an experience. The tales most anthologized in the fifteenth century—including those of the Clerk, Monk, Second Nun, and Parson, as well as *Melibee*—were established in numerous versions, and would have provided the relatively more comfortable experience which accompanies a re-encounter with generally familiar materials.

A parallel observation may be made of the generic boundaries of the tales popular in the respective centuries. Those tales popular in the fourteenth century tend toward deliberate frustration of generic expectations. *The Franklin's Tale* puts more responsibility on its audience than the lays which it purports to follow, including such open-ended questions as, "which was the mooste fre . . .?" (V, 1620). *The Pardoner's Tale* is contained within a frame which renders its impact deliberately equivocal. *The Shipman's Tale* has a hard satiric edge, less prominent in its analogues, in its insistence on the commercialization of human relations. The list could be extended, but the point is clear; each of these tales pushes against its audience's generic expectations in ways which (depending on the reader) have the potential to stimulate, to challenge, to annoy. The tales popular in the fifteenth century tend, on the other hand, to be among the most generically stable that Chaucer wrote. *The Clerk's Tale* is perhaps more an extended exemplum or simply a "moral narrative" than the *historia/hystoire* which it is styled in its continental sources, but as an internationally-known tale with an interpreter/narrator who frequently intervenes to help his audience over the rough spots, it would have occasioned no particular interpretive unease for its audience. *Melibee* was likewise an international success when Chaucer took it in hand, and even an audience encountering it for the first time would have found it familiar as a book of good counsel, leavened with certain allegorical/spiritual undertones. The patterning of the tragedies in *The Monk's Tale* is of course, so predictable that it provokes a revolt in the pilgrim audience. *The Second Nun's Tale* is a mainstream "lif and passioun" of St. Cecilia, following the dictates of the hagiographical genre and rehearsing one of the best-known stories of all. While somewhat more crowded with different kinds of content than the average vernacular sermon, *The Parson's Tale* would still have struck its audience as a coherently-formed "treatise." In short, the works popular in the fifteenth century fulfill rather than deny the general horizon of generic expectations with which their audience would have approached them, or which they evoke in their own opening lines.

The scope of this article hardly permits an adequate analysis of the content of these ten tales, but some generalizations seem possible. The tales popular in the fourteenth century all offer alternatives to social hierarchies, sworn oaths, established bonds. Of course, Chaucer's perspective differs considerably from tale to tale. *The Franklin's Tale* is essentially idealized, as *gentillesse* dissolves both the domination/submission inherent in marriage and the formal obligation of the unintended oath. *The Miller's Tale* is comic, with sexual desire acting as a triumphant leveller. In the more critical and satiric *Pardoner's Tale*, *Shipman's Tale*, and *Canon's Yeoman's Tale*, financial greed overthrows ties of friendship and hospitality and the natural hierarchy of intellect. The tales popular in the fifteenth century tend instead to reaffirm *obeisance* and subordination to the authority of lord and husband (*The Clerk's Tale*) or to Fortune (*The Monk's Tale*) or to God (*The Second Nun's Tale*) or to the domination of one's own reason over unruly impulse (*Melibee*, *The Parson's Tale*).

From the evidence of these most valued tales, two different sorts of audiences would seem to be implied—the earlier prepared to be surprised by new turns of plot and ways of shaping material and challenged by interrogation of received beliefs and values, and the later drawn more to familiar materials treated within stable generic frames and to thematic reaffirmation of divine, social, and inner hierarchies. The counter-instance to this generalization would seem, however, to be *The Prioress' Tale*, which Owen reports as the second most popular in the fourteenth century and as the most popular in the fifteenth century. The popularity of this one tale with two different audiences may simply stand as a warning of the hazards of generalization, but it may also suggest that different historically and socially defined audiences can esteem a single work of art for different reasons. *The Prioress' Tale* has been controversial in the twentieth century because critics have argued for two essentially different ways in which it can be read. One group of critics has treated the tale as a critique of the Prioress' shallow values, as revealed in the contradiction between her profession of Christian love and her grisly, excessive, and very unloving anti-Semitism.[65] Another has seen it in historically relative terms, as an embodiment of prevalent values and literary conventions of Chaucer's time.[66] In the face of this apparent contradiction, I would suggest that the tale might have been read in two different ways—that Chaucer's immediate circle might have considered it a deliberate heightening of the devices of the miracle of the Virgin (with the anti-Semitism one of the devices so heightened) in order to expose the narrowness of the Prioress,[67] while his enlarged fifteenth-century audience might have accepted it as a generically stable and fully satisfying instance of such a miracle. Such a divergence would be consistent with other evidence that Chaucer's immediate circle prized his moments of independent perspective on literary tradition, while his fifteenth-century audience inclined more toward those tales which least challenge traditional forms and values.

The obviously narrowed spectrum of taste among Chaucer's fifteenth-century readers separates them both from his primary audience and from academic audiences of today. Yet, the fact that this fifteenth-century audience found works within *The Canterbury Tales* to circulate and enjoy tells us something about the source of Chaucer's continuing appeal. The perpetuation of any work beyond the immediate social context in which it was composed must always depend on its capacity to disclose new sides of itself to subsequent readerships. Seen in this light, the locus of the "classic" or "timeless" quality in an *oeuvre* like Chaucer's might not be its capacity to speak in a single voice to subsequent readerships, but its capacity through inner complexity of form and theme to continue revealing new and pertinent aspects of itself. The presence in *The Canterbury Tales* of works which commanded the interest of Chaucer's traditionally-inclined fifteenth-century public reflects a stylistic and thematic breadth which has enabled him to attract loyal followers in each of seven very different centuries.

That Chaucer's fifteenth-century readers sought, and were able to find, different facets of his work than those esteemed by his immediate circle seems apparent enough. The difficult task is explaining *why* this new audience should have sought different values in an established work. Such an explanation must take us outside the work itself, to the social circumstances of Chaucer's fifteenth-century readership. Having earlier expressed a preference for "micro" explanations, I would prefer to treat the social situations of Chaucer's fifteenth-century readers as the sum of their individual careers. Limitations of space and evidence, however, will compel a more general level of consideration.

III. Some Tentative Explanations

According to evidence of the provenance of manuscripts of *The Canterbury Tales* assembled by Manly and Rickert, the mid-fifteenth century audience for Chaucer's work consisted not only of aristocracy, but members of the landed gentry scattered throughout England and Wales, and more than a sprinkling of prosperous merchants of London and other cities.[68] No century offers a unitary experience for all classes of persons in all decades. Most English peasants, for example, modestly increased their prosperity in the course of the century. But for those members of the landed gentry and the merchant classes most likely to read Chaucer, the mid-century was a period of pessimism, hardening class lines, and decreased economic opportunity.

M. M. Postan, whose overview of the field has been corrected in particulars but retains its broad authority, sees the fifteenth century in England as "an age of recession, arrested economic development and declining national income."[69] In the cases of both merchants and gentry, he sees a new self-protectiveness, a new concern for prerogatives, and less of the apparent optimism of their fourteenth-century counterparts. As for the merchants, Postan says that they "responded to the stability and recession of trade in the way of all merchants. They adopted the policy of regulation and restriction, impeding the entry of new recruits into commerce and attempting to share out the available trade."[70] Some features of this new restrictiveness were: monopoly and protective regulation of trade, the closing of ranks by guildsmen against guild membership or control of production by journeymen laborers, and increased middle-class landlordism.[71] These steps and others led to the formation in fifteenth-century English cities of what J. W. Thompson calls an "urban patriciate"—a closed class, practically a legal class, with mercantile and ultimately social and emotional ties with the old landed aristocracy.[72] For their part, the landed gentry responded to economic adversity by a rear-guard action in defense of traditional privileges. As Postan says, "in an age of dwindling agricultural profits seigneurial revenues derived from feudal rights and privileges were all the more valuable and all the more worth fighting for"—a situation which led to much of the "political gangsterism" of the time.[73]

Confronted with the political and economic vicissitudes of the fifteenth century, the urban merchant patriciate and the country gentry did their best to stay out of trouble. Postan pictures the urban merchant classes "in a state of solid conservative prosperity devoid of both the prizes and the penalties of the more adventurous and speculative ages."[74] C. L. Kingsford argues that the Pastons were an unusual case and that the life of one country gentry is better represented in the Stonor letters, in which "there is little suggestion of anything that broke the quiet tenor of a country gentleman's life."[75] But this kind of tranquillity has its price; a price which Kingsford reveals in what he intends as a reassuring account of the life of the Stonors:

> [T]he *Stonor Letters* afford us no evidence to suggest that either social disorder or civil war necessarily affected the lives of those who through their prudence or good fortune were not entangled in either. What we do see is a picture of the country gentleman busy with the management of his estates, taking his share in the work of local administration, living in friendly intercourse with neighbours in like circumstances to himself, growing rich with his profits as a sheep grazier, and spending money on the rebuilding of his house and laying out of his garden. Thomas Stonor had the wit to keep clear of politics; though on two occasions he was summoned for service by Edward IV, he apparently avoided compliance. He had friends in both political camps . . . but during the Lancastrian restoration managed to compromise himself with neither.[76]

Stonor's kind of prudence—together with unabashed self-interest—enabled many urban merchants and country gentry to consolidate their positions despite the hard times of the fifteenth century. It enabled some of them to own libraries and perhaps to read books. These are the people who, after all, were to form the backbone of the public for the printed book before the end of the century. But their social situation evidently disposed them to poetry in a narrower stylistic register, embodying a more restricted range of themes, than that which appealed to Chaucer's primary audience. McFarlane and Hulbert have documented the remarkable upward social mobility of Richard II's Chamber knights and of the esquires of Edward's and Richard's households,[77] and I feel comfortable in connecting the volatility of their social situations to an attraction to stylistic and thematic juxtaposition, to unresolved debate, and to the challenge of the new.[78] By the same reasoning, a readership composed of persons with a demonstrated interest in consolidating their class positions might well have inclined away from stylistic and thematic experiment. At any rate, their choices would seem to indicate a diminished capacity for all sorts of contradiction. *The Franklin's Tale* with its implied critique of *maistrie* was supplanted by *The Clerk's Tale* with its uncritical endorsement of *maistrie* and subordination in all forms; the figurative and literal "overextensions" of *The Miller's Tale* in which requittal in all forms is the ethic shared by all, were supplanted by Prudence's plea for measured self-restraint in *Melibee*; *The Prioress' Tale* was probably, as I have already suggested, read at generic face value, in a new and less taxing way. Certainly, the themes embodied in the short tales of Chaucer most popular in the fifteenth century—of mastery and subordination, of self-mastery, of the consistency of divine and earthly law—would seem highly congenial to persons in the process of constituting themselves as members of legally-sanctioned classes. Likewise, the implied continuity inherent in a return to love-visions and other genres firmly established in fourteenth-century precedent would have had its appeal for persons more interested in maintaining than in changing their status in a troubled world.

IV. CONCLUSION

Virtually every literary historian writing in the first half of this century suggests that Chaucer "exhausted" his tradition, or that his tradition had somehow "exhausted itself."[79] My own view is that artists do not exhaust traditions, nor do traditions exhaust themselves. If we suppose that Chaucer's experiments with stylistic and thematic juxtaposition were a central element of his legacy to the fifteenth century, we have no reason to suppose that the fifteenth century failed to claim them because they were used up or worn out. We can see from the richly successful experiments with stylistic juxtaposition and multi-leveled plot in fifteenth-century biblical and moral drama and in early Elizabethan tragedies like *Horestes* and *Cambyses* that the exploration of formal possibilities similar to those of Chaucer's later poetry was always subject to independent revival under new and different circumstances. Any kind of exhaustion which occurred at the beginning of the fifteenth century was not in Chaucer's poetic tradition, which remained charged with undiminished potentiality, but in the capacity of audiences to appreciate the full range of his tradition and in the capacity of new artists, working without public esteem or encouragement, to perpetuate that tradition.

Such an exhaustion, not of literary potentiality but of capacity for appreciation of Chaucer's achievement, occurred in the fifteenth century. Its immediate cause was the replacement of a closely-knit primary audience with a far-flung and disparate secondary audience. A related cause was a social situation which evidently caused the members of this secondary audience to seek different qualities in Chaucer's verse than those which had appealed to his fourteenth-century circle, and to encourage different qualities in verse written by others. This secondary audience regarded Chaucer's poetry differently not because of fatigue or capriciousness, but because of real changes in its own composition and its own world.

NOTES

1. I am paraphrasing a comment made by Ralph Cohen at an Indiana University symposium on narrative, October 1980.

2. "Literary History as a Challenge to Literary Theory," in *New Directions in Literary History*, ed. Ralph Cohen (Baltimore: Johns Hopkins UP, 1974), pp. 11-41.

3. "Art History Without Names," in *The Philosophy of Art History* (Meridian Books, 1963), pp. 207-36, 253-76.

4. Implicit in Hauser's theory is the notion that the work of art does not merely "copy" or "reflect" economic conditions, but that it is a socially-conditioned creation coordinate with other social creations. In this he anticipates such neo-Marxian theorists as Raymond William (who believes that works of art participate in patterns of hegemonic expression, which embrace the broadest range of social and cultural creations) and Fredric Jameson (whose theory of structural causality presumes the simultaneous existence within works of art of a wide variety of impulses from contradictory modes of cultural production). See Raymond Williams, *Marxism and Literature* (Oxford Paperbacks, 1977), pp. 108-14, and Fredric Jameson, *The Political Unconscious* (Ithaca & London: Cornell UP, 1981), pp. 74-102. All these formulations resist the simple assertion that an artist writes or paints in a particular way "because" he or she is a member of a particular social group. Yet at a broad level these formulations suggest a connection between the social and cultural assumptions shared by a group, the works of art being produced by those belonging to or identified with it, and the works of art enjoyed or encouraged by its members.

5. The phrase is taken from Aage Brusendorff, *The Chaucer Tradition* (Oxford: Clarendon, 1925).

6. "The Vintner's Son: French Wine in English Bottles," *Eleanor of Aquitaine: Patron and Politician*, ed. William Kibler (Austin, 1976), p. 164.

7. *Literature and History*, 5 (1977), 26-41.

8. *YES*, 7 (1977), 73.

9. (London: Routledge & Kegan Paul, 1977), pp. 194-97.

10. *The Strumpet Muse: Art and Morals in Chaucer's Poetry* (Bloomington: Indiana UP, 1976), p. 122; "Chaucer's *Envoy to Scogan*: The Uses of Literary Conventions," *ChauR*, 10 (1975-76), 46-61.

11. *Literature and Society: Selected Papers from the English Institute, 1978, NS, No. 3*, ed. Edward Said (Baltimore: Johns Hopkins UP, 1980), 15-56.

12. "Literature and Learning in the English Civil Service in the Fourteenth Century," *Speculum*, 4 (1929), 365-89.

13. Richard Firth Green, *Poets and Princepleasers: Literature and the English Court in the Late Middle Ages* (Toronto: U of Toronto P, 1980) has recently reasserted the importance of Richard II as a sponsor of Chaucer's efforts, though his argument requires that he concentrate his attention on works apparently advisory to princes, such as *Melibee* and *Boethius* (see pp. 143, 166).

14. Although Rossell Hope Robbins has cogently argued that Richard II's court was French-speaking, I would offer the counter-suggestion that, while its aristocratic members were mainly French-speaking, its knights, esquires, and other gentle members were probably mainly English-speaking. Of course, Chamber knights such as John Montagu might have been exceptions to such a rule. Still, even a generalized linguistic as well as social stratification of the sort I am suggesting would have further defined Chaucer's circle as a distinct circle. See Robbins, "Geoffroi Chaucier, Poète Français, Father of English Poetry," *ChauR*, 13 (1978), 101. On the English wills of the Lollard Chamber knights, see K. B. McFarlane, *Lancastrian Kings and Lollard Knights* (Oxford: Clarendon, 1972), 209-10.

15. Chaucer's "Complaint to His Purse," presumably written immediately after the coronation of Henry IV on September 30, 1399, embodies the Lancastrian theory of Henry's succession "by lyne and free eleccion" (1. 23). For this and all other quotations from Chaucer see *Works*, ed. F. N. Robinson (Boston: Houghton Mifflin, 1957). Chaucer received several key confirmations and grants from Henry IV in 1399 and 1400. See *Chaucer Life-Records*, ed. Martin M. Crow and Clair Olson (Oxford: Clarendon, 1966), pp. 525-34.

16. Chaucer joined Sturry for at least one visit to France (*Life-Records*, p. 50). When not otherwise annotated, material on the careers of Chaucer's associates is based on the *Life-Records*, on the *DNB*, on McFarlane, *Lancastrian Kings and Lollard Knights*, and on William Dugdale, *The Baronage of England* (London, 1675).

17. Froissart, *Oeuvres*, ed. Lettenhove (Brussels: Devaux, 1871), XV, 167.

18. Cited in McFarlane, p. 185n.

19. McFarlane, p. 214.

20. *Oeuvres*, ed. Le Marquis de Saint-Hilaire and G. Raynaud, SATF, II, 138-39; D. S. Brewer, ed., *Chaucer: The Critical Heritage* (London: Routledge & Kegan Paul, 1978), I, 39-42.

21. I, 341-42.

22. McFarlane, p. 190.

23. *The Complete Works of Geoffrey Chaucer* (Oxford: Clarendon, 1897), VII, lvii-lviii.

24. "The Authorship of 'The Boke of Cupide,'" *Anglia*, 82 (1964), 137-48. On his death see Higden, *Polychronicon*, ed. J. K. Lunby, Rolls Series, 9 (1886), p. 34.

25. *Lavision-Christine*, ed. Sr. Mary Louis Towner (Washington: Catholic UP, 1932), p. 165.

26. See above, n. 14.

27. E. F. Jacob, *The Fifteenth Century: 1399-1485* (Oxford: Clarendon, 1961), p. 25.

28. Edith Rickert, "Thou Vache," *MP*, 11 (1913-14), 209-25.

29. The tradition that the balade is addressed to the sons of Henry IV is based on manuscript headnotes, of the sort provided by Shirley in Ashmole 59: "Here folowethe nexst a moral balade to my lord the Prince, to my lord of Clarence / to my lord of Bedford and to my lord of Gloucestre . . . ," in *Chaucer According to William Caxton*, ed. Beverly Boyd (Lawrence, Kansas: Allen, 1978), p. xi. Since this headnote is confirmed by the opening lines of the text, we might choose to believe the usually unreliable Shirley.

30. See Skeat, *Works*, VII, xlii and 237-44. G. L. Kittredge cautiously withholds comment on this tradition in "Henry Scogan," [Harvard] *Studies and Notes in Philology and Literature*, 1 (1892), 109-17.

31. See E. P. Kuhl, "Chaucer's Maistre Bukton," *PMLA*, 38, (1923), 115-31; James Hulbert, *Chaucer's Official Life* (1912, rpt. New York: Phaeton, 1970), pp. 75-76.

32. "Some Friends of Chaucer," *PMLA*, 29 (1914), 273.

33. "Literature and Learning," p. 388.

34. "Some Friends of Chaucer," p. 274.

35. *John Gower: Moral Philosopher and Friend of Chaucer* (New York: New York UP, 1964), pp. 204-302, esp. 301.

36. *The Strumpet Muse*, p. 125.

37. Fisher, p. 59.

38. *DNB*, XX, 61.

39. *DNB*, V, 950-51.

40. Jerome Mitchell, "Hoccleve's Supposed Friendship with Chaucer," *ELN*, 4 (1966-67), 9-12.

41. Jacob, *The Fifteenth Century*, pp. 24-25. Page numbers for references to this work throughout the paragraph are given in parentheses in the text.

42. "Thou Vache," p. 13.

43. *Chapters in the Administrative History of Mediaeval England* (Manchester: Manchester UP, 1928), IV, 341-43.

44. David, p. 122. See also P. M. Kean, "Love Vision and Debate," in *Chaucer and the Making of English Poetry* (London: Routledge & Kegan Paul, 1972), pp. 33-38.

45. "Images of Chaucer 1386-1900," in *Chaucer and Chaucerians* (London: Nelson, 1966), p. 245. Chaucer was not, of course, a "full" member in the sense of ranking with the King's council of magnates, or other nobles, or even the knights of the household and Chamber; he was, nevertheless, in the household and on easy terms with many of its more distinguished members (not to mention his relation through marriage to John of Gaunt) in a sense which definitely sets him apart from Hoccleve and Lydgate.

46. Green, p. 211; Pearsall, p. 215.

47. *The Minor Poems*, in *Works*, ed. F. J. Furnivall, EETS, ES 61 (London, 1892), I, p. 106, l. 296.

48. Pearsall, p. 218.

49. "The Structure of Longer Middle English Court Poems," *Chaucerian Problems and Perspectives* (Notre Dame: Notre Dame UP, 1979), p. 245.

50. *Poets and Princepleasers*, p. 10.

51. *Old English and Middle English Poetry*, pp. 212-13.

52. Otto Gaertner, *John Shirley: Sein Leben und Wirken* (Halle: Von Ehrhardt Karras, 1904), p. 63. This view of Shirley has been questioned by Green, who believes him to have been an 'amateur scribe' who produced his manuscripts for "noblemen and courtiers" (*Poets and Princepleasers*, pp. 130-33).

53. "The *Canterbury Tales*: style of the man and style of the work," in *Chaucer and Chaucerians*, p. 88.

54. *Siege of Thebes*, ed. Axel Erdmann, EETS, ES 108, Pt. 1 (London, 1911), ll. 22-25.

55. To be sure, *The Siege of Thebes* announces itself as an additional Canterbury tale, with teller Lydgate cast as a pilgrim on a lean palfrey with a rusty bridle, and the early fifteenth-century *Tale of Beryn* (ed. F. J. Furnivall and W. G. Stone, EETS, ES 105 [London, 1887]) is preceded by a prologue describing certain japes of the pilgrims at Canterbury. The romance which each introduces is not, however, particularly "Chaucerian" in execution, except for the rather dim sense in which the *Siege of Thebes* may be taken as a deliberate rivalling of Chaucer's *Knight's Tale*.

56. Gaertner, pp. 21-22; Brusendorff, pp. 207-36, 453-56.

57. William McCormick, *The Manuscripts of Chaucer's Canterbury Tales* (Oxford: Clarendon, 1933), p. 200.

58. See Daniel S. Silvia, "Some Fifteenth-Century Manuscripts of the *Canterbury Tales*," in *Chaucer and Middle English Studies in Honor of Rossell Hope Robbins*, ed. Beryl Rowland (London: George Allen & Unwin, 1974), pp. 153-61.

59. John M. Manly and Edith Rickert, *The Text of the Canterbury Tales*, Vol. I (Chicago: U of Chicago P, 1940).

60. Manly-Rickert, I, 529-31.

61. Ed. Henry Bergen, Pt. 3, EETS, ES 106 (London, 1910), l. 3532.

62. McCormick, p. 200.

63. "Jean of Angoulême: A Fifteenth-Century Reader of Chaucer," *NM*, 72 (1971), 69-76.

64. Owen, "The *Canterbury Tales*: Early Manuscripts and Relative Popularity," *JEGP*, 54 (1955), 104-10; Silvia, "Some Fifteenth-Century Manuscripts," pp. 153-61. Debate continues over the authority of the textual traditions which Owen uses to determine the early popularity of the respective tales, with some holding that the proliferation of some textual traditions is less a result of authorial intervention than of scribal activity after Chaucer's death. Authority aside, however, the number of textual traditions of a tale would still seem to be a sound indicator of its popularity either before, at the time of, or soon after Chaucer's death.

65. See, for example, R. J. Schoeck, "Chaucer's Prioress: Mercy and Tender Heart," in *Chaucer Criticism*, ed. Schoeck and Taylor (Notre Dame: Notre Dame UP, 1961), I, 245-58.

66. See, for example, Raymond Preston, "Chaucer, His Prioress, the Jews, and Professor Robinson," *N&Q*, 206 (1961), 7-8. Preston suggests that the Prioress' anti-Semitism occurs within "the frame of an old folk-tale set in a remote continent," and that her denunciations reveal a variety of "childish enthusiasm."

67. I am here accepting Alfred David's "middle ground" interpretation of the impact of the tale and the character of the Prioress. See *The Strumpet Muse*, pp. 205-14.

68. Manly-Rickert, Vol. I.

69. "The Fifteenth Century," *The Economic History Review*, 9 (1938-39), 166. Postan's findings have been modified by more recent studies such as Harry A. Miskimin, "Monetary Movements and Market Structure—Forces for Contraction in Fourteenth- and Fifteenth-Century England," *Journal of Economic History*, 24 (1964), 470-90. Miskimin argues, for example, that the consequences of contraction affected different economic sectors differently, with the landed gentry feeling the blow earliest in the century. Postan's broad conclusions have, however, continued to be accepted.

70. "The Fifteenth Century," p. 166.

71. Henri Pirenne, "The Stages in the Social History of Capitalism," *American Historical Review*, 19 (1913-14), 509; Harry A. Miskimin, *The Economy of Early Renaissance Europe, 1300-1460* (Englewood Cliffs, N. J.: Prentice-Hall, 1969), pp. 110-11; R. H. Gretton, *The English Middle Class* (London: G. Bell, 1917), pp. 40, 70, 74.

72. *Economic and Social History of Europe in the Later Middle Ages* (New York: Ungar, 1960), pp. 398-403; see also Pirenne, pp. 511-13.

73. "The Fifteenth Century," p. 166.

74. "The Fifteenth Century," p. 165.

75. *Prejudice and Promise in Fifteenth Century England* (Oxford: Clarendon, 1925), pp. 33-34.

76. *Prejudice and Promise*, p. 63.

77. On the marriages of Richard II's Chamber knights see McFarlane, *Lancastrian Kings*, pp. 172-76; on the careers of Edward III's and Richard II's esquires, see Hulbert, *Chaucer's Official Life*, pp. 17-52.

78. "Chaucer's Audience," pp. 34-39.

79. See, as an example of this widely-shared tendency, Herbert Grierson and J. C. Smith, *A Critical History of English Poetry* (New York: Oxford UP, 1946), p. 43.

The Reputation and Circulation of Chaucer's Lyrics in the Fifteenth Century

Julia Boffey

This essay first appeared in The Chaucer Review *28.1 (1993): 23-40.*

THE influence of Chaucer's lyrics on the subsequent composition of poems in English, particularly those on secular subjects, has been routinely acknowledged. R. H. Robbins speaks for many other scholars when he states that "Chaucer's major influence on the fifteenth century was not through *The Canterbury Tales,* but through these formal, conventional lyrics (and his early dream visions) derived from contemporary French verse."[1] C. S. Lewis, Derek Pearsall, Denton Fox, and John Norton-Smith are among others who have discussed the importance of the forms and themes of Chaucer's lyrics for the writings of the century which followed his own.[2] While the number of surviving models is admittedly small—Pace and David's *Variorum* edition and the *Riverside Chaucer* include only twenty-two poems (including *Anelida and Arcite),* of which at least four are classed as doubtfully canonical—the testimony of both Chaucer and his contemporaries seems to indicate that the corpus once formed a significant part of his oeuvre.[3] The *Retracciouns* (I 1086), the *House of Fame* (622-23), and the *Prologue to the Legend of Good Women* (F 422-23, G 410-11) all speak of the equivalent of "many a song and many a leccherous lay," while Lydgate (in *The Fall of Princes,* I, 352-53) and Gower (in *Confessio Amantis,* VIII, 2943-47) praise Chaucer's lyric fecundity, the latter noting extravagantly that "the lond fulfild is overal" with his songs.[4] Recent suggestions that the slender body of survivals might be padded out with the addition of lyrics in French, or with the songs embedded in longer poems such as *Troilus and Criseyde* or the *Parliament of Fowls,* have attempted, with some justification, to locate further possible sources of inspiration.[5] But however flimsy and undefined this part of the canon might now appear, its impact on later Middle English poetry in general, and more specifically on the themes and forms of later lyrics, is nonetheless felt to have been significant. Consideration of the nature of this impact, in addition to its interest for literary historians, can help us to understand more clearly the forms in which Chaucer's lyrics were available to his successors and circulated amongst them.

Hard facts, of course, prove elusive. Attempts to spot echoes of Chaucer's lyrics in the poems of his successors are fraught with complications, some the routine problems which dog all source studies, others more specific to the particular features of Chaucer's oeuvre.[6] In the first category, for instance, comes the fact that what appears to be an echo of a Chaucerian theme or image may depend rather upon a common source: for example, a passage in one of the English ballades connected with Charles of Orleans:

> gret pite were hit by ihesu
> If that a lady of so gret nobles
> Shulde do hir silf refuse the coloure blew
> Which hewe in loue is callid stedfastnes.

The lines appear to recall the refrain of *Against Women Unconstant* but could just as easily have been directly inspired by the Machaut poem to which Chaucer probably alluded.[7] Amongst problems specific to Chaucer's oeuvre is the general uncertainty about authorship which hangs over so much of this part of the canon: any echo of *Against Women Unconstant* may be no more than a second-hand echo of Chaucer if the assumed model was itself in fact the work of a disciple.[8] Moreover, the duplication of stanza forms and phrasing within Chaucer's own writings may confuse the issues still further: parts of *Troilus,* for example, sound very like some of the shorter love complaints. Given the nature of the material, it seems that judgments in this area must perforce remain tentative.

The location and discussion of specific borrowings may perhaps best be introduced by illustrations rather than hypotheses. Two anonymous fifteenth-century lyrics demonstrate in a general way some of the possible areas in which Chaucer's short poems, both moral and amatory, exerted an influence. The first appears in Bodleian Library, Oxford, MS Ashmole 59:[9]

f.17v Passe forþe þou pilgryme / and bridel wele þy beeste /
       Loke not ageine / for thing þat may betyde
       Thenke what þou wilt / but speke ay wᵗ þe leeste
       Avyse þee. weele / who stondeþe þee besyde /
       Let not þyne herte / beo with þy tonge. bewryde   5
       Trust not to muche / in fayre visayginge /
       ffor peynted cheere / shapeþe efft to stynge

       Byholde þy selff / or þat þou oþer deme /
       Ne beo not gladde / whane oþer done amysse /

Sey never al þat / which wolde þee soþe seme /   10
Þou maist not wit / what þy fortune is /
ffor þere is / no wight on lyve ewysse /
Þat stondeþe sure / þer fore I rede beware
And looke aboute / for stumbling in þe snare /

Reporte not muche / on oþer mens sawe /   15
Be ay adradde / to here a wicked fame /
ffor man shal dye / by dome of goddes lawe
Þat here empeyreþe / any mans name /
f.18r   Avyse þee wele / þer fore / or þowe attame
Suche as þou mayst / never revoke ageyne /   20
A gode name / loste / is loste for ay certaine /

Pley not with pecus ne ffawvel to þy feere
Chese þou hem never yif þou do affter me
Þe hande is hurte / þat bourdeþe with þe bere
ffawvel fareþe even / right as doþe a bee /   25
Hony mowþed / right ful of swetnesse is she
But loke behinde / and ware þee frome hir stonge
Þowe shalt kache hareme / to pley w^t þeos beestis
longe /

Disp<r>eyse no / wight / but if þou may him preyse
Ne preyse no firre / but þou may discomende /   30
Weghe þy wordes / and hem by mesure peyse
Thenke þat þe gilty may. by grace amende
And eke þe gode / may happen to offende /
Remembre eke / þat what man doþe amisse
Þou haste or arte / or may be such as he is /   35

In this manuscript, which is the earliest of the three surviving copies, the
poem is headed "Balade morale of gode counseyle. made. by Gower" (the
running title has the variant "Balade of moralite made by Gower"). The
ascription is provided by the scribe, John Shirley, who copied the manuscript
probably during the 1440s when he was already of advanced age and perhaps
prey to lapses of memory.[10] Neither of the other two manuscripts in which
the poem appears (Bodleian Rawlinson c. 86 and British Library Addit.
29729) repeats the ascription, which has been generally discounted, except by
Brusendorff, who even so rather hedged his bets.[11] Stow, in British Library
MS Addit. 29729, in fact records the author as Benedict Burgh.[12]   As
Shirley's other ascription to Gower involves a stanza from *Troilus* (in San
Marino, Huntington Library MS EL.26. A. 13), which hardly inspires
confidence in this area of his knowledge, it seems reasonable to assume that
the Gower attribution is erroneous, and that the poem is the work of some
possibly anonymous fifteenth-century author.[13]

Essentially it extols the virtues of honest speech and behavior, reiterating with more verbosity the message of Chaucer's *Truth*. Its opening line, "Passe forþe þou pilgryme / and bridel wele þy beeste," recalls the exhortation of *Truth*, line 18, "Forþe pylgryme forþe forþe beste out of þi stal," and the strategies deployed throughout mimic *Truth*'s combination of command and statement. Lines 22-24, for example, are similar in structure to

> Tempest þe nouȝt al croked to redresse /
> In trust of hire þat tourneþ as a bal /
> Myche wele stant in litel besynesse.
> Bywar þerfore to spurne aȝeyns an al.
>
> *(Truth*, 8-12)

The imitator seems to have perceived the effectiveness of Chaucer's homely images and has attempted to capture his peculiarly memorable terseness. Perhaps the noticeable similarity of the piece to *Truth* prompted Shirley to head it with an extended anglicization of the title "Balade de bon conseyl" so frequently attached to Chaucer's poem.[14] It may also have caused him to think of the parallel to *Truth* in Book V of the *Confessio Amantis* (7739-41), and so have indirectly led to the Gower attribution.[15]

The second example is a love lyric, unique and hitherto unpublished, as far as I am aware, and copied onto folios 112v- 113r of Durham University Library MS Cosin V. ii. 13:[16]

f.112v	Not long a goo purposyd I and thought
	To breken of pleynly frome lusty luff*es* daunce
f.113r	And haue set all thes louears at nought
	By cawse I founde noyn to my plesaunce
	In whome I myght set my hole suffisaunce 5
	But venus whit hir smylling semblaund straunge
	Of all my purpose made a soden chaunge
	Whiche set in my sight oon so ravisshaunt
	ffull of plesaunce and of goodlynesse
	That thorught myn hert she wase so p*er*saunt 10
	She kyndly ayan my nould besynese
	And ferryd myn hert so wᵗ loueys duresse
	That for to loue I ken not me absten
	Or to sterve and dye soddenly fo peyn
	And of your good grace most it nowe p*ro*cede 15
	To cure myn hert with comforth & \<re\>leue
	Wich trymbleth and qwakith for besy drede
	ffor lake of pety nowe in this myscheffe
	Saff that it rennyth aye in my belove
	Yee will be pitous I ame so sure 20

Ye can not hurt where þat ye may cure

And I west and coude veryly conceve
That I stude in case to do you plesaunce
Or þat your benignite wolde receuc
Me to do you right lowly obseruaunce   25
Ye coud neuer better myn hert avaunce
Ne settyn itt oon a mey mery pynne
Itt wer me leuer and all þis world to wynne

ffelt ye the peynne or cowde ye it conceyve
That persith myn hert with dedely constrynt   30
To grace and mercy ye welde me receve
ffor by my trowth I can not make it qweynt
Ne my language gayly florrish & paynt
But shortly to say I ame aye þat man
That you wyll serue as suffise and can   35

Explicit

Together with Hoccleve's *Letter of Cupid* this lyric fills the blank leaves of
the final quire of a copy of *Troilus and Criseyde.*[17] One hand was probably
responsible for copying all three works; it is a neat and angular secretary,
probably of the second half of the century. The lyric, which has no title or
introduction in the manuscript, is like the "Balade morale" composed of five
rhyme royal stanzas. Its narrator briefly sketches in his personal
circumstances—he had forsworn love but suddenly finds himself unable to
resist its fiery attack—and then addresses three stanzas of petition to his lady.
In essence, although without the allegorical elaboration, it is the pattern of
Pity, and of the fourth part of *The Complaint to his Lady. Pity* is further
recalled in the images and the phrasing: Venus kindles the narrator's love as
Desire inflames the Chaucerian speaker; wounds and death and the lady's
"lack of pity" are described; the "besy peyne" of *Pity* (lines 2 and 119) seems
to underlie the "besy drede" (line 17) and the "besynesse" (line 11). The
pervasive use of rhyme-words ending in *-aunce* and *-aunt* (in the first,
second, and fourth stanzas) perhaps recalls the first part of *The Complaint of
Venus* and the more doubtfully canonical *Womanly Noblesse.* The attempt at
sophistication does not quite come off, and a kind of plain speaking
persistently erupts through the polished veneer (as in lines 32-33, "By my
trowth I can not make it qweynt / Ne my language gayly florrish & paynt"),
but this nonetheless seems a love lyric which could not have have been
conceived in English without the existence of either Chaucer's models, or a
tradition of Chaucerian lyric writing.

These two illustrations help to distinguish three particular areas in which
the influence of Chaucer's lyrics—or more broadly, their influential
authorization of certain modes of lyric writing—can be detected. The first

involves emulation of the general situations and specifically of the rhetorical strategies which he presents. In the poems which I have discussed, for instance, the author of the "Balade morale" apes the homiletic stance of the *Truth* narrator, while the speaker of the love lyric addresses his lady from the same disadvantaged position as the Chaucerian petitioner for pity. Chaucer's *Pity*, in fact, more than any other of his love-lyrics, seems to have been used as a strategical blueprint for later writers: its personified abstractions (Pity, Cruelty, Gentilesse, Curtesye, and so on); the "bill" addressed to the mistress, with its pleas and rhetorical questions; the exaggerated sentiments and the connection between lovesickness and death, all reappear.[18] Amongst other such models, the framed complaints of *Anelida and Arcite* and *The Complaint of Mars* were similarly influential,[19] while the female narrators of *Anelida* and *The Complaint of Venus* seem to have inspired some later "women's songs."[20] One of the clearest situational debts is that owed to *Fortune* by the anonymous *Lament of a Prisoner Against Fortune*, copied into three Shirley-influenced manuscripts (British Library Addit. 34360, and Harley 2251 and 7333), twice in proximity to Chaucer's own *Purse*.[21] Its debate between "The playntif" and "Fortune," like the debate in *The Complaint Against Hope*, which circulated in association with the possibly Chaucerian *Complaynt d'Amours* (in MSS Bodleian Fairfax 16 and Bodley 638, and British Library Harley 7333),[22] must surely indicate acquaintance with Chaucer's poem, although it is perhaps worth repeating (if not endorsing) Eleanor Hammond's suggestion that the piece was by Usk, and so by the reverse process available to Chaucer as a source.

The influence on later lyrics of the formal examples set by Chaucer's poems is again pervasive. His adaptations of French stanza forms—the seven-line rhyme royal stanza; different forms of eight-line ballade stanza *(ababbcbc* and *ababbccb); and variations such as those elaborated in the nine-line stanzas of the complaints of *Anelida* and *Mars*—dictated the standard forms used in fifteenth-century polite lyrics (including those lyrics intercalated in longer poems). Early examples are Hoccleve's ballades to John Carpenter, in seven-line stanzas, and to Henry Somer, in seven- and eight-line stanzas, and Lydgate's *Ballade of her that hath all virtues,* in seven-line stanzas;[23] later ones, in nine-line stanzas (and with incorporated virelai-sections on the *Anelida* model), are *The Lufaris Compleynt* and *The Lady of Sorrow* in Bodleian MS Arch. Selden B. 24.[24] The "courtly" section of any anthology of fifteenth-century lyrics reveals a preponderance of these stanza patterns. Arrangement of the stanzas into formal ballades, on the French model (with refrains sometimes linking the stanzas, and a concluding envoy) are not uncommon, and no doubt look back to a combination of French and Chaucerian influences.[25] Lydgate's *Letter to Gloucester,* with six eight-line stanzas linked by a refrain, and a concluding two-stanza envoy, is one of many later poems which fits the pattern.[26] Harder to locate are examples of the roundels and virelais which Chaucer, in the *Prologue to the Legend of Good Women* (F 422-23, G 410-11), claims to have composed. The triple roundel *Merciles Beaute,* which survives only in a late fifteenth-century copy (in Magdalene College, Cambridge, MS Pepys 2006), is not authoritatively Chaucer's,[27] and his only surviving virelais occur as part of the virtuoso stanzaic variation of Anelida's complaint. But the appearance of the forms in the fifteenth century, albeit in small numbers (Hoccleve's satirical roundels to Money and to his lady; *Earl River's Virelai)*[28] may perhaps indicate some Chaucerian precedent which has since been lost.

The matter of rhymes, thirdly, links the influence of the forms of Chaucer's models with that of their diction and phrasing. Although in the envoy to *The Complaint of Venus* Chaucer famously laments that "rym in Englissh hath such skarsete," his surviving lyrics constitute a series of virtuoso assaults on this very difficulty. The nine-line stanzas of Anelida's complaint, for instance, and the sixteen-line virelai sections, are constructed on only two rhymes per stanza; *Pity's* "Bill of complaint" is organised in three groups of three rhyme royal stanzas with a shared rhyme linking the final couplet of each group; the composite *Complaint to his Lady,* if indeed it is Chaucer's, seems to exist only as an opportunity for metrical and rhyming display.[29] Rather than following Chaucer's exploratory technical enthusiasm, many later lyric-writers seem to have preferred to adopt his rhymes wholesale (a particularly acute symptom of A. C. Spearing's Bloomian "anxiety of influence"), a practice which inevitably imparts a Chaucerian flavor to their diction.[30] The rhymes on *-aunce* and *-esse* which run through the first section of *The Complaint of Venus* and reappear throughout *Womanly Noblesse* seem to have been especially influential.[31] They appear in the lyric from the Durham manuscript discussed above; in Lydgate's *Ballade of her that hath all virtues* and some pseudo-Lydgatian poems in British Library MS Sloane 1212;[32] in some of the lyrics in Bodleian MS Fairfax 16 which have been associated with the Duke of Suffolk;[33] in the lyrics of the Findern manuscript, Cambridge University Library Ff. 1. 6;[34] and in numerous other poems.[35] Other factors, such as the common use of French-derived vocabulary in connection with courtly subjects,[36] may contribute to their preponderance, but the resemblances to Chaucer's poems seem often too close to be fortuitous.

Some more precise investigation of the chronology underlying these references to Chaucer's lyrics may help to clarify our sense of the means by which they were available to later writers, and of the forms in which they circulated. Chaucer's own personal acquaintance obviously enjoyed the most straightforward access (albeit the one whose circumstances are perhaps hardest to reconstruct). Scogan, Bukton, and Vache, recipients of the two *Envoys* and of *Truth,* presumably obtained their own copies, either by private communication or on some public occasion. That Scogan at least valued his association with Chaucer, and recorded more of his friend's lyrics, is suggested by his incorporation of *Gentilesse* in a "Moral Balade" of his own offered to the sons of Henry IV, to whom he was tutor, at a merchants' supper "in þe Vyntre in London, at the hous of Lowys Johan," some time between Chaucer's death in 1400 and his own in 1407.[37] It survives in Shirley's MS Ashmole 59 (from which I quote the introduction),[38] and in early prints by

Caxton and Thynne—versions textually distinct from Shirley's, yet repeating the attribution to Scogan, which in view of the poem's contents seems uncontroversial enough.[39] Puzzlingly, the copy of the ballade in British Library MS Harley 2251 omits the stanzas quoting *Gentilesse,* which appears independently elsewhere in the manuscript.[40] Scogan offers earnest praise of "My mayster Chaucer," calls him "this noble poete of Bretayne," (65, 126), and besides quoting *Gentillese* alludes to the *Wife of Bath's Tale* and the *Monk's Tale,* to which he evidently must have had access. One might assume similar familiarity on the part of Bukton, Vache, and presumably Gower, although of course in these cases no evidence has survived.

References in the early works of Hoccleve and Lydgate suggest that copies of Chaucer's short poems must have been circulating in some form during the first decade of the fifteenth century, unless we are to assume that these writers, like Scogan, owed their knowledge of Chaucer's texts to their personal friendship with him—a state of affairs over which there is still debate.[41] One of the earliest echoes in the works of Hoccleve would seem to involve the familiar "besy peyne" of *Pity,* which emerges in *Mother of God* (line 108)—dated by M. C. Seymour "before 1405"—a poem which itself may have been conceived in emulation of Chaucer's *ABC,* to which Hoccleve probably refers in the first *Balade to Sir Henry Somer* (line 22; compare *ABC,* line 14).[42] The notion of addressing these ballades to Somer as a means of reminding him that Hoccleve's annuity had not been paid was probably inspired, like the two roundels on "la dame monnoie," by Chaucer's *Complaint to His Empty Purse;* all three pieces are dated by Seymour around 1408.[43]

The courtly poems which Lydgate produced in the first two decades of the fifteenth century make reference to a slightly different range of Chaucerian models. *The Temple of Glass, The Complaint of the Black Knight,* and *The Flower of Courtesy* are studded with echoes of *Pity, Anelida and Arcite,* and *The Complaint of Mars.*[44] The debt appears in borrowed situations, such as the overhearing of the Valentine's Day lark which opens *The Flower of Courtesy,* on the model of *The Complaint of Mars,* as well as in matters of phrasing and diction, such as the recalling of Anelida's "swerde of sorowe" (lines 270-71) in *The Complaynt of the Black Knight* (lines 404-05). A possible echo in this poem (at line 516) of the "lyves quene" of *A Complaint to His Lady* (line 54), noted by John Norton-Smith,[45] may have some significance for assessment of the date and authorship of the latter poem, which, interestingly, seems also to have been known to the English translator of *Partonope of Blois.*[46] Lydgate evidently knew the envoy to *The Complaint of Venus* before the completion of his *Troy Book* in 1420, for he here restates Chaucer's dictum "that in ryme ynglysch hath skarsete" (Book II, line 168), a line to be echoed in *The Fall of Princes* (Book IX, line 3312).[47] By 1426-28 and the period of the execution of Thomas Montacute's commission to translate Deguilleville's *Pèlerinage de la vie humaine,* Lydgate had read Chaucer's *ABC,* for he inserted Chaucer's translation at the appropriate point in his own rendering.[48] Montacute's wife was Chaucer's granddaughter Alice, so the tribute may have been designed with more than literary motives. The contract may also have provided an exemplar, although it seems unlikely that Lydgate by this stage should not already have known a work which was apparently circulating much earlier in the century. Echoes of *Truth* in *A Pageant of Knowledge* and in *Thoroughfare of Woe,* and of *Lak of Stedfastnesse* in *The Fall of Princes* extend the range of acquaintance;[49] a reference in the latter poem to Adam as "the firste stokke" (line 36) suggests that Lydgate also knew *Gentilesse,* whether in Scogan's quotation or in an independent version.

Borrowings and echoes such as these can be traced in the output of almost every fifteenth-century writer of courtly verse. The author of *The Kingis Quair* probably knew at least *Anelida and Arcite, The Complaint of Mars,* and *Truth;* he may also, interestingly, have known *The Envoy to Scogan,* a hint that by the 1420s even the "coterie" poems, of specific and personal application to named individuals, had reached a wider public.[50] The author of the English poems associated with Charles d'Orléans again probably knew at least *Anelida, Pity,* and *Mars,*[51] the first two of which seem also to inform the translation of *Partonope.*[52] The difficulty of distinguishing between direct and mediated allusion is of course by this stage acute; Lydgate's annexation of a Chaucerian vocabulary and style was perhaps as much responsible for the Chaucerian flavor of many fifteenth-century lyrics as was direct imbibing from the "stremes hed" itself.[53] With full-scale quotation, though, we are on firmer ground. Much later in the century, the envoy to *Lak of Stedfastnesse* was appropriated to conclude the two copies of Lydgate's *Prayer for Henry VI, Queen, and People* in the fascicular Trinity College, Cambridge, MS R. 3. 21, prepared for de Worde's contact Roger Thorney;[54] it seems also to have been destined to supply a stanza on "Fortitudo" in a poem on the four virtues, partly cannibalized from Lydgate, which was copied into the former Brome manuscript (now Yale University, Beinecke Library MS. 365).[55] In Henryson's *Testament of Cresseid* a "lipper lady" recalls *Truth* as she asks Cresseid, "Quhy spurnis thow aganis the wall / To sla thy self and mend nathing at all?"[56] Part of the doubtfully Chaucerian *Merciles Beaute* was put to original use in an address to the Virgin printed in Thynne's edition of Chaucer's works.[57] The early printings of the lyrics were to make them available to a whole new audience, who sometimes copied the poems back into manuscript form (as in Bodleian MS Arch. Selden B. 10, with texts of *Fortune* and *Truth* copied from a de Worde print),[58] or used them as raw material for "new" pieces, such as the extract from *Anelida* in British Library MS Addit. 17492.[59]

How does this evidence for the knowledge and use of Chaucer's lyrics in the fifteenth-century sort with the forms and patterns of their survival in manuscripts? The manuscript tradition of these poems, partly because of their brevity and the consequent diversity of the witnesses, and partly because, as the *Varorium* editors confirm, Chaucer's "literary remains were left in no very good order," is complex.[60] The earliest survivals would seem to be the *ABC* and a group of moral and Boethian pieces: *Truth, Stedfastnesse,*

Fortune, Gentilesse, The Former Age (in Cambridge University Library MSS Ii. 3. 21 and Gg. 4. 27; British Library MSS Addit. 10340, 22139, and 36983, and Cotton Cleopatra D. vii), with odd copies of the "occasional" lyrics cropping up from time to time: *Purse* in British Library Addit. 22139, a *Confessio* manuscript, and *Scogan* in the large and more comprehensive Chaucerian anthology in Cambridge University Library Gg. 4. 27.[61] The only love lyric among this early batch is the doubtful *Against Women Unconstant* in Cotton Cleopatra D. vii. Copies of the longer courtly complaints— *Anelida, Mars,* and *Pity*—do not surface until the time of Shirley's extant manuscripts, the earliest of which, British Library Addit. 16165, cannot possibly antedate 1422-23, and could reasonably date from as late as the 1430s.[62] The appearance in the second quarter of the century of Shirley's anthologies and of the numerous lyrics in the booklets making up Bodleian MS Fairfax 16 marks the point from which circulation of an almost complete range of the poems can be charted. The only first appearances which might be later are *Rosemounde* (Bodleian Rawlinson poet. 163) and the doubtful *Merciles Beaute* (Pepys 2006) and *Womanly Noblesse* (Addit. 34360).

As far as the relative circulation of individual poems is concerned, the manuscript evidence matches fairly evenly such facts as can otherwise be deduced about which poems were known, read, and used. *Truth,* which tops the list of extant copies with twenty-two manuscripts (two with two copies), appears to have been known to Lydgate, Hoccleve, and others. Echoes of *Lak of Stedfastnesse* (the next in the list, with fifteen manuscripts) survive in *The Fall of Princes* and works from the later fifteenth century. Continuing down the list, the *ABC* (fourteen manuscripts), *Anelida* (twelve), *Purse* (eleven, one with two copies), *Fortune,* and *Gentilesse* (both with ten) are alluded to relatively early, and numerously. *Pity* (nine manuscripts), *Mars,* and *Venus* (both with seven, one with two copies of each) likewise seem to have reached an audience. The surprising feature of this comparison between manuscript survivals and allusions to the poems concerns the time-lag between Chaucer's death in 1400 and the apparent first publication of some of the lyrics in the 1420s and later. That Lydgate and Hoccleve should in the first decade of the fifteenth century have been able to quote *Purse,* or the *ABC,* or *Truth* seems reasonable enough: we know that copies were in existence, for examples have survived. But their access during this same period to *Anelida, Mars, Venus,* and *Pity* is less easy to reconstruct and seems to necessitate the hypothesis of lost manuscripts.

Part of this seeming mystery is most probably to be connected with the forms in which the lyrics came into circulation. Initially, whether designed for some occasional purpose or composed for private satisfaction, they were presumably copied onto single leaves or into small, unbound gatherings. The inventory of the library of Charles d'Orléans, one of the most prolific lyric-writers of the period, refers to such "quayers" and "feuillets" which bore "balades" and "chansons."[63] As far as we know Chaucer took no steps to organize and publish his working drafts, and the larger chaos of the surviving forms of his longer works is reflected in miniature amongst the lyrics. Pace's tentative explanation of the appearance of copies of *Fortune* and *The Former Age* in Cambridge University Library Ii. 3. 21, a *Boece* manuscript in which the lyrics are copied at the end of Book II, metre v (the source of the first of them) provides a telling illustration of the consequences of this insouciance. Following Skeat's suggestion that this manuscript's text of *Boece* was taken from Chaucer's own copy, Pace hypothesizes that "Chaucer left drafts [of the two lyrics] in his copy and that the Ii. scribe simply followed what he had before him."[64]

That short poems of this kind were registered by Chaucer on perilously unattached single leaves and fragments seems to be borne out by his practice with regard to the lyrics inset in some of the longer poems. Barry Windeatt's study of the text of *Troilus,* and of the "in-eching" process by which the composition took shape, highlights the insertion of Troilus's "song" at the end of Book III (which some manuscripts omit) as an expansion which "perhaps existed originally in the form of a physical addition to the draft which has been confused by certain scribes."[65] The textual uncertainty which hangs over the concluding roundel in the *Parliament of Fowls* may result from similar circumstances, for the two suggestions present in the manuscripts (one a variously garbled form of the lines which modern editors print as a roundel, the other a single enigmatic line of French) both have the air of solutions reached after the event.[66]

Textual complexities in and scribal uncertainties about the forms of Chaucer's lyrics are not hard to find. Several of the poems *(Truth, Fortune,* and *Purse)* exist in manuscripts both with and without envoys, as if they might have been recycled for a specific occasion at some stage after composition, and so have survived in distinct forms; the main body of *Truth,* furthermore, appears to have survived in two quite different states.[67] Confusion over the association of the narrative and lyric parts of *Anelida* has recently been signaled by A. S. G. Edwards, who argues, on the basis of the separation of the complaint from its framework in several manuscripts, and the absence of authoritative information about the authorship of the narrative section, that the work consists of two distinct components, of which only the "complaint" is Chaucerian (and this only "possibly").[68] Similar suspicions about the original distinctness of the narrative and complaint sections of *Mars* have been entertained, and the justification for the amalgamation of parts in *The Complaint of Venus* and especially *A Complaint to his Lady* has been questioned.[69] All this may have some bearing on the frequently repeated assertion that Chaucer favored framed lyrics, for it suggests that the forms in which the poems have survived can hardly be indicative of positive intentions.[70]

As a logical extension of their problems with the composite poems some scribes also appear to have had difficulty in comprehending the divisions between individual lyrics in their exemplars. The copies of *Fortune* and *The Former Age* in Cambridge University Library MS Ii. 3. 21, as Pace and David note, merge together almost as one poem. Both surviving copies of *A Complaint to His Lady* (British Library MSS Harley 78 and Addit. 34360) run this lyric indistinguishably onto *Pity*, and a note in Stow's edition of Chaucer's works (in which the text of *Pity* represents a distinct textual tradition) suggests that his copy-text preserved the two poems in the same way.[71] The early copies of *Purse, Gentilesse, Stedfastnesse*, and *Truth* which the Gower scribe used to fill a blank final leaf in British Library MS Addit. 22139 are copied consecutively, in this order, with no indication of where one text ends and another begins. Even in such a large and formally produced anthology as Cambridge University Library MS Gg. 4. 27, *Scogan* continues on into *Truth* without a break; only during the rubrication process did the scribe draw a line between the two and insert the title of the second poem, "Balade de . . . bone conseyl," in the margins on either side of its first line.[72] Such tight groupings of lyrics perhaps descended from rough exemplars in which stanzas were closely packed together and presentational niceties such as titles and colophons absent.[73]

Brusendorff proposed in the 1920s that Chaucer's lyrics circulated after his death as "fugitive texts" or in small groups, copied in unbound quires or booklets:[74] I advance nothing new in suggesting that the early exemplars were flimsy and sometimes confused or confusing. But it is salutary to discover that, in spite of the nature of the forms in which they survived, the lyrics were apparently well-known and influential at an early date. The increasing frequency of their manuscript and printed appearances after the middle of the fifteenth century does not simply mean that they suddenly sprang into circulation at this time but rather that the kinds of manuscript in which they might be carefully and lengthily preserved were gradually becoming more numerous. The fashion for fascicular manuscripts such as Fairfax 16, for anthologies of Chauceriana such as Arch. Selden B. 24 and the two parts of Pepys 2006, and eventually for small printed anthologies, such as Caxton's quartos, which could be collected one by one to form a larger volume, offered these essentially ephemeral poems a securer environment. That these codicological developments may themselves have been brought about by the very existence of Chaucer's poems is a circular but defensible proposition.[75]

NOTES

1. "The Lyrics," in *A Companion to Chaucer Studies*, ed. Beryl Rowland, 2nd ed. (Toronto, 1979), 380-402. See also Rossell Hope Robbins, "Chaucer and the Lyric Tradition," *Poetica* 15-16 (1983): 107-27.

2. C. S. Lewis, *The Allegory of Love (Oxford*, 1936), 243-59; D. A. Pearsall, "The English Chaucerians," in *Chaucer and Chaucerians*, ed. D. S. Brewer (London, 1966), 201-39; Denton Fox, "Chaucer's Influence on Fifteenth-Century Poetry," in Rowland, *Companion*, 1st ed. (Toronto, 1968), 385-402; John Norton-Smith, *Geoffrey Chaucer* (London, 1974), 16-34.

3. George B. Pace and Alfred David, ed., *A Varorium Edition of the Works of Geoffrey Chaucer, Volume V: The Minor Poems, Part One* (Norman, Oklahoma, 1982), and Larry D. Benson, ed., *The Riverside*

Chaucer (Boston, 1987). Quotations from Chaucer's lyrics cited in this article are taken from the Varorium edition, and quotations from other of his works from the *Riverside*.

4. Henry Bergen, ed., *Lydgate's Fall of Princes*, EETS, ES 121-24 (London, 1918-19), 1: 10; G. C. Macaulay, ed., *The English Works of John Gower*, EETS, ES 81-82 (London, 1900-01), 2: 466.

5. That Chaucer composed poems in French is suggested by Rossell Hope Robbins, "The Vintner's Son: French Wine in English Bottles," in *Eleanor of Acquitaine: Patron and Politician*, ed. William W. Kibler, Symposia in the Arts and Humanities, 3 (Austin, 1975), 147-72, and "Geoffroi Chaucier, Poète Francais, Father of English Poetry," *ChauR*, 13 (1978-79), 93-115; and by James I. Wimsatt, *Chaucer and the Poems of 'Ch', in University of Pennsylvania MS French 15* (Cambridge, Engl., 1982). Lyrics in the longer poems are discussed by A. K. Moore, "Chaucer's Use of Lyric as an Ornament of Style," *CL* 3 (1951):32-46, and by Robbins, "The Lyrics," in Rowland, *Companion*.

6. Similar difficulties concerning the nature of Chaucer's influence on Middle Scots poets are discussed by Walter Scheps, "Chaucer and the Middle Scots Poets," *SSL* 22 (1987): 44-59.

7. Robert Steele and Mabel Day, ed., *The English Poems of Charles of Orleans*, EETS, OS 215 and 220 (London, 1941 and 1946; rptd. as one volume, 1970), 39; Paulin Paris, ed., *Guillaume de Machaut: Le Livre du Voir-Dit* (Paris, 1875), 309. For further bibliography, see the note in Benson, *Riverside Chaucer*, 1090, and see Bartlett Jere Whiting, *Proverbs, Sentences, and Proverbial Phrases from English Writings Mainly Before 1500* (Cambridge, Mass., 1968), B384. The extent of Chaucer's debt to French lyrics which may well have been known to his English successors has been most recently demonstrated by James I. Wimsatt, *Chaucer and his French Contemporaries: Natural Music in the Fifteenth Century* (Toronto, 1991).

8. None of the three surviving manuscripts (Bodleian Library Fairfax 16, British Library Cotton Cleopatra D. vii and Harley 7578) contains an ascription to Chaucer. This first appears in Stowe's 1561 edition of Chaucer's works. Of more recent editors, only Skeat and Robinson have allowed it much weight.

9. I am grateful to the Bodleian Library, Oxford, for permission to reproduce the text from this manuscript. Manuscript contractions have been expanded according to conventional practice; in other respects, this and the transcription which follows are as far as possible diplomatic.

10. On Shirley and Ashmole 59, see Eleanor P. Hammond, "Ashmole 59 and Other Shirley Manuscripts," *Anglia* 30 (1907): 320-48, and A. I. Doyle, "More Light on John Shirley," *MÆ* 30 (1961): 93-101.

11. Aage Brusendorff, *The Chaucer Tradition* (Oxford, 1925), 235n and 252. See Macaulay, *Gower*, 1:clxxiii-v, and Max Förster, "Über Benedict Burghs Leben und Werke," *Archiv* 101 (1898): 29-64, and "Kleine Mitteilungen," *Archiv* 102 (1899): 213-14. The poem is not discussed by John H. Fisher, *John Gower: Moral Philosopher and Friend of Chaucer*

(New York, 1964), and I understand from Kate Harris that the compilers of the forthcoming *Census of Gower Manuscripts* are not including it as one of Gower's works.

12. The colophon reads "Explicit to kepe thy tonge well p*er* magi*strum* benedictu*m* burgh."

13. See the description of this manuscript in Seymour de Ricci, *Census of Medieval and Renaissance Manuscripts in the United States and Canada,* 2 vols. (New York, 1935-40) 1: 131-32. On fols. iiv-iiir occur Book I, lines 631-37 of *Troilus and Criseyde* ("A whetstone is no karving instrument. . ."), headed "Gower." I am grateful to Kate Harris for this information. The series of Gower extracts in the partially-Shirley-derived British Library MS Harley 7333 appear to fall in parts of the manuscript which were not dependent on Shirleian exemplars.

14. See Pace and David, *Minor Poems,* 59n for a list of these.

15. Much editorial effort has been expended on the question of whether Gower borrowed from Chaucer, or vice versa; see Pace and David, *Minor Poems,* 62. Ralph Hanna III, "Authorial Versions, Rolling Revision, Scribal Error? Or, the Truth About Truth," *SAC* 10 (1988): 23-40, argues that "the only actual similarity of the two passages . . . is that they share a commonplace" (29). The main thrust of Hanna's argument, that the different versions of *Truth* represent evidence of scribal transmission rather than of authorial revision (as suggested by Pace and David), does not affect my point here.

16. I am grateful to Durham University Library for permission to reproduce the text from this manuscript.

17. See the description of the manuscript by R. K. Root, *The Manuscripts of Chaucer's "Troilus,"* Chaucer Society, 1st series, 98 (London, 1914), 11.

18. All of these features are to be found in the English poems associated with Charles of Orleans; see Steele and Day, *English Poems.* For further examples, see Rossell Hope Robbins, ed., *Secular Lyrics of the Fourteenth and Fifteenth Centuries,* 2nd ed. (Oxford, 1955), nos. 128, 130, 139, 140, 154, 165, 192, 194, 195, 196.

19. See, for example, K. G. Wilson, "*The Lay of Sorrow,* and *The Lufaris Complaynt,*" *Speculum* 29 (1954): 708-26.

20. As, for instance, several of the poems copied into the so-called "Findern Manuscript" (Cambridge University Library Ff. 1. 6): see Rossell Hope Robbins, "The Findern Anthology," *PMLA* 69 (1954): 610-42.

21. In British Library Addit. 34360 and Harley 2251 the Complaint follows on without distinction from *Purse.* See the edition by Eleanor P. Hammond, "The Lament of a Prisoner Against Fortune," *Anglia* 32 (1909): 481-90, and Richard F. Green, "The Authorship of *The Lament of a Prisoner Against Fortune,*" *Mediaevalia* 2 (1976): 101-09.

22. K. G. Wilson, ed., *The Complaint Against Hope,* University of Michigan Contributions in Modern Philology, 21 (Ann Arbor, 1957). In each of the three manuscripts the *Complaynt d'Amours* follows directly after *The Complaint Against Hope.*

23. M. C. Seymour, ed., *Selections from Hoccleve* (Oxford, 1981), 24-28; Henry Noble MacCracken, ed., *The Minor Poems of John Lydgate,* EETS, ES 107 and OS 192 (London, 1911 and 1934), 2: 379-81.

24. See Wilson, "*The Lay of Sorrow.*" See also Henryson's use of nine- and ten-line stanzas in the lyric complaints of *The Testament of Cresseid* and *Orpheus and Eurydice.*

25. See further Helen L. Cohen, *The Ballade* (New York, 1915), and Albert B. Friedman, "The Late Mediaeval Ballade and the Origin of Broadside Balladry," *MAE* 27 (1958): 95-110. The material edited by Ernest Langlois, *Recueil d'arts de seconde rhétorique* (Paris, 1902), suggests the range of French models which may have been available to Chaucer's successors.

26. MacCracken, *Minor Poems,* 2: 665-67.

27. It occurs only in Magdalene College, Cambridge, MS Pepys 2006, and is not there explicitly ascribed to Chaucer.

28. On roundels and virelais, see Robbins, *Secular lyrics,* 278, and Seymour, *Hoccleve,* 125.

29. Mainly phonological features of Chaucer's use of rhyme are discussed by Masa T. Ikegami, *Rhyme and Pronunciation: Some Studies of English Rhymes from "Kyng Alisaunder" to Skelton* (Tokyo, 1984), chapter 3. See also the use of certain standard rhyme-pairs in religious lyrics, as noted by Siegfried Wenzel, *Preachers, Poets, and the Early English Lyrics* (Princeton, 1986), chapter 2.

30. A. C. Spearing, *Medieval to Renaissance in English Poetry* (Cambridge, Engl., 1985), 107ff.

31. Here perhaps already in emulation of Chaucer: testimony for his authorship consists solely of a neo-Shirleian attribution in British Library MS Addit. 34360, the unique manuscript.

32. MacCracken, *Minor Poems,* 2: 379-81, and Robbins, *Secular lyrics,* 141-43.

33. Steele and Day, *English Poems;* Henry Noble MacCracken, "An English Friend of Charles d'Orléans," *PMLA* 26 (1911): 142-80; John Norton-Smith, introd., *Bodleian MS Fairfax 16* (London, 1979): J. P. M. Jansen, "Charles d'Orléans and the Fairfax Poems," *ES* 70 (1989): 206-24.

34. Robbins, "The Findern Anthology," and Richard Beadle and A. E. B. Owen, introd., *The Findern Manuscript* (London, 1977).

35. See, for example, Robbins, *Secular Lyrics,* nos. 96, 98, 106, 151-53, 173, 191-92.

36. Compare Gower's practice, as it can be deduced from the rhyme-index provided in J. D. Pickles and J. L. Dawson, *A Concordance to John Gower's "Confessio Amantis"* (Cambridge, Engl., 1987).

37. See Walter W. Skeat, ed., *Chaucerian and Other Pieces . . . Being a Supplement to The Complete Works of Geoffrey Chaucer* (London, 1897), 237-44, and on Scogan, G. L. Kittredge, "Henry Scogan," *Harvard Studies and Notes 1* (1895): 109-17; R. T. Lenaghan, "Chaucer's *Envoy to Scogan*: The Uses of Literary Conventions," *ChauR* 10 (1975): 46-61; May Newman

Hallmundsson, "Chaucer's Circle: Henry Scogan and His Friends," *MH* ns 10 (1981): 129-39; Pace and David, *Minor Poems*, 149.

38. Shirley signals the quotation, on fol. 27r, with a marginal note: "Geffrey Chaucier made þeos / thre balades nexst þt folowen."

39. In Caxton's *Temple of Bras*, and Thynne's *The Workes of Geffray Chaucer*, see Skeat's edition (based on Thynne's text) for collations.

40. *Gentilesse* appears on fol. 48v, and *Scogan's Moral Ballade*, without the quotation (although including the stanzas in praise of Chaucer which introduce it) on fols. 153v-56r. An isolated fragment (corresponding to lines 9-24 of Skeat's text) also appears inexplicably on fol. 178v.

41. Jerome Mitchell, "Hoccleve's Tribute to Chaucer," in *Chaucer und seine Zeit: Symposion für Walter F. Schirmer*, ed. Arno Esch (Tübingen, 1968), 275-83, and Seymour, *Hoccleve*, xii, xxi; Walter F. Schirmer, trans. Ann E. Keep, *John Lydgate: A Study in the Culture of the Fifteenth Century* (London, 1961), 59, and Derek Pearsall, *John Lydgate* (London, 1970), 63-64.

42. Seymour, *Hoccleve*, 8-11, 104-05, 25-26.

43. Seymour, *Hoccleve*, 25-30, 110-12.

44. For the fullest editions of the first two, see John Norton-Smith, ed., *John Lydgate: Poems* (Oxford, 1966), 47-112; for the third, see MacCracken, *Minor Poems*, 2: 410-18.

45. Norton-Smith, *Lydgate*, 173.

46. Bartlett Jere Whiting, "A Fifteenth-Century English Chaucerian: The Translator of *Partonope of Blois*," *MS* 7 (1945): 40-54, compares line 9118 with *A Complaint to his Lady*, line 36.

47. Henry Bergen, ed., *Troy Book*, EETS, ES 97, 103, 106, 126 (London, 1906-20). The remark in *The Fall of Princes* that Lydgate "nevir was acqueyntid . . . w^t þe sovereyn balladis of Chauncer" (ix, 3401) is part of a conventional modesty topos (also disclaiming knowledge of the writings of Virgil and Ovid) designed as a rhetorical flourish rather than a statement of truth.

48. Frederick J. Furnivall and Katherine B. Locock, eds., *Deguileville's Pilgrimage of the Life of Man*, EETS, ES 77, 83, 92 (London, 1899-1904), and Pearsall, *Lydgate*, 172-77. On the question of Lydgate's authorship, see Katherine Walls, "Did Lydgate Translate the *Pèlerinage de la Vie Humaine*?" *NQ*, 222 (1977): 103-05, and Richard Firth Green, "Lydgate and Deguileville Once More," *NQ* 223 (1978): 105-06.

49. MacCracken, *Minor Poems*, 2: 734-38 (lines 134-37), and 822-28 (passim); Bergen, *Lydgate's Fall of Princes*, Book 1, 3837-43. I am grateful to Professor A. S. G. Edwards for drawing this last reference to my attention.

50. John Norton-Smith, ed., *The Kingis Quair* (Oxford, 1961): at lines 127ff., 251-52, 852; compare *Anelida*, lines 15, 97, and 250; at lines 736 and 818, compare *Mars*, lines 21 and 23; at line 1199, compare *Truth*, line 9. Line 48 of *Scogan* may be echoed at line 24, and *Scogan's* tears of Venus at lines 806-26. There may also be a general situational debt to the dialogue of *Fortune*. A ballade on good counsel, "Sen trew Vertew encressis dignytee

. . . ," described as "an obvious imitation of *Truth*," has also been ascribed to this author; see Walter W. Skeat, ed., *The Kingis Quair, together with A Ballad of Good Counsel, by James I of Scotland,* 2nd ed., STS, ns I (Edinburgh, 1911), 51-54, 99-101.

51. In Steele and Day, *English Poems,* with lines 5033-36 and 5981; compare *Anelida,* 40-41 and 211; at lines 161, 174, 1004, 3360 note general resemblances to *Pity;* with lines 3554 and 6029 compare *Mars,* 52-53 and 206.

52. Whiting, "A Fifteenth-Century English Chaucerian."

53. Pearsall, *Lydgate,* 49-63.

54. On fols. 244v-245r, and 318r-319r: collated by MacCracken, *Minor Poems,* 1:212-16.

55. Lucy Toulmin Smith, ed., *A Commonplace Book of the Fifteenth Century* (London, 1886), 18-20. It is perhaps worth remarking that the copy of the *Prayer* in Bodleian MS Fairfax 16 is followed immediately by *Truth* (the second copy of this poem in the manuscript).

56. Denton Fox, ed., *The Poems of Robert Henryson* (Oxford, 1981), 126. The resemblance is also noted by Spearing, *Medieval to Renaissance,* 185.

57. Skeat, *Chaucerian Pieces,* 281-84.

58. Pace and David, *Minor Poems,* 26.

59. Ethel M. Seaton, "The Devonshire Manuscript and Its Medieval Fragments," *RES,* ns 7 (1956): 55-56, and R. C. Harrier, "A Printed Source for 'The Devonshire Manuscript,'" *RES* ns 11 (1960): 54.

60. Pace and David, *Minor Poems,* 7.

61. See Pace and David, *Minor Poems,* 23-26, for further documentation.

62. The dating hinges on the manuscript's rubric to its copy of *Warwick's Virelai,* which must have been written after Warwick's proposal of marriage to Isabel Despenser in 1422, but before his death in 1439.

63. Steele and Day, *English Poems,* 284.

64. George B. Pace, "'The True Text of The Former Age,'" *MS* 23 (1961): 363-67.

65. B. A. Windeatt, ed., *Geoffrey Chaucer. Troilus and Criseyde: A New Edition of 'The Book of Troilus'* (London, 1984), 38.

66. See the textual note in Benson, *Riverside Chaucer,* 1150.

67. Pace and David, *Minor Poems,* 49-65, discuss and edit both versions; see further Hanna, "Authorial Versions."

68. A. S. G. Edwards, "The Unity and Authenticity of *Anelida and Arcite:* The Evidence of the Manuscripts," *SB* 41 (1988), 177-88.

69. Benson, *Riverside Chaucer,* 1079, 1078, 1081-82.

70. See, for example, Nancy Dean, "Chaucer's 'Complaint', a Genre Descended from the *Heroides,*" *CL* 19 (1967): 1-27; Pearsall, *Lydgate,* 93; and for the fullest and most recent statement, W. A. Davenport, *Chaucer: Complaint and Narrative* (Cambridge, Engl., 1988), passim.

71. In Harley 78, although there is no other indication of the division between poems, a small fleuron is drawn in the margin at the beginning of

the *Complaint;* this could of course have been added retrospectively. On Stow's copy, see Brusendorff, *Chaucer Tradition,* 225-26.

72. Malcolm B. Parkes and Richard Beadle, introd., *Geoffrey Chaucer: Poetical Works. A Facsimile of Cambridge, University Library, MS Gg. 4.27,* 3 vols. (Cambridge, Engl.,1979-80), 1: fol.8r.

73. See Norton-Smith, *MS Fairfax 16,* viii, where it is argued that some of the Chaucerian lyrics in Booklet II "show a peculiar grouping by the deliberate omission of colophons," perhaps because of an inherited characteristic in the scribe's copy which "may represent some ordering of these poems which ultimately derived from the poet's own intention." It must be added that the Fairfax lyrics *are* nonetheless separately introduced and otherwise distinguished from one another.

74. Brusendorff, *Chaucer Tradition,* chapter 4.

75. On the dissemination of Chaucer's works amongst first a "primary" audience who knew the author and later a "secondary," more disparate one, see Paul Strohm, "Chaucer's Fifteenth-Century Audience and the Narrowing of the 'Chaucer Tradition,'" *SAC* 4 (1982): 3-32, and *Social Chaucer* (Cambridge, Mass., 1989), chapter 3.

Father Chaucer

A. C. Spearing

This essay first appeared in Medieval to Renaissance in English Poetry *(Cambridge: Cambridge University Press, 1985), pp. 88-110. Minor editorial changes have been made to make the chapter more self-contained.*

*T*HE Siege of Thebes is one of the most studiedly Chaucerian of fifteenth-century poems, but in important ways it is a retrogressive work, more medieval than *The Knight's Tale*, its point of origin. The same is true of much of the poetry of Chaucer's followers, especially in England (as opposed to Scotland); measured by the doctrine of artistic progress which the Renaissance invented, they move back rather than forwards. It would be quite wrong to suppose that the transition from medieval to Renaissance in English poetry could be seen simply in evolutionary terms: on the contrary, there is a major push towards Renaissance values by Chaucer, followed by a great variety of movements in different directions, some of them (as we shall see) uninfluenced by Chaucer, others attempting to advance from his work yet actually retreating from some of the positions he had established. As J. W. Mackail put it, "whatever might have happened without Chaucer, what Chaucer did was decisive. It was even too decisive. He brought the Renaissance into England before the time. We have to wait a hundred and fifty years for the English Petrarch."[1]

If we ask why those who admired Chaucer so greatly and imitated him so diligently did not usually succeed in building on his work, the answer will no doubt have something to do with their individual capacities: none of them had Chaucer's genius. It would appear, too, that none of them had the opportunities to which Chaucer's genius enabled him to respond: there is no evidence that any of his successors before Wyatt had visited Italy or read Italian.[2] Then again, their contact with Chaucer himself was inevitably indirect. Chaucer undoubtedly wrote for readers as well as listeners, but the speaking voice was of central importance in his poetry, and his work seems to imply the existence of an intimate social circle which could respond intelligently to changing tones of voice. After his death, his work was, of course, known only in written form, and it seems clear that his tonal as much as his metrical intentions were often misjudged by his successors. But the attenuation of Chaucer's achievement among these successors must also have something to do with more general barriers in the culture of fifteenth-century England. The retreat from Chaucer's intellectual curiosity and courage must have been in part a consequence of the more restricted and repressive intellectual climate in which his successors lived; and here one may hypothesize that the fears aroused by the initial success of the Wycliffite heresy were of considerable importance. One indication in Chaucer's life of the speculative freedom that marks his literary attitude towards classical paganism may be found in his close association with the group of "Lollard knights,"[3] men of position and influence who seem to have sympathized with Wyclif's critical and questioning stance and protected his followers, without necessarily sharing his doctrinal heresies such as the denial of the real presence of Christ in the sacrament. The Sir John Clanvowe, author of *The Boke of Cupide*, the earliest Chaucerian imitation, belonged to this group, and even the apparently innocuous love-allegory of this little work may be shaped by his experience as a Lollard sympathizer. The nightingale, the proponent of courtly orthodoxy in love-matters, sounds uncommonly like a spokesperson for repressive religious orthodoxy too, for she wishes that all who reject the true religion of Cupid should be burned. That kind of joke at the expense of religious intolerance was all very well in the fourteenth century, when no one in England had been burned for heresy; but with the accession of the narrowly orthodox Lancastrians and the passing of the anti-Lollard act of 1401 which permitted the burning of heretics "that such punishment may strike fear to the minds of others,"[4] and still more after Oldcastle had associated heresy with sedition, the atmosphere was different.

The widespread fear of heresy after the opening years of the fifteenth century seems to have been shared by the English Chaucerian poets. Both Hoccleve and Lydgate in their early works had been prepared to express attitudes of the questioning kind that Chaucer had attributed to pagans or had expressed himself in *The Complaint of Mars*. The woeful lover of Lydgate's *Complaynt of a Loveres Lyf* (before 1412), echoing the betrayed pagan Troilus, demands,

> O ryghtful God, that first the trouthe fonde,
> How may thou suffre such oppressyon,
> That Falshed shuld have jurysdixion
> In Trouthes ryght, to sle him gilteles?[5]

And in *The Temple of Glass* (also before 1412) Lydgate echoes the reproaches addressed to God in *The Complaint of Mars*: how lamentable that God and Nature should

> So mych beaute, passing bi mesure,

Set on a woman, to yeve occasioun
A man to love to his confusioun.

And once more the question is asked,

> Whi wil God don so gret a cruelte
> To eny man or to his creature
> To maken him so mych wo endure
> For hir purcaas whom he shal in no wise
> Rejoise never, but so forth in jewise
> Ledin his life til that he be grave?[6]

Again, Hoccleve's *Complaint of the Virgin* (before 1405), closely translated from the French of Deguileville, begins, sensationally enough,

> O fadir God, how fers and how cruel
> In whom thee list or wilt canst thou thee make!
> Whom wilt thou spare, ne wot I nevere a deel,
> Syn thow thy sone hast to the deeth betake . . . [7]

But later both poets wrote vehement attacks on heresy, urging that it should be ruthlessly extirpated. Lydgate, in his *Defence of Holy Church* (probably 1413-14), reminds the young Henry V that heresy means treason:

> For who is blynde or haltith in the feith
> For any doctryne of these sectys newe
> And Cristes techyng therfor aside laith,
> Unto thy corone may he nat be trewe.

Henry should boldly have God's enemies killed, disregarding any feigned repentance, and let severity hold the scales of justice:

> And Goddys foon manly make to sterve,
> For any fals feynyd repentaunce:
> Of right lat rigour holden the ballaunce.[8]

Hoccleve's works are full of attacks on heresy, and in his case there is some evidence of the influence of the act *De haereticos comburendo*, for in the prologue to *The Regement of Princes* (c. 1412) an account is given of the burning of the heretic Badby in 1410. Hoccleve is urged by a beggar to take this as a warning of the danger of religious speculation, and he readily complies:

> Of oure feith wol I not despute at all;
> But, at a word, I in the sacrament
> Of the auter fully bileve, and schal,

With Goddes helpe, while life is to me lent;
And, in despyt of the fendes talent,
In al other articles of the feith
Byleve, as fer as that Holy Writ seith.   (379-85)

At the end of the *Regement* he even pauses to defend his inclusion of a
portrait of "my fadir . . ., / My worthi maister Chaucer" against those who

holden oppynyoun and sey
That none ymages schuld i-maked be:
Thei erren foule, and goon out of the wey.[9]

He addresses balades to Henry V in 1413 and 1414 urging him to support the
church "in chacyng away / Th'errour which sones of iniquitee / Han sowe
ageyn the feith," and asserting that "This yle or this had been but hethenesse"
if Henry had not acted against the heretics.[10] But his most violent assault on
Lollardy is the almost hysterical *Remonstrance Against Oldcastle* (1415), a
poem of over five hundred lines attacking the dangerous heretic from every
angle and wishing that if he does not renounce his errors, "in the fyr yee feele
may the sore."[11]

There is much evidence, then, after the opening decade of the fifteenth
century, of a growth in fear and intolerance. The determination to take shelter
within a more rigidly defined orthodoxy against what were perceived as
terrifying dangers to Church and state seems likely to have discouraged any
further development of Chaucer's questioning attitudes. Those who fear that
the country may return to heathendom if heretics are not persecuted will
naturally shy away from imaginative sympathy with even virtuous heathens.

There was a further difficulty in the relationship of Chaucer's successors
to their master, of which the source is to be found in Chaucer himself and his
attitudes towards authority. We have seen Hoccleve addressing Chaucer as
"mayster dere and fadir reverent," and from then down to Dryden's definitive
formulation, "the father of English poetry," the fatherhood of Chaucer was in
effect the constitutive idea of the English poetic tradition. There is ample
precedent for seeing the authority of the literary precursor over his successors
as analogous to the authority of the father over his sons. Lucretius refers to
Epicurus as father; Horace and Propertius both refer to Ennius as father;
Cicero calls Isocrates the father of eloquence and Herodotus the father of
history; and so on.[12] As Dryden was to put it later, "we [that is, the poets]
have our lineal descents and clans as well as other families," so that Milton
could be seen as "the poetical son of Spenser," and Spenser in turn as a son
"begotten" by Chaucer "two hundred years after his decease."[13] Descent and
inheritance from father to son provide a basic explanatory model for literary
history, and the model retains its power, for example in Harold Bloom's
conception of the tensely Oedipal relation of son to father as characterizing
the whole of English poetic history from Milton to the present.

But what kind of father was Chaucer, and what was it like for fifteenth-century poets to have Chaucer as their father? To answer these questions, we must return to Chaucer himself, and consider the role of fathers in his work and his attitude towards paternal (and thus authorial) authority. It will be helpful to begin with some thought-provoking remarks by Derek Brewer. He has noted that "Chaucer's poetry shows no sign of an imagination bothered by a dominating father-figure," and he comments especially on *Troilus and Criseyde* that Troilus "is not in the least hampered by his father King Priam, who is barely mentioned" and that in Criseyde's case it is indeed "the absence, the loss, of a father-figure, of protective authority, which is so disturbing."[14] If we look more widely, over the whole range of Chaucer's poetry, we shall find cases in which the "father-figure," the figure of "protective authority," is disturbingly absent; and other cases again in which the father-figure is present, but is presented in a distinctly unfavourable light. What is rare indeed in Chaucer is the father who is present and good, possessor of the wisdom and benevolence that a patriarchal age might have expected. One of the few Chaucerian fathers who seem unequivocally benevolent is the "noble doughty kyng" Cambyuskan of *The Squire's Tale* (V.338), but before the tale is broken off we learn nothing of the relationship between him and his children. Jill Mann has recently analysed the equivocal portrayals of fathers in *The Man of Law's Tale*, in *The Physician's Tale*, and in the section of *The Monk's Tale* concerning Ugolino da Pisa--fathers who are kind and yet cruel, or authoritative and yet subservient and whose equivocality she sees as a means by which Chaucer explores the mystery of divine providence.[15] A less serious example of an unfavourably portrayed father in *The Canterbury Tales* is Symkyn the miller in *The Reeve's Tale*. He is a ludicrously arrogant and boastful image of husbandly and paternal authority bristling with phallic weapons--

> Ay by his belt he baar a long panade,
> And of a swerd ful trenchant was the blade.
> A joly poppere baar he in his pouche
> Ther was no man, for peril, dorste hym touche.
> A Sheffeld thwitel baar he in his hose
> (I.3929-33)

--and always ready to counter any threat to his womenfolk "With panade, or with knyf, or boidekyn" (3960). All his daughter inherits from him is his "camus" nose (3934, 3974), yet he is determined to protect her virginity and marry her in accordance with his own notions of social dignity. In the end he proves incapable of asserting his own authority or of preserving his daughter's maidenhood or indeed his wife's fidelity; tyrannous paternal authority is reduced to impotence by the two young men from Cambridge.

These are literal fathers; an interesting example of the father-figure is the authoritative informant who is encountered in the type of poetic dream called the *oraculum*. This is the kind of dream defined in Macrobius's commentary on the *Somnium Scipionis* as one in which "a parent, or a pious or revered man, or a priest, or even a god" appears and gives information or advice.[16] The *Somnium Scipionis* itself belongs to this category; in it, the father-figure is Scipio Africanus the elder, who appears to his grandson in a dream and tells him of his future and of the other world. In *The Parliament of Fowls* Chaucer tells of how he read the *Somnium Scipionis*, and then had a dream influenced by it in which Africanus appeared to him. Africanus promises him a reward for his labour, shows him a gate which leads, according to the inscriptions above it, both to fulfilment and to frustration, pushes him firmly through it, comforts him in his indecision and fear by taking his hand – and then apparently vanishes, since he is mentioned no more in the whole poem. Paternal authority disappears, and Chaucer is left to deal with the uncertainties of the dream by himself. Another of Chaucer's dream-poems that evidently belongs to the same category is *The House of Fame*. Here the eagle who carries Chaucer through the heavens and instructs him in the physics of sound might be seen as a kind of comic father-figure; but at the end of Book II he too abandons him: he says he will wait for Chaucer, but he is never seen again. In Book III, just as the dreamer seems to be on the verge of obtaining the "love-tydynges" (2143) that he has been promised from one who "semed for to be / A man of gret auctorite" (2157-8) – the authoritative informant expected in the *oraculum* – the poem breaks off. We do not of course know for certain why *The House of Fame* was not continued beyond this point, or why it was put into circulation in an unfinished form, but it is surely revealing about Chaucer's attitude towards paternal or quasi-paternal authority that it should break off at this precise moment. I have suggested elsewhere that the dream in *The House of Fame* might best be seen not as an *oraculum*, but rather as an "anti-*oraculum*."[17] As such, it might be seen as representative of a general tendency in Chaucer's age to question the patriarchal, authoritarian bent of the culture that it inherited: the Wycliffite movement and the Peasants' Revolt are only the most extreme examples in public life. In literature, we might consider the case of *Piers Plowman*, with its tearing of the pardon from Truth and its reduction of Holy Church from an awe-inspiring mother-figure to a crumbling barn; or that of *Pearl*, with its reversal of expectation that makes the father the pupil and the child the teacher. But Chaucer goes further than most of his contemporaries in the persistence with which he presents paternal authority as absent or cruel.

Among the Canterbury pilgrims there are two whom we know to be fathers in the literal sense. One is the Knight, the father of the Squire; he may, for all we know, be a most benevolent parent, and certainly he exercises a quasi-paternal authority among the other pilgrims with benevolent and tactful firmness, as when he brings the Monk's dreary series of "tragedies" to an end, or when he calls on the Pardoner and the Host to kiss and make up. But, surprisingly perhaps, we see nothing of his relations with his real son, and all we are told about them is that the son acted towards him in a way appropriate for a squire in the household of his lord: he "carf biforn his fader at the table" (*General Prologue* I.100). This act symbolizes the hierarchy of the social estates, without telling us anything about the warmth or otherwise of the family relationship between the two men. The other literal father is the Franklin, and he is evidently sharply at odds with his son, whom he compares most disadvantageously with the Squire. The son cares for nothing but gaming, he loses all his money (meaning, no doubt, his father's money) at dice, and he prefers low company to that which his father thinks suitable to his rank.

> I have my sone snybbed, and yet shal,
> For he to vertu listeth nat entende,
>   (V.688-9)

says the Franklin. The blame might seem to be differently distributed if seen from the son's point of view, but there can be no doubt that, with whatever justification, the Franklin judges and speaks harshly in relation to his son.

In the company of pilgrims there is another who is a father, not literally but metaphorically--the Parson. The portrait of him in *The General Prologue* is unmistakably favourable, but it is also unmistakably negative. He is defined largely in terms of what he does not do--he does not "cursen for his tithes" (I.486), or give up visiting his parishioners because of bad weather, or leave his flock to gain greater material rewards elsewhere, and so on. Towards any obstinate sinner in his flock he engages like the Franklin in the characteristic fatherly activity of "snybbyng" or rebuke: "Hym wolde he snybben sharply for the nonys" (I.523). His Christian virtue and his noble purpose are unquestionable, but his role on the pilgrimage gives far less emphasis to attractive paternal qualities such as protectiveness, kindness, generosity, than to the negative aspects of fatherhood: his task is to forbid, to inhibit spontaneity and playfulness. In the floating link-passage which Robinson prints as the epilogue to *The Man of Law's Tale*, when the Host calls on him to tell the next tale, the Parson's response is to rebuke the Host for swearing, and thus to be classed as a "Lollere" (II.1173), a Wycliffite. But his main appearance is, of course, in the prologue to his own tale, the last of the collection as we have it. Here the Host once more calls on the Parson to tell a "fable" and thus "knytte up well a greet matteere" (X.28-9); and once more his answer has the effect of a rebuke--"Thou getest fable noon ytoold for me!" (31). He rejects fiction itself as mere *wrecchednesse*, mere *draf* (34-5), and he proceeds to offer instead the only tale of the collection that is not a tale, that has no element of narrative or fiction in it. It is indeed "Moralitee and vertuous mateere" (38), and it makes an end, as he says, to the feast of tales (47), not just by being the last course, but by negating all that has gone before, substituting a systematic treatise on human sinfulness for the unpredictable and various life of the tales, reducing verse to prose, human voices to written discourse.[18] I do not imply that Chaucer means us to criticize the Parson for doing this, only that when the time at last comes for him to exercise his paternal authority over the other pilgrims, he does so--he must do so--with an austerity that dampens the spirits, telling us that the way to eternal life is not through a tale-telling competition which ends with a jolly supper at the Tabard Inn, but "by deeth and mortificacion of synne" (X.1080).

Fear of God as father is a normal part of medieval Christianity, which we have seen exemplified in an extreme form in the lines from Hoccleve's *Complaint of the Virgin* quoted just now. The typical strategy by which the Blessed Virgin as mother is asked to shield the human supplicant from the wrath of the Father may also be found in Chaucer's *An ABC* (translated, like Hoccleve's poem, from Deguileville):

> Glorious mayde and mooder, which that nevere
> Were bitter, neither in erthe nor in see,
> But ful of swetnesse and of merci evere,
> Help that my Fader be not wroth with me,
> Spek thou, for I ne dar not him ysee,
> So have I doon in erthe, allas, the while!
> That certes, but if thou my socour bee,
> To stink eterne he wole my gost exile.
>
> Redresse me, mooder, and me chastise,
> For certeynly my Faderes chastisinge,
> That dar I nouht abiden in no wise,
> So hidous is his rightful rekenynge.
>   (49-56, 129-32)

But we have also seen that substantial passages in Chaucer's classical romances and in *The Complaint of Mars* question the combination of benevolent wisdom with supreme power that is also attributed to the heavenly Father in the traditional Christian scheme of things. To these cases can be added others. Jill Mann notes that in *The Man of Law's Tale* we are confronted with "an astonishing vision of the cosmos which presents an unnatural cruelty as fundamental to its structure and operation"--the only instance, she suggests, of a medieval writer calling the *primum mobile* "crueel."[19] In the story of Philomela in *The Legend of Good Women*, a question is put to God about the birth of the cruel rapist Tereus similar to that put by Dorigen about the black rocks in *The Franklin's Tale*. God here is *dator formarum*, the "yevere of the formes" (2228), the masculine principle that imposes shape on the shapeless feminine matter; and why, he is asked, having borne the whole created world in his thought before giving it substance, did he make or allow to be made such a poisonously evil man? If we now return for a moment to *The Knight's Tale*, and especially to Theseus's final speech, I think we shall see more clearly a major source of that poem's lasting power. In that speech Theseus envisages a different heavenly father from the one we have seen exercising authority in the situation to which the speech is designed to respond. Jupiter, the benevolent and gracious father of all things, is a mere idea in Theseus's noble mind; the reality, with whom he shadowily coexists in Chaucer's poem, is Saturn, the cruel father who does not hesitate to destroy his own children. Part of the greatness of *The Knight's Tale* surely derives from the fact that in it Chaucer has ingeniously combined his two most compelling images of paternal authority, the cruel father and the absent father.

I turn now from fathers to inheritance from the father. I suggest that Chaucer's questioning of the role of the father should be associated with his questioning of the father's power to bequeath virtue to the Son and the son's power to inherit virtue from the father. It is well known that this is a theme on which Chaucer touches rather prominently in several of his poems, though it is not of course original with him: he could have found it in Boethius, in Jean de Meun, in Dante, and doubtless in other sources too. Nevertheless, it was obviously a theme that greatly interested him, as is shown by the fact that he sometimes gives it an emphasis that seems disproportionate to its contextual relevance. In *The Wife of Bath's Tale*, for example, the Loathly Lady's lecture in bed to her reluctant husband includes a section of seventy-eight lines on the nature of true *gentillesse* (III.1109-76). (It may be worth recalling that the word *gentil* is etymologically connected with family, birth, fatherhood.) This seems an altogether excessive response to the husband's one-line complaint that she is of low birth, but Chaucer was obviously determined to set out in full the argument that our forefathers cannot "biquethe . . . / To noon of us hir vertuous lyvyng" (1121-2); that if *gentillesse* were a natural inheritance, then those of gentil birth could "nevere fyne / To doon of gentillesse the faire office" (1136-7); and that "men may wel often fynde / A lordes sone do shame and vileynye" (1150-1); so that the true definition of *gentillesse* is that "he is gentil that dooth gentil dedis" (1170). Regardless of its relevance to the tale, it is an argument appropriate to a self-made woman like the Wife of Bath, and perhaps equally appropriate to a man like Chaucer, of prosperous bourgeois family, who made his way by his own abilities into high courtly and administrative circles.

We have already seen how the Franklin, before beginning his tale, complains that his son does not possess the *vertu* that marks true *gentillesse*. We may surmise that the Franklin inwardly believes that he himself does possess that *vertu*, and that it is an understandable human weakness that leads him to feel aggrieved at his son's failure to inherit what cannot be inherited, but the burden of his tale is precisely that *gentillesse* is not derived from birth. By his deeds a squire can be as *gentil* as a knight, and a clerk as *gentil* as a squire; where moral virtue is concerned, inheritance from the father is of no significance. A very similar point is made in the ballade *Gentilesse*, but now in a way that contrasts God as father with human fathers. The "fader of gentilesse" (1) is God alone, and the man who wishes to be *gentil* must address himself "Vertu to sewe, and vyces for to flee" (4). The true heir to virtue is the man who loves virtue, whatever rank he may have inherited, for

> Vyce may wel be heir to old richesse;
> But ther may no man, as men may wel see,

Bequethe his heir his vertuous noblesse.

(15-17)

Oddly enough, Chaucer's unfavourable attitude towards the power of the father goes so far that, while denying that good qualities can be bequeathed and inherited, he occasionally asserts that evil qualities can. An example that may spring to mind is that of Criseyde, the betrayer of Troilus whose father is a traitor to Troy--though that is not a point that Chaucer ever makes quite explicitly. Unmistakably explicit is the statement at the beginning of the story of Phyllis in *The Legend of Good Women*, that the false lover Demophon was unmatched for falseness by any save "his fader Theseus" (2400), a fact which demonstrates

By preve as wel as by autorite
That wiked fruit cometh of a wiked tre.

(2394-5)

The same proverb is quoted by the Host, more jocularly, in *The Monk's Prologue*, with respect to the inheritance of sexual feebleness:

Of fieble trees ther comen wrecched ympes.
This maketh that oure heires been so sklendre
And feble that they may nat wel engendre.

(VII.1956-8)

The proverb, of course, derives from Scripture--"Sic omnis arbor bona fructus bonos facit: mala autem arbor malos fructus facit" (Matthew 7:17)-- and it is surely significant that Chaucer alludes twice to the second clause, which is unfavourable to inheritance, but never to the first, which is favourable to it.

To take this discussion a stage further, it is now necessary to reintroduce a different, metaphorical rather than literal, version of paternal authority: the authority of the literary precursor over his successors. We have seen that there is a long tradition of regarding this authority as paternal; yet Chaucer, though by far the larger part of his work is derived from existing literary sources (chiefly in Latin, French and Italian), never refers to any of his predecessors as father. Indeed, there is something peculiar about Chaucer's attitude to literary authority. He has no objection at all to disclosing that he is indebted to other writers. Sometimes this is a matter of vague references to distant predecessors from whom a story as a whole is taken--"Whilom, as olde stories tellen us. . ." (*Knight's Tale* I.1859), or

Thise olde gentil Britouns in hir dayes
Of diverse aventures maden layes
(*Franklin's Tale* V.709-10)

–while at other times it is a matter of giving references to specific sources for specific parts of a work:

> The remenant of the tale if ye wol heere,
> Redeth Ovyde, and ther ye may it leere
> *(Wife of Bath's Tale* III.981-2)

or

> In Omer, or in Dares, or in Dite,
> Whoso that kan may rede hem as they write.
> *(Troilus* I.146-7)

Like other medieval writers, Chaucer doubtless felt that his work gained prestige if it could claim to possess an ancestry and that he himself gained authority from references to authorities which would suggest that he was as much a scholar as a poet.[20] Yet Chaucer's critical attitude towards paternal authority is also reflected in his approach to the authority of those precursors to whom he might refer (as in *Troilus and Criseyde* II.18) as "myn auctour." It is rare for him to name a specific *auctor* as the authority for a complete work, as opposed to referring us to scholarly authorities for further information. One case where he does so, very straightforwardly, is *The Physician's Tale*:

> Ther was, as telleth Titus Livius,
> A knyght that called was Virginius,
> (VI.1-2)

and he proceeds to tell a story which does appear to have Livy as its ultimate source, though it is uncertain whether Chaucer's immediate source was that or the French version in the *Roman de la Rose*. But in two other cases his attitude is less straightforward. The story of Dido in *The Legend of Good Women* begins with a laudatory reference to Virgil (itself probably modelled on Dante's greeting of Virgil in the first canto of the *Inferno* and on Statius's praise of Virgil in the *Purgatorio* as the giver of light to those who follow[21]); and this is accompanied by a passing acknowledgment to Ovid too:

> Glorye and honour, Virgil Mantoan,
> Be to thy name! and I shal, as I can,
> Folwe thy lanterne, as thow gost byforn,
> How Eneas to Dido was forsworn.
> In Naso and Eneydos wol I take
> The tenor, and the grete effectes make.
> (924-9)

But the insistence that Chaucer will confine himself to the *tenor* or the *grete effectes*, the essential points, of Virgil's and Ovid's story is later developed into a sceptical and critical attitude towards his classical *auctours*. He will not repeat Virgil's explanation of how Dido came to *Libie*--"It nedeth nat, it were but los of tyme" (997), and

> I could folwe, word for word, Virgile,
> But it wolde lasten al to longe while.
> (1002-3)

When Aencas visits the temple where Dido is praying, Chaucer adds,

> I can nat seyn if that it be possible,
> But Venus hadde hym maked invysible–
> Thus seyth the bok, withouten any les.
> (1020-2)

That phrase "withouten any les" has an interesting function: it is no lie to say that Virgil asserts that Venus had made Aeneas invisible, but Chaucer evidently means to imply the possibility that Virgil is lying in making the assertion. Again, later, "oure autour telleth us" (1139) that Cupid had taken on the form of Ascanius, "but, as of that scripture, / Be as be may, I take of it no cure" (1144-5). The initial reverence for Virgil's paternal authority has been corroded by scepticism.

My other example of a questioning attitude towards a revered auctour is found in *The Clerk's Tale*. The Clerk begins with high praise of the "worthy clerk" (IV.27) from whom he has taken his story of the patient Grisilde:

> Fraunceys Petrak, the lauriat poete,
> Highte this clerk, whos rethorike sweete
> Enlumyned al Ytaille of poetrie.
> (31-3)

Yet, just as in the legend of Dido, the narrator immediately proceeds to a declaration of independence from his *auctour*. Petrarch begins, he says, with a descriptive prologue,

> The which a long thyng were to devyse.
> And trewely, as to my juggement,
> Me thynketh it a thyng impertinent,
> Save that he wole conveyen his mateere.
> (52-5)

And he therefore omits it. Throughout the tale, the Clerk continues to apply his own *juggement* to his *auctour*'s work, and to protest vigorously against the cruelty of the tale, and especially against Walter's inexplicably harsh treatment of Grisilde.[22] In this case, for reasons indicated earlier in this book, Chaucer is likely to have had the most genuine admiration for Petrarch as *auctour*, and he has not even the excuse, as he has with Virgil, that the *auctour* is pagan and therefore open to doubt. *The Clerk's Tale* indeed provides a particularly interesting example of the parallel questioning of two kinds of authority--the authorial authority of Petrarch and the husbandly and paternal authority of Walter.

Chaucer, then, seems concerned to be, or at least to present himself as being, something other than a passive inheritor of material bequeathed by his literary forefathers. It is in keeping with this that he should sometimes mystify us about his sources. The most notorious case is that of *Troilus and Criseyde*. There indeed Chaucer claims no more than to be a translator (and that is the defence of *Troilus and Criseyde* proposed in the *Prologue* to *The Legend of Good Women* against the God of Love's objection to it as heresy); but his claim is to be translating "out of Latyn" (II.14) from "myn auctour called Lollius" (I.394), not, as was in fact the case, from the Italian of Boccaccio. There are perhaps two reasons why Chaucer should attempt to deceive us in this way. One is that the claim to have a Latin source adds to the work's appearance of historical authenticity; for Chaucer, as I have argued, is really aiming to create the sense of a classical past, while at the same time indicating the scholarly effort involved in any such reconstruction of antiquity. The other reason I wish to suggest--admittedly a more speculative one--is that the supposed Lollius, like other classical authors, belongs to a remote past and constitutes no threat to Chaucer's independence; whereas Boccaccio, a vernacular author of his own century, whom he could even have met, and from whose work he learned of the very possibility of reconstructing the pagan past in a modern language, is dangerously close, a father rather than a remote ancestor. Nowhere in his work does Chaucer name Boccaccio, the *auctour* from whom he derives the three classical romances that constitute his own highest claim to poetic dignity, and, of all his sources, the one who might best be called his literary father. The name of the father, it would seem, is too dangerous to be mentioned. The other two great Italian writers of the *trecento* were less dangerous because Chaucer gained less from them in the way of specific source material. Petrarch could be mentioned as a Latin author, as the source of *The Clerk's Tale*, but there his death is so strongly emphasized that it is as if Chaucer, Oedipus-like, had killed him himself. "He is now deed and nayled in his cheste" (IV.29): the death is much to be regretted, and we shall all die in our turn, but how reassuring those nails are that keep Petrarch in his coffin! On the other hand, when Chaucer borrows from Petrarch's vernacular work, for Troilus's song in Book 1 of *Troilus and Criseyde*, his name must be suppressed and that of Lollius substituted. The influence of Dante on Chaucer is almost beyond assessment, but he was not the father of any single one of Chaucer's works (not even *The House of Fame*), and his name could therefore be mentioned several times without danger.

The present discussion has been somewhat rambling, and it may be helpful to summarize my findings so far. First, Chaucer in his work nearly always presents the father unfavourably, either as absent or as cruel. Second, he does not allow that good qualities can be inherited by sons from their fathers, though he occasionally grants that bad qualities can. Third, he is unwilling to concede authority to his major poetic ancestors, and especially to the most important of all--Boccaccio, who was of the right generation really to have been Chaucer's father,[23] and who was truly his poetic father as writer of vernacular narratives which aimed at an imaginative reconstruction of pagan antiquity. I now turn to the authority of Chaucer as author and father of his own work. Chaucer is the first secular writer in English to be known by name as the author of a body of work; yet within his work he is most unwilling to assume paternal authority. It has often been noted how modest are the roles he plays as narrator throughout his career: first a mere dreamer, a channel through which fantasy or truth is conveyed, perpetually surprised and puzzled by the events of his dreams; then a clerkly but incompetent historian, who is constantly finding that his sources (on which he is totally dependent for his knowledge of love) fail to tell him crucial things such as his heroine's age, and whether she had any children, and whether or not she really gave her heart to Diomede; last the naïve reporter of the Canterbury pilgrimage, whose own powers of poetic composition are confined to "rym dogerel" (VII.925). And it surely cannot be quite by chance that two of his most important unfinished works break off just *before* some authoritative pronouncement of meaning is to be made: *The House of Fame*, as we have seen, at the very moment when the dreamer glimpses the "man of gret auctorite," and *The Legend of Good Women*, almost at the end of the account of Hypermnestra, with the tantalizing line, "This tale is seyd for this conclusioun--" (2723). Robinson comments that "It is a little surprising that the legend should have been left incomplete, when the story was finished and a very few lines would have sufficed to make the application."[24] It is not surprising when we take into account Chaucer's pervasive unwillingness to state definitively the meaning and purpose of his writing.

It is in *The Canterbury Tales* that that unwillingness, that rejection of fatherhood, reaches its culmination. There every tale but two (the two told by the pilgrim Chaucer, one in "rym dogerel" and the other an exceptionally long "litel thyng in prose" [VII.937]), is attributed to someone other than Chaucer himself; and the mere fact of its attribution to a specific pilgrim-teller guarantees that Chaucer has no responsibility for it. The principle is stated explicitly in *The Miller's Prologue*: the "cherles tale" (I.3169) that follows is included only because the drunken Miller insisted on thrusting himself forward to tell it, much to Chaucer's regret:

> And therfore every gentil wight I preye,
> For Goddes love, demeth nat that I seye
> Of yvel entente, but for I moot reherce
> Hir tales alle, be they bettre or werse,

Or elles falsen som of my mateere

(I.3171-5)

The responsibility for the selection of tales then becomes not Chaucer's but the reader's: "Blameth nat me if that ye chese amys!" (3181). The same applies to the establishment of a tale's meaning. The teller may have a particular meaning in mind (though even that is not necessarily Chaucer's), and may direct us to it by some such remark as "Therfore I rede yow this conseil take" (*Physician's Tale* VI.285) or "Taketh the moralite, goode men" (*Nun's Priest's Tale* VII.3440) or "Lordynges, by this ensample I yow preye, / Beth war . . . " (*Manciple's Tale* IX.309-10), but it is for us to decide whether that is what the tale really means. The pilgrim-Chaucer's second tale, the tale of Melibeus, is a prose allegory which for him is evidently meant to show how a ruler can gain good counsel and learn to be merciful. But when it is finished the Host's comments make it clear that for him it was about marriage and how wives ought to behave; he wishes his own virago of a wife could be as patient as the allegorical figure of Prudence in the tale. There is no one to tell us authoritatively which is the right way to interpret the tale: Harry Bailly is not a very subtle literary critic, but then the tale is not a very coherent moral allegory, and the pilgrim-Chaucer is not a very intelligent tale-teller. We are left with a variety of possible interpretations, a variety summed up in a line which in differing forms is repeated several times in *The Canterbury Tales*: "Diverse folk diversely they seyde" (I.3857); "Diverse men diverse thynges seyden" (II.211); "Diverse men diversely hym tolde" (IV.1469); "Diverse folk diversely they demed" (V.202). Different people judge differently; and Chaucer's acknowledgment of that fact, his withdrawal of authority both from the tales and from their interpretations, amounts to what might be called a de-authorization of the whole work, or, in the terms used by some more recent theorists, to the conscious transformation of the *Tales* from a "work" to a "text."

What I have in mind may be exemplified by two of the most penetrating essays of Roland Barthes, "The Death of the Author" (1968) and "From Work to Text" (1971). Here we may find the "work" defined as writing governed and limited by the purposes of its author, while the "text" is an anonymous, fatherless space in which an irreducible plurality of meanings play against each other. "The author," writes Barthes, "is reputed the father and the owner of his work," while "As for the Text, it reads without the inscription of the Father." Again, "The Author is thought to *nourish* the book, which is to say that he exists before it, thinks, suffers, lives for it, is in the same relation of antecedence to his work as a father to his child." Thus it may be said that "a text is not a line of words releasing a single 'theological' meaning (the 'message' of the Author-God) but a multi-dimensional space in which a variety of writings, none of them original, blend and clash." To quote Barthes once more, "It is not that the Author may not 'come back' in the Text, in his text, but then he does so as a 'guest.' If he is a novelist, he is inscribed in the novel like one of his characters, figured in the carpet; no longer privileged, paternal."[25] The phrases that I have been quoting offer an extraordinarily accurate description of what Chaucer would seem to have been consciously trying to do in *The Canterbury Tales*: to relinquish his own paternal authority, and to enter the text thereby produced, that "tissue of quotations,"[26] only as a guest. Certainly the Host is someone else; and each tale is literally a "quotation," set in quotation-marks, not as the message of the Author-God, but as the potentially prejudiced statement of one of a large and various group of all-too-human pilgrims. We, looking back on Chaucer, thus confront an acute paradox. He is the first English poet to exist as an "author," the first to be known by name as the father of a body of work; and yet throughout his career he seems to be striving towards the culmination achieved in *The Canterbury Tales*, the relinquishment of his own fatherhood, the transformation of his work into a text .

That paradox was already, I believe, a source of embarrassment to Chaucer's immediate successors and may be part of the reason for their failure to build effectively on some of the most "advanced" elements in his work. The difficulty involved in being the sons of such a father was already felt by those who were the first to call him "father." Let me quote once more Hoccleve's eulogy, this time adding two lines omitted before:

> O maister deere and fadir reverent,
> My maister Chaucer, flour of eloquence,
> Mirrour of fructuous entendement,
> O universal fadir in science,
> Allas, that thou thyn excellent prudence
> In thy bed mortel mightist naght byqwethe![27]

In the following stanza of *The Regement of Princes* Hoccleve refers to Chaucer's "hy vertu," and the impossibility of the father's bequeathing his virtue to the son is undoubtedly a theme borrowed by Hoccleve from one of the Chaucer passages quoted above.[28] The son wishes to inherit the authority of a father who has denied that any such inheritance is possible and has in any case denied his own fatherhood. Chaucer seemed already to have done everything: he was truly a "universal father," whose achievement was coextensive with the whole range of imaginable possibilities for poetry in English, and whose death, as Hoccleve went on to write, "Despoiled hath this land of the swetnesse / Of rethorik."[29] What territory, what imaginative space, did this leave for would-be sons? As father, he made possible their very existence as English poets, yet, as his successors, they inevitably came too late. Like Dryden looking back at the great dramatists of the age of Shakespeare, they must have felt, "We acknowledge them our fathers in wit; but they have ruined their estates themselves before they came to their children's hands."[30] As late as the 1470s a point similar to this was being made in the anonymous *Book of Curtesye* about Chaucer, the "fader and founder of ornate eloquence," and Gower, the "auncyent fader of memorye," seen as joint originators of the English poetic tradition:

Loo, my childe, these faders auncyente
Repen the feldes fresshe of fulsomnes.
The flours fresh they gadred up, and hente
Of silver langage the grete riches.
Who wil it have, my lityl childe, doutles
Muste of hem begge--ther is no more to saye--
For of oure tunge they were both lok and kaye.[31]

And even this acknowledgment of indebtedness could not be made without incurring a further debt, for the image of precursors as reapers who have already gathered the harvest of poetry, derived originally from chapter 2 of the Book of Ruth, is itself borrowed from Chaucer's *Prologue* to *The Legend of Good Women* (F 73-7).

A consequence of this attitude towards Chaucer seems to have been a widespread anxiety among his poetic descendants about the impossibility of the task they were undertaking. In many passages scattered throughout his voluminous works Lydgate expresses his sense of inferiority as a mere star beside the sun, "compared ageyn the bemys briht / Off this poete."[32] He sees himself and other descendants of Chaucer as mere imitators, who cannot hope to match their model:

Whan we wolde his stile counterfet,
We may al day oure colour grynde and bete,
Tempre our azour and vermyloun:
But al I holde but presumpcioun--
It folweth nat, therfore I lette be.[33]

That is from Lydgate's *Troy Book*; earlier, using the same terminology of "counterfeiting" Chaucer's style, he had written in *The Flour of Curtesye*:

We may assaye for to counterfete
His gaye style, but it wil not be.[34]

A less well-known disciple of Chaucer is John Walton, composer of a verse translation of Boethius, in the preface to which he expresses a similar anxiety:

To Chaucer, that is floure of rethoryk
In Englisshe tong and excellent poete,
This wot I wel, no thing may I do lyk,
Though so that I of makynge entyrmete.[35]

Such passages are of course examples of the rhetorical topos of modesty, but that is no reason to dismiss them as meaningless. They support Harold Bloom's argument that poetic influence is accompanied by anxiety, though not his assumption that Shakespeare and his predecessors belonged to "the giant age before the flood, before the anxiety of influence became central to poetic consciousness."[36] The beginnings of English poetic history in the fifteenth century really do seem to be marked by the anxiety of influence.

For a poet to make use of a great precursor is never easy, but it was perhaps especially difficult for the fifteenth-century poets to make profitable use of Chaucer, because there had never before been such a father-figure in English. It was doubtless impossible for Lydgate, never a thinker of great resource, to envisage any form of use other than what he calls counterfeiting his master's style. There is a passage, however, in a letter of Petrarch's to Boccaccio in which he takes up this characteristically Renaissance issue of stylistic imitation and distinguishes between two kinds of similarity. He reports what advice he gave "in a kind paternal manner" to a young man much given to imitating Virgil:

> A proper imitator should take care that what he writes resembles the original without reproducing it. The resemblance should not be that of a portrait to the sitter-- in that case the closer the likeness is the better--but it should be the resemblance of a son to his father. . . . Thus we may use another man's conceptions and the color of his style, but not use his words. In the first case the resemblance is hidden deep; in the second it is glaring. The first procedure makes poets, the second makes apes.[37]

Lydgate's use of the language of painting in the lines quoted above from the *Troy Book* (lines incorporating a familiar pun on "colour" as a rhetorical term, which is also present in Petrarch's letter) strongly suggests that for him the ideal goal of Chaucerian imitation was identicality, literal counterfeiting. He may have seen Chaucer as father, but he did not really want to be his son; he simply wanted to be Chaucer. This may enable us to return to *The Siege of Thebes* and see it in a new light. We saw that when Lydgate described himself as meeting the Canterbury pilgrims, there was no Chaucer among them. It is as if Lydgate, in his wishes at least, has succeeded in *becoming* Chaucer; and, as we observed, the nearer *The Siege of Thebes* gets to *The Knight's Tale*, the more of Chaucer's actual words Lydgate takes over. The reader begins to suspect that an ideal culmination of Lydgate's enterprise might be simply a recomposition of *The Canterbury Tales* analogous to the recomposition of *Don Quixote* imagined by Borges as the goal of his Pierre Menard.

Harold Bloom sees the poetic influence which constitutes poetic history in Oedipal terms. The literary son feels that his authority is lessened by the imaginative area already occupied by the literary father, and he must, if he is himself a "strong poet" or "major aesthetic consciousness,"[38] adopt one or more of a variety of modes of misreading in order to gain for himself the already occupied space. It is difficult, no doubt, to see Lydgate, whose strength is a matter of mild persistence rather than of heroic courage, as a "major aesthetic consciousness" engaged in a life-or-death struggle to win authority from his powerful ancestor, but it is worth bearing in mind that *The Siege of Thebes* includes a retelling of the story of Oedipus. It is tempting to suppose that in the early part of the *Siege* Lydgate was unconsciously dramatizing precisely the innocent destructiveness he had to engage in himself in order to survive a father as powerful yet benevolent as Chaucer. In order to live as a poet, he had to kill Chaucer--unknowingly, of course, but then Oedipus did not know that it was Laius whom he had killed at the crossroads. First, he had to remove Chaucer silently from his own Canterbury pilgrimage, then, casting him as Laius, he had to conceal from himself what he was doing by ensuring that the Oedipus legend should be deprived of all mythic power. This is no more than a fantasy, of course, but even fifteenth-century monks had unconscious minds.

In a way, it might have been easier for Chaucer's poetic descendants to follow him if he had been more willing to play the role of father that they thrust upon him. Lydgate in particular, when he is striving hardest to be Chaucerian, tends to impose on his work a didacticism--"the 'message' of the Author-God"--very different from Chaucer's indeterminacy of ultimate meaning. D. H. Lawrence wrote in a letter to Edward Garnett, "We have to hate our immediate predecessors, to get free from their authority."[39] Who could possibly have hated the Chaucer who appears only as a guest in his own work, the Chaucer rightly described by Lydgate as "gronde of wel-seying"?--

> Hym liste nat pinche nor gruche at every blot,
> Nor meve hym silf to parturbe his reste
> (I have herde telle), but seide alweie the best,
> Suffring goodly of his gentilnes
> Ful many thing enbracid with rudnes.[40]

A Chaucer who had insisted more sternly on his parental authority might have provoked a healthy rebelliousness in his sons. Whatever the reason, it was not until nearly a century after his death that Chaucer's descendants were able to free themselves from the gentle bond of their universal father, his "repressive tolerance." Then John Skelton was able to make radically new use of the Chaucerian inheritance, for example by his comparative assessment of Chaucer and of Lydgate in *Phyllyp Sparowe*, and later by suggesting in *The Garland of Laurel* that the true purpose of the English poetic tradition that sprang from Chaucer was that it should culminate in the laureation of John Skelton. The "strong" way out of the son's relation to the father is the kind of respectful repudiation practised, from the safe distance of Scotland, by Robert Henryson: even while praising "worthie Chaucer glorious," he dared to ask, "Quha wait gif all that Chauceir wrait was trew?",[41] and proceeded to write an alternative ending to *Troilus and Criseyde*. A little later Gavin Douglas was to judge, boldly but justly, that

Chaucer "standis beneth Virgill in gre" and that his legend of Dido quite misrepresents the account given by that "prynce of poetis" in the *Aeneid*.[42] Skelton, Henryson and Douglas were truly the sons of Chaucer in daring to be themselves, to adopt a sceptical independence of judgment that is genuinely Chaucerian but that could not be passively inherited from father Chaucer.

NOTES

1. *The Springs of the Helicon* (London, 1909), p. 17.

2. Margaret Aston notes that, so far as fifteenth-century learning in general is concerned, "The earliest indigenous exponents of learning in the north were those who . . . had experienced Italian culture firsthand" ("The Northern Renaissance," in *The Meaning of the Renaissance and the Reformation*, ed. Richard L. DeMolen (Boston, 1974), pp. 71-129; p. 75).

3. See K. B. Mcfarlane, *Lancastrian Kings and Lollard Knights* (Oxford, 1972), pp. 137-226.

4. *Documents of the Christian Church*, ed. Henry Bettenson, 2nd edn. (Oxford, 1963), p. 182.

5. *John Lydgate: Poems*, ed. J. Norton-Smith; lines 269-72. Cf. *Troilus and Criseyde*, V.1706-8.

6. Ed. Norton-Smith, lines 226-8, 234-9.

7. *Selections from Hoccleve*, ed. M. C. Seymour, lines 1-4. The opening six stanzas of this poem are omitted from Huntington MS HM 111.

8. Ed. J. Norton-Smith, lines 92-5, 103-5.

9. Thomas Hoccleve, *The Regement of Princes*, ed. F. J. Furnivall, vol. III, EETS E.S. 72 (London, 1897), lines 379-85, 4982-3, 5006-8.

10. *Hoccleve's Works: The Minor Poems*, eds. F. J. Furnivall and I. Gollancz, rev. Jerome Mitchell and A. I. Doyle, EETS E.S. 61 and 73 (London, 1970), pp. 40, 41.

11. Ibid., p. 18

12. *De rerum natura* III.9; Horace, *Epistles* I.xix; Propertius III.iii.6; *De oratore* II.10; *De legibus* I.5. I am much indebted to Dr. James Diggle for supplying me with these references.

13. "Preface to Fables Ancient and Modern," in John Dryden, *Of Dramatic Poesy and Other Critical Essays*, ed. George Watson (London, 1962), vol. II, p. 270.

14. *Chaucer and his World* (London, 1978), p. 43.

15. "Parents and Children in the *Canterbury Tales*," in *Literature in Fourteenth-Century England*, eds. Piero Boitani and Anna Torti (Tübingen, 1983), pp. 165-83.

16. Macrobius, *Commentary on the Dream of Scipio*, trans. William H. Stahl (New York, 1952), p. 90.

17. *Medieval Dream-Poetry* (Cambridge, 1976), p. 11.

18. For an excellent study of this aspect of *The Parson's Tale*, see Lee W. Patterson, "The 'Parson's Tale' and the Quitting of the 'Canterbury Tales,'" *Traditio* 34 (1978), p. 331-80.

19. "Parents and Children in the *Canterbury Tales*," pp. 169-70, quoting *Man of Law's Tale* II. 295.

20. For a valuable study of the medieval conceptions of *auctoritas* which form the background to Chaucer's attitude, see M.-D. Chenu, *Introduction à l'étude de saint Thomas d'Aquin* (Montreal and Paris, 1950), chapter 4.

21. *Inferno* I.82; *Purgatorio* XXII.67-9.

22. For more detailed discussion see my *Criticism and Medieval Poetry*, 2nd edn. (London, 1972), chapter 4.

23. Boccaccio was born in 1313, John Chaucer between 1310 and 1312.

24. *The Works of Geoffrey Chaucer* (London, 1957), p. 854.

25. Roland Barthes, *Image-Music-Text*, trans. Stephen Heath (London, 1977), pp. 160, 161, 145, 146, 161.

26. Ibid., p. 146.

27. *The Regement of Princes*, lines 1961-6.

28. Henry Scogan also recalls this theme from Chaucer's *Gentilesse* in his *Moral Balade*, in *Chaucerian and Other Pieces*, ed. W. W. Skeat (Oxford, 1897), lines 65-104.

29. *Regement,* lines 2084-5.

30. *Of Dramatic Poesy and Other Essays*, ed. Watson, vol. 1, p. 85.

31. *Caxton's Book of Curtesye*, ed. F. J. Furnivall, EETS ES 3 (London, 1868), lines 330, 324, 400-6.

32. *Fall of Princes*, ed. H. Bergen, EETS E.S. 121-4 (London, 1918-19), II.999-1000.

33. *Troy Book,* ed. H. Bergen, EETS E. S. 97, 103, 106, 120 (London, 1906-20), II.4715-19.

34. *Chaucerian and Other Pieces*, lines 239-40.

35. II.33-6, in *English Verse Between Chaucer and Surrey*, ed. Eleanor P. Hammond (Durham, North Carolina, 1927), p. 42.

36. *The Anxiety of Influence* (New York, 1973), p. 11. I note with interest, however, that in more recent work Bloom announces that he has changed his mind and now acknowledges that "the anxiety of influence ... is crucial in Euripides confronting Aeschylus or in Petrarch dreaming about Dante" (*The Breaking of the Vessels* [Chicago, 1982], p. 15).

37. *Familiarium rerum libri* XXXII.19, trans. Morris Bishop, *Letters from Petrarch* (Bloomington, 1966), pp. 198-9. The distinction Petrarch draws here is itself imitated from a classical author, the younger Seneca, to whom indeed he refers immediately after the passage quoted. Seneca writes:

> Even if there shall appear in you a likeness to him who, by reason of your admiration, has left a deep impress upon you, I would have you resemble him as a child resembles his father, and not as a picture resembles its original; for a picture is a lifeless thing (*Epistulae*

Morales, ed. and trans. R. N. Gumere [Cambridge, Mass., 1970], no. 84).

38. *The Anxiety of Influence,* p. 6.

39. *The Letters of D. H. Lawrence,* vol. 1, ed. James T. Boulton (Cambridge, 1979), p. 509.

40. *Troy Book* V. 3519-26.

41. *Testament of Cresseid,* lines 41, 64, from *The Works of Robert Henryson,* ed. Denton Fox (Oxford, 1981).

42. *The Proloug of the First Buke of Eneados,* in *Virgil's Aeneid,* ed. David F. C. Coldwell (Edinburgh, 1957), vol. II, lines 407, 418.

The Scottish Chaucer

Louise O. Fradenburg

This essay first appeared in Proceedings of the Third International Conference on Scottish Language and Literature *(Stirling and Glasgow: William Culross & Son, Ltd., 1981), pp. 177-90.*

T HE nature of Chaucer's influence on the Middle Scots poets has vexed scholarship for many years. Recent critics have been less concerned with quantifying that influence than with assessing its quality. We are more and more hearing statements that run something like this: "The Scottish poets of the fifteenth century found in Chaucer an important model, but they used that model to serve their own purposes." Certainly the more we understand about the workings of literary tradition in the Middle Ages, the less will Middle Scots poetics seem exceptionally, perhaps embarrassingly, derivative. We can usefully declare the Middle Scots poets to be as independent-minded as one could wish, and the scholarly renascence in this field has gone a long way in helping us to recognize the nature of that independence by pointing out the ability of Middle Scots poets to read critically and to depart from Chaucerian models.

We would be further helped in our understanding of "Scottish Chaucerianism"—that perilous phrase—if we inquired more energetically into the following matters: first, the nature of literary influence itself; second, the historicity of fifteenth-century Scotland—i.e., those features, if any, that distinguish the period from the rest of the Middle Ages; third, and finally, the interdependence of literary influence and historicity. The ways in which the Scottish poets of the fifteenth century read, and revised, Chaucer, differ significantly from the ways in which English poets of the sixteenth century received Chaucerian texts. We need, then, better to understand the nature of Chaucer's influence within the context of a fifteenth-century poetics of "intertextuality"—within the context, that is, of the way fifteenth-century Scottish poets rewrote, and hence wrote criticism about, their literary past.

One of the features most distinctive of the critical discourse—by which I mean the influenced text—of fifteenth-century Scotland is its frequent self-designation *as* critical discourse. All medieval texts refer to other texts in one way or another; all medieval texts recreate other texts in one way or another. What seems peculiar about fifteenth-century critical discourse is the frequency, again, with which it calls attention to its status as creative response. One thinks of the figure of Aesop in Henryson's fables, of Mapheus Vegius in the thirteenth book of Douglas's *Aeneid*; of the frequent allusions to Chaucer that signify real intertextual quarrels and reconciliations, instead of Chaucer's own allusions to mythical "auctours"; of the texts that, like the *Testament of Cresseid*, depend on a Chaucerian text for the completion of their meanings, but which in doing so complete the meanings of the Chaucerian text. These texts are "inscribed" with a consciousness of their relations to other texts; they frequently take, as a subject of their discourse, the nature of literary revisionism.

Fifteenth-century critical discourse tends to ask itself more explicitly what it is doing when it recreates past literature than do earlier medieval texts. And it also frequently calls attention to the pastness of its literary past. Though it is the sixteenth century that views Chaucer as the master of an age qualitatively different from its own—because misty, dark and savage—the fifteenth century nonetheless shows the dawning of a consciousness that Chaucer lived some time ago, and thus shows the beginnings of a new attention to its own historicity. By the fifteenth century, Chaucer has already become an "auctour," dignified by the passage of time. Dunbar's roll-call of poets in the "Lament for the Makars" begins with Chaucer and the Chaucerian language of praise; the "Lament" is, in part, a piece of literary history. The critical discourse of fifteenth-century Scots poets is often a historical discourse as well: it enacts a sense of the past, and a desire for the past.

The fifteenth century is also, in many respects, a century of experimentation—of what we should have to call "play." There is, in the fifteenth century, much raw newness to master. It is a transitional and hence duplicitous, Janus-like period; if we grant this duplicity we can grasp more fully why experimentalism goes hand in hand with a desire for the past in fifteenth-century critical discourse. The fifteenth-century poet often creates and explores new demands for meaning by picking apart earlier poetry, by decomposing it into fragments and then recomposing it, in order to see more clearly how it used to work; to see whether it can be pushed now in this direction, now in that; to make poetry out of the attempt. One of the features then, that distinguishes fifteenth-century revisionism is the pressures put upon the significance of the text by rapid and profound historical change— by, for example, the advent of printing, or by growing national aspirations. Mediation between past and present becomes unusually problematic. Fifteenth-century poets thus allude to Chaucer because, as a charismatic figure of literary authority who pioneered in their own language, he could consecrate their poetic experiments and speculations at a time of shifting power bases, intellectual and doctrinal pluralism, and their own growing claims to authority and recognition. Chaucer helped to satisfy their desire for the past, their wish to be connected to it. At the same time, his texts seemed lavishly to provide questions begging for answers, and models of discourse to be picked apart and re-analyzed.

What Chaucer also provides is *a* text, *a* discourse; a text that is, unmistakably, Chaucerian. The recognizability of the text, the text with a signature, is becoming a central ideal in the fifteenth century, and we see this both in the ways Chaucer is revised and the way he is emulated. Thus, alongside an implicit participation in the continuous re-creation of the matter of Troy, a work like the *Testament of Cresseid* answers explicitly and significantly to *Troilus and Criseyde*, by Geoffrey Chaucer. And fifteenth-century Scottish poets care about making their own texts recognizable. This desire should not be confused with Renaissance conceptions of textual heterocosms, self-sufficient "little worlds" of language; the fifteenth-century text is still open, on one side, to the past. But the fifteenth-century text, interestingly, often asserts itself *as* conclusion, and moreover rejects the distinctive Chaucerian strategy of palinode. Fifteenth-century critical discourse fills in the gaps which it discovers for itself in the Chaucerian text, and styles itself, often, as palinode *to* that text by offering it closure. Again, beyond that, the conclusive discourse of the fifteenth century rarely invites the revisions of later texts; when the invitation occurs, it is often oblique.

Thus, in the closing stanzas of the *Kingis Quair*, the poet-narrator directs his book to

> . . . pray the reder to haue pacience
> Of thy defaute, and to supporten it,
> Of his gudnesse thy brukilnesse to knytt
> And his tong for to reule and to stere
> That thy defautis helit may bene here.[1]

The poet, in an apparent gesture of humility, invites the reader to revise and improve the versification of his poem. But the *Kingis Quair*, it will be remembered, is very much taken up with the subject of how to "reule" and "stere" the unruly, so that the reader who may heal its faults can only do so in the metaphoric terms generated by the poem itself. The metaphors of the poem, as it were, try to maintain their control of the text even in performance. What, then, appears to be a modest recognition of poetic fallibility, and an invitation to further revision, becomes a means of asserting the continuing authority of the poem's rhetoric. The poet does not "retract" his earlier confidence in his text.

Fifteenth-century critical texts, then, both proclaim and deny their participation in an ongoing tradition of "Inglis" poetry. We can begin to explain this duplicity by reminding ourselves that the imperative behind much of Scottish revisionism in the fifteenth century was the enrichment, even the development, of a sophisticated vernacular culture. Several critics have noted that the historical task of the Middle Scots poets closely resembled Chaucer's own: all are writers engaged in the development of vernacular resources and the translation and adaptation of foreign literary models. This literary project was itself part of a larger imperative: the fifteenth century in Scotland was a period marked by a growing, and inevitably double, awareness both of national goals and European horizons. With all their foibles, most of its kings both responded to, and initiated, its challenges by experimenting energetically with the social, political, and economic materials to hand.

Not surprisingly, James I, long prisoner in England, made experimentation into something like a program. However straitened and confined the circumstances of his captivity must often have been, he demonstrated, upon his return to Scotland in 1424, that he had learnt more than one political lesson from the Lancastrian experiment—and that he had the zeal and the ambition immediately to put his knowledge into practice. By destroying, shortly after his return, the politically dangerous Albany Stewarts—and by accordingly revitalizing the crown's failing finances—he showed that he understood well the need to consolidate royal authority. His legislative practices, moreover, also demonstrate the influence of English models. The relatively pluralistic, localized nature of Scottish political power made wholesale adoption of the English model of centralized and intensive government an unlikely possibility, but James, however misguided, was an optimist. Gower called him Scotland's "'law-making king'";[2] and the articles of his first parliament, incongruously intermingling, as Ranald Nicholson puts it, provisions "that were to bring revolutionary political changes [with] . . . others that ordered the destruction of rooks' nests and of all fish weirs in tidal waters" indeed suggest that, for James, nothing "was too momentous or too inconsequential to escape legislation."[3] One scholar has called the *Kingis Quair* the "literary counterpart" of James's attempt to legislate into being a bicameral parliament.[4] James's plan for a parliament modelled on English lines, and the *Quair*'s encouragement of "songis new" inspired by foreign literary models, both attest a kind of pioneering spirit.

Significantly, James's legislation often bespeaks what Nicholson calls a "sense of national identity." It points clearly, in fact, to an exhaustive program of fully national scope, one which would regulate husbandry and the economy, and centralize the forms of political power—all for the greater glory and enrichment of Scotland and its king. James, in short, wanted to build a state that could rival in strength and prestige the other emergent nations of an increasingly new Europe.

The cultural language of James's court life articulates an identical message. When Linlithgow castle was destroyed by fire, James eloquently replaced it with "an imposing royal residence, more palace than castle."[5] We know, too, that James's court was likely a literary one, if only because his daughters Margaret and Eleanor both wrote and translated poetry. The financial records are also eloquent on the sums expended for continental luxuries and entertainment. However limited the Scottish crown's resources in comparison to England or France, the cultural life of James's court suggests a desire to emulate the leisured culture of rival courts. The code of aristocratic consumption in the new Europe spoke political volumes; its nostalgic pageantry symbolized the aspirations of the present as much as the desire for the past.

However limited the practical results of James's centralizing policies, his dedication to the Europeanization of Scotland lends special weight to MacQueen's contention that James pursued a literary policy—that the *Quair*, in particular, urges something like a rebirth of Scottish vernacular literature, to be inspired by foreign literary models.[6] The *Quair* should indeed be read within the context of fifteenth-century Scotland's increasing self-awareness, and its corresponding willingness to appropriate what it could from its neighbors—within the context of new concepts of a national polity and centralized authority.

One of the important points, too, that this context helps us to clarify, is that the desire for the past in Scottish critical discourse of the fifteenth century includes the desire for *a* literary past. It is in fact a desire to incorporate the literary past of its European rivals, the desire to create for itself an impressive tradition that it can, then, reinterpret or "finish." The fifteenth-century Scottish pioneers of vernacular humanism articulated for themselves a celebrated poetic genealogy precisely because their own discourse was experimental and, again, to some degree nationalistic. Dunbar's "Lament" argues the stellar origins of Middle Scots poetry by asserting an unbroken line of achievement in sophisticated genres from Chaucer, "of makaris flour," to himself; it is a piece of historical revisionism, but a piece which makes clear the enabling function of both Chaucerian allusion and Chaucerian text. In a Scottish text, the Chaucerian allusion is mythopoetic.

The legend of James I's cultural achievements plays a similar role in the fifteenth century's interpretation of Scottish literary history. By using the word "legend" I do not mean to raise doubts about James's authorship of the *Kingis Quair*. I mean instead to suggest that, whether or not he wrote the *Quair*—or any other poem, for that matter—some important fifteenth-century writers and readers wished to believe that he did; and that wish is itself of historical significance. These fifteenth-century writers and readers may, of course, have been correct in attributing such literary accomplishments to James I; what matters in the present context is how the fact of his authorship, if it be fact, was perceived and interpreted by his contemporaries. The fifteenth century's desire for the Chaucerian text is, as I have suggested, enacted in mythopoesis, and the belief that Scotland's law-making king was also a makar becomes embedded in its own turn in the historical discourse of manuscript and chronicle. The *Quair* itself, that is, becomes an important part of the vernacular culture's need to dignify itself with a tradition.

Bower, in praising James's musical and scholarly talents, employs the trope of Egyptian gold, derived ultimately from the *De doctrina christiana* and often used in defenses of poetry. He describes James "'translatus in Angliam, tanquam alter Josephus ductus in Aegyptum.'"[7] This trope, used in the context of the *Scotichronicon*, triumphantly revises James's eighteen years of captivity into a promise of Scotland's future cultural and political greatness; Scotland's greatness, the trope implies, will incorporate and supersede that of England, the old land of exile. Something like this propagandistic spirit inspires Dunbar's genealogy of poets.

One of the most important pieces of evidence we have for James's authorship of the *Quair* is the testimony of the manuscript that contains the only surviving copy of the poem (Selden Arch. B 24, in the Bodleian library). Evidence in the manuscript tells us that it was probably commissioned by Henry, third Lord St. Clair; that it was in the possession of, and read by, members or the St. Clair family for quite some time. One of the poem's recent editors suggests that a St. Clair wrote the heading to the poem: "'Heireftir followis the quair Maid be/King James of scotland the first.'"[8] James's authorship, then, appears to have been a St. Clair family tradition, if not a matter of historical fact; and the St. Clairs were incontestably a cultured, well-read family, important patrons of Scottish vernacular humanism from early on in the fifteenth century. This, again, does not prove that James wrote the *Quair*; it proves that, when the St. Clairs read the poem, they were pleased to believe that they were reading a poem by James I—our early hero of Scottish culture. For the St. Clairs, at least, Chaucerianism was sanctioned by Stewart authority. That we find James's name thus embedded in the Selden manuscript—the "largest single source" of English poems "'translait' into Scots"[9]—tells us much about historical myth-making in fifteenth-century Scottish literature.

The Selden manuscript was largely the work of the scribe James Gray, whom MacQueen describes as a "specialist" in vernacular literature. Gray is known to have served, besides the St. Clairs, Archbishop Schevez—"the king of early Scots [book] collectors"[10] who participated in the "outburst of liturgical and devotional nationalism" at the close of the fifteenth century by conducting a search for the relics of St. Palladius.[11] These facts suggest that the manuscript was compiled within the context of a deliberate, energetic enrichment of Scots vernacular resources .

The manuscript itself contains several works by Chaucer "translait" into Scots—among them the *Parliament of Fowls*, the *Legend of Good Women*, and the *Troilus*, with which last the manuscript begins. It also contains several works attributed to Chaucer but not in fact by him—Lydgate's *Complaint of the Black Knight*, for instance. The Chaucerian pieces take up the first part of the manuscript; the two major works which conclude the manuscript are the *Kingis Quair* followed by the *Quare of Jelusy*. The latter poem is itself indebted to the *Kingis Quair*.

As part of the new vogue in manuscripts devoted exclusively, or largely, to genuine or purported works by Chaucer, the Selden manuscript attests the centrality of the Chaucerian text to the aspirations of Scottish culture. By bringing together Chaucer's important courtly works—the colophons are careful to name him, and to title his poems—with two later Scots Chaucerian pieces, the manuscript historicizes revisionist poetics in a bound volume.

Here we see the manuscript as historical discourse—like Dunbar's "Lament," helping Scottish vernacular poetry to a celebrated literary past.

The *Kingis Quair* and another poem in the Selden manuscript, "Blak be thy bandis," can illustrate for us at least one of the distinctive features of fifteenth-century historical discourse: the desire to "finish" the Chaucerian text. The following stanza, written by the scribe James Gray, follows the manuscript's text of the *Troilus*:

> Blak be thy bandis/and thy wede [also]
> Thou soroufull book of mat*er* disesparit
> In tokenyng of thyn inward mortall wo
> Quiche is so bad/þ*at* may not been enparit
> Thou oughtest neu*er* outward ben enfarit
> That hast within /so many a sorourull cl . . . .
> Suich be thyne habyte as thou hast thy . . . . [12]

These lines suggest the self-awareness of fifteenth-century discourse. The scribe poses the rhetorical question of whether the *Troilus* ought to be published, so to speak, at all; so great is the poem's "inward wo" that it should perhaps remain a private experience. But the very language of Gray's own commentary on the *Troilus* derives in part from the *Troilus*, as the following lines make clear:

> For wel sit it, the sothe for to seyne,
> A woful wight to han a drery feere,
> And to a sorwful tale, a sory chere. [13]

In Gray's metaphor, black bindings and "wede" become editorial "tokenyngs," representations of the poem's meaning—of its "inward mortall wo." The metaphor of the book's black weeds becomes, in fact, a kind of pun, a concretization of the principles of Chaucerian literary decorum—a sorrowful tale should have a sorrowful "chere"—and hence becomes a means of fulfilling, of "finishing," the Chaucerian intention which the scribe has read in—or into—the *Troilus*.

Interestingly, the dominant tone of Gray's reading of the *Troilus* is one of grief and loss—not, as seems to be true of certain modern readings of the poem, one of ironic distance from the miserable sufferings of the heathen. Gray's reading seems, in fact, to have been largely unaffected by the palinode which occupies the close of the *Troilus*. It is therefore no accident that Gray should have chosen to place, after his own stanza of lamentation, Chaucer's "Truth"—with its rhetoric of urgent exhortation and its message of consolation: "trouthe thee shal delivere, it is no drede." The strategy of this "Balade de Bon Conseyl," in urging "thou Vache" to "leve thyn old wrecchednesse" and turn instead to prayer—"Crye him mercy, that of his hy goodnesse/Made thee of noght"—repeats the strategy of the *Troilus*'s palinode, in which the "yonge, fresshe folkes" are urged to reject feigned loves and to trust instead in the love of Christ. For the scribe of the Selden manuscript, "Truth" becomes part of a pattern of compensation for the betrayal of language and of intimacy—of "trouthe," in fact—documented by the closing book of Chaucer's poem. Inscribed into the Selden text of "Truth" is the devastating emotionality of Troilus's loss; the "I-thou" address of "Truth" reinforces the grammatical shift toward the audience at the end of the *Troilus*, so that the affect generated by the *Troilus* and concretized in Gray's own stanza is subjected to new scrutiny. By placing "Truth" after his own poem, Gray tries to finish editorially what Chaucer had begun in the palinode to the *Troilus*.

The *Kingis Quair* itself is closely related to three important Chaucerian texts: the *Parliament of Fowles*, the *Knight's Tale,* and perhaps most importantly, the *Troilus*. One crucial feature of the *Quair*'s critical poetics is the revision of Chaucer's lyric strategies. Chaucer seems always to have felt dubious about, or troubled by, the courtly lyric. Few of his survive, and those which he embeds in his narratives tend to have an uncomfortable relationship with their surroundings. The beautiful song sung by Troilus at the close of Book III—"Love, that of erthe and se hath governaunce"—is difficult, for some readers at least, to re-read without an accompanying sense of confusion and loss, and perhaps irony. The final stanza runs as follows:

> So wolde God, that auctour is of kynde,
> That with his bond Love of his vertu liste
> To cerclen hertes alle, and faste bynde,
> That from his bond no wight the wey out wiste;
> And hertes colde, hem wolde I that he twiste
> To make hem love, and that hem liste ay rewe
> On hertes sore, and kepe hem that ben trewe.
> (III, 1765-71)

Read within the context of Troilus's story—how he fell "Fro wo to wele, and after out of joie"—this lyric becomes a desiring text whose desire is finally left unfulfilled; and it becomes an idealizing text whose language describes the might-have-been and the ought-to-have-been, but not things as-they-came-to-be. The referent for this lyric within the larger narrative is problematic and ambiguous; the lyric voice that speaks this text is alienated from the narrative intention that gives rise to it.

The poet-narrator of the *Quair* experiences, as several scholars have noted, the reverse of Troilus's fortunes in love, to the point where the new Troilus appeals to the happiness of his love as justification both for writing a poem about himself and persuading others to love. His suggestion that others follow his example is legitimated by the *Quair*, whereas Troilus's prayer that "colde hertes" be made to love as he loves is at least questioned by the surrounding narrative. The *Quair*-poet accordingly revises Troilus's song so that it becomes virtually the last word on love. He poses the following rhetorical question:

Eke quho may in this lyfe haue more plesance
Than cum to largesse from thraldom and peyne,
And by the mene of luffis ordinance,
That has so mony in his goldin cheyne.

(st. 183)

The poet-narrator makes this ebullient remark towards the close of his narrative, after we have been assured of the happy outcome of his love. In this passage, Troilus's heavenly words have a clearly defined referent: the poet-narrator himself, whose narrative of discipline in the service of a Christian love fully legitimates his own lyricism. The lyricism of Book III in the *Troilus* is an "entremes," a "respit"; in the *Quair* it enables closure because it is not alienated from, but rather is the culmination of, the narrative intention.

The concluding stanzas of the *Quair*, moreover, offer a prayer of thanksgiving—to the nightingale, who sings to the poet of love; to the allegorical guides who taught him love's service; finally to God himself "that all oure lyf hath writt." The move to prayer repeats the move to prayer at the end of the *Troilus*, but here the rhetorical shift does not threaten to erase the preceding narrative. This is no palinode, for though the poem's conclusion transcends its beginnings it also grows unambiguously out of them. Whereas Chaucer's prayer to the Trinity seems to ask us to "quit" the narrative, to make a fresh start away from the sobering lessons of human desire and human poetry, the *Quair*-poet's prayer—addressed to a poet-God—closes the narrative of desire that precedes it by authorizing that narrative. In doing this, the *Quair*-poet redefines the possibilities for poetic closure offered by the *Troilus*.

Here we must remember James Gray's decision to repeat Chaucer's final prayer by placing "Truth" after his own woebegone comment on the *Troilus*. This gesture, importantly, expresses agreement less with the *Quair*'s themes of "trouthe" in human love than with its strategy of reinforcing closure. The redefinition of Chaucerian closure is a central feature of the critical poetics of the fifteenth century. It reveals a desire to re-write, or to write again, the Chaucerian text; it reveals a desire to align fifteenth-century texts with the Chaucerian text, but a desire also to re-finish that text, and hence to disclose new narrative purposes or emphasize anew the potentialities of older ones. The redefinition of closure thus helps Scottish poets of the fifteenth century to enact their literary and historical aspirations. It enables them to create a dignified literary past which they can then reinterpret, and bring to what they see as a new fullness, a newly meaningful end. For the fifteenth-century Scottish poets, Chaucer is neither a poet to be slavishly imitated, nor simply a text to be plundered or ignored at will; instead, through a richly complicated process of historical revisionism, Chaucer's text authorizes, and helps to articulate, the dream of a sophisticated vernacular poetry in "Scottis."

1. St. 194. Citations from the *Kingis Quair* are to *The Kingis Quair of James Stewart*, ed. Matthew P. McDiarmid (Totowa, NJ:Rowman and Littlefield, 1973).

2. W. Goodall, ed. *Johannis de Fordun Scotichronicon cum Supplementis et Continuatione Walteri Bower* (Edinburgh, 1759), II. 482; quoted by Ranald Nicholson, in *Scotland: The Later Middle Ages* (Edinburgh: Oliver & Boyd, 1974), p. 305.

3. Nicholson, p. 305.

4. Gregory Kratzmann, *Anglo-Scottish Literary Relations: 1430-1550* (Cambridge: Cambridge University Press, 1980), p. 34.

5. Nicholson, p. 319.

6. John MacQueen, "The literature of fifteenth-century Scotland," in *Scottish Society in the Fifteenth Century*, ed. Jennifer Brown (London: Edward Arnold, 1977), p. 188.

7. See *Scotichronicon* XVI 28, 30; quoted by E. W. M. Balfour-Melville, in *James I, King of Scots: 1406-1437* (London: Methuen & Co., Ltd., 1936), pp. 52-53.

8. McDiarmid, p. 5.

9. Kratzmann, p. 14.

10. John Durkan and Anthony Ross, *Early Scottish Libraries* (Glasgow: John S. Burns & Sons, 1961), p. 6.

11. Nicholson, p. 560.

12. Ed. Robert Kilburn Root, *The Manuscripts of Chaucer's Troilus*, Chaucer Soc.,1st Ser., No. 98 (London and Oxford: Kegan Paul, Trench, Trübner & Co., Limited, and the Oxford University Press, 1914 [for 1911] , rpt. 1967), p. 43.

13. I, 12-14. Citations from Chaucer's works are to *The Works of Geoffrey Chaucer*, 2nd ed., ed F. N. Robinson (Boston: Houghton Mifflin Company, 1957).

Textual Authority and the Works of Hoccleve, Lydgate, and Henryson

Tim William Machan

This essay first appeared in Viator *23 (1992): 281-99.*

C HAUCER'S legacy to fifteenth-century vernacular writers was manifold and includes the decasyllabic line, a distinctive poetic persona, vivid characterization, and, perhaps most importantly, what A. C. Spearing has called an *"idea* of English poetry."[1] As a vernacular writer working within cultural constraints which typically reserved "auctor" as an honorific for select ancient and Christian Latin writers, Chaucer often explored this idea in his comments on the relations between his own compositions and the literary traditions to which they respond. Such relations are examined in the extra-dream frame, windows, and tapestries of the *Book of the Duchess,* in the description of "Fames halle" in the *House of Fame,* in the account of the "Dream of Scipio" in the *Parliament of Fowls,* and in the discussion of experience and authority in the prologue to the *Legend of Good Women.* In these instances, in various ways, Chaucer explicitly juxtaposes his compositions (and himself) with the prior texts which enable and inform his works. By medieval standards, it is these prior texts of classical poets and learned commentators which are typically judged the only authoritative texts both in the sense of being original creations and in the sense of having the unimpeachable "auctoritas" of an "auctor." But if Chaucer's affirmation of such authoritative intertextual fields legitimizes his work as a vernacular writer, his self-conscious confrontation of these writers and texts bespeaks an awareness of the complex and potentially problematic nature of concepts like textual authority and authorship.

It is in the *Troilus,* where Chaucer utilizes the fiction of Lollius and his text, that the various relations between the modern vernacular work and the ancient authorial book are most fully explored. In the poem's famous conclusion, for instance, Chaucer affirms the culturally subordinate status of vernacular poetry by admonishing his "Litel bok" to

subgit be to alle poesye;

And kis the steppes where as thow seest pace
Virgile, Ovide, Omer, Lucan, and Stace.
(5.1790-1792)[2]

At the same time, however, he validates his own composition by situating it in this literary tradition only one step below these culturally recognized "auctores." And the implication is that Gower, inasmuch as Chaucer sends the book out to him, is not even on the staircase.

Many (if not most) medieval vernacular writers depict themselves as inheritors and translators of prior books, but to Chaucer this relationship offered both thematic potential and a way to define a suitable literary role for himself within the constraints of late medieval culture. His writings, consequently, could serve as a model for vernacular writers with similar metatextual interests. In the fifteenth century, in fact, the "*idea* of English poetry"—and, more particularly, Chaucer's desire to invest vernacular works with textual authority—was understood, accepted, and implemented in varying ways. Here, I am concerned with three fifteenth-century writers— Hoccleve, Lydgate, and Henryson—and with the question of how the concept of an authorial book that a vernacular writer translates or extends functions thematically and rhetorically in select works.

For Hoccleve, the issue of textual authority was perhaps of little importance, since much of his poetry was contemporary and topical. His works, that is, often rest on their own textual authority or on the authority of history without explicitly confronting the metatextual issues I mentioned at the outset. His various begging and commemorative poems, for example, respond to contemporary, historical issues and therefore need not concern themselves with the intertextual fields from which they emerge. Even in a poem like that on Henry V's accession to the throne, which might invite the use of a variety of exempla, Hoccleve focuses as much on the here and now as he does in a poem like the "Balade to My Maister Carpenter," wherein he entreats Carpenter to intercede between him and his debtors. Furthermore, while a work like the *Regement of Princes* may itself respond to a long literary heritage, this response is compromised by poems like the balades to Edward, duke of York, and John, duke of Bedford; as envoys to presentation copies, they recuperate the *Regement* as primarily a topical work.

All that being said, however, it must also be said that when Hoccleve does turn his eye to the issue of textual authority, he does so with sometimes startling clarity. Whatever the historical value of the numerous autobiographical passages,[3] for example, they necessarily show an awareness—perhaps learned from Chaucer—of a narrator's rhetorical presence in his own narration. The sequence of poems known as the *Series,* moreover, is, to use John Burrow's phrase, "to an unusual degree preoccupied with the business of its own composition."[4] The design of the *Series* in fact encourages "the reader to feel as if he were looking over the poet's shoulder as it took shape."[5] In this regard, one should also note the interplay in the *Series* between Hoccleve as vernacular poet and his Friend as the voice of literary tradition or textual authority, which typically predetermines what the vernacular writer will compose. It is the Friend, for instance, who in the "Dialogue" advises Hoccleve not to publish the "Complaint" (25-35)[6] and who inquires what Hoccleve intends to write next (199-202). But the relationship between the Friend and Hoccleve is, significantly, a dialectic in which each party contributes to the composition of the *Series*. The Friend, that is, appears in part as a literary adviser who presents the vernacular poet with the books he is to transmit, but Hoccleve actively engages these books and shapes them to his own designs. For example, the *Series* de facto overrules the Friend's advice against publication of the "Complaint," and ultimately the Friend affirms Hoccleve's control over the work he is producing:

> Do foorth in goddes name / & nat ne woonde
> To make and wryte / what thyng þat thee list.
> ("Dialogue" 523-524)

This literary dialectic is similarly apparent when the Friend, specifying only that Hoccleve write something favorable of women (785-786), leaves to Hoccleve the choice of which work to compose. Hoccleve exercises his literary authority by writing the "Tale of Jereslaus's Wife," but the Friend returns a week or two later to discover that the poem has no "moralizynge" and asks:

> . . . was ther noon in the book
> Out of the which / þat thow this tale took?
> (epilogue to the "Tale" 13-14)

He produces another book with the requisite moral—which Hoccleve translates—and thereby demonstrates the strength of literary tradition.[7] But Hoccleve then reasserts his own authority by eventually translating the Latin treatise *Learn to Die,* which in the "Dialogue" he had proposed to do (204-206); and he advances his own claim to authority perhaps even more strongly in the work itself, for after translating part of the piece he observes the labor is "so greet thyng / to swich a fool as me" (921) that he substitutes a prose translation of the ninth lesson of All Hallow's Day for the final three parts of the treatise. Nonetheless, the vernacular poet remains in a dialectic with tradition, for when the lesson is completed Hoccleve notes:

> This booke thus to han endid had y thoght,
> But my freend made me change my cast,
> Cleere out of þat purpos hath he me broght.
> (1-3)

And indeed the Friend as textual authority sends to Hoccleve yet another book (82-84): "The Tale of Jonathas." As Burrow notes, "The *Series* is . . .

designed both to affirm [Hoccleve's] recovery and also, by its very existence, to prove it by showing that he can indeed talk sense again."[8] It is important to recognize, however, that such talk, as the *Series* constitutes it, is not a monologue but a dialogue with old books and literary tradition.

In the *Regement of Princes* Hoccleve confronts the issue of textual authority on a number of occasions but never, I think, exploits the thematic potential of his material to the extent that he does in the *Series*. He is careful, for instance, to itemize his three sources (2038-2053, 2108-2114),[9] but he does not subsequently involve these books and their authors thematically—as Chaucer does with Lollius or Henryson with Aesop—and in fact he mentions them only sporadically. For example:

> Aristotle amonestith wonder faste,
> In his book whiche to Alisaundre he wroot.
> (3109-3110)

To be sure, Hoccleve does present himself as rather actively engaging literary tradition in a Chaucerian vein. He describes Chaucer as the Virgil of English poetry (2085-2086), and also makes his own identity dependent on a connection with Chaucer. When the Beggar asks him his name, that is, and the poet replies, "Hoccleue, fadir myn, men clepen me" (1864), the Beggar recognizes him through his association with the premier English poet:

> Sone, I haue herd, or this, men speke of þe;
> Þou were aqueynted with Caucher [*sic*], pardee.
> (1866-1867)

The poem literally inscribes, then, an idea of English poetry which conceives Chaucer as the fountainhead and Hoccleve as one of the rivulets, though the topic is never examined in detail.

Hoccleve's ambivalence towards the issue of textual authority—his simultaneous recognition and only mild interest—is clearest in the treatment of the famous Chaucer portrait introduced in stanza 714.[10] In the portrait in Harley 4866, Chaucer, who "fayn wolde han . . . taght" (2078) Hoccleve, emerges from a windowlike picture frame in the page to point to the lines which refer to him. The very existence of this unusual marginal portrait of an actual historical writer pointing self-reflexively at the verses which describe him is itself a testament to the extraordinary status Chaucer as an individual poet had already acquired among certain fifteenth-century writers.[11] Even more suggestive, however, is the placement of the figure: the head and torso are within the frame, while the right arm extends naturally outside and across the frame to enable the index finger to direct the reader's gaze to the text of Hoccleve's poem. Imagistically, Chaucer thus stands behind the text on the page but also emerges to constitute a connection between Chaucer and his texts—which inspired Hoccleve—and Hoccleve's poem. This image is thus potentially a richly symbolic representation of both the intertextual fields from which any work emerges and of the nascent establishment of an idea of English poetry which is mediated not simply by works or themes but also by individual writers. As provocative as this juxtaposition of text and picture in the *Regement* might be, however, what is perhaps most striking about the passage is the fact that Hoccleve does so little with it. He incorporates the picture primarily to point to something extratextual—the reality of the historical Chaucer—just as

> The ymages þat in þe chirche been,
> Maken folk þenke on god & on his seyntes.
>   (4999-5000)[12]

In fact, as I have just suggested, the text which the picture helps to create is itself latent with symbolic potential, and the sense here of a missed—or unnoticed—opportunity becomes strongest if one speculates on what Chaucer might have done with a portrait of Lollius at the end of the *Troilus*.

Of the three writers with whom I am concerned, Lydgate is by far the one most given to references to the books and authors on which his compositions depend. And it is not simply the larger size of his poetic output which accounts for these references, for he insistently returns to the topic in poem after poem. What also differentiates Lydgate from Hoccleve, however, is the greater superficiality of his treatment. At the risk of using a cliché of Lydgate criticism, I would suggest that it is as if Lydgate, more so than Hoccleve, recognized the fact that Chaucer was interested in textual authority but not the thematic and rhetorical strategies which defined his interest.[13] Here I will confine my remarks to the *Siege*, the minor poems, and the *Fall of Princes*.

The *Siege of Thebes,* of course, is Lydgate's contribution to the *Canterbury Tales* and purports to be the first tale told on the return portion of the pilgrimage. By writing himself into the fiction of Chaucer's poem, Lydgate necessarily foregrounds the fact that he is responding to another's book. The story he chooses to tell, moreover, is one of the oldest and most popular in western European literature, so that subject matter as well as narrative frame implicitly emphasize the existence of preceding textual authorities. Lydgate's most immediate source is a French prose version of the *Roman de Thebes,* his treatment of which further seems to project an awareness of the issue of textual authority. As Derek Pearsall points out,

> Lydgate was well aware of the inferior "authority" of
> such vernacular romances; he makes no specific mention
> of his source, but laces the narrative with more or less
> relevant passages from the encyclopedic works of
> Boccaccio, to whom he alludes frequently, so that the
> uninitiated reader might assume that his source was
> Boccaccio throughout.[14]

Given Boccaccio's accomplishments as one of the premier vernacular writers,[15] Lydgate may well have intended to encourage such an assumption in order to give his poem a greater claim to authority; and the explicit connection to Chaucer and the *Canterbury Tales* might serve much the same purpose.

While Lydgate takes a number of liberties with his source, throughout the *Siege* it is his dependence on its textual authority and his role as mere translator that he stresses. He does not, for instance, indicate the way in which Edippus kills Laius, because "the story / writ not the maner howh" (582),[16] nor does he describe what happens after Polyneices and Tideus go to bed with Adrastus's daughters, "For it is nat declared / in my boke" (1505). The limitations imposed by the authorial book are also clear in the account of the battle between the Thebans and the Greeks in part 3, where Lydgate declares:

> But al the maner / tellen I ne may
> Of her fightyng / nor her slaughter in soth,
> Mor to declare / than myn Autour doth.
> (4252-4254)

There is, as I have suggested, something arch in this posture, for the *Siege* is scarcely a slavish translation. But more importantly, if there is a thematic purpose in the leitmotif of references to Lydgate's author and book, it is never clear what it is. Much of the time, indeed, these references are essentially metrical fillers which rather statically occupy a half-line before or after the caesura but which are not extensions of the surrounding themes or narrative matter. For example, in a brief "occupatio" after Eteocles expresses his disappointment that Polyneices should want to claim the throne and banish him from Thebes the reference to Lydgate's "story" exists solely for the rhyme it enables:

> Al that he spak, / who that couth aduerte,
> Of verrey scorn, Rooted in his herte;
> As it sempte /, the story can ȝou teche,
> By the surplus / sothly of his speche.
> (1993-1996)

Similarly, there is no metatextual significance when Lydgate refers to himself as reader in his account of Tideus's encounter with Ipsiphyle and King Lycurgus's son:

> And in hir Armes / a litil child hadd she . . .
> Sone of the kyng / born forto succede,
> Called ligurgus / in story as I rede.
> (3030, 3033-3034)

Other rhyme-motivated references to Lydgate's author or book or to other books include: "the story kan reherce," "the story telleth vs," "be recorde of wryting," and "as bookes specifye." In all, there are some twenty-six such post-caesura half-lines in the *Siege* which exist apparently only for the sake of rhyme.[17]

In eight instances, it is the half-line before the caesura which contains the metrically motivated metatextual allusion.[18] In describing the guests summoned by Adrastus to his daughters' weddings, for example, Lydgate notes:

> And thyder cam ful many lusty knyght,
> Ful wel beseyn / and many lady briȝt,
> From euery Coost / and many frecssh sqwyer,
> Þe Story seith / and many comunere.
> (1657-1660)

Or when Tideus first appears in the tale, Lydgate observes:

> Of aventure / ther cam / a knyght ryding,
> The worthiest in this world lyvyng,
> Curteys, lowly / and right vertuous,
> As seith myn autour / Called Tidyus.
> (1263-1266)

On eighteen occasions, these references occupy an entire line, as in the record of Edippus's reign:

> And as myn autour writ / in wordys pleyn,
> by Iocasta he had sones tweyn.
> (877-878)[19]

And at the conclusion to the second part of the poem, Lydgate's metatextual digression fills three lines:

> As the story / shal clerly determyne,
> And my tale / her-after shal ȝou lere,
> ȝif that ȝow list / the remenaunt for to here.
> (2550-2552)[20]

Even in these longer passages, the references are self-contained and could be removed without the poem being materially affected. The filler quality of Lydgate's allusions to authors and books perhaps becomes clearest, however, when one compares them to Chaucer's treatment of the same topic. For instance, the famous stanza about Lollius which introduces the "Canticus Troili" of book 1 of the *Troilus* is thematically significant in the way in which it juxtaposes incongruent theory and practice: Chaucer insists there is only a "tonges difference" between himself and his Latin "auctor," when in fact he here blends one of Petrarch's sonnets into Boccaccio's *Il Filostrato.*[21] And this juxtaposition, in turn, figures in a larger thematic exploration of the narrator's role in the poem. To be sure, not all of Chaucer's metatextual references are thematically motivated. For instance, the fact that the Franklin, in dating the concealment of the rocks off the coast of Brittany to December, chooses the date "as thise bookes [him] remembre" (5.1243) seems in no way significant. What is significant, though, is the desultory appearance of such perfunctory remarks; when Chaucer repeatedly refers to his sources—as is the case in the *Troilus* but not the *Franklin's Tale*—there is always a discernible purpose.

Another type of passage in the *Siege* which suggests a perfunctory interest in the "auctor" and his book is that which juxtaposes the "auctor's" book with other accounts of the same story. After attributing the building of Thebes to King Amphioun, for instance, Lydgate asserts:

> But sothly ʒit / Some expositours,
> Groundyng hem / vpon olde auctours
> Seyn that Cadmvs / the famous olde man,
> Ful longe afor / this Cite first began.
> (293-296)

Or when discussing Ipsiphyle's lineage Lydgate states:

> Hir fadres name / of which also I wante,
> Thouh some seyn / he named was Thoante,
> And some bokes · vermes ek hym calle.
> (3194-3196)

It is apparent in these allusions that Lydgate perceives unanimity among these varying authorial books. Even when the accounts diverge, Lydgate attempts to reconcile or downplay the differences, as if to imply that textual authority and authorial opinions are by nature consistent with each other because they reflect the transcendent truths of life.[22] For instance, when Tideus, one of the poem's heroes,[23] enters Argos, Lydgate is careful to qualify any moral disapproval which might attend his banishment from Caledonia:

> And he, allas / out of that Regioun
> Exiled was / for he his brother sclowe,
> As Stace of Thebes / writ the manere howe,
> Al be that he / to hym no malys mente.
> (1270-1273)

The books cannot be reconciled in the account of Tideus's refusal to enter Thebes in part 3, which some books are said to attribute not to prudence but to folly. There, Lydgate relies on the immediate textual authority of his "book" and simply states the difference of opinion without exploring the thematic potential of such differences:

> Though some bookes / the contrarye seyn:
> But myn Autour / is platly ther-ageyn,
> And affermeth / in his opynyoun,
> That Tydeus / of hegh discrecioun,
> Of wilfulnesse / nor of no folye,
> Ne wold as tho put in Iupartie
> Nowther hym-silf / nor non of his ferys.
> (3971-3977)

A useful way to approach such metatextual passages, again, is through comparison to similar passages by Chaucer. Book 5 of the *Troilus,* for instance, is in part characterized by the various ways in which the narrator distances himself from his story by stressing its conditional nature: his tale, he insists, is only one version of one historical incident, created from complex and sometimes discordant intertextual fields. For example, the narrator alerts the reader to some stories, which he cannot confirm, that indicate Criseyde gave Diomede "hire herte" (1050); in Cassandra's lengthy equation of Diomede with the boar in Troilus's dream (1457-1519), the poem foregrounds the complex narrative background and potential of the smallest part of any story; the conditional nature of this *Troilus and Criseyde* is again apparent when the narrator refers readers interested in Troilus's "worthi dedes'' to other versions of the story (1770-1771) and also gives notice of his own future compositions (1772-1778); and he underscores this conditionality when, as I noted at the outset, he affirms a place for his text in a literary tradition in which the *Troilus* coexists with the other works to which he has alluded. Such metatextual motivations, however, are entirely lacking in corresponding passages in Lydgate's *Siege.* The conflicting views about the founder of Thebes or the name of Ipsiphyle's father seem more idle curiosity than inquiry into the problematic nature of origins; Statius's account of Tideus's exile, latent with potentially negative criticism, is quickly bypassed, so that his account becomes consonant with Lydgate's; and the blatantly differing versions of Tideus's motivation in part 3 are simply stated and thus accommodated without consideration of the limitations of a narrator's viewpoint or the conditionality of any narrative.

In the minor poems there is a similar pattern of incorporation but not integration of references to authors and their books. "The Kings of England Sithen William Conqueror," for example, is a 210-line stanzaic poem which itemizes the accomplishments of all the English kings from Alfred the Great to Henry VI.[24] It is thus explicitly dependent on textual authorities for its content and structurally patterned in a way that emphasizes this dependence. References to chronicles, books, and authors, moreover, permeate the poem. In the poem's 210 lines, in fact, there are twenty-nine metrically motivated lines or half-lines of the sort I noted earlier, including "as seith myn auctor," "as bookys speceffye," "as I reede," and "as seith the Cronycleer."[25] The reader is thus continually aware of the intertextual fields from which the poem emerges, but, because the references are so perfunctory, they cease to point to the texts which precede them and become merely rhetorical flourishes. A case in point is the following passage on William Rufus, who

> xiiij yeer bar his crown in deede,
> Buried at Wynchestir, þe cronycle ye may reede.
> (118-119)

One other feature common in the minor poems merits consideration here: Lydgate's dismissal of his own "book" in an envoy. His inspiration for such dismissals, again, was almost certainly the famous line at the end of Chaucer's *Troilus:* "Go, litel bok, go, litel myn tragedye" (5.1786).[26] In Chaucer's poem the thematic purposes of the line are manifold: it furthers the narrator's withdrawal from the poem and, concomitantly, solidifies the conception of the *Troilus* as a completed literary artifact; it places this artifact in a literary tradition; and, for these and other reasons, it furthers the metatextual themes of the poem. In short, it is part of a grand and eloquent conclusion to a grand and eloquent poem which imputes textual authority to Chaucer's own composition.

Lydgate seems to have been particularly struck by this line, one of the most profoundly metatextual in the Chaucerian canon. In fact, 19 of the 146 numbered poems in MacCracken's two-volume edition conclude with an envoy beginning something like "Goo litel tretys," "Go, lytil pistel," "Go, lyitill byll," ". . . go forth, litle Table," "Go, lytel balade," or "Go, litel quayre."[27] There may well be a thematic appropriateness in the reification such a dismissal occasions in "The Complaint of the Black Knight" or in the precatory "To Mary, the Queen of Heaven": in each case the text of the poem is both a message and a missive. But it is not at all clear why the collection of commonplaces entitled "That Now Is Hay Some-Tyme Was Grase" invites the intimate self-referentiality of "Go forth anon, thou short dite" (129), or why "Look in Thy Merour, and Deeme Noon Othir Wight," another collection of commonplaces that stresses the intrinsic value of all people and counsels mercy and virtue, should end with the following paradoxical affirmation and denial of itself as a poetic object: "Go litel bille withoute title or date" (209). Similarly paradoxical is the dismissal in the envoy of "Stans Puer ad Mensam," a didactic poem on manners and etiquette only ninety-nine lines long: "Go, Iytel bylle, barren of elloquence" (92). Here, an eloquent conclusion is adapted for a brief, avowedly ineloquent poem on mundane matters. In general, the effect of such inappropriate dismissals is much like that of the repeated references to books and authors in "The Kings of England Sithen William Conqueror": they are rhetorical rather than metatextual, and in no case do they appropriate textual authority for the poems themselves, as does the dismissal in the *Troilus.* Thus what Pearsall has observed of another aspect of Lydgate's poetic technique holds true for these metatextual allusions as well: "Luxuriance of language and metaphor easily passes over into mere flamboyant display."[28]

Over 36,000 lines in length, the *Fall of Princes* offers ample opportunity to consider Lydgate's treatment of a variety of issues relating to an authorial book, his own composition, and the relations between the two. Lydgate drew directly on Laurent de Premierfait's *Des cas des nobles hommes et femmes*, which is itself derived from Boccaccio's *De casibus virorum illustrium*.[29] It is the latter text, which he calls "Bochas's book," that Lydgate presents as his primary source, though even this book as Lydgate translates it is in a sense the product of three authors: "Bochas," Humphrey, duke of Gloucester, and Lydgate himself all make competing demands on the text Lydgate produces.[30] As in the *Siege of Thebes*, however, Lydgate downplays the significance of his own narrative role and explicitly stresses his fidelity to Bochas and his responsibility to Humphrey. Thus, in his account of Lucrece Lydgate notes:

> And for that Bochas remembreth pitousli
> Hir dedli sorwe and lamentacioun,
> Writ hir complent in ordre ceriousli,
> Which that she made for hir oppressioun,
> I folwe muste and make mencioun,
> Afftir myn auctour parcel rehersyng,
> Touchyng hir woordis said in hir deieng.
> (3.974-980)[31]

And Humphrey's material effect on the translation is evidenced in his directive that Lydgate include a "remedie" after each of Bochas's tales (2.141-154) and in his monetary grant which enables the poor and aged Lydgate to complete the translation (3.64-84).[32]

The dynamics of the creation and transmission of both an authorial text and a vernacular recension are thus inherent in the *Fall*. Bochas, for instance, is sometimes depicted as producing stories from his own imagination and sometimes in response to the competing demands of literary tradition, as in book 1. There, Bochas is about to write an account of Theseus when Thyestes appears to him and exclaims:

> My will is this, that thou anon proceede
> To turn thi stile, and tak thi penne blyue,
> Leue Theseus, tak now off him non heede,
> But my tragedie first thou descryue.
> (3865-3868)

Bochas complies by letting Thyestes speak, just as later in book 1 he similarly responds to divergent intertextual demands when, having produced a diatribe against women, he sees Queen Althea and decides to tell her story

(4845-4865). But never does Lydgate exploit the metatextual potential of these dynamics; never does he indicate a thematic purpose behind his disingenuous insistence that he is only operating under the directions of Humphrey and Bochas,[33] and never does he address his own, frequently ambiguous role in the production of the *Fall.* In fact, those occasions on which the effects of his presence are undeniable are bypassed in silence. Thus, when faced with contradictory demands from his patron and his authorial text, Lydgate chooses the former without any real explanation and without exploring the significance of such decisions in the creation of literary works:

> But at Lucrece stynte I will a while,
> It were pite hir story for to hide,
> Or slouthe the penne of my reude stile,
> But for hir sake alle materis set a-side.
> Also my lord bad I sholde abide,
> By good auys at leiser to translate,
> The doolful processe off hir pitous fate.
>   (2.1002-1008)[34]

Lydgate's disinterestedness here in the relationship between his text and the books to which it responds is particularly striking. First, this is in fact the first of two versions of Lucrece's story in the *Fall* (a portion of the later one is quoted above), though Lydgate does not acknowledge as much. Second, the two versions structure the story quite differently; in book 2, Bochas narrates the rape, and Lucrece devotes her complaint to explaining why her loss of honor necessitates her death, while in book 3 the entire story is told through Lucrece's complaint, which concomitantly focuses far less on the nature of honor. And third, the above quoted passage occurs after Lydgate has observed that he will *not* write of Lucrece

> Sithe that Chaucer, cheeff poete off Bretayne,
> Wrot off hir liff a legende souerayne.
>   (2 .979-980)

Indeed, in Lydgate's view, Chaucer has written so many stories so well,

> Wherfore yiff I sholde my penne auaunce,
> Afftir his makyng to putte hem in memorie,
> Men wolde deeme it presumpcioun & veynglorie.
>   (2.992-994)

Using Collucius (that is Collucio Salutati) as his source (2.1009), Lydgate nonetheless, in accordance with Humphrey's wishes, does tell the story.[35] Together, the two Lucrece passages thus offer the opportunity to discuss a variety of metatextual issues, including the divergence of prior texts, the relationship between the *Fall* and these competing textual demands, and the implications of one writer's recuperation of the same story twice. None of these opportunities, however, is exploited.

Even when forced to disagree openly with his authorial text, Lydgate does do so for the most part unobtrusively. In the account of King John of France's capture by Edward of England, for instance, Bochas favored John. Lydgate is compelled to suggest the inadequacy of this position, but this disagreement, despite the mild irony in which Lydgate indulges, is not treated with any thematic significance:

> Thouhe seide Bochas floured in poetrie,
> His parcial writyng gaf no mortal wounde . . .
> Wher was Bochas to helpe at such a neede?
> Sauff with his penne he maade no man bleede.
> (9.3169-3170, 3181-3182)

As in the *Siege,* then, implicit in the *Fall* is a belief in the transparency and consistency of authorial texts and truths.[36] Complications and differences are bypassed or smoothed over, and though the complexity of the relationship between Lydgate's *Fall* and its source is continually apparent to the reader, it is persistently left undeveloped. Lydgate is never consistent, for example, in his presentation of just what the *Fall* purports to be: sometimes he models it as a straight translation of Bochas's text, other times he expressly supplements this text (as in the account of Lucrece), and still other times it appears as a metatextual account of Bochas producing his book, as in this passage on Julian the apostate:

> With this tiraunt Bochas gan wexe wroth
> For his most odious hateful fel outrage.
> And to reherse in parti he was loth
> The blasfemyes of his fell langage.
> (8.1653-1656)

Also as in the *Siege*—and to the same effect—Lydgate both alerts readers to competing versions of a story and refrains from considering the implications of such differences or utilizing their thematic potential. Thus after Thyestes, in a passage noted above, tells his story to Bochas, Atreus appears, calls Thyestes a liar, and proceeds to tell his side of the story. Both Bochas and Lydgate respond with bored silence:

> When Iohn Bochas fulli hadde espied
> Off these too brethre thaccusiouns,
> And how thei hadde maliciously replied
> Ech ageyn other in ther discenciouns,
> He gan dulle to heere ther mociouns,
> Put vp his penne, & wrot nat mor a woord

Off ther furie nor off ther fals discord.
(1.4208-4214)

Similar undeveloped recognitions of competing versions occur in the
accounts of Atlanta (1.4915-4928), Dido (2.1989-2009), Belgius (4.3570-
3590), and Henry, the son of Frederick II (9.1730-1743).
The overall effect of the *Fall* in this regard, as with the overall effect of
much of Lydgate's poetry, is curiously twofold: on the one hand, one is
continually struck by the number of metatextual issues, themes, and
references, but on the other, one is equally struck by the limited ways in
which they are developed. Like Chaucer in the *Canterbury Tales* and the
prologue to the *Legend*, Lydgate incorporates references to his own poems,[37]
but unlike Chaucer he does not acknowledge his own role as writer of the text
before the reader or the fact that his own works necessarily have some
relation to the tradition of books. One telling passage occurs at the beginning
of book 6, another at the conclusion of the *Fall*. In book 6, the goddess
Fortuna appears to Bochas and inspires him to vow to finish the book.
Bochas responds with a complex image about the relations between writers
and their texts which literally inscribes his book on his tomb, just as he is
figuratively inscribed in the book itself:

> And lest my labour deie nat nor apalle,
> Of this book the title for to saue,
> Among myn othir litil werkis alle,
> With lettres large aboue vpon my graue
> This bookis name shall in ston be graue,
> Hou I, Iohn Bochas. in especiall
> Of worldli princis wrytyn haue the fall.
> (6.225-231)

And at the conclusion of the poem, Lydgate again draws on Chaucer's
dismissal of the *Troilus* by observing: "With lettre & leuys go litil book
trembling" (9.3589). What is striking in the passage in book 6 is that nothing
in the image accommodates Lydgate's own role in the production of the *Fall;*
if authorial books are consistent and transparent, so evidently does Lydgate
judge himself to be.[38] And the dismissal is instructive because of the way it
collapses and conventionalizes its source. Chaucer's conclusion confidently
allocates a place for the *Troilus* in the steps of literary tradition at the same
time it problematizes such traditions through references to the transcendent
power of God. Lydgate, on the other hand, utilizes the self-validating
dismissal to insist on the "reudnesse" of his own composition. He implies
"Laureat poetes" had some role in "forthring" his poem but does not specify
just what this role was, so that the step metaphor which he borrows from
Chaucer (3605) becomes, again, merely a rhetorical flourish. And when he
incorporates the religious elements of Chaucer's conclusion, Lydgate does so
in a way which unproblematizes them by making them, through a request that

God strengthen his overtly moralizing poem, expressly consistent with his production:

> I do presente this book with hand shaking,
> Of hool affeccioun knelying on my kne,
> Praying the Lord, the Lord oon, too & thre,
> Whos magnificence no clerk can comprehende,
> To send you miht, grace and prosperite
> Euer in vertu tencressan & ascende.
>
> (9.3599-3604)

Robert Henryson, the latest of the three fifteenth-century writers with whom I am concerned in this paper, is the one who most fully exploited the metatextual references and themes which pervade Chaucer's poetry. In both the *Testament of Cresseid* and the *Moral Fables* Henryson displays a sophisticated understanding of the complex nature of textual authority and of its significance for a vernacular poet attempting to create his own texts. Indeed, in some ways, particularly in the *Testament*, Henryson explores textual authority even more intently than Chaucer and thereby advances a conception of the vernacular "book" even more modern than his predecessor's.

It is the *Moral Fables*, however, which in some ways offers Henryson's most extended examination of literary authority. Though the work purports to be merely a translation undertaken by the "requeist and precept of ane lord" (34),[39] it is in fact a strikingly original composition both in its individual fables and in its overall structure: several of the fables are original reworkings of widespread stories;[40] the *moralitates*, far from being didactically prescriptive, expose the multiple meanings latent in any story;[41] and the ordering of the tales bespeaks a thematic design absent in Gualterus Anglicus's Latin text—one of Henryson's sources—or in the similar productions of Caxton and Lydgate.

It is in the seventh fable, "The Lion and the Mouse," where Henryson most intently examines—in fact dramatizes—the relationship between his poem and the textual authority from which the prologue claims it derives. The fact that this dramatization occurs at the "sovereign mid-point" of the *Fables* suggests that Henryson regarded the issue as particularly important.[42] In the prologue to this fable, Henryson has a dream in which he encounters his author and master Aesop, a meeting which is unprecedented in both the Aesopic tradition in general and the *Moral Fables* in particular. The thematic complexity of the encounter, moreover, distinguishes it from even vaguely similar meetings, such as those between Dante and Virgil,[43] Gavin Douglas and Mapheus Vegius,[44] or more to the point of this paper, either Petrarch or Dante and Bochas in the *Fall of Princes*.[45] Neither of the Italian writers, for instance engages in a metatextual discussion with Bochas (or Lydgate); Petrarch appears to spur Bochas on by reminding him of the virtuous effects of writing, while Dante tells Bochas his next subject should be Duke Gualtier, whose life will reveal the friends and foes of Florence. Henryson's extensive dialogue with Aesop, however, constitutes an examination of the relationship between vernacular writers and the authorities and books to which they respond. The result of this examination is a demonstration that the former are as entitled as the latter to authorial voice and authority—that the vernacular writer can speak on his own without following what a book, imagined or real, specifies.

This demonstration is accomplished in three ways. First, by placing Aesop in a work which purports to be a translation of Aesop's text, Henryson explicitly renders his *author* part of the fiction. And if the source of Aesop's words here is in effect Henryson himself, then Aesop's book is also exposed as a fiction: it, Aesop, and the *Moral Fables* must all originate with Henryson. At the same time he fictionalizes Aesop, indeed, Henryson here underscores the rhetorical role any narrator necessarily has in the tale he tells by speaking directly to the characters for the first and only time in the *Fables.* This meeting between "auctor" and "makar," in other words, elevates the status of the latter in the production of literary works.

A second way in which Henryson dramatizes the transference of textual authority from traditional authors and books to vernacular writers is in his assumption of the dominant role in the dialogue. Henryson, purportedly the translator, initially demands a composition from his author. Then, when Aesop wonders,

> . . . quhat is it worth to tell ane fenȝeit taill,
> Quhen haly preiching may na thing auaill?
> (1389-1390)

the vernacular writer is able to override the "auctor's" objections. Henryson's dominance here becomes even more significant when one realizes that Aesop, curiously, now resides in Heaven and that he never objects to the criteria Henryson advances for the "taill"—that it be simultaneously rhetorically and ethically pleasing (1386-1387)—or to Henryson's right as a vernacular writer to advance such positions. In effect, Aesop's acquiesence provides divine as well as authorial validation of Henryson's literary views.

The third way this fable suggests the creation of vernacular textual authority is the story Aesop eventually tells. Moralized as an account of the ideal balance between king and commons, "The Lion and the Mouse" is the most explicitly political tale in the *Fables.*[46] Consequently, since Henryson has already imaged himself as the originator of his author's dialogue and book, in this way he assumes responsibility for an "auctor's" characteristic of ethical utterance. It is such responsibility which Aesop in fact stresses in his final remarks to Henryson:

> . . . My fair child,
> Perswaid the kirkmen ythandly to pray
> That tressoun of this cuntrie be exyld,

>   And iustice regne, and lordis keip thair fay
>   Vnto thair souerane lord baith nycht and day.
>   (1615-1619)

In effect, Henryson's meeting with Aesop in the "Lion and the Mouse" projects textual authority and vernacular language as the parents of the "makar" and thereby dramatizes the creation of vernacular authorship.[47] But in dramatizing such authorship, Henryson simultaneously undermines the need—theoretical or practical—for an author and authorial book which a vernacular writer translates or extends.[48]

This need is further undermined—perhaps obviated—in the opening of the *Testament of Cresseid.* There Henryson describes how one day, in a "doolie sessoun" (1), he began to read "ane quair . . . Writtin be worthie Chaucer glorious" (40-41). Significantly, he depicts Chaucer with the qualities Chaucer himself had reserved for the genuine "auctores." That is, the identification of writer with book implies Chaucer's right to authorship, while his authority is affirmed by his "gudelie termis" and "ioly veirs" (59) and also by the fact that his *English* text serves as the textual authority for another vernacular work. In an implicitly similar situation in the *Siege of Thebes,* Lydgate unquestioningly accepts the authority of Chaucer's book, which he in fact uses as a means to legitimate his own text. Henryson, however, uses the conditionality of the *Troilus* to legitimate the equally conditional *Testament.* He picks up "ane vther quair" and exclaims:

>   Quha wait gif all that Chauceir wrait was trew?
>   Nor I wait nocht gif this narratioun
>   Be authoreist, or fenȝeit of the new
>   Be sum poeit, throw his inuention
>   Maid to report the lamentatioun
>   And wofull end of this lustie Creisseid,
>   And quhat distress scho thoillit, and quhat deid.
>   (64-70)

Since afterward Henryson begins his own version of Cresseid's "wofull end," this second "quair" presumably not only is in the vernacular but also is the *Testament* itself. Hence one finds Henryson comfortably using the language of Latin literary criticism ("authoreist," "poeit," and "inuention") in a discussion of vernacular writers and also, more importantly, explicitly presenting his book as its own source.[49] At the same time, however, he questions the truthfulness of these new, vernacular authorities, whom Henryson sees as valid if competing voices in an unquestionably valid *vernacular* intertextual field. In the *Troilus,* by comparison, the books with which Chaucer's text competes are in Latin, the traditional authorial language. In the seventy or so years since Chaucer's death, then, the nature of the critical issue had evolved from the implicit questioning of the exclusive right of traditional "auctores" to authority, to a position which assumes that this right belongs to vernacular writers as well as to the "auctores," and then questions the nature of authority itself.

General conclusions from a study as selective as this one must be tentative. What does emerge clearly, however, is a sense of the evolving way in which the *"idea* of English poetry" was recognized and utilized during the fifteenth century. Hoccleve, Lydgate, and Henryson, for example, all recognized Chaucer's interest in the authorial "book," but each utilized the potential of such books in his own distinctive fashion. In the works of Hoccleve and Lydgate, we see recognition of Chaucer's metatextual concerns, while in Henryson's work we see acceptance and in fact extension of the Chaucerian view of literary history. This is a view which finally obviates the need for the authorial "book" and consequently enables modern—that is, post-Renaissance—poetry .

It is inappropriate, of course, to make value judgments about Hoccleve, Lydgate, and Henryson on the basis of how they respond to Chaucer's interest in textual authority: all writers are entitled to their own thematic and stylistic preferences. But it is appropriate to point out, I think, the inconsistent fashion in which the *"idea* of English poetry" developed in the fifteenth century: the writers whom we typically and justifiably see as most responsible for the transmission of Chaucerian poetics and an English literary tradition were not ubiquitously responsive to that aspect of Chaucer's writing which perhaps best justified this same poetics and literary tradition. Such inconsistency, however, may be characteristic of literary history. Writers are generally free to focus on whatever themes or issues they like, and so to fault a medieval writer for not pursuing an *"idea* of English poetry" may well be to fault him for not being interested in something which was justly of no concern to him. Indeed, the identification of a specific literary tradition among the divergent interests of a given period's divergent writers inevitably formulates the growth of the tradition in bits and pieces. Since identification of such traditions is inherently retrospective, moreover, it is quite likely that the tradition which a critic locates in bits and pieces is in such condition precisely because the issues involved are far more interesting to the present than they were to the past. But this, of course, is one of the reasons we read old poems in the first place, and if there is misprision in the way poets clear imaginative spaces for themselves, there can also be misprision in the way critics construct literary history—that is, through what they make of earlier books made by what those books' writers made of still earlier books.

NOTES

1. *Medieval to Renaissance in English Poetry* (Cambridge 1985) 34. I am happy to thank Helen Cooper and A. S. G. Edwards for their encouragement and interest in this paper.

2. All citations of Chaucer's poetry are from *The Riverside Chaucer*, ed. Larry D. Benson (Boston 1987).

3. See Jerome Mitchell, *Thomas Hoccleve: A Study in Early Fifteenth-Century Poetic* (Urbana 1968) 1-19; John Burrow, "Autobiographical Poetry in the Middle Ages: The Case of Thomas Hoccleve," in *Middle English Literature, British Academy Gollancz Lectures*, selected and introduced by John Burrow (Oxford 1989) 223-246; D. C. Greetham, "Self-Referential Artifacts: Hoccleve's Persona as a Literary Device." *Modern Philology* 86 (1989) 242-251.

4. "Hoccleve's *Series:* Experience and Books," in *Fifteenth-Century Studies: Recent Essays*, ed. Robert F. Yeager (Hamden, Conn. 1984) 260.

5. "The Poet and the Book," in *Genres, Themes and Images in English Literature: From the Fourteenth to the Fifteenth Century*, eds. Piero Boitani and Anne Torti, Tübingen Beiträge zur Anglistik 11 (Tübingen 1988) 245.

6. All citations of the minor poems are from *Hoccleve's Works: The Minor Poems*, ed. Frederick J. Furnivall and I. Gollancz, EETS e.s. 61 (1892), 73 (1925); rev. Jerome Mitchell and A. I. Doyle (Oxford 1970). I do not include diacritics in the quotations.

7. Such a demonstration may itself be problematized by the ambiguity it reveals in literary tradition. That is, the Friend had asked for something favorable of women, but "the *moralizacio* of *Jereslaus Wife* by allegorizing the story (with the Emperor as Christ, his brother as man's body, his wife as the soul), undermines the apparently 'real' narrative of the perfect long-suffering woman in the tale" (Greetham [n. 3 above] 250 n. 22).

8. "Hoccleve's *Series*" (n. 4 above) 260.

9. The edition I cite is *Hoccleve's Works*, ed. F. J. Furnivall, EETS e.s. 72 (1897). I again omit the diacritics.

10. It is entirely appropriate to speak of the portrait as part of Hoccleve's design for the poem. It survives only in London British Library MS Harley 4866, where the figure points to line 4996, in B. L. MS Royal 17.D.6, where it points to lines 4997-4998, and in Philadelphia, Rosenbach MS 1083/30, where the figure—apparently traced from the Harley manuscript as an afterthought, perhaps as recently as the nineteenth century—points to the space between stanzas 712 and 713. The Royal picture, unlike those in Harley and Rosenbach, is not framed and gives a full frontal view of the poet standing. It is nonetheless latent with some of the symbolic potential I note in Harley, for the Royal picture does show Chaucer pointing to the lines referring to him. Traces of the portrait appear in B. L. MS Harley 4826. The relevant leaf has been excised from B. L. MS Arundel 38, and the pertinent five stanzas are missing from Cambridge, University Library MS Gg.6.17; the Arundel manuscript suggests the picture had been present and was the

reason the page was excised, and the Cambridge manuscript that something similar to this happened to the exemplar of the manuscript. Six manuscripts which never contained the picture nonetheless do have marginal notes referring to it. Thus, in the words of Aage Brusendorff, though the majority of *Regiment* manuscripts lacks the portrait, it is "beyond doubt that Hoccleve in the copies of his poem made under his direct supervision caused a portrait of Chaucer to be inserted here" *(The Chaucer Tradition* [1925; repr. Oxford 1968] 14). Also see Mitchell (n. 3 above) 110-115; and David Anderson. *Sixty Bokes Olde and Newe* (Knoxville. Tenn. 1986) 113-115.

11. Perhaps the "typical" author portrait of the fifteenth century was that of a writer presenting his book to a patron; such pictures exist, for example, for both Hoccleve and Lydgate. See Michael Seymour, "Manuscript Portraits of Chaucer and Hoccleve, *Burlington Magazine* 124 (1982) 618-623. And marginal illustrations of Middle English works were certainly not unknown in the fifteenth century. See Kathleen L. Scott, "The Illustrations of *Piers Plowman* in Bodleian Library MS. Douce 104," *The Yearbook of Langland Studies* 4 (1990) 1-86. The closest parallel to the marginal Chaucer illustration in the *Regement* may be the picture of Chaucer beside the *Tale of Melibee* in the Ellesmere manuscript of the *Canterbury Tales,* though the larger design of this manuscript indicates that the Chaucer depicted there is not so much the historical poet as the fictional pilgrim.

12. For a discussion of this function of the Chaucer portrait see James H. McGregor, "The Iconography of Chaucer in Hoccleve's *De Regimine Principum* and in the *Troilus* Frontispiece," *Chaucer Review* 11 (1977) 338-350.

13. This is not to say, of course, that Lydgate had no theory of poetics. For an attempt to define his theory, see Lois A. Ebin, *Illuminator, Makar, Vates. Visions of Poetry in the Fifteenth Century* (Lincoln, Nebr. 1988) 19-48.

14. *John Lydgate* (Charlottesville, Va. 1970) 153.

15. See, for example, David Wallace, *Chaucer and the Early Writings of Boccaccio* (Woodbridge, Suffolk 1985).

16. All citations of the *Siege* are from *Lydgate's Siege of Thebes,* ed. Axel Erdman, EETS e. s. 108 (1911: repr. London 1960).

17. These references occur at lines 225, 427, 761, 1507, 1541, 1547, 1874, 1995, 2563, 2599, 2809, 3005, 3015, 3034, 3171, 3188, 3520, 3831, 3839, 3848, 3862, 4193, 4452, 4465, 4554, 4622. Similar post-caesura rhyme-motivated references to authors and books frequently occur in Lydgate's *Saint Albon:* 1.38, 1.48, 1.619, 1.706, 1.708, 1.743, 1.818, 2.159, 2.1015, 2.1192, 2.1248, 2.1300, 2.1313, 2.1547, 3.128, 3.139, 3.325, 3.696. At 2.1316 an entire line is devoted to such a reference. See *"Saint Albon and Saint Amphibalus" by John Lydgate,* ed. George F. Reinecke (New York 1985).

18. The relevant lines are 1059, 1266, 1660, 1679, 1716, 2144, 2612, 4235.

19. The other passages are at lines 199, 213, 307, 582, 874, 880, 1002, 1003, 1505, 1637, 2887, 3154, 3197, 4232, 4426, 4437, 4611.

20. Other longer, though still self-contained, metatextual passages occur at lines 293, 1270, 3195, 3201, 3510, 3537, 3971, 4541.

21. For a useful discussion, see the notes in Benson (n. 2 above) 1028.

22. Such beliefs reflect Lydgate's view of the writing and reading of poetry, which he sees as unambiguously moral activities. In Ebin's analysis: "Unlike Chaucer, who repeatedly questions the relation between appearance and reality, experience and authority in his writing and the limitations the poet's craft imposes on his effort to create a truthful vision, Lydgate neither doubts the inherent truthfulness of good poetry, nor does he question the master poet's intentions" ([n. 13 above] 32). Also see the rest of her discussion, 32-39 and her comments in *John Lydgate* (Boston 1985) 16, 42.

23. See Pearsall (n. 14 above) 155-156, and Ebin, *John Lydgate* (n. 22 above) 56-57.

24. This poem exists in three versions, only one of which (the first printed by MacCracken) is the focus of my discussion. The stanzas recounting the kings from Alfred the Great to William the Conqueror (which constitute the first 105 lines in MacCracken's edition) may well be late additions by someone other than Lydgate, and the second version printed by MacCracken is almost certainly by someone else. See Linne R. Mooney, "Lydgate's 'Kings of England' and Another Verse Chronicle of the Kings," *Viator* 20 (1989) 255-289; and Alan Renoir and C. David Benson, "John Lydgate," in *A Manual of Writings in Middle English 1050-1500*, gen. ed. Albert E. Hartung (New Haven 1980), 7.1864-1865. If the initial 105 lines are not in fact by Lydgate, the remaining 105 nonetheless amply demonstrate the technique with which I am here concerned; and the use of this technique by someone other than Lydgate in adapting Lydgate's poem would in fact reflect a good sense of his style. All citations of the minor poems are from *The Minor Poems*, ed. Henry W. MacCracken, EETS e.s. 107 and o.s. 192 (1911, 1934; repr. Oxford 1961, 1962).

25. There are twenty-four of the post-caesura rhyming half-lines: 1, 14, 29, 33, 37, 42, 13, 45, 49, 55, 62, 82, 84, 88, 112, 119, 123, 125, 139, 156, 160, 175, 182, 185. On one occasion, at line 28, the half-line before the caesura is involved, and four times references occupy the entire line: 60, 107, 136, 171.

26. The formula, which was also used by Boccaccio, has a long history and goes back, ultimately, to Ovid. See the note on line 1786 in Benson (n. 2 above) 1056. Given the extent of Lydgate's debt to Chaucer, however, there seems no reason to credit any other source. And it is therefore Chaucer's use of the dismissal which is most important for comparative purposes. It should be noted that Lydgate was not alone among fifteenth-century writers in his superficial use of the phrase. See R. J. Schoeck, "'Go Little Book'—A Conceit from Chaucer to Meredith," *Notes and Queries* 197 (1952) 370-372.

27. The number 146 includes as one poem those which exist in multiple versions. The dismissals I cite occur in the following poems: "A Prayer to St. Thomas of Canterbury," "The Legend of St. Austin at Campon," "Cristes Passioun," "The Fifteen Joys and Sorrows of Mary," "To Mary the Queen of Heaven," "An Epistle to Sibile," "Poems on the Mass," (which is in fact two poems, here counted as one, both of which have the dismissal), "A Ballade of Her That Hath All Virtues," "The Complaint of the Black Knight," "My Lady Dere," "A Lover's New Year's Gift" (in which the dismissal occurs twice near the end of the poem), "The Churl and the Bird," "Stans Puer ad Mensam," "Look in Thy Merour, and Deeme Noon Othir Wight," "That Now Is Hay Some-Tyme Was Grase," and "The World Is Variable."

28. *Old English and Middle English Poetry* (London 1977) 235.

29. A convenient discussion of the sources is Renoir and Benson (n. 24 above) 1838.

30. For discussions of Lydgate's original contributions in the *Fall*, see Pearsall (n. 14 above) 230-241, and Ebin, *John Lydgate* (n. 22 above) 64-47.

31. Cf. 1.442-448, 5.2537-2543. All citations of the *Fall* are from *Lydgate's Fall of Princes,* ed. Henry Eergen, EETS e.s. 121, 122, 123, 124 (London 1924, 1927).

32. A still useful discussion of Humphrey's role in the production of the *Fall* is E. P. Hammond, "Poet and Patron in the *Fall of Princes,*" *Anglia* 38 (1914) 121-136.

33. In this regard, one might compare the thematic and creative opportunities the pose of close translator afforded Chaucer. See my "Chaucer as Translator," in *The Medieval Translator: The Theory and Practice of Translation in the Middle Ages,* ed. Roger Ellis (Woodbridge, Suffolk 1989) 55-67. More generally, see Rita Copeland, *Rhetoric, Hermeneutics, and Translation in the Middle Ages: Academic Traditions and Vernacular Texts* (Cambridge 1991).

34. Lydgate similarly diverges from his "auctor" without comment at 8.1170-1176.

35. Eleanor Prescott Hammond suggests that Humphrey overrode Lydgate's decision to omit the story; she speculates that "it must have been he who permitted the recently written refusal of the task to stand—perhaps because of its language" ("Lydgate and Collucio Salutati," *Modern Philology* 25 [1927] 57).

36. Again, Lydgate's belief in the essential morality of poetry is relevant here. Cf. Pearsall's observation on Lydgate's additions in the *Fall:* "With this moralistic conception of poetry at the back of his mind, always extruding itself through the varied landscape of Bochas, it is not surprising that the most overwhelming of Lydgate's amplifications in the *Fall* are in the form of moralisation" ([n 14 above] 235).

37. Lydgate names and summarizes the *Siege of Thebes* at 1.3708-3815 and the *Troy Book* at 1.5937-6042.

38. Though Lydgate, of course, could not control how readers responded to his poem after his death, Lydgate's silence on his own role in the

production is all the more striking in view of the fact that in England the *Fall* ultimately became synonymous with Boccaccio's *De casibus* and was the primary form in which Bochas's book was read. See A. S. G. Edwards, "The Influence of Lydgate's Fall of Princes c. 1440-1559: A Survey," *Mediaeval Studies* 39 (1977) 424-439.

39. All citations of Henryson's poems are from *The Poems of Robert Henryson*, ed. Denton Fox (Oxford 1981).

40. E.g. "The Cock and the Jasp" and "The Cock and the Fox."

41. See Spearing (n. 1 above) 192-195.

42. See A. C. Spearing, "Central and Displaced Sovereignty in Three Medieval Poems," *Review of English Studies*, n.s. 33 (1982) 247-261.

43. *The Inferno* 1.61-87.

44. "The Thirteenth Book of the Aeneid," prologue, lines 75-154.

45. Petrarch appears at 8.57-189, Dante at 9.2509-2559.

46. A variety of readings, all of which agree on the political nature of the fable, are Spearing (n. 42 above); Denton Fox, "The Coherence of Henryson's Work," in *Fifteenth-Century Studies* (n. 4 above) 275-281; C. David Benson, "O Moral Henryson," ibid. 215-235; and George D. Gopen, "The Essential Seriousness of Robert Henryson's *Moral Fables*: A Study in Structure," *Studies in Philology* 82 (1985) 42-59.

47. On the theoretical underpinning of authorship in the Middle Ages see A. J. Minnis, *Medieval Theory of Authorship, Scholastic Literary Attitudes in the Later Middle Ages* ed. 2 (Aldershot 1988). On the political advisory role poets began to acquire in the late Middle Ages, see Richard Firth Green, *Poets and Princepleasers: Literature and the English Court in the Later Middle Ages* (Toronto 1980).

48. For further discussion of these points see my "Robert Henryson and Father Aesop: Literary Authority in the *Moral Fables*," *Studies in the Age of Chaucer* 12 (1990) 193-214.

49. Cf. Paul Strohm's comment: "in setting aside Chaucer's book in favor of his new narration he both learns from Chaucer's example and shows full independence of it" ("Fourteenth- and Fifteenth-Century Writers as Readers of Chaucer," in *Genres, Themes and Images in English Literature* [n. 5 above] 100).

The Tale of Beryn and The Siege of Thebes: Alternative Ideas of The Canterbury Tales

John M. Bowers

This essay first appeared in Studies in the Age of Chaucer 7 (1985): 23-50.

I T is safe to say that few people have read John Lydgate's *Siege of Thebes* or the anonymous *Tale of Beryn,* two fifteenth-century attempts to continue the literary journey and tale-telling of Chaucer's unfinished masterpiece.[1] Yet in a real sense very few people have read *The Canterbury Tales.* What they have experienced is a modern fabrication by Skeat, Robinson, Baugh, Fisher, and other editors who offer the poem as a single work, albeit marred by gaps and rough edges, but nonetheless recounting what was said on a one-way trip from Southwerk to the outskirts of Canterbury. This is technically a fabrication because no surviving manuscript arranges the fragments in an order which gives perfect geographical support to this design—not without the notorious "Bradshaw shift"—and no single manuscript, not even Ellesmere, contains all the tales and links to be found in a modern edition with its scholarly conflations.

To recognize and investigate a recoverable "idea" of this assemblage, as Donald Howard has done so provocatively, really means to grant full confidence to the authority of Ellesmere, a manuscript that implies but by no means specifies a one-way journey.[2] His and other unity studies have proceeded with the assurance that Ellesmere preserves the poet's own final arrangement of the *Canterbury* fragments, despite the fact that this confidence was not shared by an earlier generation of textual scholars at work analyzing the full range of surviving manuscripts. Brusendorff, Tatlock, Manly, and Dempster reached a critical consensus in concluding that none of the manuscript sequences, however attractive, had any final authority in determining the order of the groups.[3] Largely excluding the testimony of these textual experts, unity studies have also tended to fall prey to a circularity in their own logic. A typical argument begins with the assumption that there must be an orderly and meaningful arrangement of details in the frame narrative, proceeds to set Ellesmere's time and place references in a naturalistic sequence—leaving the pilgrims unnaturalistically outside Canterbury (or the Celestial Jerusalem) without the return to the Tabard announced in *The General Prologue*—and then concludes that the frame narrative does indeed have an orderly and meaningful arrangement which gives rise to an aesthetic unity.[4]

In a recent return to the manuscript evidence, Larry Benson has sought to confirm the belief that Ellesmere does indeed preserve Chaucer's own final arrangement of fragments, although his argument is made problematic by the findings of a new generation of textual critics.[5] Norman Blake and most of the scholars working on the Variorum Chaucer, while disagreeing on particulars of production, agree on the following points: (1) Hengwrt and Ellesmere were copied by the same scribe, (2) Hengwrt is the older of the two manuscripts, (3) the Ellesmere arrangement is derived from Hengwrt, and (4) Hengwrt's readings are superior to Ellesmere's and therefore it is preferred as a base text. While Benson's argument combines the virtues of intellectual thoroughness and speculative zeal— "Anything is possible," he writes—he does not finally resolve the paradox of having a single scribe produce a good text with a muddled order of fragments, then a poorer text with a restored, definitive order.

The appeal of Ellesmere to modern critics is partly explained by its undeniable appearance as a book in the medieval as well as the modern sense. Parkes and Doyle have broken new ground in exploring the processes by which such a book was produced, finding that Ellesmere fits best into the category of *compilatio*, a genre developed in academic and legal circles during the thirteenth century for bringing together authorities in a systematic and accessible format.[6] While a compiler was constrained in what he could add, he was free to rearrange his materials by imposing a new *ordinatio*. Instead of transmitting Chaucer's own structure and apparatus—though including glosses which are perhaps the poet's own—the Ellesmere scribe emerges as an intelligent person who developed the inchoate structure of Chaucer's unfinished work in a conventional form. Rather than perfectly preserving the poet's structural intentions, then, Ellesmere takes its place among other early manuscript collections as the enterprise of a proto-editor coming to terms with the challenge of ordering a large work which, when all the pieces were put together, was still painfully incomplete.

Over the past three decades a case for questioning the authority of Ellesmere and the one-way design which it implies has been steadily argued by Charles Owen: "The text of the *Canterbury Tales* nowhere supports the theory so popular with critics that Chaucer abandoned the homeward journey."[7] Lydgate's *Siege of Thebes* and the Northumberland manuscript of *The Canterbury Tales*, which contains the unique copy of *The Tale of Beryn*, offer supporting testimony that two capable readers working in the first decades after Chaucer's death did indeed take the announced plan of *The*

General Prologue at face value, if not in the actual number of tales to be told, at least in a narrative outline which would have the pilgrims turn their backs on Canterbury and set off toward London.[8] The *Beryn* poet brings the pilgrims to their goal in the cathedral, allows them an overnight stay during which the Pardoner has a misadventure with a local tapster, and then puts them back on the road to Southwerk. In the *Prologue* to *The Siege of Thebes*, Lydgate places himself in Canterbury as a pilgrim who falls in with Chaucer's merry band. As they set off toward London the next morning, the monk of Bury is invited to tell a tale and complies with a 4,500-line version of the ancient romance of Thebes.

The purpose of this paper is to investigate the alternative "ideas" of *The Canterbury Tales* arrived at by these two fifteenth-century readers, who clearly understood the unfinished outline of the collection differently from Ellesmere and Professor Howard. Their efforts as continuators represent editorial decisions and critical responses which are nearly contemporary with Chaucer—Lydgate may have known the poet himself—and therefore deserve more recognition than has hitherto been granted to them.[9] Once we have grudgingly accepted the grafting of inferior poetry to a work of literary genius, it is worth exploring three aspects of each continuator's enterprise: (1) his sense of a round-trip journey not ending with the pilgrimage's goal in Canterbury Cathedral, (2) his attitude toward characterization and fictional coherence within the frame narrative, and (3) the contextualization of each supplemental tale within the frame narrative which has been newly expanded to contain it.

I

The *Beryn* poet was a scrupulous, discerning reader of the *Canterbury* fragments which came down to him. Though lacking his master's gifts as a versifier, he had a fine ear for colloquial dialogue, as well as real talents for inventing and staging comic action. Unlike Chaucer's own brief, sometimes very sketchy links, his continuing frame narrative of 732 lines has a sophisticated structure which alternates episodes featuring various pilgrims with scenes comprising the Pardoner's fabliau adventure with a local tapster and her paramour. Even without the Pardoner interludes, the *Prologue* to *The Tale of Beryn* is more eventful than even *The General Prologue*, which constitutes over a quarter of the entire frame narrative of the Canterbury collection but in which the pilgrims actually do very little besides dine, chat (none of the table talk is directly quoted), and agree to the Host's diversion of tale-telling. My review of that invented action in the following paragraphs is designed not so much to document the Beryn poet's ingenuity as to illustrate his grasp of the characterizations and the narrative strategies of the original poem into which his continuation is fitted.

The poet shows a solid understanding of Chaucer's characterizations in *The General Prologue* as well as the links. The Monk has a "manly chere" (*Beryn* 138), and the lecherous Friar wants to sprinkle holy water on the pilgrims so that he will have a chance to get a better look at the Nun's face (lines 141-44). The Prioress behaves "as vomman tauȝt of gentil blood & hend" (line 287), while the pious Knight takes charge of leading the procession to the shrine in the cathedral, where the Miller and other "lewde sotes" wander about as if they were gentlemen trying to identify coats of arms and interpret the images in the stained glass (lines 147-56). After their religious duties are fulfilled, the Knight and his son change their clothes, since the Knight had set out wearing a humble tunic soiled by his coat of mail and the fashion-conscious Squire has a stylish wardrobe to show off. Father and son then go out to study the city's fortifications, which would be of professional interest to men of arms. The Squire pays careful attention to his father's long-winded lecture (the Knight has told by far the longest tale so far), while his youthful thoughts are constantly fixed upon the "lady þat he lovid best," who kept him awake at night (lines 231-50).

The *Beryn* poet also recalls prior altercations from the links. The Summoner is still stinging so much from the tale told at his expense by the Friar that he plans to repay him in kind, once again, "yf it hap[pene] homeward þat ech man tell his tale" (lines 184-90). The Pardoner also takes pains to avoid the Host, who had so roundly cursed him after his tale of the three rioters (lines 19-21). Wherever characters appear inconsistent with their former selves, the poet seems to be poking fun rather than betraying carelessness.[10] When we are told that the Wife of Bath is so tired that she prefers to sit in the kitchen garden with the Prioress, and later in the parlor with the innkeeper's wife, surely we are meant to smile at this middle-aged woman who had talked a good show earlier but has now run out of steam. Her lustiness was all verbal, and this woman who claimed to know wandering by the way now has "no will to walk" (lines 281-86).

In a far more pointed manner, the *Beryn* poet's recollection of Chaucer's original description of the Pardoner changes his present slapstick fabliau into a more savage farce. He shows too much familiarity with the other pilgrims not to know that the figure chosen to play the major role in his addition was described in *The General Prologue* as "a geldyng or a mare" (*GP*, I, 691). Whether this means the Pardoner was a eunuch or homosexual—or both—he is certainly a candidate foredoomed to failure in his amatory assault upon a barmaid.[11]

Almost the instant that the pilgrims arrive at their inn in Canterbury, the Pardoner makes an unambiguous pass at Kitt the tapster, who represents herself as a young widow and coyly leads him on. After visiting the cathedral, he returns to the inn and surprises her in her bedroom, not leaving until he has won her permission to return that night after the others have gone to bed. When he does contrive to sneak back after the candles have been extinguished, Kitt is in bed with her real lover, who proceeds to beat the Pardoner over the back and head with the pilgrim's staff which he had left behind earlier. (Readers of the *Roman de la Rose* will not miss the symbolism of the pilgrim's staff as a phallus, here amputated and turned back upon its original owner.)

If the Pardoner is meant to be seen as a homosexual posing as a ladies' man, he comes off as the same sort of ineffectual fop as Absolon kneeling outside Alison's window in *The Miller's Tale* (cf. 493-507). But if he is indeed a recognizable eunuch, whose appearance and temperament conform to the medieval pathology as it has been explored by Walter Curry, then medical treatises help explain his compulsive behavior which leads nowhere. One medieval physician described the *eunuchus ex nativitate* as "a man beardless by nature [who] is endowed with a fondness for women and for crafty dealings, inasmuch as he is impotent in performing the works of Venus."[12] If he hopes to sleep with Kitt to assuage his lust, he reveals that aspect of his personality which is self-deceptive and self-destructive. His *Prologue* and *Tale*, placed just before *The Canon's Yeoman's Tale* in preceding *The Tale of Beryn* in Northumberland, depict him as a person capable of castrating himself metaphorically by first admitting to the falseness of his relics and then soliciting a donation from the Host. This had been a prior instance of his inviting the abuse which he was self-destined to receive. Learning nothing from his own sermon and exemplum, this licentious, debauched figure plunges into the scheming life of the tavern, "that develes temple," which had been the undoing of the three rioters in his tale. At minimum, his prior delight in relics and money bespeaks a sterility of spirit which is taken up by the *Beryn* poet: when the Pardoner enters the cathedral, his interest is fixed upon the stained-glass windows; as he leaves, he steals some Canterbury brooches.

What is most important for our purposes, whether we see him as an anatomical or spiritual eunuch, is the reliance of this comic enrichment upon an understanding of how the Pardoner had already been portrayed by Chaucer. Thus the story of his bitter experience with Kitt and her lover cannot be fully appreciated as an independent piece. The fabliau episodes have been fused with the *Prologue* to *The Tale of Beryn*, and the *Prologue* has been fully integrated into the whole of the frame narrative of the *Canterbury* collection as it was understood by a skillful storyteller attempting to fill the central gap in the design which Chaucer had originally announced. The fact that he locates almost all the action at the "Cheker of the Hope," with only momentary regard for the shrine of Saint Thomas (lines 163-70), suggests that the *Beryn* poet was concerned not so much with the spiritualized pilgrimage as with the secular, nonreligious, and even grossly irreverent quality of a frame story which had its beginnings in an inn in Southwerk.

Another indicator of the *Beryn* poet's capability of adapting his skills to Chaucer's narrative strategy shows in the way he has paired the teller with the tale—the Merchant with the adventures of young Beryn. While Chaucer was masterful in the prologues and tales devised for the Wife of Bath and the Pardoner, for example, other instances are less impressive, and the assignments of tales to the Shipman and the Second Nun are notoriously makeshift. Nothing in *The General Prologue*'s description of the Merchant prepares the reader for the sardonic tale of January and May which he offers, and the *Prologue* to the *Merchant's Tale* itself, with the unhappy man's lament over his two-month marriage to a shrew, comes off as a lackluster introduction probably added in rough-draft fashion following "Lenvoy de Chaucer" at the end of *The Clerk's Tale*.[13] The tale of the young merchant Beryn, however, is very nicely suited to a pilgrim whom *The General Prologue* had described as "sownynge alwey th' encrees of his wynnyng" (*GP*, I, 275) when actually he had fallen into debt. It incorporates the lurking anxieties which a merchant must have felt whenever his ships set sail for a foreign port—that they might be shipwrecked along the way, that they might arrive safely only to fall victim to local regulations, or that the citizenry might conspire to cheat him of his vessels and cargo. The story ends with a wish-fulfilling victory on the part of the young merchant, who thwarts the schemes of the locals, redeems his five ships, doubles his investment, and ends up marrying the king's beautiful daughter.[14]

This outcome is doubly appropriate for the altered version of the Merchant, since Northumberland (fol. 71[r-v]) follows the practice of Hengwrt and other manuscripts of the *d*-order in substituting *The Franklin's Prologue* for the original *Merchant's Prologue*.[15] The resulting view of the Merchant, not as a shrew-ridden husband but as a father upset by his son's misconduct, makes almost poignant his interest in the young Beryn, a prodigal son who causes *his* father much grief until the trials of his mercantile adventures succeed in reforming his character. Though the tale itself offers no competition to the brilliance of Chaucer's performance in *The Merchant's Tale*, it lends itself admirably to the hopes and desires of the teller, while Beryn's difficulties with the people of Falsetown also complement in normal diptych fashion the Pardoner's bitter experiences as a stranger in Canterbury.

While the *Beryn* poet fully grasped the narrative strategy of Chaucer's tales as accesses to the personalities of the tellers and as digressive commentaries on the frame action, he was also alive to the realism of the "roadside drama" which critics earlier in our own century perceived as the unifying principle in Chaucer's work.[16] The arrival of the pilgrim band in Canterbury is not transformed into an ascent to the Heavenly Jerusalem. It is the arrival of thirty-two merry travelers in the medieval equivalent of a tourist town, one which would have been known as a solid secular reality to the poet who, the colophon leads us to believe, was himself a Canterbury monk.[17] A "mydmorowe" entry into town (*Beryn* 13) allows the action to follow smoothly from *The Canon's Yeoman's Tale*, which was begun "in the morwe-tyde" at Boughton-under-Blean and was meant to last until the pilgrims reached Canterbury (*CYP*, 588, 556, 623-26). Harry Bailey goes off to secure lodgings for the night, religious duties are quickly followed by various forms of relaxation—as befitting a narrative more concerned with "game" than "ernest"—and early the next morning the group starts its journey back to Southwerk.

Only at this point, with the start of the return half of the trip (lines 683-97), does the poet allow himself an imitation of the springtime opening of *The General Prologue*. As a clever twist, this description of twittering birds and a flowering landscape is put into the mouth of the Host, who ends by insisting that they turn again to the tale-telling competition which had enlivened their outward voyage (*Beryn* 699-702):

> Now, sith almy3ty sovereyn hath sent so feir a day,
> Let se nowe, as covenaunt is, in shorting of þe way,
> Who shall be the first that shall vnlace his male,
> In comfort of vs all, & gyn som mery tale?

The Host decides that they should not draw lots this time, because the cut might fall to someone sleepy or half-drunk—perhaps recalling an earlier episode in the journey when the drunken Miller shouted down the Monk in following the Knight—and so he calls for a sober volunteer instead. The Merchant, known by the Host to have retired early the night before, speaks up and the 3,300-line tale begins.

We cannot say with any certainty how the *Beryn* poet first came in contact with *The Canterbury Tales*, whether as scattered pieces which he or an acquaintance had collected from a variety of sources, as an existing collection which had been tossed together in some hopelessly chaotic sequence, or as a compilation having the careful elegance of Ellesmere yet still without satisfying the formal intentions stated in *The General Prologue*. We cannot even be sure whether he inherited a complete series of links. The situation is permanently clouded because the Northumberland manuscript is a mutilated descendant of the "edition" in which *The Tale of Beryn* first appeared.[18] Yet it is hard to imagine that the poet-continuator himself did not have a hand, probably a strong one, in arranging the fragments in an order which suited his concept of a round trip:[19]

I (A):	*GP-KnT-MilL-MilT-RvL-RvT*
II(B[1]):	*MLT*
V-IV (F[a]-E[b]):	*SqT-MerL-MerT*
III (D):	*WBT-FrT-SumL-SumT*
IV (E[a]):	*ClL-ClT*
V (F[b]):	*MerE-FranT*
VIII (G[a]):	*SNT*
VII (B[2b]):	*PrT*
VI (C[a]):	*PhyT*
VII (B[2ac]):	*ShT-Th-MelL*-2-line addition to *Thopas-MelL*
VI (C[b]):	*PardT*
VIII (G[b]):	*CYL-CYT*

Prologue and *Tale of Beryn*
[*SumT*, III (D), 2159-2294: misplaced conclusion]

VII (B[2def]):	*Mel-MkL-MkT-NPL-NPT*
IX (H):	*ManT*
X (I):	*ParsL-ParsT*

The geographical references in the outward-bound links chart a linear movement from Deptford and Greenwich (*RvP*, I, 3906-3907) to Sittingbourne (*WBP*, III, 847) to Boughton-under-Blean five miles from Canterbury (*CYP*, VIII, 556), and the three time references fit into the scheme of a two-day trip with an arrival on the morning of the third.[20] Events which are implied to have taken place before the band reaches Canterbury—notably the "flyting" tales of the Friar and Summoner and the altercation between the Host and the Pardoner—do indeed occur in fragments assigned to the first leg of the trip. What is more, if the same scrutiny were applied to Northumberland as has been focused on Ellesmere, other signs of critical insightfulness could be found, as in the editorial decision to have *The Second Nun's Tale* followed by *The Prioress' Tale* and *The Physician's Tale*, forming what might be called the "Martyrdom Group."[21] The intelligence behind this thematic rearrangement most likely belonged to the continuator himself, since his supplement to the frame narrative would make little sense unless he could be assured, by his own disposition of materials, that tales besides *Beryn* would be assigned to the homeward journey.

The fragments allotted to this homeward ride seem to confirm the poet's care for geographical references, though also raising questions about the degree of corruption in the Northumberland manuscript. The last 135 lines of *The Summoner's Tale* have clearly been inserted out of place following *The Tale of Beryn*.[22] What, then, are we to make of the second part of fragment VII (B²) which comes next? Is this another scribal blunder? Far more likely the original editor, searching for homeward tales, decided to separate *Melibee* from *Thopas* so that Chaucer the pilgrim, like the Merchant in the continuation, would tell one tale going and another tale returning. If so, the editor has also eliminated the geographical inconsistency which would otherwise have resulted if the Host's reference to Rochester (*MkP*, VII, 1926) had come after the Summoner's mention of Sittingbourne (*WBP*, III, 847). And since this manuscript lacks the *Manciple's Prologue*[23] with its troublesome reference to "Bobbe-up-and-down" (*ManP*, IX, 2-3)—if this has been correctly identified as Harbledown, less than two miles out of Canterbury—then the "Northumberland shift" of the second half of fragment VII (B²) solves all the geographical problems of the frame narrative for the return as well as the outward journey.

With the deletion of *The Manciple's Prologue* and its allusion to the Cook sleeping "by the morwe" (*ManP*, IX, 16), fragment X (I) with its afternoon setting follows smoothly after fragment IX (H) as the first line of *The Parson's Prologue* indicates: "By that the Maunciple hadde his tale al ended." Four o'clock in the afternoon is a credible time to begin a tale which will last until the pilgrims reach Southwerk at sunset, and the "thropes ende" which they are approaching (*ParsP*, X, 12) could be any of several villages on the outskirts of London, whereas no such thorp seems to have existed at the Canterbury end of the road.[24] Indeed, Harbledown (*ManP*, IX, 2) is the village where pilgrims normally dismounted to continue humbly on foot (a practice not observed here by Chaucer's travelers) because it was so close to Canterbury that the towers of the cathedral were within easy view—so close, in fact, that no intervening thorp, if there were room for one, would be worth mentioning by the Parson.[25] The appearance of Libra overhead and the Parson's promise "to knytte up al this *feeste* and make an ende" (*ParsP*, X, 47) suggest Harry Bailey's weighing of the best tale and the final meal which the pilgrims had agreed to share before disbanding.

Yet despite the *Beryn* poet's proven talents for inventing scenes of human comedy, he does not appear to have composed an end frame for the travel narrative, although this is far from certain because the manuscript itself breaks off before the conclusion of *The Parson's Tale* (X, 989). Perhaps there once was a marvelously funny resolution to the story. Perhaps the wily Host found a way to render his verdict without offending his other twenty-nine paying customers, while his wife Godelief, wielding a medieval rolling pin, came elbowing her way to center stage. Or perhaps the Parson's long sermon had such a sobering influence on the pilgrims that they bypassed the Tabard and returned directly home filled with the piety and resolve described as appropriate by Christian Zacher.[26] It is not likely that we shall ever know. The manuscript pages missing from the last quire of Northumberland were sufficient to contain the remainder of *The Parson's Tale* as well as the *Retraction*, but this does not foreclose the possibility that an additional quire, or perhaps more, once followed at the end.

Taken as it survives, without any supplementary close-frame, the narrative of a return to London does not altogether nullify the Parson's intent (*ParsP*, X, 49-51):

> To shewe yow the wey in this viage
> Of thilke parfit glorious pilgrymage
> That highte Jerusalem celestial.

The classical expression of this *peregrinatio* image had first appeared in *The Knight's Tale*: "we been pilgrymes passynge *to and fro*" (I, 2848). Pagan Egeus, who voices this doctrine without necessarily asserting final authority over it, nonetheless speaks in accordance with the Christian commonplace that man is "bondon to goye here in þis world and not to rest but to traveyll . . . for here to stonde is to vs impossible."[27] Because the pilgrimage of man's life is temporal rather than spatial—and therefore it does not matter whether the tale-tellers are moving toward or away from the actual city of Canterbury—the eschatological implications of *The Parson's Prologue* would remain undiminished. Indeed, there is an aptness in having the Parson return to this theme while the band approaches London, as if to say that the physical trip is over but the true spiritual pilgrimage is only beginning.[28] As Daniel Knapp has remarked, "it seems to me that if a redirection of piety by the Parson was to close the world of tales—and to my knowledge no one contests this—such a redirection would have had more force if made after the shrine than if made before."[29] It would also be apt, aesthetically as well as geographically, for the *peregrinatio* image to be raised again on the same stretch of highway where the Knight had introduced it at the start of the literary journey.

Manuscripts of the family to which the text of Northumberland belongs normally end with the Retraction, taking up as it does the themes of "verry penitence, confessioun, and satisfaccioun" from *The Parson's Tale*. If this is the conclusion which the *Beryn* poet accepted,[30] the Host is deprived of the privilege of judging the tale of best "sentence" and most "solaas" as Chaucer proceeds to his own verdict, which gives a sense of closure to *The Canterbury Tales* by dismissing them as "endityinges of worldly vanitees." While we cannot be certain, given the mutilated condition of the manuscript, Northumberland may very well have offered the same ending as Ellesmere, leaving audiences to decide whether the Parson spoke for Chaucer and whether the poet's formulaic disavowal in his Retraction should be read as ironic or sincere—but leaving the pilgrims outside London instead of Canterbury.

II

In the *Prologue* to *The Siege of Thebes*, the fifty-year-old poet John Lydgate projects himself as a pilgrim giving thanks for his recovery from a recent illness by making the journey to Canterbury, where he falls in with Chaucer's band of pilgrims, who have been lingering there, as it were, like unquiet spirits for the two decades since the death of their creator. The Host invites him to join the company and provide a merry tale, and when they set off the next morning for London, he obliges by offering an account of the ancient city of Thebes from its founding by Amphion to its destruction by Theseus.

As one of the great Chaucerians of the early fifteenth century, Lydgate proved himself a devoted imitator of literary forms in works such as *The Temple of Glas* and *A Complaynt of a Loveres Lyfe*, but he otherwise professed a reluctance to cover the same material which his master had already treated. In *The Pilgrimage of the Life of Man*, for example, he chose to graft Chaucer's lyric "Of Our Lady the ABC" to his text rather than undertake his own translation of these lines from Deguilleville.[31] Permission to exercise this borrowing and any other manner of artistic license may have come directly from Chaucer himself, as *The Troy Book* implies: "For he þat was gronde of wel seying / In al his lyf hyndred no makyng."[32] Yet rather than usurp the historical materials or foreign sources which Chaucer had already used, Lydgate seems to have preferred "to magnifie" or to "extende the goodlynesse"[33] of Chaucer's work, as he did by continuing the journey of the Canterbury pilgrims.

The manuscripts and early printed texts reflect the ambiguous claims of this work. Is it designed as an independent piece or as an organic continuation of *The Canterbury Tales*? Of the twenty-three manuscript witnesses from the fifteenth century, five actually attached *Thebes* to

Chaucer's poem.[34] In British Library Additional 5140, *The Canterbury Tales* ends with a Latin explicit noting that this has been the last of the tales composed by Chaucer, but it is followed by an incipit announcing the final tale *translata et prolata* by John Lydgate while returning from Canterbury.[35] Whereas Christ Church (Oxford) 152 is careful to introduce the work as "the monk of Buryys tale of the Sege of Tebes," the Ingilby manuscript contains no rubric separating the two works, concluding only with a colophon that reads: "Heere endith the laste tale of Canterbury maad and told bi Dan John Lidgate Mon. . . ."[36] If the Erdmann-Ekwall stemma is correct, the texts of these manuscripts descend from ancestors, or belong to family groups, in which *Thebes* survives as an isolated work.[37] This line of descent raises the possibility that some of these earlier specimens might also have been bound as continuations but, owing to their size and internal unity, were physically cut away for independent circulation.

Perhaps encouraged by such couplings in the manuscripts which came to them as copy texts, the early editors Stow (1591), Speght (1598, 1602, 1687), and Urry (1721) followed their instincts as compilers, no doubt with an eye to commercial advantage, and printed the work along with the rest of the Chaucer canon.[38] In light of this steady testimony that Lydgate's poem claimed some legitimacy as a continuation of *The Canterbury Tales*— whether or not the fifteenth-century poet expected an actual physical joining of the two works—it is worth evaluating the "idea" that results from the new Lydgatian ending.

As a resurrection of the roadside drama, Lydgate's *Prologue* fails in nearly every way that *The General Prologue* and *Beryn* succeed. The poet had not read closely, did not remember clearly, or (as I shall argue) did not care greatly about the details in *The General Prologue* and the links that comprised the frame narrative.[39] He has confused the description of his Pardoner with Chaucer's Summoner as well as with Symkyn the miller from *The Reeve's Tale* (*Thebes* 32-34; cf. *GP* 624 and *RvT* 3935), and he mistakenly alludes to the Friar's altercation with the Pardoner instead of with the Summoner (*Thebes* 35). Nor does he show a concern for the consistency of time and place references. The astrological setting in the opening of his Prologue does not accord with Chaucer's,[40] and later he states that *The Knight's Tale* was told as the pilgrims passed Deptford (line 4523), when in fact that locale was mentioned in connection with *The Reeve's Tale* (I, 3906). These blunders are all the more baffling when we consider that Lydgate knew his master's poetry so thoroughly, line by line and phrase by phrase, that he seems under a divine decree to write only in echoes.

The verisimilitude of his own fiction is likewise frail. As pilgrim-narrator, he stays in Canterbury for a shorter period than we would expect of a devout monk.[41] He announces that his tale will last for "the space as I suppose of vii. Myle" (line 324), but when they reach Boughton-under-Blean five miles along the road, he has finished only one-quarter of the story (lines 1044-46).[42] Yet if Lydgate's talents were not primarily exercised in creating a lively, credible fiction, this is not sufficient reason to dismiss the value of his enterprise. As C. S. Lewis once noted, "The stupidest contemporary, we may depend upon it, knew certain things about Chaucer's poetry which modern scholarship will never know,"[43] and John Lydgate was not the stupidest of Chaucer's readers.

"The [*Thebes*] Prologue is not very merry and not very funny," Derek Pearsall has rightly observed; "The surprising thing is to find it being done at all."[44] Clues for discovering some of Lydgate's motives are to be found partly in his characterization of the Host and partly in his digressive homage to Chaucer. Harry Bailey is the shadow of his former self. As the sole member of the original cast with a speaking role, he is brought forward only as the agent of the tale-telling, the function he had performed in *The General Prologue* when he instigated the game. Here he is vulgar without charm, talkative without energy or life, his character emerging from the topics and tone of his conversation. He rattles away with recommendations for lodging and dining, which are the specialties of his profession, but he does so in peculiar slang which must have been for Lydgate a calculated exercise in what he thought to be Chaucer's low style.

However sincerely this imitation may have been meant as flattery, Lydgate reserved outright praise for the twenty-line digression congratulating Chaucer as the "Floure of poetes thorghout al Breteyne" (line 40) and the "chief Registrer of þis pilgrimage" (line 48). This intrusion has the unsettling effect of reminding us that we are reading an account altered by the absence of its original pilgrim-narrator. Lydgate creates an additional paradox by disrupting the story to commend its original fabricator as the man who remembered and rehearsed these tales, as if they had actually been told along the road to Canterbury. This passage points beyond itself to the true nature of Lydgate's indebtedness. Just as the Host's identity is established by verbal style, the Prologue presents itself as a network of verbal borrowings rather than a coherent fiction—as an artifact made from a Chaucerian artifact, not from real life.[45] Lydgate's concerns were insistently verbal, ultimately philosophical, and in any case different from the creation of a believable story. If the *Prologue* is badly done, it is probably because his interest was not fiction at all but rather *history*, which for him meant the lessons that could be drawn from the past and transmitted by writers. This is why his emphasis, as well as care for details, is influenced more strongly by the historical *Knight's Tale* than the fictitious *General Prologue*.

It has often been noted that Lydgate wrote *Thebes* without the sort of noble patron for whom he produced *The Troy Book* and later *The Fall of Princes*.[46] As such, this "poet's poem" can be viewed as an affectionate gesture toward Chaucer, but it might also be regarded as a critical response to what Lydgate found most profitable in the kind of poetry compiled in *The Canterbury Tales*, particularly *The Knight's Tale*. Robert Ayers argues that Lydgate, while believing that it was chronicle fact, offered his account of the rise and fall of Thebes as a *speculum principis*, with the practical lesson—which is also a moral lesson—that a ruler can best avoid misgovernance if he is truthful and constant in his dealings with others:

The unity of the *Siege of Thebes* then, centers in the moral idea, and no episode, no characterization, and no tonal feature of the poem is extraneous to this essential moral purpose of the plot pattern.[47]

Far from being some private commerce between a poet and his dead master, Lydgate's work fits Anne Middleton's description of a public poetry which is morally pious and yet whose "central pieties are worldly felicity and peaceful, harmonious communal existence."[48]

It remained for Lois Ebin to draw attention to Lydgate's self-conscious attitude toward poetry's "unique powers to bring concord out of discord, order out of disorder, civilization out of chaos" which is dramatized nowhere better than in his *Thebes*.[49] Departing from his sources, Lydgate recounts how Amphion founded Thebes solely through power of language (lines 286-91):

> I take record / of kyng Amphyoun,
> That bylte Thebes be his elloquence
> Mor than of pride / or of violence,
> Noble and riche / that lik was nowher non,
> And thus the walles / mad of lym and stoon
> Were reised first / be syngyng of this kyng.

In another original stroke, he reports that the Muses refused to lend their presence at Edippus's incestuous wedding as they had at the nuptials of Mercury and Philology in the allegory by Martianus Capella (lines 830-40). This immoral marriage, so shunned by the high priestesses of poetry, sets off a political chain-reaction which leads to the extinction of the city, described in some of Lydgate's more touching verses (lines 4554-61):

> But Theseus / myn Autour writ certeyn,
> Out of the feld / or he fro Thebes wente,
> He bete it downe / and the howsys brente,
> The puple slough / for al her crying loude,
> Maad her wallys / and her towrys proude
> Rounde aboute / euene vpon a rowe,
> With the Soyle / to be laide ful lowe
> That nou3t was left / but the soyle al bare.

Refining Ayers's insights, Ebin finds that the conflicts of the poem are not so much between individual characters as between the word and the sword.[50] After Jocasta has failed to persuade her son Polyneices to reconcile himself with his brother Eteocles (lines 3726-3821), the final victory goes to weapons instead of words, and the siege continues until both sides are wasted.

When Thebes is finally leveled and its population slaughtered, the poet looks forward four hundred years to the founding of Rome, which will, of course, suffer its own decline and fall, and he ends with an appeal for "pees and quyet / concord and vnitè" (line 4703), echoing the language of the Treaty of Troyes which England had recently signed with France. As Walter F. Schirmer has noted, "While other poets wrote panegyric poems to Henry V, sang praises of the battle of Agincourt, or, like John Page in his poem *The Siege of Rosten* (1418-19), gave expression to his people's romantic and patriotic mood, Lydgate looked on the affair *sub specie aeternitatis*, in an epic seemingly valid for all time."[51] The optimism of this plea for peace, however, veils the warning that his own state had the potential to follow the same tragic course as Thebes and Rome. Like a dutiful expounder of history, Lydgate insists that those who do not learn from the past are condemned to hear those mistakes repeated.

Much more can be said about *Thebes* as a separate work, but it is peculiarly interesting to explore the invitation, offered implicitly by Lydgate and accepted by certain scribe-editors and Renaissance printers, to see the poem as a completion of *The Canterbury Tales*. As mentioned earlier, the poet seems to have had a faulty recollection of *The General Prologue*, but his knowledge of *The Knight's Tale* is so thorough that Ekwall theorizes that he retrieved a copy of Chaucer's poem before he finished his own but never bothered to return to his *Prologue* and make the necessary adjustments.[52] This hypothesis seems farfetched; Lydgate's familiarity with the contents of so many other tales, not to mention his understanding of the outline of the frame narrative, makes it highly improbable that he worked from a manuscript such as Longleat 257 or Harley 1239 which contained only a small selection of tales.[53] Special affinities between *Thebes* and *The Knight's Tale* should come as no surprise since both poems concern the destruction of the same Greek city, with Chaucer following Boccaccio's *Teseida* while Lydgate worked from a lost French history containing material closely related to the surviving *Roman de Edipus* and *Histoire de Thebes*.[54]

In ten specific passages toward the end of his continuation, however, Lydgate drew material directly from Chaucer, even if he was not always recounting the same events. When describing how Adrastus stopped the duel between Polyneices and Tideus (lines 1377-86), Lydgate echoed Chaucer's description of the bloody fight between Palamon and Arcite in the grove outside Athens (*KnT*, I,1704-13); when describing the funeral rites performed for those who died in the siege, he borrowed freely from the depiction of Arcite's funeral (*KnT*, I, 2949-61). Because of these borrowings as well as the interrelation of the two plots, Alain Renoir has called *Thebes* a companion piece to *The Knight's Tale*, while Derek Pearsall has characterized it as "a new and improved version" of Chaucer's first Canterbury tale. More nearly contemporary in its response, Longleat 257 copies *The Knight's Tale* as a sequel to *Thebes* or, in current terminology, Lydgate's poem as a "prequel" to Chaucer's.[55]

What has not been fully appreciated is the structural relationship of the two poems within the context of the complete *Canterbury* collection as it has been expanded and redefined. At the point in the action when Theseus intervenes at Thebes on behalf of the noble widows, the two narratives begin to run concurrently. Lydgate switches his sources and twice reminds his audience that he is repeating what has already been heard in *The Knight's Tale* (lines 4520-24, 4531). Thus the stories dovetail with one another, as Lydgate uses narrative congruence and verbal echoes to knit up the end of his tale with the beginning of Chaucer's. A "retrospective patterning" emerges that gives a new but not wholly unexpected shapeliness to the enlarged work.[56] Lydgate sought to remind his audience of the geographical setting where the Knight had told his tale, as if to say that this return to the subject matter of the first fiction of the series parallels the pilgrims' physical return toward London. Since *The Troy Book* speaks of following Chaucer's "tracis" or footsteps, it would appear that Lydgate was familiar with the topos of a literary work as a *via* or journey.[57] The tale-telling, then, like the journey itself, has come full circle. The end is made to join with the beginning, and the new structure suppresses the apocalyptic in favor of the cyclical.

John Norton-Smith has observed that Lydgate was not normally gifted with "creative intuition," or what Geoffrey of Vinsauf had termed *archetypus*.[58] Yet the ending of *Thebes* suggests levels of significance which may have extended beyond the poet's conscious intention and therefore invite application of the archetypal criticism of our own century. On the face of things, a journey into the Kentish countryside and a return to the English capital suggest the basic pattern for a quest romance, and indeed Lydgate's work conforms almost perfectly with what Northrop Frye has described as the last or *penseroso* phase of romance, "a tale in quotation marks, where we have an opening setting with a small group of congenial people, and then the real story told by one of the members." The effect is to present through a leisurely contemplative haze a story which entertains its audience without unnerving them with the harsh confrontation of tragedy.[59] Social cataclysms assume reality only within the inner fiction, while the cozy audience within the frame narrative proceed with their lives in some privileged spot. So with Lydgate's *Thebes* there is no close frame. The circular return to *The Knight's Tale* bypasses Chaucer's *General Prologue*, whose colorful characters had been so carelessly reproduced in Lydgate's own *Prologue*, because these jangling pilgrims belong to the world of "game" which Lydgate dismisses in preference for the "ernest" of the kind of poetry for which he so valued Chaucer (lines 54-57).

The hero who is exalted at the end of Lydgate's poem is not the protagonist or the storyteller or even the audience, but rather the nation of the audience. This peculiar *anagnorisis*, or recognition of a communal heroism, should come as no complete surprise, since the pilgrims who travel through the English countryside have been presented from the beginning as a microcosm of the English nation. For the audience of readers as for the audience of pilgrims, the death struggle of the city of Thebes has taken place as a mental excursion recalling the fates of Athens and Rome while leading inexorably back to the present reality, which is none other than London, the *civitas* of their origins—or, as T. S. Eliot put it, "the nearest, in place and time, now and in England."

Frank Kermode has brilliantly demonstrated that the apocalyptic "sense of an ending," because it accords with the Judeo-Christian view of history as a rectilinear rather than cyclical movement of time, stood as the dominant mode of literary closure up to the twentieth century.[60] Western writers observed a pattern in historical events free from the repetitions of ritual. Lydgate's *Thebes* presents a different pattern. Putting aside the apocalyptic implications of the *Parson's Prologue* and Chaucer's *Retraction*—the one public, the other private—Lydgate produces a story which formed part of a historical fabric composed of countless repetitions. The Lydgatian *Canterbury Tales* imposes on itself a circular structure for much the same purpose as *Finnegans Wake*. Each work's circularity reflects its author's vision of a historical past in which heroes and their civilizations constantly reenact the ritual of rise and fall upon Fortune's wheel. Lydgate learned this lesson in *The Monk's Tale*; later he would hammer away at it in his own *Fall of Princes*.[61]

This circularity does not mean that the end of Lydgate's *Thebes* totally lacks apocalyptic features. The obliteration of a city and the slaughter of its people certainly gives a sense of finality, and the concluding plea for love to awaken in men's hearts and for nations to live together in "pees and quyet / concord and vnytè" has strong millennial overtones. This epilogue, which is Lydgate's own invention, ends with a prayer to Christual through the intercession of the Virgin Mary, thereby creating a mixed ending of the sort predicted by Frye as the conclusion to a poetic symposium such as *The Canterbury Tales*. The reader reaches a point at which "the undisplaced apocalyptic world and the cyclical world of nature come into alignment," a point which might properly be called an epiphany.[62] While God's help is called for, specifically through Mary as an intermediary between the divine and the human, the primary request is "to sende vs pes / her in this lyf present" (line 4713). Divine grace comes as the final reinforcement of practical wisdom. While some may view a return to London as a return to spiritual exile, in accordance with the romance pattern used by T. S. Eliot in "Journey of the Magi," the spiritual lessons taught by the poem form an ethical consolation, a rule for present conduct, and a standard for future judgment. A return to the real world is, paradoxically, a return to fiction, because an enclosed form cannot avoid being a statement about literature itself. Many modern works end upon the promise of returning to the point in time where they begin, although this Proustian paradigm is by no means exclusively modern. *The Consolation of Philosophy*, *The Wanderer*, and *The Divine Comedy* stand in a line of works—including Chaucer's own *Book of The Duchess* ("I wol by processe of tyme / Fonde to put this swevene in ryme")—in which the hero-narrator undergoes a series of educating traumas which finally render him capable of writing the piece which the reader has just finished reading. Yet unlike these works, we must remind ourselves, the Lydgatian *Canterbury Tales* is actually a reader's round trip formed from two books, the second continuing and redefining the first. As a critical response, *Thebes* almost instinctively repeats the performance of the New Testament as "a book which rewrites and requites another book," reaching concord with its intentions rather than assaulting its truths.[63]

While there is no climactic scene in which Harry Bailey announces who has earned a free meal at the Tabard Inn, Lydgate renders his own literary judgment by way of the structure which his supplemental tale has created. The ending of his *Thebes* encourages the reader to begin *The Canterbury Tales* anew, for the simple reason that they are worth re-reading. Chaucer's characters have life, his histories speak, and the cumulative lessons of his poetry can and must be applied—so long as we focus on ethical poetry like *The Knight's Tale*, not *The General Prologue* and links featuring the low style of the visceral Host. That Lydgate's poem feeds upon these literary materials rather than immediate experience may seem sterile to some modern readers—again the paradigm is the New Testament, also a dense mass of quotations and allusions in which Jesus says over and over "as it is written"[64]—yet for all its aesthetic self-containment, the Lydgatian collection offers hardheaded advice. The echoic character of his verse becomes a stylistic reflection of his inherent confidence, voiced also by Chaucer in *The Parliament of Fowls* (lines 22-28), that poetry has the power to preserve past knowledge while offering renewal to the world which it serves. For all of the high praise bestowed upon Chaucer as the "Floure of poetes thorghout al Breteyne," Lydgate made a finer commendation by producing a conclusion which suggests that the reader turn back the leaves and begin again the literary journey.

III

The purpose of this article has been to extend a different kind of journey, by continuing along the path already charted by textual scholars, old and new, who have argued that all early-fifteenth-century collections of the *Canterbury* fragments represent the editorial labors of scribes and their supervisors. Unity studies based on Ellesmere's arrangement have an undeniable validity, but only insofar as they deal with a nearly complete proto-edition which came close to reflecting what were probably Chaucer's final intentions. By contrast, Lydgate and the *Beryn* poet gave priority to the poet's earlier intentions, as established in *The General Prologue* by the Host's plan for a tale-telling competition. Their continuations, while usually dismissed as spurious accretions to a masterpiece, bear witness to the ways some medieval readers were responding to the *Canterbury* collection in the first decades after Chaucer's death. Lydgate's concern for ethical poetry, for instance, led him to neglect the mimetic reality of the pilgrims in the frame narrative, while the *Beryn* poet invested some of these same pilgrims with more dramatic vitality than they display in Chaucer's own links. Yet what these two continuators shared—and what modern critics must recognize—was an authentically medieval English sense that a pilgrimage narrative could describe a round trip and not only a one-way passage to some cathedral shrine or the Celestial Jerusalem that lay beyond.

NOTES

1. John Lydgate, *Siege of Thebes*, ed. Axel Erdmann and Eilen Ekwall, 2 vols., EETS, e.s., nos. 108, 125 (London, 1911, 1930); and *The Tale of Beryn with a Prologue of the Merry Adventure of the Pardoner with a Tapster at Canterbury*, ed . F. J . Furnivall and W. G. Stone, EETS, e.s., no. 105 (London, 1909). Chaucer quotations and lineations are from Geoffrey Chaucer, *The Complete Poetry and Prose*, ed. John H. Fisher (New York: Holt, Rinehart and Winston, 1977).

2. Donald R. Howard, *The Idea of the Canterbury Tales* (Berkeley: University of California Press, 1976), pp. 212-13 et passim, accepts the Ellesmere order as the starting point for his critical discussion. In his chapter "The Idea of an Idea," pp. 1 -20, he distinguishes an idea as something different from the author's intention, genre, style, language, tradition, values, mental archetype, and cultural mythology—yet including all of these: "This whole is an idea" (p. 19).

3. Aage Brusendorff, *The Chaucer Tradition* (Oxford: Clarendon Press, 1925), pp. 119-20, 125-26; J. S. Tatlock, "The Canterbury Tales in 1400," *PMLA* 50 (1935): 105-06, 131-33; John M. Manly and Edith Rickert, eds., *The Text of the Canterbury Tales: Studied on the Basis of All Known Manuscripts*, (Chicago: University of Chicago Press, 1940), 2:475-94 (hereafter Manly and Rickert); and Germaine Dempster, "Manly's Conception of the Early History of the *Canterbury Tales*," *PMLA* 61 (1946): 384, 386-89, alluding to Tatlock, pp. 106, 131. Robert A. Pratt, "The Order of the *Canterbury Tales*," *PMLA* 66 (1951):1141-67, proceeds under the proviso that his conclusions have merit only "if Chaucer had a definite intention" (p. 1142).

4. The search for an aesthetic wholeness not based on the older principle of roadside drama was begun by Ralph Baldwin, *The Unity of the Canterbury Tales* (Copenhagen: Rosenkilde and Bagger, 1955), and has been most recently extended, in ways both learned and beautiful, by V. A. Kolve, *Chaucer and the Imagery of Narrative: The First Five Canterbury Tales* (Stanford, Calif.: Stanford University Press, 1984). Scholars who have entered into the discussion of ordering include Stanley B. Greenfield, "Sittingbourne and the Order of *The Canterbury Tales*," *MLR* 48 (1953):51-52; William Witherle Lawrence, *Chaucer and the Canterbury Tales* (1950; reprint, New York: Biblo and Tanner, 1969), pp. 90-118; Lee Sheridan Cox, "A Question of Order in the *Canterbury Tales*," *ChauR* 1 (1967): 228-52; E. Talbot Donaldson, "The Ordering of the *Canterbury Tales*," in Jerome Mandel and Bruce A. Rosenberg, eds., *Medieval Literature and Folklore*

Studies: Essays in Honor of Francis Lee Utley (New Brunswick, N. J.: Rutgers University Press, 1970), pp. 193-204; James H. Wilson, "The Pardoner and the Second Nun: A Defense of the Bradshaw Order," *NM* 74 (1973): 292-96; James Paul, "A Defense of the Ellesmere Order," *RLSt* 5 (1974): 118-20; Edward S. Cohen, "The Sequence of the *Canterbury Tales*," *ChauR* 9 (1974): 190-95; and George R. Keiser, "In Defense of the Bradshaw Shift," *ChauR* 12 (1977): 191-201. Arthur K. Moore, "Medieval English Literature and the Question of Unity," *MP* 75 (1968): 285-300, has launched a general but lucidly articulated assault against "the unchecked flow of unity studies" (p. 300) in the field.

5. Larry D. Benson, "The New Order of *The Canterbury Tales*," *SAC* 3 (1981): 77-120. He responds (pp. 101-10) to N. F. Blake, "The Relationships Between the Hengwrt and Ellesmere Manuscripts of the *Canterbury Tales*," *E&S* 32 (1979): 1-18; and A. I. Doyle and M. B. Parkes, "Paleographical Introduction," in Paul G. Ruggiers, ed., *The Canterbury Tales: A Facsimile and Transcription of the Hengwrt Manuscript, with Variants from the Ellesmere Manuscript* (Norman: University of Oklahoma Press, 1979), pp. xix-xliii. N. F. Blake, "On Editing the *Canterbury Tales*" in P. L. Heyworth, ed., *Medieval Studies for J. A. W. Bennett* (Oxford: Clarendon Press, 1981), p. 101, poses the paradox involving Hengwrt and Ellesmere: "It has never been satisfactorily explained (indeed the question has rarely been asked) why one manuscript should have the best text and another the best order." Roy Vance Ramsey's potentially earth-shaking argument, based on the techniques of compository identification in "The Hengwrt and Ellesmere Manuscripts of the *Canterbury Tales*: Different Scribes," *SB* 35 (1982): 133-54, maintains "the very high quality of the text of the Hengwrt manuscript and the many dangers of too great a reliance on and trust in the text of the Ellesmere manuscript" (p. 154) and therefore leaves the paradox intact, whether one or several scribes are presumed.

6. A . I . Doyle and M. B. Parkes, "The Production of Copies of *The Canterbury Tales* and *the Confessio Amantis* in the Early Fifteenth Century" in M. B. Parkes and Andrew G. Watson, eds. *Medieval Scribes, Manuscripts, and Libraries* (London: Scholar Press, 1978), pp. 163-710, esp. pp. 190-92. This continues the work of M. B. Parkes in "The Influence of the Concepts of *Ordinatio* and *Compilatio* on the Development of the Book" in J. J. G. Alexander and M. T. Gibson, eds., *Medieval Learning and Literature: Essays Presented to Richard William Hunt* (Oxford: Clarendon Press, 1976), pp. 115-41.

7. Charles A. Owen, Jr., "The Alternative Reading of the *Canterbury Tales*: Chaucer's Text and the Early Manuscripts," *PMLA* 97 (1982): 237-50, esp. pp. 243, 247. Earlier arguments for assigning certain fragments to the return to London had come from Robert K. Root, "The Manciple's Prologue," *MLN* 44 (1929): 493-96. John M. Manly, "Tales of the Homeward Journey," *SP* 28 (1931): 613-17; James A. Work, "The Position of the Tales of the Manciple and the Parson on Chaucer's Canterbury Pilgrimage," *JEGP* 31 (1932): 62-65; and Manly and Rickert, 2:493.

8.   Most forceful among recent exponents of the pilgrims' one-way journey has been Donald Howard, *The Idea of the Canterbury Tales* pp. 28-30, 67-74 and Donald Howard, *Writers and Pilgrims: Medieval Pilgrimage Narratives and Their Posterity* (Berkeley: University of California Press, 1980), which draw upon 526 accounts documented by Reinhold Röhrich in *Bibliotheca Geographica Palaestinae: Chronologisches Verzeichnis der von 333 bis 1878 verfasster Literatur über das Heilige Land mit dem Versuch einer Kartographie* (1890; reprint, Jerusalem: Universitas Booksellers, 1963). However, D. J. Hall, *English Mediaeval Pilgrimage* (London: Routledge & Kegan Paul, 1966), p. 17, notes that the significance of a journey to a native holy place was very different from a pilgrimage to Jerusalem, thus undermining Howard's reliance upon guidebooks and diaries concerning these special Jerusalem pilgrimages.

9.   It has recently been drawn to my attention that just such an investigation has been called for by Judson Boyce Allen and Theresa Anne Moritz, *A Distinction of Stories: The Medieval Unity of Chaucer's Fair Chain of Narratives for Canterbury* (Columbus: Ohio State University Press, 1981), p. 41 n. 70. In general their study argues that "normative arrays of exempla" in the Canterbury collection generate explicitly Christian meanings and yield an ethical unity which does not rely upon any sequential unity within the frame narrative (pp. 68-74) and therefore all surviving manuscripts should be studied so that the question of ordering might be approached on firmer medieval grounds (pp. 98-99). Other critical issues are raised by Harold Bloom, *The Anxiety of Influence* (New York: Oxford University Press, 1973), although the author himself maintains that there was "a great age before the Flood" extending from Homer to Shakespeare when a master such as Chaucer "moved his ephebe [*sic*] only to love and emulation and not to anxiety'" (p. 122). Yet any reader of fifteenth-century English literature will recognize how wrong this cavalier dismissal is, although such an explanation of medieval manifestations of poetic anxiety must await future studies.

10.   E.J. Bashe, "The Prologue of *The Tale of Beryn*," *PQ* 12 (1933):1-16, has great praise for the poet's consistency in back reference to Chaucer—90 percent according to his reckoning (p. 11)—but without appreciating the possible humor intended when a pilgrim appears inconsistent with his or her former self.

11.   The case for eunuchhood is made by Walter Clyde Curry, *Chaucer and the Medieval Sciences* (Oxford: Oxford University Press, 1926), pp. 54-70 ("The Pardoner's Secret"), while another view is presented by Monica E. McAlpine, "The Pardoner's Homosexuality and How It Matters," *PMLA* 95 (1980): 8-22, with generous documentation of all studies relevant to the issue of his sexuality. An interpretation more patristic than physiological has been voiced by Robert P. Miller, "Chaucer's Pardoner, the Spiritual Eunuch, and *The Pardoner's Tale*," *Speculum* 30 (1955): 180-99. In *Beryn*, the Pardoner's sexual failure seems to reflect complementarily his nature as a spiritual eunuch totally alienated from the sacral dimension of pilgrimage, as the

alternating episodes make clear by isolating him in the web of his own gross folly.

12. Curry, *Chaucer and the Medieval Sciences*, p. 58. He goes on to state that the *Beryn* poet successfully incorporates the Pardoner's physical and psychological impairments into a comedy which is turned darker and more sardonic as a result (p. 68).

13. Manly and Rickert, 2:266-67. For conjecture on Chaucer's earlier intention to give the tale to the Friar, see Albert C. Baugh, "The Original Teller of the Merchant's Tale," *MP* 35 (1937): 15-26.

14. For an examination of the tales as entries into the psychologies of the tellers, see Wolfgang E. H. Rudat, "The *Canterbury Tales*: Anxiety Release and Wish Fulfillment," *AI* 35 (1978): 407-18. The hazardous livelihood of a fourteenth-century merchant is suggested by Muriel Bowden, *A Commentary on the General Prologue to the Canterbury Tales*, 2d ed., rev. (New York: Macmillan, 1967), pp. 146-54; and Kenneth S. Cahn, "Chaucer's Merchants and the Foreign Exchange: An Introduction to Medieval Finance," *SAC* 2 (1980): 81-119.

15. Manly and Rickert, 6:569; the origin and significance of this transposed link have been discussed in careful detail by Benson, "The Order of *The Canterbury Tales*," pp. 102-106.

16. Esteem for the dramatic unity of the frame narrative came from George L. Kittredge, *Chaucer and His Poetry* (Cambridge, Mass.: Harvard University Press, 1915), pp. 154-55; John L. Lowes, *Geoffrey Chaucer and the Development of His Genius* (Boston: Houghton Mifflin, 1934), p. 164; and R. M. Lumiansky, *Of Sondry Folk: The Dramatic Principle in the Canterbury Tales* (Austin: University of Texas Press, 1955), pp. 15-28.

17. *The Tale of Beryn*. pp. vi, 137, offer Furnivall's comments on the colophon (p. 120): "Nomen Autoris presentis Chronica Rome / Et translatoris / Filius ecclesie Thome."

18. The best account of the Northumberland manuscript is offered by Manly and Rickert, 1:387-95. They state that the entire text is written in "one stiff book hand, ugly and awkward" (p. 388), although I detect the entry of a second hand, smaller and neater, commencing with *Sir Thopas* (fol . 158r).

19. The contents of the manuscript are most easily surveyed in ibid., vol. 2, in "Chart II" on the second unnumbered page following p. 494. Gaps in the manuscript have resulted in the loss of *GP*, I, 1-156; *MilT*, I, 3217-83; *RvT*, I, 4228-4324 and *MLP*, II, 1-316 (or *RvT*, I, 4228 to *CkT* 4422 and *MLP*, II, 99 to *MLT* 316, depending on whether the text once included *MLH*, II, 1-98); *ClT*, IV, 57-142; *SqT*, V, 328-672; and *ParsT*, X, 142-275 and X, 332-959. Manly remarks that the Northumberland scribe "was certainly not the author or translator of *Beryn*" (1:389).

20. A variety of time schemes are examined by John S. P. Tatlock, "The Duration of the Canterbury Pilgrimage" *PMLA* 21 (1906): 478-85, but Manly and Rickert, 2:493, insist upon two days of journeying each way, based on Rickert's extensive collection of records on travel in the fourteenth century.

Such a schedule for a five-day round trip, with the third day spent in the cathedral town, has been explored by Charles A . Owen, Jr., "The Plan of the Canterbury Pilgrimage," *PMLA* 66 (1950): 820-26. While Hall, *English Mediaeval Pilgrimage*, laments that "no complete diary of a pilgrimage in England has yet come to light" (p. 17), there are expense records such as the one kept by Nicholas Harewode in 1415, which is intriguing because all of his stopping places are mentioned also by Chaucer: dinner at Dartford, supper at Rochester; dinner at Ospringe, supper at Canterbury; and, on the return, dinner at Sittingbourne, supper at Rochester; dinner at Dartford, supper at London; see F. J. Furnivall and R E. G . Kirk, eds., *Analogues of Chaucer's Canterbury Pilgrimage*, Chaucer Society, 2d ser., no 36 (London, 1903), pp. 5-6. Manly and Rickert, 5:387, note incorrectly that *RvP*, I, 3906, with its reference to Deptford, has been omitted from Northumberland (fol. 50v).

21. Allen and Moritz, *A Distinction of Stories*, pp. 101-102, suggest just such a thematic grouping of these three tales.

22. Manly and Rickert, 6:173, note that there is a complete family of manuscripts which lacks this final episode (*SumT*, III, 2159-2294), a fact that suggests an earlier Chaucerian version of the *Summoner's Tale* which ended with the donation of the fart. The Northumberland scribe seems to have received the account of the fart's division too late to insert it in its proper place

23. Manly and Rickert, 8:142.

24. Manly, "Tales of the Homeward Journey," pp. 613-14.

25. Ward, *The Canterbury Pilgrimages*, p. 280.

26. Christian Zacher, *Curiosity and Pilgrimage: The Literature of Discovery in Fourteenth-Century England* (Baltimore, Md.: Johns Hopkins University Press, 1976), p.49, draws upon the researches of Edward L. Cutts, *Scenes and Characters of the Middle Ages*, 5th ed. (London Simpkin, Marshall, Hamilton, Kent, 1925), pp. 189-90.

27. Woodburn O. Ross, ed., *Middle English Sermons*, EETS, o.s., no. 209 (London, 1940), p. 74.

28. A similar scene is registered by Raymond S. St.-Jacques, "Conscience's Final Pilgrimage in *Piers Plowman* and the Cyclical Structure of the Liturgy," *Studies in Medieval Culture* 4 (1974): 387. Gale C. Schricker, "On the Relation of Fact and Fiction in Chaucer's Poetic Endings," *SP* 60 (1981): 13-27, argues persuasively that "it is indeed a structural principle that the endings in Chaucer's poetry treat the speakers' return to a factual, quotidian reality following the extraordinary experience of being totally immersed in the fiction of a dream or story" (p. 14). If the *Retraction* might be compared to the final prayer in *TC*, the setting of the *Prologue* to The Parson's Tale might be likened to the preceding stanza (*TC*, V, 1856-62) with its reference to Gower and Strode, known friends of Chaucer the man, which returns the focus of the narrative to the factual reality of their common city, London.

29. Daniel Knapp, "The Relyk of a Seint: A Gloss on Chaucer's Pilgrimage," *ELH* 39 (1972): 23.

30. Interpretations of Chaucer's ending are reviewed by James Dean, "The Ending of the Canterbury Tales: 1952-1976," *TSLL* 21 (1979): 17-33, with recent contributions coming from Georgia R. Crampton, "Other Senses of Ending," *Spenser: Classical, Medieval, and Modern*, ed. David A. Richardson (Cleveland, Ohio: Cleveland State University Press, 1977), pp. 132-42; and Michael Holahan, "'Swich fyn . . . swich fyn': Senses of Ending in Chaucer and Spenser," in ibid., pp. 116-31. A study especially valuable for its review of prior criticism is Lee W. Patterson, *"The Parson's Tale* and the Quitting of the *Canterbury Tales,"* *Traditio* 34 (1978): 331-80. Commentary on the *Retraction* and its sincerity can be examined in James D. Gordon, "Chaucer's Retraction: A Review of Opinion," in MacEdward Leach, ed., *Studies in Medieval Literature in Honor of Albert Croll Baugh* (Philadelphia: University of Pennsylvania Press, 1961), pp. 81-96; and in Olive Sayce, "Chaucer's 'Retraction': The Conclusion of the *Canterbury Tales* and Its Place in Literary Tradition," *MÆ* 40 (1971): 230-48.

31. Caroline F. E. Spurgeon, ed., *Five Hundred Years of Chaucer Criticism and Allusion, 1357-1900*, 3 vols. (Cambridge: Cambridge University Press, 1925), 1:35: "In thys book I wyl hym sette, / And ympen thys Oryson / Affter hys translacion." In excluding Chaucer's histories from *The Troy Book*, Lydgate remarked, "To take on me it were but hi3e foly / In any wyse to add more þer-to" (ibid., 3:3).

32. Spurgeon, ed., *Five Hundred Years*, 1:25.

33. These passages from *The Troy Book* and *The Courte of Sapyence* are quoted in ibid., pp. 25 and 16, respectively.

34. Since publication of the full Erdmann-Ekwall edition, a new manuscript of the *Thebes* has been unearthed by A. I . Doyle and George B. Pace ("A New Chaucer Manuscript," *PMLA* 83 [1968]: 25).

35. Lydgate, *Thebes*, 2:36-37. *The Canterbury Tales* ends on fol. 257v: "Explicit narracio Rectoris et ultima inter narraciones huis libri de quibus composuit Chauucer cuius anime propicietur deus. AMEN." *Thebes* begins on fol . 258r: "Incipit ultima de fabulis Canturarie translata et prolata per Dompnum Iohannem Lidgate monachum in redeundo a Cantuaria."

36. The Christ Church MS is described in ibid., 2:211-17. The Ingilby MS (ibid., 2:47-48) has found its way to the British Library and has been renamed Egerton 2864. It is described, with slightly different foliation, by Manly and Rickert, 1:143-47. Royal MS 18.D.II., though not physically connecting the two works, contains two rubrics acknowledging the fictive relationship: "In this preamble shortly is comprihendid A Mery conseyte of Iohn lydgate Monke of Bury declarynge how he aionyde þe sege of Thebes to the mery tallys of Caunterburye" (fol. 147v); "Here begynneth the Segge of Thebes ful lamentably tolde by Iohn lidgate Monke of Bury anneyynge it to þe tallys of Canterbury" (fol. 148r). See Lydgate, *Thebes* 2:56. Not mentioned here is a fourth manuscript, Longleat 257, in which *The Knight's Tale* follows as a sequel to Lydgate's poem. In a forthcoming study Daniel W. Mosser argues persuasively that the Cardigan copy of Y also originally

preceded that manuscript's copy of *The Canterbury Tales*, whose writing and collection were not adequately assessed by Manly and Rickert, 1:71-78.

37. Lydgate, *Thebes*, 2:94, 213.

38. Eleanor Prescott Hammond, "Lydgate's Prologue to the Story of Thebes," *Anglia* 36 (1912): 361-62.

39. In *Thebes*, 2:96, editor Ekwall remarks upon Lydgate's "confused and faulty remembrance" when writing his *Prologue*.

40. Ibid., p. 95.

41. Ibid.

42. Ibid., p 107.

43. C. S. Lewis, *The Allegory of Love: A Study in Medieval Tradition* (Oxford: Oxford University Press, 1936), p. 163.

44. Derek Pearsall, *John Lydgate* (Charlottesville: University Press of Virginia, 1970), pp. 66-67.

45. Ibid., pp. 85-86. Hammond, "Lydgate's Prologue," p. 361, remarks that it would be "an exercise for the student of Chaucer to trace this prologue, phrase by phrase and idea by idea, to its sources in the *Canterbury Tales*."

46. Lydgate, *Thebes*, 2:9; Pearsall, *John Lydgate*, p. 151; Walter F. Schirmer, *John Lydgate: A Study in the Culture of the XVth Century*, trans. Ann E. Keep (Berkeley: University of California Press, 1961), p. 65; Alain Renoir, *The Poetry of John Lydgate* (Cambridge, Mass.: Harvard University Press, 1967), p. 111.

47. Robert W. Ayers, "Medieval History, Moral Purpose, and the Structure of Lydgate's *Siege of Thebes*." *PMLA* 73 (1958): 474 and generally 464-68; see also Schirmer, *John Lydgate*, pp. 63-64.

48. Ann Middleton, "The Idea of Public Poetry in the Reign of Richard II," *Speculum* 53 (1978): 95.

49. Lois Ebin, "Lydgate's Views on Poetry," *AnM* 18 (1977): 97. Judson Boyce Allen, *The Ethical Poetic of the Later Middle Ages* (Toronto: University of Toronto Press, 1982), argues that nearly all poetry of the period shared this obligation.

50. Lois Ebin, "Chaucer, Lydgate, and the 'Myrie Tale,'" *ChauR* 13 (1979): 331-32.

51. Schirmer, *John Lydgate*, p. 62. Using this allusion to help date the poem, Ekwall, in Lydgate, *Thebes*, 2:8, quotes from the twenty-fourth paragraph of the Treaty of Troyes concluded between England and France in May, 1420: "Item, ut Concordia, Pax, & Tranquillitas inter praedicta Franciae & Angliae Regna perpetuo futuris temporibus observentur." Mindful of the vulnerability of even the world's greatest empire, Lydgate around 1400 had written a work entitled *The True History or Mappe of Romes Ouerthrowe*, during which he was reminded of Chaucer's compendium of tragic falls in *The Monk's Tale*; see Spurgeon, ed., *Five Hundred Years*, 1:14. Allen and Moritz, *A Distinction of Stories*, p. 26, call for further study of the relationship between the *Siege* and *The Knight's Tale*, since both poets are primarily concerned with establishing a normative definition of human society: "Every city, every civilization, faced the

temptation to become a Thebes. John Lydgate saw this very clearly when he inserted his story of Thebes as another, and final, Canterbury tale."

52. Lydgate, *Thebes*, 2:96 and 134.

53. References in other Lydgatian poems, particularly the *Temple of Glas* and *Fall of Princes*, indicate a knowledge of at least nine other tales; see Spurgeon, ed., *Five Hundred Years*, 1:17-18, 35-43. *Thebes* itself (lines 18-26) praises the diverse subject matter and moral tone of the "Canterbury talys / Complet and told at many sondry stage."

54. Ibid., pp. 6-7; Alain Renoir, "The Immediate Source of Lydgate's *Siege of Thebes*," *SN* 33 (1961): 86-95.

55. Renoir, "The Immediate Source," pp. 113-14; and Pearsall, *John Lydgate*, p. 153. Longleat 257 is described by Manly and Rickert, 1:339.

56. I am indebted for this term to Barbara Herrnstein Smith, *Poetic Closure: A Study of How Poems End* (Chicago: University of Chicago Press, 1968), p. 212. Baldwin, *The Unity of the Canterbury Tales*, p. 15, remarks that the formal circularity proposed by Chaucer (and produced by Lydgate) would give the work the "englobed and polished *ratio* lauded by the medieval literary theorists."

57. Spurgeon, ed., *Five Hundred Years*, 1:25.

58. John Lydgate, *Poems*. ed. John Norton-Smith (Oxford: Clarendon, 1966), p. x.

59. Northrop Frye, *Anatomy of Criticism: Four Essays* (Princeton, NJ.: Princeton University Press, 1957), pp. 202-203. Morton W. Bloomfield, "Contemporary Literary Theory and Chaucer," in Donald M. Rose, ed., *New Perspectives in Chaucer Criticism* (Norman, Okla.: Pilgrim Books, 1981), pp. 32-33, has predicted that interpretative advances will be made in the kind of structural analysis "similar to the basic approach of a critic like Northrop Frye or an archetypal critic who is concerned with the basic patterns whether they be deep or surface ones."

60. Frank Kermode, *The Sense of an Ending: Studies in the Theory of Fiction* (Oxford: Oxford University Press, 1967), pp. 3-31.

61. Spurgeon, ed., *Five Hundred Years*, 1:36-37, quotes Lydgate's acknowledgment of *The Monk's Tale* as a model for his *Fall of Princes*, as well as his use of roadway imagery — "this world is a thurghfare ful of woo" (p. 36)—to describe the tragic patterning of history.

62. Frye, *Anatomy*, p. 203.

63. Kermode, *The Sense of an Ending*, p. 59.

64. Morton W. Bloomfield, "Allegory as Interpretation," *NLH* 3 (1972): 302. Northrop Frye, *The Great Code: The Bible and Literature* (New York: Harcourt Brace Jovanovich, 1981), p. 79; the implications of these verbal back references are explored throughout the latter half of this volume, as well as in the second volume promised by the author.

Critic and Poet: What Lydgate and Henryson Did to Chaucer's *Troilus and Criseyde*

C. *David Benson*

This article originally appeared in Modern Language Quarterly *53 (1992): 23-40.*

A LTHOUGH Chaucer's *Troilus and Criseyde* is cited and used by many English writers in the fifteenth and sixteenth centuries, the two major reworkings of the love story before Shakespeare are by John Lydgate in his *Troy Book* (1412-20) and by Robert Henryson in his late fifteenth-century *Testament of Cresseid*.[1] Lydgate and Henryson are perhaps the most prominent representatives of the English and Scottish Chaucerian traditions, and their two Trojan works had great influence. Lydgate's massive *Troy Book*, commissioned by Henry V when still Prince of Wales, became the standard history of the Trojan War in English (as its patron hoped it would) and is one of the sources for Shakespeare's *Troilus and Cressida*. It survives in more manuscripts than does Chaucer's *Troilus*. Henryson's short poem had an even more eventful career. First produced in relative obscurity (no early manuscripts survive or separate prints before 1593), Thynne included it following *Troilus* in his 1532 edition of Chaucer's works (apparently as an afterthought). As a result, it was widely accepted as the genuine conclusion to Chaucer's poem into the eighteenth century. Henryson's tabloid-like revelations about Cresseid's private life (that after being rejected by Diomede she became a prostitute and finally died of leprosy) were the most memorable incidents of the story for many later readers. Until the time of Shakespeare and well beyond, reference to Chaucer's love story almost always includes, and is often dominated by, Henryson's account of Cresseid's end.

Although it is fashionable today to assume a writer's deep Oedipal anxiety as he tries to match a great predecessor (and there is evidence of such feelings toward Chaucer by other writers of the period), neither Lydgate or Henryson seems especially intimidated by *Troilus and Criseyde*. Instead, both appear invigorated by the challenge of adding to Chaucer's achievement and produce some of their finest work, though the results are very different. Put most crudely, Henryson is a great poet and Lydgate is not; the former creates a small tragic masterpiece, the latter a pseudohistory of interminable length.[2] It tells us much about the literary judgment of each that Lydgate's response to Chaucer's eight-thousand-line Trojan poem was a work almost four times as long (over thirty thousand lines), whereas Henryson had the shrewd tact to respond with just over six hundred lines. In light of these numbers, the difference between Lydgate and Henryson has often been thought as one of quantity versus quality. Although there is some truth in this judgment, it is finally too simple and obscures the separate motives and accomplishments of each.

Lydgate approached Chaucer's story of *Troilus and Criseyde* as a scholarly commentator ready to annotate, reinforce, and provide his readers with the historical context to Chaucer's work; Henryson's response is to exploit in his own original way Chaucer's innovative literary devices, including the characterization of Criseyde. It is as if each were attempting to rectify a different absence in *Troilus*. For Lydgate, it is Chaucer's announcement early in the poem that his subject is not the war or destruction of the city and that anyone who wants to know about

> the Troian gestes, as they felle,
> In Omer, or in Dares, or in Dite,
> Whoso that kan may rede as they write.
> (1.145-47; cf. 5.1770-71)[3]

Homer is just a name in the Middle Ages, but Lydgate had read Dares and Dictys in the authoritative redaction of Guido delle Colonne and is prepared to recount all to his audience. The Chaucerian absence that Henryson wants to fill is the narrator's admission that he does not know what Criseyde felt in her heart toward Diomede and the refusal of *Troilus* to tell the end of her story: "Men seyn—I not—that she yaf hym hire herte" (5.1050). Criseyde's heart, mind, and soul (and what happened to her among the Greeks) are the subject of the *Testament*.

Lydgate's *Troy Book* is a careful, if expanded, translation of Guido delle Colonne's late thirteenth-century *Historia destructionis Troiae*. Although the learned *Historia* is actually a sober Latin adaptation of Benoît de Sainte-Maure's inventive French romance, *Le Roman de Troie* (ca. 1180), it was widely accepted in the late Middle Ages as the true history of the Trojan War based on the supposed eyewitness journals of Dares on the Trojan side and Dictys on the Greek.[4] Benoît, followed by Guido, transforms the sparse accounts of Dares and Dictys into an epic narrative that opens with Jason's pursuit of the Golden Fleece and ends only with the return of the Greeks after the final destruction of Priam's city. Like Benoît, who invented the episode, Guido includes the story of Troilus and Briseida (as Criseyde is there called). Recounted in several separate episodes that tell us almost nothing about the beginning and growth of Troilus's love affair, Guido's narrative begins with Briseida's departure from Troy to the Greek camp at the request of her traitor father Calchas. Both lovers lament their separation, but once among the Greeks Briseida immediately wins and soon accepts the affections of Diomedes (allowing Guido to moralize on the frailty of women), while Troilus is left to revenge himself with limited success against his rival on the battlefield until he himself is killed in ambush by Achilles.

Lydgate clearly accepted the authority of the *Historia*, regarding it, as Walter Schirmer has noted, as a "historical work containing all the moral and political lessons which history was expected to teach."[5] Lydgate changes nothing essential in Guido's factual matter, though everything is developed at greater length. The story of the separated lovers is especially enlarged because of Lydgate's knowledge of *Troilus and Criseyde*, which he praises extravagantly. Indeed it may well have been the impact of Chaucer's poem that inspired Lydgate and the future Henry V (who himself owned a copy of it) to have the full story of Troy told in English. To many modern readers, Lydgate's tributes to Chaucer are irritating at best because the monk of Bury seems to have captured nothing of the psychological depth, imaginative empathy, tragic intensity, or literary power of his model. Derek Pearsall has compared part of the initial description of Criseyde in the *Troy Book* (2.4736-62) with Chaucer's portrait of her near the end of his poem (5.806-26). Although Lydgate borrows heavily from his predecessor (who in this passage is uncharacteristically formal and distant), much is lost: "Gone are the distinctive tone of voice, the pure felicity of diction, the asides, the sweet smoothness of line flowing into line; in their place the generalized epithet, the conventional image, the loose syntax, the lame metre, the patches of decoration, the pretentious abstraction."[6] The reader may all too easily agree with Lydgate himself a few lines earlier when, in a formula often used by Chaucer, he says that to try to imitate his master's description of Criseyde is "hiȝe foly" (2.4682).

The harsh assessment that Lydgate has so often received from later readers is in a sense unfair because it comes from judging him as a poet. Lydgate has his virtues, but exceptional skill at poetry is not one of them. In a recent article, Pearsall usefully sees Lydgate as a mediator rather than a creator: "What Lydgate did was to absorb Chaucer to the official taste of the fifteenth century, by praising and imitating him in ways that were acceptable to that taste."[7] It might be even more appropriate for us to think of Lydgate not so much as a poet but as a critic. He often recognizes what Chaucer has done, even if he cannot do it himself. He would have been the appropriate first holder of a chair in Chaucer studies (his interest in Chaucer is surely more academic than Boccaccio's was in Dante). To be quite frank, Lydgate is one of us. Instead of kissing the steps trod by Virgil, Ovid, Homer, Lucan, and Statius, he is more easily imagined in conversation with the president of the Modern Language Association. Whenever we are tempted to condescend to Lydgate, we should stop and consider whether any of us could equal even his modest poetic attainments should the *Modern Language Quarterly*, for instance, like the fifteenth century, demand that our response to Chaucer be written in verse. No doubt some of our number could equal him in prolixity.

Lydgate's praise of Chaucer during his description of Criseyde and later when he comes to tell of the lovers' parting (3.4237-63) shows that he recognized his predecessor's greatness. It will be the argument of the rest of this section that Lydgate understood much, though certainly not all, of what Chaucer had accomplished in *Troilus and Criseyde*, even if he was incapable of equaling it in his own verse. In a brilliant essay that still remains influential today, C. S. Lewis (one modern critic who could write good Middle English poetry) identified four elements in *Troilus* that Chaucer had added to his immediate source, Boccaccio's *Il Filostrato*: history, rhetoric, doctrine, and courtly love.[8] Except for the problematic issue of courtly love, most Chaucerians today would agree that these elements are indeed important in Chaucer's version of the story. That they also mark Lydgate's treatment of the love story indicates that he was a better reader of *Troilus* than has sometimes been recognized.

Lewis first demonstrates that Chaucer "approached his work as an 'historical' poet contributing to the story of Troy." He expected his audience to be interested not only in "the personal drama between his little group of characters" but also in "that whole world of story which makes this drama's context" (p. 10). Chaucer indeed adds material from the medieval history of Troy to Boccaccio's poem, as I have discussed elsewhere, but Lydgate takes this process much further.[9] The *Troy Book* puts the love story of *Troilus and Criseyde* back into the context of the history from which Boccaccio had freed it. In contrast to Chaucer's use of Troy as background, Lydgate retells Guido delle Colonne's entire *Historia destructionis Troiae*. Responding to and going beyond the historical element in *Troilus*, Lydgate provides readers of Chaucer's poem with the full Trojan context, much as certain university teachers spend weeks on the *General Prologue* and on an exhaustive exposition of fourteenth-century English life as a prelude to reading the *Canterbury Tales*.

Lydgate's commitment to the historical truth of Troy, as he understood it, is fundamental. Unlike Chaucer, he does not feel free to omit or completely invent episodes, though he does expand and interpret.[10] For all his praise of Chaucer's style, it is Guido's order of presentation of the love story that Lydgate chooses to follow (Torti, p. 182). Like Guido, he first describes Troilus and Criseyde separately and only mentions the affair as the lovers are about to part (3.4077ff.). He does supplement the *Historia* with a brief (for him) digression on how the relationship began, taken from the first three books of Chaucer's *Troilus*, with most of the attention on how Troilus was smitten at his first sight of Criseyde (3.4201-23). By identifying the digression as Chaucerian, Lydgate seems to deny any responsibility for its historical truth. Just as Chaucer had urged those who wanted to learn more about the Trojan War to read Dares and Dictys, Lydgate, the more historical poet, urges those who want to learn more about the love story to turn to Chaucer: "þe hoole story Chaucer kan ȝow telle / ȝif that ȝe liste—no man bet alyue" (3.4234-35). Lydgate's commitment to Guido's history, for all his praise of Chaucer's love story, can also be seen in his characterization. Lydgate does use Chaucer's name for Guido's Briseida, but the name Pandarus appears in the narrative, as it does in the *Historia*, as that of a king who came to fight on the Trojan side (2.7626). The role of Pandarus in the love affair is mentioned only in passing during the summary of *Troilus* (3.4216). Similarly, Lydgate's Diomede is a noble fighter and sincere lover of Criseyde (see, for example, 3.4820ff.), as he is in Guido, rather than Chaucer's smooth seducer. Chaucer may be "historical," but Lydgate is much truer to the medieval history of Troy.

Lewis also shows that Chaucer "approached his work as a pupil of the rhetoricians" who "found his original too short and proceeded in many places to 'amplify' it" (p. 11). No reader of the *Troy Book* will need to be told that Lydgate responded to and amplified the rhetoric of Chaucer's *Troilus*. Pearsall notes that throughout his career Lydgate "uses academic rhetoric to fortify and improve upon successive Chaucerian models" ("Chaucer and Lydgate," p. 52), even though the improvement may be only in his own eyes. In two passages during his retelling of the story of *Troilus and Criseyde* that specifically praise Chaucer (2.4694-4719; 3.4237-63), it is not the older poet's humor, colloquialism, learning, or irony that Lydgate celebrates (as we might), but rather his "gold dewe-dropis of rhetorik so fyne, / Oure rude langage only tenlwmyne" (2.4699-4700). Lydgate recognizes that Chaucer's command of rhetoric had finally made English a serious literary language, and he develops this idea in a second tribute that compares his predecessor to Petrarch (3.4351), whom Chaucer's own Clerk in the *Canterbury Tales* had cited as "the lauriate poete" whose "rethorike sweete / Enlumyned al Ytaille of poetrie" (4.31-33):

> For he owre englishe gilte with his sawes,
> Rude and boistous firste be olde dawes,
> Þat was ful fer from al perfeccioun,
> And but of litel reputacioun,
> Til þat he cam, &, þoruȝ his poetrie,
> Gan oure tonge firste to magnifie,
> And adourne it with his elloquence—
> To whom honour, laude, & reuerence,
> Þoruȝ-oute þis londe ȝoue be & songe,
> So þat þe laurer of oure englishe tonge
> Be to hym ȝoue for his excellence.
> (3.4237-47)

Far from being intimidated by Chaucer, Lydgate seems grateful that the older poet had made English literature, including the *Troy Book*, possible. In imitating and inflating Chaucer's rhetoric, Lydgate was responding to only one part of the achievement of *Troilus*, and his practice does not begin to equal his model, but the result is instructive, as the work of a modern critic who analyzes only one aspect of Chaucer is instructive.

The third element identified by Lewis in *Troilus* that was not in Boccaccio's *Filostrato* results from the fact that "Chaucer approached his work as a poet of doctryne and sentence." Lewis quotes Hoccleve's praise of Chaucer for this quality and warns us not to be astonished "that the fifteenth century should imitate those elements of Chaucer's genius which it enjoyed instead of those which we enjoy" (p. 12). As an example of doctryne and sentence in *Troilus*, Lewis mentions Chaucer's long Boethian addition on free will and Fortune in book 4, a theme that appears throughout the poem.[11] Anna Torti has noted the prominent role of Fortune in the *Troy Book* (p. 181), and indeed Lydgate prefaces his first and longest discussion of the affair (when the lovers part) with a lament against Fortune and her changeable wheel that reminds us specifically of the opening of book 4 of *Troilus:*

> Allas! Fortune, gery and vnstable,
> And redy ay for to be chaungable;
> When folk most triste in þi stormy face,
> Liche her desire þe fully to embrace:
> Þanne is þi Ioye aweye to turne & wrype,
> Vp-on wrechis þi power for to kipe—
> Record on Troylus, þat fro þi whele so lowe
> By fals envie þou hast ouer-þrowe,
> Out of þe Ioye which þat he was Inne,
> From his lady to make him for to twynne
> Whan he best wende for to haue be surid.
> (3.4077-87)

Lydgate is a poet of *doctryne* and sentence in a more limited way than Chaucer. The older poet adds to his poem a range of philosophical and religious issues not found in Boccaccio without providing clear answers, whereas Lydgate, as tends to be true with critics even in our postmodern age, is anxious to draw moral or political meaning from the story and to explain why things happen as they do. For example, Lydgate must find a reason for the death of Hector, the event that seals Troy's destruction. Without changing Guido's facts, he interprets Hector's actions just before his death as covetousness and thus by the crudest application of the notion of a "tragic flaw" is able to identify the cause that lay behind this crucial event: Hector's moral error exposed him to death (Benson, *History of Troy*, pp. 124-29). Writing about a similar analysis of another incident in the *Troy Book*, Pearsall notes that "such moralising is often highly inappropriate, indeed . . . totally destructive of any values for which the story itself might stand" (*John Lydgate*, p. 131). In retelling the love story of *Troilus and Criseyde*, Lydgate must explain the betrayal of Criseyde, to which I shall turn in discussing the fourth element that Lewis found added to *Troilus*.

In the last and longest section of his essay, Lewis says that "Chaucer approached his work as the poet of courtly love" (p. 14). Courtly love has become a problematic term for contemporary readers of Chaucer, and, whatever one's definition, few would find it much in evidence in the *Troy Book*. Nevertheless, Lydgate does respond to an undoubted courtly element in *Troilus*: the ennobling of Troilus and Criseyde. The purest hero in the *Troy Book* is not Hector, who brings on his own death, but Troilus, whose "epic status" is noted by Torti (p. 174). Troilus's prowess in battle is stressed when he is first mentioned in the *Troy Book*, and, bringing a phrase forward from Guido in all seriousness that Chaucer uses somewhat mockingly, Lydgate calls him "Hector þe secounde" (2.288). When next mentioned, Troilus is described as "ȝong, fresche, and lusty, & coraious also" (2.2995). The first two adjectives especially, so reminiscent of Chaucer's idealistic and innocent hero, are used formulaically for Troilus throughout the *Troy Book* (e.g., 2.4865, 8629; 3.173-74, 2387; 4.1638). Lydgate's formal portrait of Troilus, much expanded from the *Historia*, stresses his accomplishments as a warrior (the deeds that Chaucer mentions but never develops are fully recounted in the *Troy Book*); and whereas Guido notes merely that Troilus was popular with women because of his reserve, Lydgate adds lines that remind us of Chaucer's steadfast Troilus, who could not stop loving Criseyde for a quarter of a day: "þer-to in loue as trewe as any stele, / Secre and wys"; and "He was alwey feithful, iust, & stable, / Perseueraunt, and of wil inmvtable / Vp-on what þing he onys set his herte" (2.4874-75, 4879-81). The death of Lydgate's perfect knight results from no fault of his own, but from the false treachery of Achilles, whose wickedness is much developed from Guido (e.g., 4.2668ff., 2768ff.), and the woe thereby occasioned is the subject of a long, learned, and original lament by Lydgate (4.3004-70)—the kind Chaucer makes fun of at the end of the *Nun's Priest's Tale*.

If Troilus is truly ennobled in the *Troy Book*, Criseyde only seems to be. The antifeminist lesson that Lydgate draws from Criseyde's betrayal, though clear enough in the end, is complicated by his use of a prominent narrative voice, reminiscent of that in Chaucer's *Troilus*, which appears to offer sympathy to the heroine. After telling us that the lovers must part and praising Chaucer, Lydgate's narrator notes that his source blamed Troilus for loving Criseyde and then reports at length all the terrible things that Guido had to say about women: they are like serpents; they are never satisfied with one man; they continually sell themselves; they change like the moon, and so on (3.4264-4342). The English narrator is careful throughout the diatribe to note that these are Guido's opinions ("as seith Guydo"), and at the conclusion he insists, "þus techeþ Guydo, God wot, & not I!" (3.4343). The narrator pretends to be indignant with Guido ("ful euel mote he þriue!" [3.4355]) and affirms "by þe rode" that he himself believes that for every bad woman there are a hundred good ones, citing various holy women (3.4361-97). He returns to Guido's complaint that women are naturally double and uses this as a final defense: if nature made them this way, how can they be responsible: "For ȝif wommen be double naturelly, / Why shulde men leyn on hem þe blame?" (3.4408-9). A similar argument is repeated at the end of the entire passage (3.4441-45).

As Gretchen Mieszkowski has fully explained, the joke here is not only that Lydgate's final "defense"—that women are false by nature—is really the deepest insult but also that Guido's reported attacks against women, which the narrator pretends to disdain, are greatly expanded in the *Troy Book*, even by Lydgate's standards.[12] Although there is some genuine literary play here, A. C. Spearing is justified in finding Lydgate's irony "a coarse-grained misreading of Chaucer's tone."[13] In contrast to Chaucer's genuine sympathy for Criseyde, Lydgate's is merely superficial; as Pearsall notes, "He reabsorbs Criseyde into the conventional stereotypes of medieval anti-feminism" ("Chaucer and Lydgate," p. 48). Yet Lydgate has not misunderstood Chaucer completely. He has clearly reproduced the separation in *Troilus* between the poet's own views and those of his narrative voice, an aspect of Chaucer's achievement recognized only fairly recently by modern critics (Mieszkowski, p. 126). Lydgate also deserves credit for seeing the humor in the account of the affair in *Troilus*, perhaps Chaucer's most striking contribution to the love story, even if his attempt to equal his predecessor hops far behind. Like much academic humor, Lydgate's comedy is forced and its effectiveness diluted by repetition—he uses the same kind of mock defense for other women in the *Troy Book* (Mieszkowski, pp. 123-24; Pearsall, *John Lydgate*, pp. 134-36).

When Criseyde finally betrays Troilus, Lydgate's pretended sympathy is more subtle and more nasty, reminiscent of the narrator's attitude toward May in the *Merchant's Tale*. Criseyde is said to visit Diomede "of verray womanhede" (4.2132) and sit on his bed "benignely" (4.2139). When she gives him "Hooly hir herte" (4.2147), the narrator replaces Guido's brief direct attack on women with a long passage that marvels at "what pite is in wommanhede, / What mercy eke & benygne routhe— / þat newly can al her olde trouthe" (4.2148-50). Humor has been left far behind, and two extraordinary images follow (4.2154-59): women change more easily than money in Lombard Street, and "So þat þe wynde be redy and þe tyde, / Passage is ay, who-so list to passe!" (Would it be too much to claim that Lydgate is thinking of the *stilnovo* images of sailing that run through *Troilus*?) He concludes with these malicious lines:

> For leuere she had chaunge & variaunce
> Were founde in hir þanne lak of pite,
> As sittyng is to femynyte,
> Of nature nat to be vengable,
> For feith nor ope, but raþer mercyable
> Of mannys lyf stondyng in distresse.
> (4.2172-77)

Criseyde is never mentioned again in the *Troy Book*. She has been taken back into the inexhaustible well of medieval antifeminism. Lydgate understands much of what Chaucer had done in *Troilus*, but not the remarkable sympathy for his fallen heroine.

What happened to Criseyde in the Greek camp after Diomede is told by Robert Henryson in his *Testament of Cresseid*. Henryson may be a more intelligent reader of Chaucer's *Troilus* than Lydgate, but of more significance is his different approach.[14] In contrast to Lydgate's academic treatment of *Troilus*, Henryson responds as a poet. By that I mean that he does not attempt to contextualize, expand, or explain elements and techniques in Chaucer's poem, but instead these elements inspire him to produce something original. Rather than retell the love story so that it becomes more conventional, Henryson produces a new narrative that is fully worthy of its source.

The ultimate tribute to Henryson's success is that the *Testament* was for so long regarded as Chaucer's own despite clear signals to the contrary in the poem. At the beginning of the *Testament*, the narrator says that he was reading a book "Writtin be worthie Chaucer glorious / Of fair Cresseid and worthie Troylus" (ll. 41-42).[15] He then claims to have taken up "ane vther quair" that told of "the fatall destenie / Of fair Creisseid [*sic*], that endit wretchitlie" (ll. 61-63), and he makes a remarkable statement about the two texts:

> Quha wait gif all that Chauceir wrait was trew?
> Nor I wait nocht gif this narratioun
> Be authoreist, or fenȝeit of the new
> Be sum poeit, throw his inuentioun.
> (ll. 64-67)

Many critics, noting the audacious questioning of Chaucer's reliability, have detected the beginnings of a new conception of literature here that heralds the Renaissance, one based on the poet's own invention rather than the repetition of approved sources. The contrast with the *Troy Book* is stark: Lydgate goes back behind Chaucer to the authoritative history of Guide delle Colonne; Henryson goes forward to tell an original story about the most vulnerable character.

Some of the ways that Henryson's response to *Troilus and Criseyde* differ[s] from Lydgate's can be seen if we consider again the four elements that Lewis identified as distinguishing Chaucer's version of the love story: history, rhetoric, doctrine, and courtly love. Perhaps the clearest difference between the *Troy Book* and the *Testament* is that whereas Lydgate tells the history of the Trojan War from its earliest causes to the Greek returns, Henryson's poem, like Chaucer's, keeps the war in the background. And yet, as Lewis and others since him have noted, even if Chaucer's use of Trojan history is selective, it carries much more meaning than in his immediate Boccaccian source. Chaucer does not recount the whole history of Troy, but he does evoke that history at significant moments. The love of Troilus and Criseyde develops in the shadow of the Greek siege, and the end of the affair presages the destruction of the city. The war is mentioned much less frequently in the *Testament* than in *Troilus*, but, as I have argued elsewhere, Troilus's noble generosity near the end of the poem toward the begging lepers (including the unrecognized Criseyde) seems undercut by our knowledge that the secular aristocratic values he represents (reminiscent of Hector's ineffectual chivalry toward Criseyde in book 4 of *Troilus*) will soon be overwhelmed by the utter ruin of Troy.[16] Henryson's use of the Trojan historical context in the *Testament* is purely suggestive and nothing like the full record provided by Lydgate.

Henryson's use of the events of the "history" of *Troilus* itself is equally selective and inventive. For example, Tillyard long ago argued that the nonrecognition of the lovers just discussed (their first and last encounter in the *Testament*) depends on our recollection of the crucial moment in book 2 of Chaucer's poem when Criseyde sees Troilus ride under her window as he returns from battle.[17] Although J. A. W. Bennett strongly denied the resemblance between these two scenes, unconvincingly in my opinion, he himself went on to argue for other Chaucerian echoes, and Douglas Gray, among others, has suggested further similarities between the two works.[18] The difficulty we have in being sure about whether a particular incident in the *Testament* is truly based on something in *Troilus* is itself revealing. Lydgate, being careful not to compromise the truth of Guido's history, regularly signals and annotates his borrowings from Chaucer, such as his account of how Troilus first saw Criseyde (3.4201-13). Henryson is less explicit, and his transformations of what are likely to be Chaucerian hints make the extent of his obligations harder to assess. The word *parliament* suggests what I mean. Chaucer employs this familiar English political term nine times to describe the Trojan council that decides to send Criseyde over to the Greeks (4.143, 211, 217, 218, 344, 377, 559, 664, 1297). Lydgate, apparently showing his awareness of Chaucer's practice, uses the term throughout the *Troy Book* for similar councils, including the one that decides Criseyde's fate (3.3747). Henryson uses the term only once, and then not for a political gathering but for the assembly of gods that meets to punish Cresseid with leprosy (1.266). Although the parallel is not as direct as in the *Troy Book*, Henryson's use of Chaucer's term is much more suggestive: it asks us to compare and contrast the two different parliaments, one human and the other cosmic, that bring such misery to Cresseid.

Henryson is not as committed to the historical record as Lydgate, and, like Chaucer, he is willing to change Guido's authoritative facts for his own purposes. Unlike Diomede in the *Troy Book*, who is the sincere lover of the *Historia*, Henryson's Diomeid is Chaucer's practiced seducer: "Quhen Diomeid had all his apetyte, / And mair, fulfillit of this fair ladie, / Vpon ane vther he set his haill delyte" (ll. 71-73). Calchas in the *Testament* is different from the seer in both Guido and Chaucer; not only is he a noticeably sweeter and more concerned parent (if no more effective), but he is made a priest of Venus instead of Apollo.[19] What Henryson has done, I believe, is to combine Calchas with the third major character in *Troilus* who has no function at this point in the story: Pandarus. Chaucer's Pandarus is a priest of Venus, in practice and deed even if not formally ordained. Moreover, Henryson's Calchas shares his love of proverbs, however inappropriate; when Cresseid reports her rejection from Diomeid, he replies, "Perauenture all cummis for the best" (l. 104). Calchas's ignorance about what has happened and will happen to his daughter (and his inability to do anything about it) seems to suggest Henryson's view of the futility of those in *Troilus* like Calchas and Pandarus who believe that they can know and control the future.

Although Lydgate lavishly praises his master's rhetoric (the second element that Lewis found added to *Troilus*), it is Henryson who is able to imitate Chaucer's command of a range of appropriate styles. In contrast to the relentless rhetorical expansion of the *Troy Book*, one of Henryson's most impressive accomplishments in the *Testament*, as A. C. Spearing has so well demonstrated, is a conciseness that "depends upon precision and completeness; it compresses much explicit meaning into as few words as possible."[20] This, of course, is the antithesis of Lydgate's sometimes empty embellishments in the *Troy Book*. But Henryson's conciseness does not mean that he entirely avoids the rhetorical dignity that Lydgate correctly saw as one of Chaucer's genuine contributions to English verse. The most obvious example of stylistic display in the *Testament* is the great set piece of Cresseid's vision, which occupies fully one-third of this short poem, in which the pagan gods/planets descend to debate and judge the woman's supposed blasphemy (ll. 141-343). The detailed portraits of these benevolent and malevolent forces are as learned as they are elaborate.[21] Henryson's mastery of appropriate styles is also seen in the complaint of Cresseid (ll. 407-69), written in an unusual stanza form apparently invented by Chaucer in "Anelida and Arcite," whose rhetorical elaborateness may, as Lee Patterson has suggested, lead us "to see it as a performance."[22] There does seem a deliberate contrast here to the starkness of her subsequent acceptance of responsibility (l. 574) and final testament (ll. 577-91). Henryson is a rhetorical poet, but, like Chaucer, he plays more than one note.

Perhaps nowhere is Henryson's similarity to Chaucer and difference from Lydgate clearer than in the third element Lewis found added to *Troilus*: *doctryne* and sentence. Although a judgmental tone has been detected by some in the *Testament* (sometimes identified as a kind of premature Presbyterianism; see, e.g., Sklute), the moral seriousness of Henryson's poem, whatever we take to be its final views, has little in common with the conventional lessons presented in the *Troy Book*. Lydgate's major characters are often thoroughly noble (Troilus) or wicked (Achilles, Criseyde); any apparent complexity is relatively superficial, as we have seen: the narrator pretends to defend Criseyde, who is indefensible, or a hero like Hector falls by committing a moral fault. No reader is left in much doubt about the message that Lydgate has to teach. In contrast, Henryson, like Chaucer, draws no clear moral from the story of *Troilus and Criseyde*. Some have seen the poem as bitterly critical of Cresseid (this is the way it seems to have been read by most in the late Middle Ages and Renaissance),[23] but many modern interpreters have noted the number of open questions in the poem, including the role of the gods, the justice of Cresseid's guilt and punishment, and the extent of her moral growth before her death.

The curtness of the ending of the *Testament*, which is concise even by Henryson's usual standard, dramatizes the difficulty that Henryson's various voices have as they try to make sense of Cresseid's experiences. Troilus, who is largely ignorant of the punishment his beloved has suffered and her response to it, has little to say—and most of that is about his own feelings: "I can no moir; / Scho was vntrew and wo is me thairfoir" (ll. 601-2). The tomb he has constructed is even more reticent: it notifies "fair ladyis" that Cresseid, once the flower of women, "Vnder this stane, lait lipper, lyis deid" (l. 609). The concluding voice of the narrator, who is not at all personalized as at the beginning of the poem, offers the most banal of morals ("Ming not 3our lufe with fals deceptioun") before lapsing into silence: "Sen scho is deid I speik of hir no moir" (ll. 613-16). Douglas Gray begins his discussion of the *Testament* by noting that it "has provoked an amazing variety of interpretations" (p. 162), and Malcolm Pittock has recently declared, with some exaggeration, that the poem "is unique among British medieval texts in the diametrically opposed interpretations it has occasioned."[24] Although the meaning of the *Testament* has occupied modern critics more than any other single topic, just as the lessons of the Troy story are a major concern of that critic-*manque* Lydgate, Henryson seems less interested in delivering a didactic message than in involving his readers in a series of complex moral issues. As he announces in the first stanza, the *Testament* is a "tragedy," which is what Chaucer finally calls *Troilus*. Genuine tragedy, in contrast to the sententious history of Lydgate, offers no lessons except the untrustworthiness of the world and the foolishness of regarding anyone as happy (or damned) before death.

The fourth and most questionable element that Lewis found added to Chaucer's *Troilus* is courtly love. Even more so than in the *Troy Book*, the attractiveness of the romantic love between *Troilus and Criseyde* is reduced to ashes in the *Testament*. Whether we find Troilus's chivalry at the end of the poem noble or deluded, his great love affair now exists only as a distant memory ("Sa deip imprentit in the fantasy / That it deludis the wittis outwardly" [ll. 508-9]) prompted by the sight of a pitiful leper met begging on the road. Though neither lover recognizes the other, that leper is, of course, Cresseid, whose physical beauty is turned before our eyes into terrible ugliness (ll. 337-50)—the epithet "fair" used so often to describe her becomes increasingly ironic. Nothing good is said about courtly love in the *Testament*, whose perspective is established early by the old narrator whose devotion to Venus is supported by a warm fire and the hint of aphrodisiacs (ll. 22-35). But if the *Testament* is no celebration of courtly love, as Lewis believed *Troilus and Criseyde* to be, Henryson learned much else from Chaucer as he transformed his Trojan love story.

We have already seen Henryson's re-creation of Calchas, who evokes both Chaucer's seer and, even more interestingly, the absent Pandarus. The old narrator just mentioned has often been seen as influenced by Chaucer's complex narrative voice in *Troilus*, though his fascination with the young lovers may remind us of Pandarus or even the nasty narrator of the

Merchant's Tale. The *Testament* is a masterly reworking not only of *Troilus* but of other Chaucerian poems as well. The bitter Spring at the beginning of the *Testament* seems to play with the opening of the *Canterbury Tales* (and other poetic springs): the Canterbury "shouris soote" (1.1) are replaced by Scottish "Schouris of haill" (l. 6). Spearing has convincingly compared Cresseid's complaint to Dorigen's in the *Franklin's Tale* (*Medieval to Renaissance*, pp. 184-85). If such moments are debts that Henryson owes to Chaucer, they are hard for modern critics to calculate, because instead of Lydgate's faithful treatment of Guido and Chaucer, they are the inspirations that one great poet finds in another. For instance, Henryson seems to have responded to Chaucer's careful attention to physical space, not found in Boccaccio's poem: examples include Troilus's room, Criseyde's garden and chamber, and the small private bedroom in which the love is consummated and which is successively enclosed by a larger room, Pandarus's house, the city, and the besieging Greek army. Henryson not only creates similarly enclosed spaces (the narrator's oratory and the secret oratory within Calchas's house in which Cresseid meets her doom from the gods) but also contrasts these with the open road on which Troilus and Cresseid meet for the last time.

Undoubtedly the most powerful example of the way that Henryson both acknowledges and renews Chaucer is the character of Cresseid herself. Especially at the beginning of the *Testament* she retains many of the qualities of her model, such as a dependence on male help, a fear of public exposure, and self-regard. But as she approaches her pitiful end, Henryson's Cresseid not only transcends Lydgate's antifeminist cliché but also becomes in some ways more interesting and certainly braver than Chaucer's heroine. *Troilus* makes us wonder what Criseyde really thinks and feels by constantly preventing access to her innermost self: we never know when or even if she ever fully loves *Troilus*, for example, and must be content with her ambiguous public statements.[25] Henryson does explore Cresseid's heart and soul; we know everything she thinks and feels. In a reversal of Chaucer's practice, it is Cresseid's private experience we know, whereas Troilus remains a more distant public figure. Henryson's Cresseid has a more detailed moral life than Chaucer's. Spearing correctly notes that the *Testament*, as an intelligent reading of *Troilus*, is "a deeply compassionate poem" (*Medieval to Renaissance*, p. 179), but Henryson goes beyond compassion to respect; he shows his heroine moving from self-pity to responsibility: "Nane but my self as now I will accuse" (1. 574). Cresseid descends from Criseyde, but the Scottish heroine achieves a literary and moral life distinctly her own. Both Lydgate and Henryson followed Chaucer's *Troilus* and, in their different ways, understood his accomplishment. We should honor Lydgate for his critical acumen (and consider him the patron saint of academic Chaucerians), but Henryson is more than a Chaucerian; he is the English writer's true poetic successor.

NOTES

1. For some of these other English responses to Chaucer's story, see Hyder E. Rollins, "The Troilus-Cressida Story from Chaucer to Shakespeare," *PMLA*, 32 (1917): 383-429, and my essay "True Troilus and False Cresseid: The Descent from Tragedy," in *The European Tragedy of Troilus*, Piero Boitani (Oxford: Clarendon, 1989), pp. 153-70.

2. My debt to Anna Torti's authoritative article "From 'History' to 'Tragedy': The Story of Troilus and Criseyde in Lydgate's *Troy Book* and Henryson's *Testament of Cresseid*," in Boitani, pp. 171-97, will be obvious. I am also grateful to Nicholas Watson for allowing me to read an advance copy of his stimulating essay on the same subject delivered as a talk at the Medieval Institute, Western Michigan university, in 1992 and soon to appear in the Elizabeth Kennedy festschrift.

3. All quotations from Chaucer are taken from *The Riverside Chaucer*, ed. Larry D. Benson et al., 3rd ed. (Boston: Houghton Mifflin, 1987).

4. For Guido and his English translators see my *History of Troy in Middle English Literature* (Cambridge: Brewer, 1980).

5. *John Lydgate*, trans. Ann E. Keep (Berkeley: University of California Press, 1961), p. 44.

6. *John Lydgate* (Charlottesville: University Press of Virginia, 1970), pp. 55-58. All quotations from Lydgate's *Troy Book*, cited by book and line number, are from the edition of Henry Bergen, EETS, ES, 97, 103, 106, 126 (London, 1906-20).

7. "Chaucer and Lydgate," in *Chaucer Traditions: Studies in Honour of Derek Brewer*, ed. Ruth Morse and Barry Windeatt (Cambridge: Cambridge University Press, 1990), p. 39.

8. "'What Chaucer Really Did to Il Filostrato," *Essays and Studies*, 17 (1932): 56-75; quoted from its reprinting in *Critical Essays on Chaucer's "Troilus and Criseyde" and His Major Early Poems*, ed. C. David Benson (Toronto: University of Toronto Press, 1991), pp. 8-31.

9. See chapter 4, "Troy," in my *Chaucer's "Troilus and Criseyde"* (London: Unwin, 1990).

10. When Lydgate announces that he is tempted to omit the description of Criseyde because Chaucer has done it better, he concludes that he cannot because if he did he would "þe trouþe leue / Of Troye boke" and omit matter presented "As Guydo doþ in ordre ceryously," thus committing an offense "þoruʒe necligence or presumpcioun" (2.4687-92).

11. See chapter 7, "Fortune," of my *Chaucer's "Troilus and Criseyde."*

12. "The Reputation of Criseyde: 1155-1500," *Transactions of the Connecticut Academy of Arts and Sciences*, 43 (1971): 117-22.

13. *Medieval to Renaissance in English Poetry* (Cambridge: Cambridge University Press, 1985), p. 181.

14. For two discussions of Henryson as a reader of Chaucer, see Denton Fox's introduction to his *Testament of Cresseid* (London: Nelson, 1968), pp. 21-24, and Spearing, *Medieval to Renaissance*, pp. 165-69.

15. All quotations from the *Testament* are from *The Poems of Robert Henryson*, ed. Denton Fox (Oxford: Clarendon, 1981).

16. "Troilus and Cresseid in Henryson's *Testament*," *Chaucer Review*, 13 (1979): 263-71, reprinted in *History of Troy*, pp. 143-50. My argument has been challenged by Spearing: "Troilus's moral status is never questioned or even discussed in the *Testament*" (Medieval to Renaissance, p. 351 n. 34). I would agree that Henryson makes no explicit criticism, but knowledge from the history of Troy that Troilus's extinction is almost as imminent as Criseyde's might make readers wonder if he is as prepared as she is for death. If my argument has validity, Henryson's evocation of the Trojan context is Chaucerian in its subtlety and in the demands it makes on the reader; it is completely different from Lydgate's historical literalness.

17. *Poetry and Its Background* (London: Chatto and Windus, 1955), p. 9.

18. Bennett, "Henryson's *Testament*: A Flawed Masterpiece," *Scottish Literary Journal*, I (1974): esp. 5, 11; Gray, *Robert Henryson* (Leiden: Brill, 1979), esp. pp. 169, 172-73, 179.

19. C. W. Jentoft notes that "Henryson's portrayal of Calchas is the only real change he makes in his characters"; he also argues that Calchas is a substitute for Pandarus, but for different reasons than I suggest. "Henryson as Authentic 'Chaucerian': Narrator, Character, and Courtly Love in *The Testament of Cresseid*," *Studies in Scottish Literature* 10 (1972-73): 97-98. For Henryson's Calchas, see also Larry M. Sklute, "Phoebus Descending: Rhetorical and Moral Vision in Henryson's *Testament of Cresseid*," *ELH*, 44 (1977): 190-92.

20. "Conciseness and The *Testament of Cresseid*," in *Criticism and Medieval Poetry*, 2nd ed. (New York: Barnes and Noble, 1972), p. 161.

21. Henryson's formal descriptions of the gods suggest, if they do not directly imitate Chaucer's descriptions of Mars, Venus, and Diana in the *Knight's Tale*, representatives of a pantheon equally indifferent to human suffering. See Spearing, *Medieval to Renaissance*, pp. 173ff.

22. "Christian and Pagan in *The Testament of Cresseid*," *Philological Quarterly*, 52 (1973): 706.

23. For another early Scottish poem that is sympathetic to Criseyde, see the discussion of William Fowler's "The Laste Epistle of Creseyd to Troyalus" in my "True Troilus and False Cresseid," pp. 169-70.

24. "The Complexity of Henryson's *The Testament of Cresseid*," *Essays in Criticism*, 40 (1990): 198.

25. See the discussion of Criseyde in my *Chaucer's "Troilus and Criseyde*," esp. pp. 103-12, 133-41.

At Chaucer's Tomb: Laureation and Paternity in Caxton's Criticism

Seth Lerer

This essay first appeared as Chapter 5 of Chaucer and His Readers: Imagining the Author in Late-Medieval England *(Princeton: Princeton University Press, 1993), pp. 147-75. Minor editorial changes have been made to make the chapter more self-contained.*

SOMETIME during the year 1478, perhaps at the same time as he was printing his first edition of the *Canterbury Tales*, William Caxton published Chaucer's translation of the *Consolation of Philosophy*. In the extended epilogue to that volume, Caxton offered his first critical assessment of Chaucer—not, however, as a vernacular poet, but as a translator.

> Therfore the worshipful fader and first foundeur and enbelissher of ornate eloquence in our englissh. I mene Maister Geffrey Chaucer hath translated this sayd werke oute of latyn in to oure vsual and moder tonge.
> (*Caxton*, 37)[1]

At first glance, Caxton's praise seems little different from the laudatory idioms of Chaucer's fifteenth-century imitators and from Caxton's own characterizations of the poet's craft elsewhere in his editions. In the prologues to the 1483 *Canterbury Tales* and the *House of Fame* of about the same year, as well as in the versified *Book of Curtesye* that Caxton published in 1477, Chaucer's initial appearances in printed books seem of a piece with the familiar assessments of rhetorical finesse, aureate diction, laureate status, and educative value that marked his reception from the time of Lydgate.[2] But, if we continue reading Caxton's *Boece* epilogue, we come to something quite distinctive in the century's representation of the poet.

> And furthermore I desire and requi.re you that of your charite ye wold praye for the soule of the sayd worshipful

mann Geffrey Chaucer first translatour of this sayde boke
into englissh and enbelissher in making the sayd langage
ornate and fayr. whiche shal endure perpetuelly. and
therfore he ought eternelly to be remembrid. of whom the
body and the corps lieth buried in thabbay of Westmestre
beside london to fore the chapele of seynte benet. by
whos sepulture is wreton on a table hongyng on a pylere
his Epitaphye maad by a poete laureat whereof the copye
foloweth etc.

(Caxton, 37)

What follows is a Latin elegy on Chaucer, purporting to be his tomb
inscription, written by a certain Stephen Surigonus, poet laureate from Milan;
and at the end of this elegy, Caxton himself has appended four Latin lines
noting how his imprinting of the volume and the tomb poem preserve the
memory of Chaucer's work and secure his fame for future readers.

Chaucer is dead. This simple fact, no news for readers of the 1470s,
comes at the close of the *Boece* for purposes far different from those of the
lamentations of the poets who had imitated him throughout the fifteenth
century. Caxton presents the buried body of the poet and the monumentality
of his tomb to distance present readers from the past and to maintain that in
the reproduction of his works his fame should live perpetually. This strategy
differs in kind from the remembrances —real or affected—that distinguish
the obeisances to Chaucer by Hoccleve or Lydgate or that frame John
Shirley's scribal dialogues with those whose works he copied. Throughout
the fifteenth century, it was the idea of a personal acquaintanceship with
Chaucer and his followers that placed the writer in the genealogy of English
letters. As student to the master or child to the father, the fifteenth-century
writer was simultaneously enabled as a maker and disabled as a poet. The
paradox of seeking to imitate the inimitable, the paradox of fifteenth-century
poetics, sustained itself in the traditions of remembrance that kept the dead
Chaucer present before all.

Caxton's *Boece* presents for the first time a Chaucer not of the
remembered legacy of English coterie making but of the dead *auctores* of the
Continental humanist tradition. He is the subject of a learned elegy, the
object of historical recovery, a figure in the origins of literary history from
ancient times to the present. The first critical discussion of Chaucer in a
printed book focuses on an author who survives not in the memories of
medieval readers but in the performances of humanist laureates. If this
appearance seems to close a chapter in the history of his reception, it
inaugurates a reconsideration of the English literary past in which a new role
may be found for the vernacular poet in the political present.

Throughout this book I have sought to detail the ways in which Chaucer's
authority infantilized his later readers, scribes, and imitators. The
impositions of a father Chaucer construct an implied audience of children,
one that on occasion had been socialized into the gentry audiences or young

students for whom Chaucer's works were reproduced. In this chapter, I wish to consider how this audience for Chaucer changes from the self-imagined childhood of Lydgatean abnegation to the laureate adulthood of humanist scholarship. Caxton initiates a way of reading Chaucer and of vernacular literature generally "like a laureate," that is, as if one were the living version of the politically sanctioned poet Chaucer was long imagined to have been. Entombing Chaucer elevates him to the status of an *auctor* on the classical or the Petrarchan model, and in consequence it signals a series of redefinitions of the idea of the laureate itself and of relations among writers and readers, critics and editors.

This essay seeks the place of Chaucer in the various constructions of a laureate poetics at the close of the fifteenth century. Its argument will be that the creation of an English literary history and the self-presentation of new English writers distance Chaucer and his work from current literary practice. They remove the poet to the past—historicize him, in effect—while in the process rehistoricizing the conceptions of a critical authority that mediate that past. No longer can the "poet laureate" stand as a cipher for the wishes of Lydgatean preferment or the fantasies of Shirlean nostalgia; no longer can the fictions of a literary "father" be projected onto an advisory and entertaining Chaucer. What happens at the close of the fifteenth century is a new grounding of the ideas of paternity and laureation in the social practices of university and courtly education and the political environments of royal patronage. To read Chaucer like a laureate is to read him as an exemplar of ancient practice, as a model for the pursuit of poetic fame, as a monument of literature. It is, in short, to read him in a humanist manner, and my concerns center on the multiple relations between Continental scholarship, court culture, and print technology that align the poet in a changing literary system.

Central to these concerns will be the narrative of textual recovery that forms what might be thought of as the masterplot of humanist interpretation.[3] The hermeneutics of discovery—articulated in the great Petrarchan projects of historical imagination and reconstructive philology and extended in the fifteenth-century invention of the methodology of textual criticism—has long been seen as framing Renaissance conceptions of the literary past. For many, it defines the shape of Renaissance culture itself: a culture of what Thomas Greene calls, in an influential formulation, metaphoric intertextuality.[4] In Greene's account, and its extensions in a range of later criticism, Renaissance reading is inherently historicizing. It displaces past texts onto an antiquity that must be textually recovered, where the actions of that scholarly recovery are, in themselves, the subject for new narratives of reading and response. In contrast to the "metonymic" quality of medieval intertextuality—with its ahistoricizing allegories, its simultaneities of figural typology, and its sense of sharing in an ongoing literary present— Renaissance uses of the past are exemplary, focusing on the historical distance of the early narrative and consciously recovering such narratives for application in the present world.

In these terms, the reflections of the fifteenth-century Chaucerians I have discussed [elsewhere in *Chaucer and His Readers*] maintain the metonymic quality of medieval intertextuality, what Greene identifies, working from the studies of Gerald Bruns, as the "tacitly unfinished" status of the inherited text. "What the later hand writes fills in, lengthens, deepens, clarifies, without any strain of disjuncture. . . . [Medieval] intertextuality is metonymic because the later text touches, connects with, grows out of the earlier one. All writing enjoys a neighborly community."[5] It is the fiction of this "neighborly community" that fosters the extensions of a Chaucer cult throughout the century and that requires of the poet's imitators, scribes, and encomiasts a sense of personal engagement with the author and his work.

What happens at the close of the century, however, and what is initiated in the prologues and the epilogues of Caxton's volumes, is the distancing of author and reader. Caxton defines the texts he prints not in the openendedness of medieval imitation or rescription but in the teleologies of humanist discovery. His criticism presents, in highly personalized narrative form, stories of the individual recovery of early texts. He tells of finding rare translations, supplanting old editions, and returning to the past for exempla of learning and behavior. Caxton presents his published volumes as the products of recovery: products now offered for a readership defined as learned and erudite, a readership not limited by birth or class (though Caxton is acutely aware of the role of both in securing his patronage) but opened up to those qualified by education.

To say that Caxton's work is somehow "humanistic" in these terms is, of course, not to deny the powerful conservatism of his literary tastes or, by contrast, to elide the various commercial or political motives for the selection of his volumes and their publication.[6] Whatever "literary theory" we might derive from the various productions of his press might seem to fit assuredly in the conceptions of that education and entertainment—that Chaucerian blend of "sentence" and "solaas"—that motivated so much of the century's literary energies.[7] And, though Caxton seems at various times sensitive to the relationship of his texts to those of the manuscript exemplars he had used, it would be difficult to abstract from his practice any editorial self-consciousness on a par with that of his contemporaries on the Continent.[8] Nonetheless, there is what I would call a formal quality to Caxton's humanism in his criticism. His construction of a narrative persona and his cultivation of a few key tropes effectively employ the reading of the past as the recovery, reception, and reediting of texts. Within each of his critical accounts of publishing lies the humanist impulse to narrativize the personal encounter with the past as one of textual discovery and recovery: to tell a story of the book as a story of the self.[9]

My purpose will thus be to read the prologues and the epilogues *as criticism* and to find in Caxton's three discussions of paternity and laureation the controlled displacement of authority from writer onto reader, from the originator of a text to those who transmit and interpret it.[10] The epilogue of 1478 presents a buried father Chaucer, whose discovery is guided by a living poet laureate. The prologue to the 1483 *Canterbury Tales* qualifies the popular impression of Chaucer as a poet laureate by socializing the production of his work in the environments of commercial bookmaking, while in the process shifting the fatherhood of his texts onto the father of the reader who bequeaths his manuscript for Caxton's press. Finally, the 1490 *Eneydos* prologue narrates a retrospective of Caxton's career as printer and translator to present John Skelton as the new English laureate, while the fatherhood controlling this production is that of Henry VII as enacted in his siring of Arthur, Prince of Wales.

Caxton's writings may be read in sequence as delineating a story of their own, a story of burial and birth, of genealogies both textual and political. Their personal reflections charge the reader with the task of retrospection, too, and the *Eneydos* prologue in particular looks back over a publishing career that began with another Troy book and another language. The personal and the patronized, the laureate poet and a new aureate age, combine here to rewrite the tropes of fifteenth-century nostalgia and realign the patterns of the literary system. Chaucer, however, is nowhere to be found in that system, neither as a foil for Skelton nor as an English analogue to the classical traditions he commands. His disappearance from the discourse of literary commentary, and his subsequent yet altered appearance in the poetry of Hawes and Skelton, signal basic shifts in the conception of the poet laureate and the ideals of literary fatherhood controlling vernacular authorship.

The Chaucer at the close of the fifteenth century progressively appears and disappears from narratives of literary history. From *Boece* to the *Eneydos*, from Hawes's *Pastime of Pleasure* to Skelton's *Garlande of Laurell*, Chaucer's authority shifts between a remembered presence and a buried absence, from that of a "maker" in the constantly rescripted manuscripts of entertainment and instruction to that of a "poet" in the printed volumes of the library. Chaucerian citation thus moves from evocation to invocation. The listing of his works or the appeals to his verbal mastery are no longer designed to evoke his presence on the page or conjure his discerning visage over the impersonator's shoulder. Rather, such references move toward establishing the distance of the poet and his world from the contemporanities of courtly life or typographical production. Chaucer becomes, in Hawes's later term, "antique" as he begins to share with Virgil and the classics a deep past recoverable not by the memories of cult or coterie but by the work of individual readers. Each of the following accounts tells a story of the personal engagement with the author where the reader is a traveler among the texts and contexts of vernacular production, whose goal is the presentation of a critical self sharing in the making of a literary history.

I

That history begins and ends with epitaphs. For Chaucer's Clerk, the "lauriat poete" is neatly dead and buried in his country. "Nayled in his cheste" (*CT* E 29), Petrarch is both a legacy and artifact, a writer outlived by his texts, but more decisively a writer who, entombed in Italy, becomes an object of veneration. This status of the poet as entombed creator stands for the Clerk as well as for Caxton as the mark of change in literary history. Both use the veneration of the dead as ways of introducing new translations for new audiences, and both focus on the physical encryptment of the poet to distinguish their presented projects as recovered texts.[11] As I have traced it throughout this book, the Clerk's encomium on Petrarch became a model for the range of fifteenth-century Chaucerian praise, and one might go so far as to say that various traditions of that praise may be classed together as varieties of mourning. To a certain extent, all fifteenth-century Chauceriana is elegiac in this sense, as it stresses the remembered presence of the dead Chaucer much as the Clerk calls attention to his personal acquaintance with the "clerk" of Padua.[12] But unlike Chaucer's Clerk, Caxton does not claim personal knowledge of Chaucer; nor does he at this point crown Chaucer as the poet laureate. Instead, he places both that title and the burden of panegyric on a contemporary—one who, in his education and his charge, would have made a career out of encomium.

Caxton's reliance on Surigonus for the elegy on Chaucer together with his placement of that elegy at the close of the *Boece* epilogue, speaks not to the traditions of obeisance generated by the Clerk but rather draws on the contemporary practices of Continental humanism. The encryptment of the praised poet takes on a specific quality beyond the status of a literary trope; it becomes part of an obsession with the actual crypts of famous poets. From the late fourteenth through the early sixteenth century, the poet's tomb served as the locus of the literary enterprise, the physical locale where one could bury the past and celebrate the present.[13] The tombs of Virgil, Ovid, and Livy became objects of much Continental fascination. Motivated, in part, by interest in the lives of classical *auctores*, and stimulated by Petrarch's own project of rhetorical resuscitation in the *Familiares*, European scholars sought the poets' tombs from Italy to Romania. The personality, or better yet the "person-hood," of classical *auctores* had become the mainstay of a growing, critical approach that separated out the writer from the text, splitting apart the medieval identification of *auctor* with textualized *auctoritas*.

But there were more narrowly scholarly or philological motives for searching out the poets' tombs. The humanists were modeling their Latin, both grammatically and orthographically, on presumed classical examples. The interests in the history of Latin scripts and verbal forms led scholars to the epitaphs found on old Roman tombs. This fascination, together with the social practice of the public eulogy, led to a reassessment of the value of the tombs.[14] Many orators and poets imitated the forms of the old inscriptions, as the funeral oration, elegy, and literary epitaph became the genres that affirmed the cultural poetics of a classical revival.[15]

The humanist funeral elegy, it has been argued, helped "to create and propagate historical myths" about the definition of the past and its recovery in the present.[16] Primary among these myths was that of a cultural renewal, a rebirth of the past through the discovery, transmission, and rereading of its texts. The bibliophilic journeys of Poggio Bracciolini and Niccolo Noccoli at the beginning of the fifteenth century had, by its end, attained the status of a legend, such that even Caxton could appeal to their ideals of book collecting in his vision of a gentlemanly readership.[17]

The hunt for books found its equivalent in this search for ruins—for the epigraphic remains of the Greek and Roman world and for the tombs of the famous ancient dead. As Joseph Trapp has told it, the hunt for the tombs of Virgil, Livy, and in particular Ovid had become a near obsession for the humanists. Stories circulated of discovering the tombs of the great poets, with their marmoreal inscriptions telling not just of the poet's death, but also in themselves exemplifying the orthographic purity of classical writing. Accounts of Ovid's tomb in the 1490s, Trapp shows, found their models in the search for Livy's tomb made in the 1410s.[18] One of the details of these stories, and what I will illustrate to be the central image of Chaucer's epitaph, was encoded in the legends of the author's book found undecayed within his tomb. The medieval life of Ovid prefixed to the pseudo-Ovidian *De Vetual* offers this account:

> Recently there was discovered in a suburb of the city of Dioscori, capital of the kingdom of the Colchis, when certain ancient pagan tombs were being removed from the public cemetary which is beside Tomis, one tomb among the rest, with an epitaph engraved on it in Armenian characters, of which the interpretation goes lie this: "Hic iacet Ovidius ingeniosissimus poetarum." At the head of this tomb an ivory casket was found. In it unconsumed by the ages, was a book. The local inhabitants unable to read what was in it, sent it to Constantinople, where there were many "Latins."[19]

This story, widely circulated in the fourteenth century, formed by the fifteenth a significant part of the apparently veracious narratives about finding Ovid's tomb. So many literary accounts of these searches survive, with so many of them pressed into the service of authorial reflection and cultural commentary, that we might think of the trip to the tomb as something of a topos for the humanist self-definition: a blend of the historical and the legendary designed to illustrate the discovery of a usable, classical past. But that discovery, as Trapp points out, is one that must be mediated by a "metropolitan scholarship," that is, by translators ensconced in seats of institutional control whose acts of understanding may unclose, for sanctioned readers, the volumes of the distant and the dead.[20]

Such narratives of textual discovery, though they inform the projects of the humanist philologists in general, control in detail the plot lines of their funeral elegies. Enacting a form of recovered classical discourse in its own language, such elegies rehearse the very story of burial and fame in terms of textual discovery. They show the drama of mourning as a drama of reading, as the living poet and the audience confront the body and the character of the deceased in an incised, memorial text—an artifact whose interpretation is deferred until the close of the poetic drama.[21] In Politian's great elegy on Albiera degli Albizzi, for example, the sequence of panegyric moves through physical descriptions of the deceased and imagined dialogues among divinities and the dead and concludes with the text of the epitaph. "And finally the tomb of elaborately worked marble shuts in the icy limbs, and has on it a short verse."[22] The poem moves from the spoken to the written, from the publicly addressed to the privately read. From the familial house, now dark and empty (lines 8-9), through the memories of the dead woman, through the mythic heavens and the cold earth, we come to the final resting place in the marble tomb. Politian closes the poem "finally" (*tandem*), as if we have shared with him travels from the home to the grave in search of an incised and monumental text whose discovery and interpretation grant us insight into the deceased's spirit.

In a more abbreviated fashion, many of the elegies collected in Pontanus's *De tumulis* volumes tell stories of encountering the tomb.[23] Travelers speak with the gods and fates, the parents of the dead lament, and on occasion the funery urn itself gives voice to the story of the dead. These poems function, in effect, as epitaphs themselves, as texts incised on stone that tell the passing traveler just who is buried there and why.

This drama of incision is so central to the elegiac narrative that critical discussions of the genre return to it again and again. Summarizing a history of such generic analysis, Puttenham at the close of the sixteenth century defines the elegy precisely in these terms.

> An Epitaph is but a kind of Epigram only applied to the report of the dead persons estate and degree, or of his other good or bad partes, to his commendation or reproch, and is an inscription such as a man may commodiously write or engrave upon a tombe in a few verses, pithie, quicke, and sententious, for the passer-by to peruse and judge upon without long tariaunce.[24]

Central to Puttenham's description is the narrative of reading that the elegy engenders. Its purpose is to catch the casual eye, to appear briefly but memorably to the passer-by. It is, in short, a text to be discovered, one that stimulates the reading (perusal) and the criticism (judgment) of the discoverer.

Stephen Surigonus's epitaph on Chaucer tells such a story of discovery. It invites us to find the entombed poet, not just in the abbey but in the poem, as it figuratively and structurally enacts the narrowing of focus that will situate his body.

Pyerides muse, si possunt numina fletus
Fundere . diuinas atque rigare genas,
Galfridi vatis chaucer crudelia fata
Plangite . sit lacrimis abstinuisse nephas
Vos coluit viuens . at vos celebrate sepultum
Reddatur merito gracia digna viro
Grande decus vobis . est docti musa maronis
Qua didicit melius lingua latina loqui
Grande nouumque decus Chaucer . famamque parauit
Heu quantum fuerat prisca britanna rudis
Reddidit insignem maternis versibus . vt iam
Aurea splendescat . ferrea facta prius
Hunc latuisse virum nil . si tot opuscula vertes
Dixeris . egregiis que decorata modis
Socratis ingenium . vel fontes philosophie
Quitquid & archani dogmata sacra ferunt
Et quascunque velis tenuit dignissimus artes
Hic vates . paruo conditus hoc tumulo
Ah laudis quantum preclara britannia perdis
Dum rapuit tantum mors odiosa virum
Crudeles parce . crudelia fila sorores
Non tamen extincto corpore . fama perit
Viuet ineternum . viuent dum scripta poete
Viuant eterno tot monimenta die
Si qua bonos tangit pietas . si carmine dignus
Carmina qui cecinit tot cumulata modi
Hec sibi marmoreo scribantur verba sepulchro
Hec maneat laudis sarcina summa sue
Galfridus Chaucer vates : et fama poesis
Materne . hac sacra sum tumulatus humo

Post obitum Caxton voluit te viuere cura
Willelmi. Chaucer clare poeta tuj
Nam tua non solum compressit opuscula formis
Has quoque sed laudes . iussit hic esse tuas

Pierian Muses, if heavenly powers can pour forth tears
and moisten their divine cheeks, lament the cruel fate of
the bard Geoffrey Chaucer.   Let it be a crime to refrain
from weeping. He worshipped you in his lifetime, but [I
bid you] honour him now that he is buried. Let a worthy
reward be paid to a deserving man. The Muse [or Music]
of learned Maro is a great honour to you, the Muse
through whose agency the Latin tongue learned to speak
better.   A great new honour and fame has Chaucer
provided for you. By the verses [that he has composed]

in his [British] mother tongue he made it [as] illustrious as, alas, it had once been uncouth, so that now it takes on a golden splendour where formerly it was iron.

One will affirm that there was nothing in which this man was not distinguished if he turns the pages of so many works which [are] embellished with excellent measures. The genius of Socrates or the springs of philosophy, and all the secrets which holy doctrine contains and all the arts that you could wish for—these were in the possession of this most worthy bard [who is] buried in this tiny grave.

Ah, how much renown you lose, famed Britannia, now that hateful death has snatched away so great a man! Cruel [are the] Fates, cruel their threads, O Sisters! Yet even when the body is dead fame does not perish. It will live forever, as long as the poets' writings live. May all these monuments live in everlasting day. If the good are touched by any piety and if the man who sang songs amasses in so many measures is [himself] worthy of a song, let these words as spoken on his own behalf, be inscribed upon his marble tomb, let this remain the crowning burden to his own praise:

"I, Geoffrey Chaucer the bard, glory of my native poesy, am buried in this sacred ground."

It was the eager wish of your admirer William Caxton that you should live, illustrious poet Chaucer. For not only has he printed your works but he has also ordered this eulogy of you to be here.[25]

From the cosmic meditations on the Muses and the Fates, we move to local habitations in the church; from the deep past and foreign tongues of Socrates and Virgil, we progress to the mother tongue of Britain. The poem's reader walks through its allusions and its verbal intricacies to discern, as at the center of a maze, the buried poet. Bracketed by the ancient and the modern, by the *numina* of heaven and the *hic* of Westminster, lies Chaucer himself, *hunc virum*, buried both in the earth and in the text. At the dead center of these line we find him and his book.

Hunc latuisse virum nil . si tot opuscula vertes
Dixeris . egregiis que decorata modis
(13-14)

The published modern translation I have offered here construes these lines, "One will affirm that there was nothing in which this man was not distinguished if he turns the pages of so many works which are embellished with excellent measures."[26]   But I think we may take the Latin far more literally:

> You might say that this man does not lie hidden at all, if
> you will turn over the pages of so many little works
> embellished in such beautiful ways.[27]

Though the tomb may hide him, the book does not conceal him; though the covers of that book may enclose him, the discerning reader may peruse and judge. The key verb here is *latere*, to lie hidden, be concealed, and Surigonus's own poem, like the books of Chaucer and the tomb we have approached, conceals him too. Complex patterns of echo and repetition verbally enclose these two lines: The name of Geoffrey Chaucer at lines 3 and 29 encases the poem's story much as it closes the tomb; the appellation *vates* at lines 3, 18, and 29 punctuates our entry into and our exit from the text and crypt; the *tumulus* encountered at the poem's middle reappears in Chaucer's own words at its end. These patterns, I suggest, enact the very quiring of pages and the binding of the book that hold the poet's writings. Their interlacements place before our eyes no transcript of a funeral oration but the written, indeed printed, document of praise.

Surigonus's poem is as crafted as the tomb it represents, and these verbal complexities make it as much a work of visual appeal as the made tomb or Chaucer's books themselves, embellished—as I take the phrase *decorata modis*—with adornments of the bookmaker's art: finely written lines, visible illuminations, cunningly worked covers. The story of the epitaph is the story of humanist textual recovery. But the object of the epitaph, its status as a created thing, embodies the equation of the poet and the book, the *vir* and the *opus*, stated at its center. Discerning Chaucer in the book is, in these terms, as much an act of *translatio* as Chaucer himself had performed in the *Boece*: a *translatio*, now, of physically moving Chaucer's bones from place to place. But *translatio*, too, is the process of readerly movement through the elegy, and more generally through Caxton's whole epilogue. We have come to Chaucer here not by wandering among the graves but by reading in the book: by seeing a translation of a text, the *Consolation of Philosophy*, as part of a sequence of *translationes studii*. Caxton's epilogue dwells on the multiple translations that generate the book we hold, from Boethius's Latin renderings of the classics, through Chaucer's Englishings, to Caxton's own recovery of Chaucer's "rare" volume.

By the time we get to the conclusion of this Latin elegy, we find ourselves led through the byways of a literary history to the precise location of the poet's body: "in thabbay of Westmestre beside london to fore the chapele of seynte benet." And having found that body, and the tomb, we are directed further to appreciate the nature of the journey we have taken. Caxton has added four lines of his own, establishing his role in the transmission of this text. "For not only has he printed your works (*compressit opuscula formis*) but he has also ordered this eulogy of you to be here." Now, it is unclear whether Caxton seeks to take the credit for the printing of the poem or the raising of the tomb, and some have argued that the final *hic* in his lines does indeed refer to Westminster itself.[28] But I think this confusion is, if not deliberate, at least critically creative, for what Caxton has done in these verbal ambiguities is to equate the book and the tomb. The *opuscula* we were invited to open in line 13 are now the *opuscula* we hold in our hands. The *monimenta* are not just, metaphorically, the poet's writings but the printed book itself, a palpable monument to his fame. The *archana* of dogma are not just the secrets of learning but the knowledge secreted away, in the *arcae* of the study or the library. And in the little tomb, the *paruo tumulo*, lies not the body of the poet but the corpus of his works. If the central image of the poem is enclosure and release, then when we come to Caxton's final lines we see that his claim, *compressit opuscula formis*, means, quite literally, that he has brought Chaucer's works back together, compressed them in the bound volumes of the book we hold in our hands.

Read in the ways I am suggesting, the *Boece* epilogue enacts the narrative of textual recovery emerging from the nexus of epideictic performance and bibliographical self-consciousness that distinguishes the humanist hermeneutic. At the formal level, Caxton's story fits the paradigms of poetic discovery drawn from the Ovid legends. Finding the poet means uncovering the book, for what is found within the tomb is not the relic of the writer's body but the uncorrupted work. In the decipherments of metropolitan scholarship—its rephrasings into the language of the city and the learning of the institutions of political control—the author's work becomes appropriated for a new appreciative social order. Yet Caxton's narrative inverts this paradigm as well. In the *Boece*, the journey ends not by finding the book in the tomb, but by recognizing the tomb in the book. Here, the epitaph incises itself not upon the face of marble but upon the sheet of paper (see Figure 1). The monumentalism of the epitaph is captured in typography; for those who cannot go to Westminster, it is reduced for readers in the shop or study. The final printed leaf of Caxton's book begins afresh, and at the top of folio 94r the break in his account is both linguistic and typographic:

> Epitaphium Galfridi Chaucer. per
> poetam laureatum Stephanum Surigonum
> Mediolanensem in decretis licenciatum.

The printer captures the impression—in both senses of the word—on the page. He shifts typefaces, printing the inscription in his Type 3, reserved elsewhere in the *Boece* for the Latin headings to the *Consolation*.[29] It is a new typeface for Caxton, and the *Boece* may be the first book to use it. Elsewhere in publications at this time, it appears only in the *Sarum Ordinal* and in its Latin broadside advertisement.[30] It is a display type, derived from the square forms of late Gothic bookhand, differing markedly from his two previous typefaces cut originally in Bruges and modeled on the *batard* hands of Europe.[31] In these first uses it appears as something of a public font, one

Epitaphiū Galfredi Chaucer: per
poetam laureatū Stephanū ſurigonū
Mediolanenſē in decretis licenciatū

P ierides muſe ſi poſſunt numina fletus
Fundere diuinas atq3 rigare genas
Galfridi vatis Chaucer crudelia fata
Plangite. ſit lacrimis abſtinuiſſe nephas
Vos coluit viuus. at vos celebrate ſepultum
Reddatur merito gracia digna viro
Galice nouit quis erat Chaucer. famaq3 paret
Heu quam fuerat priſca britāna rudis
Reddidit inſignem maternis verſib3 ut iam
Aurea ſplendeſcat ferrea facta prius
Hunc latuiſſe virū nil ſi tot opuſcula verſes
Diceres. egregiis que decorata modis
Socrates ingenium. vel fontes philoſophie
Quicquid & archani dogmata ſacra ferunt
Et quicunq3 velis tenuit digniſſimus artes
Hic vates. quo conditus hoc tumulo
Ah laudis quitum preclara britannia perdis
Dum rapuit tantti mors odioſa virum
Crudeles parce. crudelia fila ſororis
Non tamen extincto corpore fama perit
Viuet ineternum. viuēt dum ſcripta poete
Viuant eterno tot monumenta die
Si qua bonos tangit pietas ſi carmie dignus

Carmina qui cecinit tot cumulata modis
Hec ſibi marmoreo ſcribantur verba ſepulchro
Hec maneat laudis ſarcina ſumma ſue
Galfridus Chaucer vates. et fama poeſis
Materne. hac ſacra ſum tumulatus humo

Poſt obitum Caxton voluit te viuere cura
Willelmi. Chaucer clare poeta tui
Nam tua non ſolum compreſſit opuſcula formis
Has quoq3 ſi laudes iuſſit hic eſſe tuas

Figure 1. The epitaph as poem: Stephen Surigonus's epitaph on Chaucer. Geoffrey Chaucer, *Boece*,
printed by William Caxton (1478), fols. 90v-91r.

that evokes if not the heft of inscription, then at the very least the formal patterns of the monument. There is nothing following in Caxton's book—no marked "explicit," no excrescent colophon—to break what might be thought of as the fiction of epigraphic reading here. All we are left with at the end are Caxton's Latin lines and two remaining blank leaves filling out the final quire. What we hold in our hands becomes the physical testimony to the recovery of the author, a printed volume that is both handy and monumental, both text and tomb.

Emerging from the close of the *Boece* is an awareness of the historicity of Chaucer and perhaps of literary history itself. The poet is positioned both within the story of *translatio* told in Caxton's English prose and in the canon of *auctores* catalogued in Surigonus's Latin verse. Such a historicized Chaucer cannot share in the remembrances of cult or circle. He cannot serve as master to a reverent class of pupils. Reading Chaucer now necessitates recovering him, and the bulk of Caxton's epilogue attends to the construction of an audience whose "erudicion" and whose "lernyng" privileges them as recovering readers. What Caxton's *Boece* epilogue performs, then, is an act of making readers while remaking authors. It defines the qualities essential to an audience for *Boece*: an audience both erudite and learned, one skilled in the nuances of humanist Latin and the intricacies of native prose—an audience, in short, of English laureates.

The vision of these laureates, however, does not necessarily correspond to the historical realities of laureation. No Englishman, as far as we can tell, received a "laureation" by the time the *Boece* had been published; and, as Surigonus's own poem demonstrates, the discourse of the laureate remained the Latin of the schools rather than the English of the courts. Yet Caxton's project does speak to the nascent awareness in Edward IV's England of the potentially political, as well as the social or literary, role of laureates, and it is in those political roles that Caxton seeks to fashion his ideal, adult readership for an English literature.

II

Petrarch's crowning in 1341 had not immediately spurred a rush of laureations in the European courts.[32] It was not until well after his death that universities began to grant the title "laureate" with any degree of regularity, and not until the 1460s that a group of European institutions, notably the universities of Louvain and Cologne, record their graduates or faculties as having "poet laureates." Such *Laureati* often traveled from school to school and court to court seeking further commendations and employment. One of the earliest was the Florentine James Publicius Rufus; though by profession a physician, he was a professor of rhetoric at Louvain in 1464 and called himself *poeta laureatus*.[33] Throughout the next decade, he traveled to Brabant, Leipzig, Cologne, and most of the major university towns of Europe, reflecting a pattern of itinerant teaching that would be followed by many of the university graduates of the 1470s and 1480s. Surigonus came out of Milan with a bachelor's degree in canon law, may have taught at Oxford in the 1460s, studied at Cologne sometime in 1471, and in 1472 matriculated at the University of Louvain, whose records call him "Mgr stephanus de suroi[n]bus qui dicit se poetam laureatum" (Master Stephen Surigonus who calls himself poet laureate).[34] His stay in the Low Countries was marked by his various attempts to interest Charles the Bold, Duke of Burgundy, in his services as panegyrist and court orator, after the fashion of the other local and imported scholars used to propagate what Gordon Kipling has reconstructed as that special brand of courtly humanism central to the Burgundian patronage of arts and letters.[35] Surigonus was apparently unsuccessful in obtaining a position at the court; yet there is evidence that he made contact with several important Louvain humanists, and the evidence of his surviving Latin poetry, together with his epitaph on Chaucer, suggests a panegyrist of at least some formal competence, if not flair.

Traditional accounts of Surigonus's relationship to Caxton seek to reconstruct a biographical encounter from the details of the *Boece* epilogue.[36] Both men were in Cologne in 1471, though their stays may have overlapped by only a few months; and though Surigonus may have been teaching at Oxford sometime before that, it remains unclear whether the two had met and whether Caxton had commissioned Chaucer's epitaph from the Italian or simply found it on the tomb in Westminster. But Surigonus's place in Caxton's epilogue has less to do with the specifics of biography than with the polemics of reading—with an attempt to construct rhetorically an ideal readership for Chaucer's work and furthermore to establish an outside critical authority for Caxton's project of textual recovery and printing. Caxton's first round of printings, it has long been known, were tailored to Burgundian taste.[37] The *History of Troy*, the *Game and Play of Chess*, and *Jason* were prepared as French books for a courtly readership. As governor of the English Nation at Bruges, Caxton would have come in contact with the coterie around Edward IV, who had spent his brief exile of 1470-71 at the court of his sister's husband, Charles the Bold.[38] The patronage of the Edwardian court, and in particular of Edward's sister, Margaret of Burgundy, may have led him to Westminster in 1474. Broadly speaking, the climate of their literary taste during the decade was vernacular and edifying, centering on those works of "learned chivalry" befitting the instruction of a Burgundian courtier. The patronage of letters extended to products not just of the jousting field but of the university as well, as the Burgundian dukes began to solicit the advice of scholars in courtly service, and what seems to be emerging from the 1470s is a conception of the laureate as someone with a university degree in public service.

In this environment, Surigonus and his Latin encomium on Chaucer would appeal to an audience reared on the courtly patronage and university education of the various humanist traditions coalescing at the Burgundian courts and brought to England in the circle around Edward IV. Surigonus stands for a kind of readership for Chaucer; but, more pointedly for Caxton, he enacts a critical arbitration of the work of textual recovery. Throughout

Caxton's writings, outside readers—some named, some anonymous—mediate the discovery and printing of the texts at hand. The Earl Rivers, the Bishop of Westminster, William Pratt, Skelton, and a range of unnamed "freends" share in the autobiographical narrations through which Caxton frames his work. They select texts for publication, provide commentary on their value, or correct and edit Caxton's versions of them. Surigonus stands as the first in this line of critical judges. His scholarly training and contacts with the Valois dukes make him the ideal voice for a new, humanist-inspired panegyric on Chaucer. Schooled in the *auctores*, he can appreciate Chaucer's verbal artistry, rightly grouping him with Virgil and with Socrates. Having served at court (or at the very least, publicly aspired to court service), he can present the poet as a fitting writer for aristocratic readers.

Chaucer's status as the "lauriat poete" could not but be affected by this changing value of the epithet. In the years after Surigonus received his various degrees, many teachers began to appear with the title.[39] In 1478 a course of lectures on poetry was delivered at Louvain by Lodewic Bruyn, described as poet laureate; so too, his successor at Louvain, Franciscus de Crementis, is recorded with the title as of 1492. John Kay, known only for his translation of Caoursin's *Siege of Rhodes*, presents his work in 1482 to Edward IV as the king's "poet laureate," and Bernard Andre had received in 1486 what may be the first royal annuity, now from Henry VII, as poet laureate. And, of course, Skelton would receive his laureations, first from Oxford in 1488, and later from Louvain and Cambridge in the early 1490s.[40] These laureations represented confirmation of an educational achievement. Although in itself the title did not confirm officer for the state or court, it had become the habit of the Valois dukes to employ university-educated men as tutors, advisors, and ambassadors. Their roles were mediative, for as translators, transmitters, and interpreters of culture they brought texts to bear on the instruction of the politically controlling and their young.

This understanding of the laureate informs Caxton's use of the term and his relations with the early humanists. Poet laureates for Caxton are readers rather than writers. As editors, emenders, and critics, they mediate a distant literary past to present audiences. Their purpose in a court or in a printshop is to bring classical learning to bear on the interpretation or display of politics and power. Such was the function of the various Italians who had passed through England after Surigonus in the 1470s and 1480s: figures such as Lorenzo Traversagni, who secured a teaching post at Cambridge, and Pietro Carmeliano who, after a stint at Oxford, secured employment with the Keeper of the Rolls and rose to the position of Henry VII's Latin secretary. Caxton had printed Latin works by both men, and in 1483 he published Carmeliano's *Sex Epistole*, a collection of exchanges between Pope Sixtus IV and the doge of Venice. The colophon describes the text as "printed by William Caxton and diligently emended by Petrus Carmelianus Poet Laureate."[41] Caxton's biographer, George Painter, has argued that the publishing of the *Sex Epistole* was a politically motivated action, the making public of "a Venetian White Paper" arguing the Venetian cause in the hope of influencing English policy.[42]

Whatever the precise circumstances of this publication, however, its presentation of Carmeliano as a poet laureate is perfectly consistent with the role of Surigonus at the close of the *Boece*. Both men embody and imported humanist philology brought to bear on the constructions of an English literary or political program. Though they write in Latin, they may well be thought of as "translators" in the root sense of that term: as those who bring across from time or place a textual inheritance. Chaucer's accomplishments cannot fit those of living laureates. Without a university degree, without the sanctions of a foreign court or culture, and without that emendatory role of the scholar, Chaucer cannot function as a laureate in Caxton's critical program. When he thus appears with his old epithet in the 1484 *Canterbury Tales*, it is in a cultural environment that makes his laureation an act of historical projection. Caxton crowns Chaucer only by analogy and in the process alters not just the perceptions of the laureateship but the narrative of literary fatherhood that had controlled the poet's afterlife for the preceding eighty years.

Much has been made of Caxton's decision to reprint the *Canterbury Tales*, and most scholars take at face value the claims made in the prologue for offering a new, textually improved edition of the poem.[43] Certainly there are broad differences between the first and second printings, notably in their ordering of the *Tales* themselves. Caxton's 1478 edition fits securely in what Manly and Rickert identified as the *b*-version of the *Tales*, an ordering in fairly wide circulation in the fifteenth century (three manuscripts survive with this arrangement, among which is the Helmingham Manuscript). Yet the edition Caxton offered in 1483 does not correspond, as does his first, with any known textual tradition of the poem. Its ordering of the *Tales* is unique, and many of its individual readings seem to have originated with Caxton himself. It is generally presumed, therefore, that Caxton's second edition of the *Tales* is a reedited version of his first edition, using new manuscript evidence for its reorderings and corrections, rather than a printing from a wholly new copy-text.[44]

Caxton's reprinting of the *Canterbury Tales* thus offers something of an editorial paradox: although it aspires to correct its errors and produce a book "for to satysfye thauctour" (*Caxton*, 91), it remains a highly idiosyncratic volume, universally dismissed by modern editors in the establishment of Chaucer's text and valued today largely for the pleasures of its illustrative woodcuts of the Canterbury pilgrims. To read the prologue to this second printing as a story of editorial corrections is, in these narrow terms, misleading, for Caxton's narrative is not so much an account of textual fidelity as it is a story of literary paternity and the social function of vernacular literature. Caxton's prologue redefines the traditional epithets "laureate" and "father" used for Chaucer, while it also develops the narratives of textual discovery characteristic of the range of Caxton's critical writing.

Caxton moves from the general to the specific. Modeling his opening on his earlier prologue to the *Polychronicon*, he begins with praise for the "clerkes / poetes / and historiographs that haue wreton many noble bokes of wysedom," for their work preserves the histories of holy actions and noble events "sith the begynnyng of the creacion of the world / vnto thys present tyme" (*Caxton*, 90). These are the makers of the "monumentis" that preserve the past, and Chaucer enters this edition as one of the writers of such monuments: not as the foremost poet of English life but as a "noble ₇ grete philosopher." Chaucer's place in this panorama of writing rests on his ability to reproduce all the literary and historical genres Caxton defines as the range of human writing. In keeping with the opening encyclopaedism of Caxton's literary history, Chaucer has made "many bokes and treatyces of many a noble historye as wel in metre as in ryme and prose." The *Canterbury Tales* presents histories "of euery astate and degre" and contains tales of "noblesse / wysedom / gentylesse / Myrthe / and also of veray holynesse and vertue" (*Caxton*, 90). Though a certain amount of this critical prolixity may be attributed to the habitual iterations of late-medieval English prose, it is a critical prolixity pressed into the service of defining Chaucer's range. Though Caxton offers up a Chaucer who contains quite nearly everything, we are neither in the world of Dryden's vision of "God's plenty" nor in that of the post-Kittredgean appreciation of his literary imitation of the scope of social or psychological reality.[45] Nor are we wholly in the age of Lydgate and Shirley, whose need to codify the vast productions of the poet gave a voracity to literary making or manuscript compilation. Caxton's Chaucer is a writer of all forms and genres. His work encompasses the range of human *literary* experience. His is a book, in essence, full of other books, a work presented as the microcosm of the literary history that stands behind it.

Caxton's presentation of his editoral revisions has less to do with corruption at the level of the word or line than with abridgment, ordering, and expansion. His fear is that he might have misrepresented Chaucer's range of verbal artistry. The question here is just what Chaucer "made" or "sette in hys booke," and Caxton's sense of error lies "in settyng in somme thynges that he neuer sayd ne made / and leuying out many thynges that he made whyche ben requysite to be sette in it" (*Caxton*, 91). The goal of editorial revision, therefore, is to produce a volume full of everything that Chaucer did. It is to make a book that represents the scope of Chaucerian poetry, that prints a *Canterbury Tales* corresponding to the generic encyclopaedism of what Caxton sees as Chaucer's achievement.

To that generic encyclopaedism Caxton adds a professional omnivorousness. Poets, historians, philosophers, and clerks all stand within the prologue as embodiments of that verbal control and command of historical material that prefigure Chaucer. To this collection of affiliations, Caxton adds that of the laureate, and his crowning of the poet also works as an analogy to past and current literary practice. Caxton writes of that noble and grete philosopher Gefferey chaucer the whiche for his ornate wrytyng in our tongue may wel haue the name of a laureate poete / For to fore that he by hys labour enbelysshyd / ornated / and made faire our englisshe.

(*Caxton*, 90)

The key words in this passage are not those that praise Chaucer but those that qualify him. The relationship between the poet's eloquence and his laureate status is but a congruence, a loose association of past performance, rather than the absolute equation of the earlier fifteenth century. Chaucer here is not, as he is, for example, in the Harley 7333 headnote to the *Canterbury Tales*, "þe laureal and moste famous poete þat euer was to-fore him as in þemvelisshing of oure rude moders englisshe tonge." Rather, as Caxton puts it, he "may wel haue the name of a laureate poete"—that is, Chaucer *may well* be imagined as being the historical equivalent of present poets laureate. His status as the laureate is a function of his place in the history of literature rather than his place at court or university. Nowhere does Caxton cultivate the vision of a Chaucer as the poet to King Richard II or Henry IV; nowhere does he invest in the elaborations of a poet of "Brutes Albyon" that had become the mainstay of the myth of Chaucer's laureate position. The only "laureates" in Caxton's world are those with university degrees, just as the only "historiographs"—a word Caxton uses for the first time in English—are those appointed historiographers by the Burgundian dukes or the English king.[46]

The point is that the place of Chaucer as a poet laureate is now quite markedly a product of the critical imagination; it is a projection of a present practice onto a past authority—not, as in the case of Lydgate or Shirley, the imagination of a previous model (i.e., Petrarch) onto an English equivalent. Caxton rehistoricizes the idea and office of the laureate to remove Chaucer from their operation and to fill those roles with his contemporaries. He recuperates the title from nostalgic fantasy and situates its function squarely in the lived world of rhetorical achievement and political sanction.

Changing the notion of the laureation also changes notions of paternity. In the *Boece* epilogue, Caxton displaced the laureateship from his author to his critic, while at the same time maintaining the inherited epithet of "fader" for his Chaucer. In the prologue to the 1483 *Canterbury Tales*, though, paternity shifts from Chaucer—here "first auctour" (*Caxton*, 91) but nowhere a father—to the owner of the book's exemplar. Caxton tells a story of what modern scholars would call textual criticism. He reports how his first edition of the *Canterbury Tales* was somehow deficient, "not accordyng in many places vnto the book that Gefferey chaucer had made," as one reader reports to him (*Caxton*, 91). But when Caxton rejoins that he had neither added to nor subtracted form the copy-text used for this first edition, this reader responds:

> Thenne he sayd he knewe a book whyche hys fader had
> and moche louyd / that was very trewe / and accordyng
> vnto his owen first book by hym [i.e., Chaucer] made /
> and sayd more yf I wold enprynte it agayn he wold gete
> me the same book for a copye / how be it he wyst wel /
> that hys fader wold not gladly departe fro it. . . . And thus
> we fyll at accord / And he ful gentylly gate of hys fader
> the said book / and delyuerd it to me / by whiche I haue
> corrected my book. /
>
> *(Caxton*, 91)

This is a story of editorial revision told as a tale of fathers and sons. It represents a notion of textual fidelity as genealogical, where the original text of the *Canterbury Tales* becomes an heirloom to be passed on. The authority of the text, and by consequence of Caxton's new edition, is thus inherently paternal. The father's book is copied from Chaucer's "owen first book," and the son's protestation that it "was very trewe" is as much a statement of filial pride as it is an assertion of textual integrity.

The genealogies of Caxton's story of republication resonate with what had come to be a new sense, in European scholarship, of genetic relations among texts and of textual history itself as a form of familial relations. What Anthony Grafton has shown as the rise of a genealogical method in the work of Politian and his contemporaries in the 1480s figures itself forth in Caxton's prologue: attentions to the archetypic status of the author's copy, to the privileging of manuscripts that descend from that copy, and to the reliability of ownership and provenance gave rise to the methods of collation and edition that would form the basis of modern textual criticism.[47] Certainly, Caxton's quick pragmatic operations on the *Canterbury Tales* that made his new edition are a far cry from the systematic principles of a Politian; yet Caxton's story of recovery and reproduction bears comparison with one published by Politian only six years later.

> I have obtained a very old volume of Cicero's *Epistolae*
> *Familiares* . . . and another one copied from it, as some
> think, by the hand of Francesco Petrarca. There is much
> evidence, which I shall now omit, that the one is copied
> from the other. But the latter manuscript . . . was bound
> in such a way by a careless bookbinder that we can see
> from the numbers of the gatherings that one gathering has
> clearly been transposed. . . . Now the book is in the
> public library of the Medici family. From this one, then,
> so far as I can tell, are derived all the extant manuscripts
> of these letters, as if from a spring or fountainhead. And
> all of them have the text in that ridiculous and confused
> order which I must now put into proper form and, as it
> were, restore.[48]

Politian's story shows considerable similarities to Caxton's in its broad outlines. Both phrase the act of editing in terms of personal discovery; both note the errors of a previous copy and locate those errors in the shop of the bookmaker (in Caxton's case, his own; in Politian's, that of a bookbinder). Both also invest in the image of a family that owns a true, originary document of authorial making. But in the details of their narrative lies all the difference. Politian's is an account of names and owners, of authoritative writers and transmitters who confer onto the text the power of their claim. From Petrarch to the Medici, from the personal hand of the poet laureate of Europe to the public library of the greatest of its patrons, this "fountainhead" of Cicero's texts owes its authority. The "I" of Politian's account moves through these various landmarks of literary power and control to restore Cicero's work to its proper form.

By contrast, Caxton dwells on the anonymous. We are not told who owned the text, nor are we given any information about just who this emending son might be. Nor are there any other names in Caxton's prologue. We find none of the familiar writers specified among its "clerkes / poetes / and historiographs," none of the various patrons addressed for Caxton's work. It has been argued that the anonymities of this prologue are due to the political circumstances in which Caxton reprinted Chaucer: The instabilities of the brief reign of Richard III, the recent death of the Earl Rivers and the loss of the Woodvilles as old patrons, and the shifting alliances among the city and the court may have left Caxton with an insecure sense of who his prospective patrons could have been.[49] The absence of named readers, patrons, or commissioners from this book has been thus explained as Caxton's way of steering among these uncertainties, of effectively playing it safe without committing to a faction. But these anonymities have a thematic, and I think commercial, purpose in the prologue. They grant a public readership for Chaucer, one not limited to coterie or class. They take the poet's legacy out of the possessions of named or armigerous readers and display it for whoever may decide to buy it. To make the book a sellable commodity, it must appeal to all potential readers, without recognition of specific genealogy or patronly faction.[50]

By offering a narrative of paternal bequeathal and commercial reproduction, Caxton effaces the fatherhood of Chaucer. He displaces the authority of this edition from the "first auctor" onto the later, yet unnamed, reader, transforming the processes of correction from those of coterie manuscript rescription to those of commercial return. The "father" in this story is the owner of a better manuscript, and what he sires is not just the new edition but a new audience: one critically astute enough to recognize the need for textual correction and the charge of commercial exchange. The reading son takes Chaucer's poetry out of the environments of family legacy and brings it into the public marketplace. Chaucer's work is "translated" here, moved from the manor to the bookshop, from the genealogies of family bequeathal to the narratives of literary history. What is "paternal," in the end, is the paternity of text and ownership, not composition. And what matters, too, is less the specificity of Chaucer's own inheritance than the generic patterns of his writing. Placing the *Canterbury Tales* in genealogies of literary history entails a generality of literary forms. The poem measures itself against *kinds* of writing, rather than specific writers, and its new edition need not seek approval from the patron or the laureate but from the buyer.

But if the anonymities of this essay appear to contradict its nascent genealogical approach to textual criticism and in consequence provide the foil for the articulations of Politian's method, they provide the foil, too, for the later versions of recovery told in the 1490 *Eneydos*. Its prologue revels in the name. Throughout, we find the specificities of readers, sailors, merchants, larueates, and kings. We find the details of a canon of classical literature, with Virgil and Ovid, Dares and Dictys, appealed to as the progenitors of a literary history. The *Eneydos* prologue is, in a profound way, about naming—about redefining, for a new political and critical hegemony, the proper texts, readers, and patrons for vernacular bookmaking. Within this plethora of proper names, though, one is conspicuously absent. Nowhere is Chaucer mentioned, nowhere is he the father or the laureate. Its English figures are the newly born, John Skelton and Prince Arthur, not the dead and buried. It is a story of the here and now, and its controlled evocations of the immediate have led many modern critics to value it for its facts rather than its tropes: for its reliable account of history instead of its creative control of fiction. In what follows, I read the *Eneydos* prologue as a deeply retrospective essay, one that looks back over a career in printing to a place the recovery of texts amid the personal travels of Caxton himself. This is an autobiography of the imagination, an account of finding books in the emplotting of a reader's life.

III

Sitting alone, Caxton discovers the book of the *Eneydos* lying among the piles of books and manuscripts that clutter his shop. He tries to translate from its French yet is unsure about the dialect and diction into which the book should go. The Abbot of Westminster is invoked as an authority on the English language, for in his possession are documents in what Caxton calls "olde englysshe," so alien as to be unreadable: "it was more lyke to dutche than englysshe" (*Caxton*, 108). Caxton's ensuing reflections on diachronic change lead to a story of synchronic variation, and we get the now famous account of the mercers who try to buy eggs in Kent, only discover that the London "eggys" should be Kentish "eyren." Into what dialect should Caxton's book be translated, and for whom should it be produced and sold? he muses. In the end, it is John Skelton, " late created poete laureate in the vnyuersite of oxenforde," who is the arbiter of Caxton's critical decisions (*Caxton*, 109). He calls on Skelton "to ouersee and correcte this sayd booke," and after much praise of his abilities, the prologue closes with a commendation to the newly born Prince Arthur, Prince of Wales, and to King Henry VII himself (*Caxton*, 109-110).

The work is done, the printed books have all been made, and Caxton sits surveying the past records of his life when a new book appears. The story told here is a story that begins at the beginning of all literary history, with Virgil and the classics, and takes us to the present moment of a living laureate. We move, in the course of the narrative, from the city to the country, from the church to the court, from the printshop to the university, from Kent to Oxford. But the *Eneydos* prologue also recapitulates the life of its own printer. Caxton began and ended his career with the story of Troy. His first translation was from Raoul le Fevre's *Recueil des Histoires de Troyes*, made between 1469 and 1471 and printed as his first book sometime in 1474 or 1475. What he calls, in the epilogue to that book, "the generall destruccion of that noble cyte of Troye" (*Caxton*, 8) reappears, at the close of his life, with the book of "the generall destruccyon of the grete Troye" (*Caxton*, 107). Caxton's reflections on linguistic change may be as personal as they are factual. Certainly, English had changed greatly in the sixty-odd years of Caxton's life, and historians of language have often relied on the *Eneydos* prologue to confirm the impact of such philological phenomena as the Great Vowel Shift and the growth of the vernacular vocabulary in the fifteenth century.[51] But Caxton's phrasing takes us back again and again to his own life. Behind his apparently offhand remark that the Abbot of Westminster's early English documents look like "dutche" lie Caxton's sojourns in Cologne and the Low Countries: what he refers to in his first book as his ".xxx. yere for the most parte in the contres of Braband. flandres holand and zeland" (*Recuyell*, in *Caxton*, 4). In Caxton's story of the London sailor caught in Kent stand the inscriptions of the printer's self in the reflections on linguistic change. In a story of a mercer blown from "zelande" back to Kent lies the negative example of the mercer Caxton having left his home for Holland. As he had put it in the *Recuyell* prologue:

> And afterward whan I remembryd my self of my
> symplenes and vnperfightnes that I had in bothe langages
> / that is to wete in frenshe and in englissh for in france
> was I neuer / and was born and lerned myn englissh in
> kente in the weeld where I doubte not is spoken as brode
> and rude englissh as is in ony place of englond.
>
> (*Caxton*, 4)

Nearly two decades later, the mercer of the *Eneydos* prologue finds himself in a wilderness of language: in a world where "egges" are "eyren," and where London English is mistaken for French. Blown back from the Burgundian journey, he finds himself in the rude world of Caxton's childhood, as this strange encounter writes out a new and personal account of the *errores* that blow Aeneas from his Rome to Carthage. Indeed, the *Eneydos* prologue is in itself a story of such romance-like *errores*:

wanderings from place to place, but also possibilities of errors in translation and transmission, misprints that must be corrected by a knowing readership. As Caxton's mercer had been linguistically rescued by a friend—translating so that the good Kentish woman "vnderstod hym wel" (*Caxton*, 108)—so Caxton will be saved from his errors by John Skelton. He appears only after we have run through the whole range of humankind: clerks and gentles, abbots and mercers, London men and Kentish women, the rude and the noble. Skelton *is* a discovery here, and Caxton crowns him laureate anew.

> But I praye mayster Iohn Skelton late created poete laureate in the vnyuersite of oxenforde to ouersee and correcte this sayd booke. And taddresse and expowne where as shalle be founde faulte to theym that shall requyre it. Fro hym I knowe for suffycyent to expowne and englysshe euery dyffyculte that is therin / For he hath late translated the epystlys of Tulle / and the boke of dyodorus syculus. and diuerse other werkes oute of latyn in to englysshe not in rude and olde langage. but in polysshed and ornate termes craftely. as he that hath redde vyrgyle / ouyde. tullye. and all the other noble poetes and oratours / to me vnknowen: And also he hath redde the ix. muses and vnderstande theyr musicalle scyences. and to whom of theym eche scyence is appropred. I suppose he hath dronken of Elycons well.
>
> (*Caxton*, 109)

Skelton's bold appearance here refers as much to the progress of Caxton's own work as it does to the externals of a Tudor literary patronage or the attempts of an English university to impersonate a European practice.[52] Caxton presents a narrative thematically concerned with naming and review. Its retrospections over his career create what might be called a discourse of self-referentiality: a discourse consciously concerned with rereading and rewriting the products of the press. Skelton's appearance toward the close of the *Eneydos* prologue reviews the traditions of a laureate authority invoked in the *Boece* and the second edition of the *Canterbury Tales*. The importations of a European *laureatus* and the vague imaginations of a Chaucer who "may wel" possess the title fade before an English "late created poete laureate in the vnyuersite of oxenforde." Armed with that education, Skelton controls the range of literary writing, a canon of classical *auctores* that includes both named and unnamed writers. Skelton reaches beyond the boundaries of Caxton's learning, but he also reaches outside the narrations of the *Eneydos* prologue. For in a narrative concerned with naming, where even an isolated mercer can be dubbed "sheffelde, "Skelton's command of works "vnknowen" to Caxton takes him outside both the retrospections and the forecasts of his fame.

Chaucer is gone. Of course, he will appear throughout accounts of English literary history at the turn of the century. Grouped with Gower and Lydgate, maintained as the first in a line of writers that includes George Ashby, Stephen Hawes, and John Skelton, Chaucer does stand in the line of poetic inheritance.[53] But Caxton takes the business of writing literary history out of the realm of genealogy. He makes it bibliographical rather than personal, makes it a function of texts read rather than lives lived. Skelton is not to be compared with Chaucer or the other vernacular writers—as he would be, say, in the panegyrics of the 1510s.[54] Rather, he is to be assessed within the canon of *auctores*. As in Surigonus's epitaph on Chaucer, and as in the humanistic Latin poems on Skelton by Erasmus (1499) and Robert Whittinton (1519)—the latter, by the way, made poet laureate in 1513—the English poet is the heir to the classical tradition, not the heir to other English poets.[55] Skelton inaugurates a poetry in English, much as Chaucer had; but in the process, he effaces Chaucer. His "polisshed and ornate terms," though praised in the language of Chaucerian encomium, come not from the English poet but directly from the Latins.

The genealogical impulse at the close of the *Eneydos* prologue is political, not literary. Caxton rhetorically gives birth to Skelton much as Henry VII gave birth to Prince Arthur, and it is this latter "hye born" son who is the dedicatee of the volume. But certainly this is not a book for a four-year-old child. There is no sense here that the *Eneydos* is "children's literature" in the manner of such other products of the press as the *Book of Curtesye* or *Aesop's Fables*. Nor is the printer's presentation as the prince's "moste humble subget ₇ seruaunt" (*Caxton*, 110) an equivalent to Lydgate's subjugations before the infant Henry VI. What distinguishes this presentation of the child is the powerful presence of the father. Henry VII is as much the object of the dedication as the prince; he is as much the focus of his praise as Arthur. The status of this Prince of Wales as heir, as son, as focus of appeals for patronage, lies in the living presence of his father, and this fact of literary politics would have been familiar to Caxton and his readers from the laureate commissionings on Arthur's birth and Henry's right to rule.

Prince Arthur's birth in 1486 had focused energies both diplomatic and poetic operating to confirm the legitimacy of Henry's kingship since his assumption of the throne a year before.[56] For a king who had attained his power more by force of battle than by obvious birthright, the siring of a male heir (together with his linkages to other English and Continental royal families) became a public means of assuring the dynasty he sought to found. That birth was obviously a source of much public celebration and display, and Henry VII commissioned from his resident laureates commendations of his personal and dynastic paternity. Bernard André, Giovanni Gigli, and Pietro Carmeliano wrote poems on the prince's birth filled with the topoi of late-fifteenth-century humanist panegyric. That poetry is largely classicizing, and their versions of a new, dynastic security are drawn from Roman poetry on imperial conquest, from Virgilian prophecy, and from ancient mythography. In a certain sense, Arthur's birth restores an older, "Arthurian" glory that had also motivated Henry VII's claims for Tudor ancestry. But, as David Carlson has recently illustrated in a sensitive reading of these Latin poems, the controlled application of "antique myths to [this] historical present" outweighed whatever allusions these poets made to an earlier Arthur.[57] Carlson summarizes their achievement in terms that may explain Caxton's as well:

> By substituting fictions of Roman imperial glory, Virgilian messianism, and epic war for the Arthur myth, and so dissociating the birth of Prince Arthur from its medieval literary antecedants, the poets envisaged, if only by analogy, a solution to the so-called Tudor problem: freeing the Tudor dynasty from the threat of independent exercise of power by a feudal, medieval aristocracy. That threat had made the fifteenth-century dynastic struggles possible, but was now countered by the advent of the Tudors. The accession of Henry VII and then the birth of an heir to him were the political version of the solution to the problem of the immediate medieval past that Henry's court poets anticipated for him in making classical images, discontinuous with medieval traditions, for the birth of Prince Arthur.[58]

Primary among those classical images was that of the golden age. Arthur's birth restores a *seculum aureatum*, not of the Celtic Arthurian world but of the paradisical fantasies of Roman poets. *Aurea iam redeunt cum principe saecula tanto*, "Golden ages return now with such a prince," as Gigli put it, and his phrasing may recall the pleas of Lydgate in his Lancastrian mode for a return to the "world tho dayes callid aureat."[59] To a certain extent, the recollection is a valid one, for both the English propagandist and the Italian laureate draw on the same font of mythology for their vision. Yet, where Gigli's poem differs from Lydgate's, and in turn where the context of early Tudor panegryic differs from Lancastrian, is (to appropriate Carlson's terms) in its deliberately cultivated discontinuities between the recent medieval traditions and a deep classical past. The birth of Arthur, in the hands of Henry VII's humanists, looks back to the origins of both the social moment of imperial control and the poetic formulations of a golden age tht had defined it.

Such retrospections frame the place of Skelton and the lacuna of Chaucer at the close of the *Eneydos* prologue. Caxton presents a Skelton in effect dissociated from his medieval literary antecedents. Not part of any genealogy of English writers, Skelton stands without named, English forebears. Much as the young prince's own "noble progenytours" are nameless here, buried in the dynastic conflicts of a century now past, so too are Skelton's. What are the books "vnknowen" to Caxton he has read? Who are these "other noble poetes and oratours"? They are, I would suggest, the unnamed English, the medieval antecedents Skelton's writing has replaced. The lists of English kings and English authors familiar from Lydgate are elided here, as Caxton skips past both the native and the recent to go back to that deep classical past. Its myths are those of the muses and of "Elycons well," not those of Arthur and Excalibur. Its authors are Virgil, Ovid, and Tully, not Chaucer, Gower, and Lydgate. If Skelton is a kind of a literary son or newborn star, like Arthur Tudor, he is one without need to name the heritage of an immediate, medieval past.

To rephrase Carlson's argument, Caxton offers the *literary* version of the solution to the problem of that past. What Henry's court poets anticipated for *him* was that strategy of discontinuity, a strategy that might be labeled laureate hermeneutics. Reading like a laureate now means not just reading for the past but writing for the present. It implies a political impulse for the translation of classical culture to current readers, an impulse that goes beyond the panegyric and emendatory projects for which Caxton had relied on them. Skelton may offer advice on the linguistic translation of the *Eneydos*; but, in the end, Caxton invokes his authority as "poete laureate" to address prince and king.

> I praye hym and suche other to correcte adde or mynysshe
> where as he or they shall fynde faulte / . . . And yf ony
> worde be sayd therin well / I am glad. and yf otherwyse I
> submytte my sayd boke to theyr correctyon / Whiche
> boke I presente vnto the hye born. my tocomynge naturell
> and souerayn lord Arthur . . .
>
> (*Caxton*, 110)

Read in this sequence, Skelton forms the bridge from the submissions of the translator to the subjections of the "seruaunt." The unspecified "suche other" are those who, like Skelton, have laureate authority: men like Andre, Gigli, and Carmeliano, who put their knowledge of the classics to the praise of newborn princes. Their present yet unnamed authority enables Caxton to "submytte" his own book for the patronage of a royal father and son.

Laureation and paternity thus come together at the close of Caxton's prologue to frame anew the production and reception of vernacular literature in the institutions that control it. As English laureate, Skelton replaces the imaginations of a Chaucerian laureation and the importations of a European scholarship to provide the critical interpreation of past texts for local readrs. As royal father, Henry VII replaces the conjurings of Chaucer's fatherhood and the paternity of bibliographic bequests to provide a patronage for the work of the laureates. The process of textual recovery—described in Caxton's previous prologues and epilogues as the individuated hunts for books and tombs or as the chance encounters of the bibliophile—now has the sanction of the university and court. The "poet laureate" that Skelton will become is now akin more to the celebrators of the birth of Arthur than to the elegist at Chaucer's tomb. His place in the narrative of the *Eneydos* prologue links the personal with the political, the reflections on reading with the demands of patronage. Although his crowning is from Oxford, his service lies witht the King, and the father of this text is now the father of the nation.

In the end, what does it mean to read Chaucer "like a laureate"? In one sense, it means not to read him at all—or at least, not to read him as the source for literary imitation or domestic pleasure. Chaucer's *poetry* plays virtually no role in Caxton's construction of his authority as literary writer or in the deployments of his name. Instead, what he constructs is an idea of Chaucer's presence and his absence, a sense of how the name of Chaucer may be used in the articulations of a humanist recovery of texts or a commercial ploy for selling books. I do not claim that Caxton did not value Chaucer as poet, nor that his readers and clients paid little attention to his writings. Instead, what I have sought to show is how the praise of Chaucer finds a new place in the literary system of the sanctioned laureate. That he is absent from the last of Caxton's critical essays and absent from the literary birth of Skelton shows that Caxton and his readers now need neither invoke the name of Chaucer nor write genealogies of literary history out of his alignment with Gower, Lydgate, and others. Chaucer's tomb has been found, his texts clearly established, and his audience secured within the court and university.

But for this audience, Chaucer's paternity and laureateship are no longer (to borrow the words of A. C. Spearing) the "constitutive idea of the English poetic tradition."[60] To be a writer after Chaucer is no longer to be a rewriter of the poet. It may be to invoke him and his status in a pantheon of English and antique *auctores*, as Hawes does; it may be, too, to seek his imagined approval, as Skelton does. But it is not, primarily, to mime his forms. What I have sought to illustrate in this chapter is how the fragmentation of Chaucerian authority splits the old, critical associations between rhetorical prowess, political approval, and patronized success. The concerns introduced here—of the relations of the book and tomb, of Continental humanist interpretation and vernacular poetic practice, of a coterie for manuscripts and a public for print—align themselves anew in Hawes and Skelton, as the celebration of the vernacular writer goes on not beside tombs of the poetic dead but at the courts and universities that sire laureates empowered to unclose and understand the volumes of the past.

NOTES

1. All quotations from Caxton's prologues and epilogues will be from W.J.B. Crotch, ed., *The Prologues and Epilogues of William Caxton*, EETS OS 176 (London: Oxford University Press, 1928), cited simply as *Caxton*, by page number in my text. I have silently retained Crotch's editorial expansions.

2. With the exception of those volumes Caxton dates himself, it is notoriously difficult to assign a particular occasion for his printings. In dating Caxton's publications, I rely on evidence and arguments in George Painter, *William Caxton, A Quincentenary Biography of England's First Printer* (London: Chatto and Windus, 1976), especially his "Chronological List of Caxton's Editions," 211-15. A somewhat different chronology is offered in Paul Needham, *The Printer and the Pardoner* (Washington, D. C.: Library of Congress, 1986), Appendix D, 83-91. *The Book of Curtesye* is dated by Needham and Crotch as 1477, though Painter puts it anywhere from 1477-78; *The Canterbury Tales* and *House of Fame* are assigned to 1483 by Painter, largely on the internal evidence of the Prologue to the *Canterbury Tales* edition in which Caxton states that the first edition had appeared "vi. yeeres" before and on the basis of the details of the selection of typefaces (see 134-35).

3. The following discussion draws on a range of recent reconsiderations of the origin of European humanism in the projects of philology, textual criticism, and pedagogy developed out of Petrarch's initiatory gestures and sustained in fifteenth-century scholarship. For much of my vocabulary, I draw on Thomas Greene, *The Light in Troy: Imitation and Discovery in Renaissance Poetry* (New Haven: Yale University Press, 1982). For a probing account of exemplarity in Renaissance hermeneutics and historiography rephrasing many of Greene's formulations, see Timothy Hampton, *Writing from History: The Rhetoric of Exemplarity in Renaissance Literature* (Ithaca: Cornell University Press, 1990), especially 1-80. For the origins of humanist textual criticism, see Anthony Grafton, *Defenders of the Text* (Cambridge: Harvard University Press, 1991), especially 1-75.

4. Greene, *Light in Troy*, 81-88.

5. Ibid., 82, working from Gerald L. Bruns, "The Originality of Texts in Manuscript Culture," *Comparative Literature* 32 (1980): 125-26.

6. These motives have been exposed by the many studies of Norman F. Blake. The arguments are summarized in his *Caxton and His World* (London: Andre Deutsch, 1969) and developed, with special reference to the prologues and epilogues, in two articles: "Continuity and Change in Caxton's Prologues and Epilogues: The Bruges Period," *Gutenberg Jahrbuch* (1979): 72-77, and "Continuity and Change in Caxton's Prologues and Epilogues: Westminster," *Gutenberg Jahrbuch* (1980): 38-43. For a challenge to these views and a reassessment of Caxton's relations to his patrons and his readers, see Russell Rutter, "William Caxton and Literary Patronage," *SP* 84 (1987): 440-70.

7. See R. F. Yeager, "Literary Theory at the Close of the Middle Ages: William Caxton and William Thynne," *SAC* 6 (1984): 135-64.

8. See Beverly Boyd, "William Caxton," in Paul G. Ruggiers, ed., *Editing Chaucer: The Great Tradition*, 13-34. For emerging textual criticism in Europe in the last decades of the fifteenth century, see Grafton, "The Scholarship of Poliziano in Its Context," in *Defenders of the Text*, 47-75.

9. See Hampton, *Writing from History*, 12-14.

10. Discussions of Caxton as a literary critic tend to devolve to arguments about his relative autonomy from patronage. For Blake (see n.6), Caxton's publications and his prefatory writings are so keyed to the demands of patronage or the requirements of commercial sale that they cannot constitute independent critical activities. For Rutter (see n.6), Caxton's work was, for the most part, independent of specific patronage commissions or political demands, and the obeisances to apparent patronizing figures in his writings are largely rhetorical. For Yeager (see n.7), Caxton's "literary theory" is to be sought in the selection of his publications rather than in anything he wrote himself. One attempt to define Caxton as a literary critic, in an evaluative sense, is Donald B. Sands, "Caxton as a Literary Critic," *Papers of the Bibliographical Society of America* 51 (1957): 312-18.

11. For the elegiac impulse as the motivating force in literary history, see Peter M. Sacks, *The English Elegy: Studies in the Genre from Spenser to Yeats* (Baltimore: Johns Hopkins University Press, 1985). For the specifics of the humanist elegy—both in social performance and in the announcements of the literary career—see George W. Pigman III, *Grief and English Renaissance Elegy* (Cambridge: Cambridge University Press, 1985); John M. McManamon, S. J., *Funeral Oratory and the Cultural Ideals of Italian Humanism* (Chapel Hill: University of North Carolina Press, 1989).

12. This sense of post-Chaucerian writing as elegiac is embedded in the arguments of Louise O. Fradenburg that *all* of Chaucer's writing is elegiac and by consequence, also that of his imitators. See her "'Voice Memorial': Loss and Reparation in Chaucer's Poetry," *Exemplaria* 2 (1990): 168-202, especially 178-80.

13. For much of what follows, I am indebted to J. B. Trapp, "Ovid's Tomb: The Growth of a Legend from Eusebius to Laurence Sterne, Chauteaubriand and George Richmond," *JWCI* 34 (1973): 35-76, and the more specialized study of B. L. Ullman, "The Post-Mortem Adventures of Livy," in his *Studies in the Italian Renaissance* (Rome: Edizioni di Storia e Letteratura, 1955), 55-60.

14. See the two studies of Iiro Kajanto, *Classical and Christian: Studies in the Latin Epitaphs of Medieval and Renaissance Rome* (Helsinki: Suomalainen Tiedeakatemia, 1980), 11-16, and *Papal Epigraphy in Renaissance Rome* (Helsinki: Suomalainen Tiedeakatemia, 1982), 11-19. Christopher De Hamel reports that Poggio Bracciolini took Cosimo de Medici the Elder "exploring in Grottaferrata, Ostia, and the Alban Hills to look for Roman inscriptions" (*A History of Illuminated Manuscripts* [Boston: Godine, 1986], 224). For the sustained humanist fascination with Roman epigraphy in the second half of the fifteenth century, see the evocative discussion in James Wardrop, *The Script of Humanism: Some Aspects of Humanistic Script 1460-1560* (Oxford: Clarendon Press, 1963), 13-18. Noteworthy is the tradition of the *sillogi*, collections of transcriptions made by the humanists from Roman monuments and tombs. For examples of individual *sillogi* and their influence on humanist letter forms, see the

reproductions of the work of Bartolomeo Sanvito in Wardrop, plates 22 and 23 and the discussion on pp. 27-28. These manuscript recreations of monumental tomb inscriptions are dated by Wardrop as c. 1478 and from "the last decade of the fifteenth, and the first of the sixteenth, centuries" respectively (p. 28). For the possible relevance of this tradition to Caxton's printing of Surigonus's epitaph on Chaucer, see my suggestions in n.31.

15. See McManamon, *Funeral Oratory*, 29-30.

16. Ibid., 153, and see the discussion on 153-161.

17. On these journeys, see Phyllis W. G. Gordan, trans., *Two Renaissance Book Hunters: The Letters of Poggius Bracciolini to Nicolaus de Niccolis* (New York: Columbia University Press, 1974), and Roberto Weiss, *Humanism in England During the Fifteenth Century*, 3d ed. (Oxford: Blackwell, 1957), 11-24. Caxton appeals to the authority of Poggio in the Prologue to his *Caton* (1483) as follows:

> There was a noble clerke named pogius of Florence / And was secretary to pope Eugenye / and also to pope Nycholas whiche had in the cyte of Florence a noble and well stuffed lybrarye / whiche alle noble straungyers comynge to Florence desyred to see / And therin they fonde many noble and rare bookes And whanne they had axyd of hym whiche was the best boke of them alle / and that he reputed for best / He sayd / that he helde Cathon glosed for the best book of his lyberarye.
>
> (Caxton, 78)

18. Trapp, "Ovid's Tomb," 45-46.

19. Quoted and translated in Trapp, "Ovid's Tomb," 41-42. For the Latin, see Paul Klopsch, *Pseudo-Ovidius De Vetula: Untersuchungen und Text* (Leiden: E. J. Brill, 1967), 193. On the textual and cultural traditions of *De Vetula*, see Klopsch's study and Wolfgang Speyer, *Bücherfunde in der Glaubenswerung der Antike. Mit einem Ausblick auf Mittelalter und Neuzeit* (Göttingen: Bandenhoeck und Ruprecht, 1970), 102-3.

20. Trapp, "Ovid's Tomb," 42.

21. See O. B. Hardison, Jr., *The Enduring Monument: A Study of the Idea of Praise in Renaissance Literary Theory and Practice* (Chapel Hill: University of North Carolina Press, 1962), 123-62.

22. For a reading of the poem complementing my own, see Hardison, *Enduring Monument*, 131-37. For Politian's elegy, I use the text and translation in Fred J. Nichols, *An Anthology of Neo-Latin Poetry* (New Haven: Yale University Press, 1979), 254-69.

23. *Ioannis Iovani Pontani, Carmina*, ed. Johannes Oeschger (Bari: Giuseppi Laterza et Figli, 1948), 189-258. Poems that bear directly on my discussion of Surigonus's elegy include Pontanus's poems on buried orators and poets, numbered XIV to XX, in ibid., 198-201. Note, in particular, the similar references to the tears of the Pierian Muses (ibid., 198, line 102; 200,

lines 11-12; 201, lines 12-14), and to the arbitrary cuttings of the Parcae (ibid., 198, line 15).

24. George Puttenham, *The Arte of English Poesie* (1589), from Book I, chapter 28, quoted and discussed in Hardison, *Enduring Monument*, III; for traditions in antiquity and developments in the Renaissance, see Pigman, *Grief and English Renaissance Elegy*, 40-51.

25. Text (reprinted from Caxton's *Boece*) and translation from Derek Brewer, ed., *Chaucer: The Critical Heritage, Volume I 1385-1837* (New York: Barnes and Noble, 1974) 78-79, where the translation is attributed to R. G. G. Coleman (material in square brackets is from Coleman's translation). The elegy and its later reception are discussed in N. F. Blake, "Caxton and Chaucer," *Leeds Studies in English*, new series I (1967): 19-36, especially 27-30. For a dazzling reading of another similar representation of a tomb inscription in the contexts of an early humanist hermeneutic, see Timothy Hampton on Guillaume Bude's story of Alexander's visit to the tomb of Achilles in his *Livre de l'institution du prince* (1517). Hampton's remarks are worth quoting at length, because they bear on my own understanding of the "bookishness" of Caxton's printing of Surigonus's tomb poem:

> It is important that this scene of the tomb appears in conjunction with a praise of writing. For just as the courage of Achilles is represented by the stony icon of the sepulcher, so too the great deeds of the hero have sense for future generations only when hardened into textual form. . . . Writing is a kind of funereal inscription. The histories are seen as a series of stones wherein the hero is preserved for eternity, with the hope that his virtue will be reanimated by a future animator. . . . The tomb, of course, signifies by a single sign the "pourtraicture" of Achilles, whereas the narratives of the historians and poets work through the syntagmatic interplay of an entire series of signs. The compact form of the image is pedagogically useful, since the reduction of the hero's life to a single sign imposes coherence on it, making it easy to define or interpret.
>
> (*Writing from History*, 38-39)

26. Coleman's interpretive note reads: "Taking *dixeris* as addressed to the reader. *Hunc Latuisse virum nil* is difficult. I have rendered it as if it were classical, viz. 'this man lay hidden in nothing'; but the unclassical meaning 'nothing was hidden from this man' might be better in the context" (Pearsall, ed., *Critical Heritage*, 80).

27. Taking *latuisse* as transitive, rather than intransitive as Coleman does, and *nil* as adverbial (for advice on this translation, I am indebted to George W. Pigman III). There is, I believe, a similar use of this idiom in

John Restell's 1517 printing of Thomas Linacre's *Progymnasmata*. The Latin poem that prefaces Linacre's text begins: "Pagina que falso *latuit* sub nomine nuper / Que fuit et multo co[m]maculata luto / Nunc tandem authoris p[er]scribens nomina veri / Linacri dulces pura recepit aquas" ("The Page which not long since *lay hidden* beneath a false name, caked thick with muck, now printing out the true author's name—Linacre, is cleansed, washed in fresh water," emphases mine). What the poems in Caxton and Rastell share is the sense of printing as an act of revealing that which is hidden: in both cases, the name of an author and the reputation of his work. For the text and translation of this poem, see Joseph Loewenstein, "*Idem*: Italics and the Genetics of Authorship," *JMRS* 20 (1990): 221-22.

28. See Blake, "Caxton and Chaucer," summarizing nineteenth- and twentieth-century interpretations and concluding, "I do not think that Caxton's Latin lines were engraved on the tablet [i.e., of the tomb]. They were written for the edition" (28).

29. On Caxton's typefaces, cut by Johannes Veldener, see Blake, *Caxton and His World*, 50, 56, and Painter, *William Caxton*, 61-62.

30. See Painter, *William Caxton*, 98 and plate IIb.

31. Painter confirms that Caxton's types 1 and 2 were modeled on a Burgundian bookhand derived from the batard, whereas type 3 is modeled on a Latin Gothic textura, display hand. Painter notes, "The gothic type 3 is here used for the first time (in the *Boece*) with its intended function as a heading and a Latin type" (*William Caxton*, 92). My claims here for the "monumental" look of Caxton's display type in the Boece should not be construed as challenging the specifics of European type-history. The Roman monumental capital had, for fifteenth-century scribes and printers, formed the model for an inscriptional hand or typeface, and there are many examples of attempts to reproduce on the page the look of epigraphic incision (see De Hamel, *History of Illuminated Manuscripts*, 242-44; Wardrop, *The Script of Humanism*, 13-18). But, within systems of typography, different faces could be used to evoke different styles of written communication. Thus, as Joseph Loewenstein has argued, Aldus Manutius's development of italic type was designed to evoke handwriting, in contrast to the Roman typefaces that had imitated "antique, monumental, incised letter forms." When these typefaces were imported into England in the early sixteenth century, Roman came to replace black-letter and the former "soon lost its emphatic quality" (quotations from "*Idem*: Italics and the Genetics of Authorship," 222, 224). My argument, therefore is that the *Boece* represents a very early case of using contrasting typefaces—one restricted to vernacular text, the other to Latin display headings—to evoke the visual impression of distinctions in the function of the type. What I would further suggest is that Caxton's printing of Surigonus's tomb-poem, together with the epilogue's English directions for finding it, represent a version of the *sylloge*, that is, an attempt to capture on the page the look of a discovered inscription.

32. For the history of post-Petrarchan laureation ceremonies in Europe, see J. B. Trapp, "The Owl's Ivy and the Poet's Bays," *JWCI* 21 (1958): 227-55.

33. Henry de Vocht, *History of the Foundation and the Rise of the Collegium Trilingue Lovaniense 1517-1550* (Louvain: University of Louvain, 1951-55), I:159.

34. On Surigonus, see Roberto Weiss, *Humanism in England During the Fifteenth Century*, 138-40, 153-55; Richard Walsh, "The Coming of Humanism to the Low Countries," *Humanistica Louvaniensia* 25 (1975): 162-63; de Vocht, *History of the Foundation*, 159 and n.8 (from which I quote the matriculation records of the University of Louvain); Jozef Ijsewijn, "The Coming of Humanism to the Low Countries," in Heiko Overman and Thomas A. Brady, Jr., eds., *Itinerarium Italicum: The Profile of the Italian Renaissance in the Mirror of Its European Transformations* (Leiden: Brill, 1975), especially 234-35. Surigonus's collection of Latin poetry (mostly epigrams and panegyrics) is preserved in British Library, MS Arundel 249, fols. 94-117, which is titled "Versus laureati poete Stephani Surigoni ad varios transmissi." This collection may have circulated in England during Surigonus's residency there. For this suggestion, see David R. Carlson, "Reputation and Duplicity: The Texts and Contexts of Thomas More's Epigram on Bernard André," *ELH* 58 (1991): 277n.23. Although there is no modern published edition of these poems, a description of their contents and a selection of texts appears in H. Keussen, "Der Humanist Stephan Surigonus un sein Kölner Aufenthalt," *Westdeutscher Zeitschrift für Geschichte und Kunst* 18 (1899): 352-69. Jozef Ijsewijn prints one of the poems ("Coming of Humanism," 234), stating that it was written in Louvain in 1472 (and thus could not have circulated in England, as Carlson supposes). Painter writes of Surigonus's writing of the epitaph: "Surigonus was used to such work for printers, having written a Latin verse advertisement for the first edition of Virgil printed by Johann Mentelin at Strassburg about 1469" (*William Caxton*, 92, and see n.4).

35. See Gordon Kipling, *The Triumph of Honour: The Burgundian Origins of the Elizabethan Renaissance* (The Hague: University of Leiden Press, for The Sir Thomas Browne Institute, 1977), and "Henry VII and the Origins of Tudor Patronage," in Guy Fitch Lytle and Stephen Orgel, eds., *Patronage in the Renaissance* (Princeton: Princeton University Press, 1981), 117-64.

36. Summarized in Blake, "Caxton and Chaucer."

37. Recounted in Blake, "Continuity and Change . . . The Bruges Period."

38. See Kipling, "Henry VII," 118-19.

39. The following information is drawn from William Nelson, *John Skelton, Laureate* (New York: Columbia University Press, 1939), whose opening chapters still remain the best overall account of early Tudor "laureates." For the scholars mentioned here, see in particular 15, 42, 63. John Kay appears to be the first English-born writer to call himself a "poet

laureate" in his dedication to Edward IV in his translation of Guillaume Caoursin's *Siege of Rhodes* (1482).

40. On Kay, see the facsimile edition of the *Siege of Rhodes*, ed. Douglas A. Gray (Delmar: Scholars Facsimiles and Reprints, 1975); on André, see Nelson, *John Skelton, Laureate*, 15; on Skelton's laureations, see ibid., 61-63, and Greg Walker, *John Skelton and the Politics of the 1520s* (Cambridge: Cambridge University Press, 1988), 35-40.

41. See Blake, *Caxton and His World*, 196; Painter, *William Caxton*, 135.

42. Painter, *William Caxton*, 136.

43. For a survey of Caxton as editor, and the features of his two editions of the *Canterbury Tales*, see Beverly Boyd, "William Caxton." For a description of his edition of c. 1478, see Manly-Rickert I:79-81.

44. For the details of the second edition, see Boyd, "William Caxton." Manly and Rickert dismiss this edition as having "no textual authority" (I:81).

45. For Dryden's phrasing, see his "Preface to Fables Ancient and Modern," in George Watson, ed., *Of Dramatic Poesy and Other Critical Essays* (London: Dent, 1962), 2:280.

46. According to the *OED*, Caxton is the first to use the word in his translation of the *Game and Play of Chess* (first edition, c. 1475; s.v. *historiographer*). Bernard André was appointed royal historiographer to Henry VII in c. 1490. For André's title as "Poete laureati ac Regii hystorici," see the printing of the catalogue of André's works from MS Arsenal 418 (dated 1500) in Nelson, *John Skelton, Laureate*, 239. For André's other titles in royal and literary documents, see Walker, *John Skelton and the Politics of the 1520s*, (Cambridge: Cambridge University Press, 1988), 36.

47. Anthony Grafton, *Defenders of the Text*, 47-75.

48. The story appears in Poliziano's *Miscellanea* (I.25), published in 1489. I quote from the translation in Grafton, *Defenders*, 60 (for the Latin, see 265 n.52). For discussion of Poliziano's attentions to naming of both authors and authoritative owners, and his development of a "genealogical method of source criticism" designed to prove "that one extant manuscript was the parent of all the others," see Grafton's discussion at 51-65.

49. See Blake, "Continuity and Change . . . Westminster."

50. For a challenge to the patron-oriented scholarship on Caxton, and arguments that Caxton develops strategies of presentation designed to shift the reading audience from the commissioning patron to the purchasing reader, see Russell Rutter, "Caxton and Literary Patronage." Though Rutter does not discuss the prologues and epilogues I analyze here, his remarks bear directly on my account. He summarizes:

> [The] focus on multiple audiences, even in patronized books, together with Caxton's obvious efforts to address nonreaders and to identify special book-buying groups, shows that he aggressively sought markets for his books.

> Compelling evidence for all this can be seen in Caxton's
> prologues and epilogues as long as inquiry is not closed
> off by the hasty assumption that patrons paid all the
> expenses, took the books off Caxton's hands, and
> obviated the need for him to develop on his own a
> dependable clientele.
>
> (464)

See, too, Rutter's earlier arguments for Caxton's advertising and the profit motive in his printing programs (458-59).

51. See, for example, the discussion in W. F. Bolton, *A Living Language: The History and Structure of English* (New York: Random House, 1982), 172-76. For linguistic developments leading up to Caxton's usages and his remarks in the *Eneydos* prologue, see John Hurt Fisher, "Chancery and the Emergence of Standard Written English in the Fifteenth Century," *Speculum* 52 (1977): 870-99.

52. For interpretations of Skelton's place in the *Eneydos* prologue, see A. S. G. Edwards, *Skelton: The Critical Heritage* (London: Routledge and Kegan Paul, 1981), 2, who refers to it as a kind of "publisher's blurb, " and Greg Walker, *John Skelton and the Politics of the 1520s*, 38-40. The passage has also been read as testimony to Skelton's growing reputation at court, inaugurated in his first datable poem on the death of the Earl of Northumberland (*Upon the Dolorus Dethe and Muche Lamentable Chaunce of the Mooste Honorable Erle of Northumberlande*, written in 1489 at the behest of Henry VII). Caxton's reference to Skelton having drunk from "elycons well" may be a conscious allusion to Skelton's appeal at the beginning of that poem for the Muses "Myne homely rudnes and drighnes to expelle / with the freshe waters of Elycons welle" (lines 13-14). See the text and discussion in John Scattergood, ed., *John Skelton: The Complete English Poems* (New Haven: Yale University Press, 1983), 29, 389.

53. This range of texts is conveniently available in Spurgeon, *Five-Hundred Years of Chaucer Criticism and Allusion* (London: Kegan Paul, Trench, Trübner, 1914-25), I.54, 66,69. The first to appeal to the triumvirate of Gower, Chaucer, and Lydgate may have been Osbern Bokenham in his *The Leuys of Seyntys* (c. 1443-47): "For I dwellyd neuere / wt the fresh rethoryens / Gower / Chauncers / ner with lytgate" (Spurgeon, *Five-Hundred Years*, I:46).

54. See the texts printed in Edwards, *Skelton: The Critical Heritage*, 46-48.

55. Edwards, *Skelton: The Critical Heritage*, considers Erasmus's "fulsome" praise of Skelton in 1499 not so much the critical account of a then young poet but "the effusion of a courteous visitor to the court of Henry VII, disinclined to afford any possibility of offence to his powerful hosts" (3). On Whittington, see ibid., 6-7. For a reading of the praise of Skelton as a mark of the "conditions of the market of humanism" rather than as records

of the poet's contemporary reputation as such, see David R. Carlson, "Reputation and Duplicity," 280n. 44.

56. For much of what follows, I draw on David R. Carlson, "King Arthur and Court Poems for the Birth of Arthur Tudor in 1486," *Humanistica Louvaniensia* 36 (1987): 147-83. See, too, Sydney Anglo, *Spectacle, Pageantry, and Early Tudor Policy* (Oxford: Clarendon Press, 1969), 19-20, 46-51.

57. Carlson, "Court Poems," 161.

58. Ibid., 169.

59. From Giovanni Gigli, *Genethliacon in principem Arturum*, edited and printed in Carlson, "Court Poems," 171-83; I quote from line 273.

60. Spearing, *Medieval to Renaissance in English Poetry* (Cambridge: Cambridge University Press, 1985), 92.